ENGLISH LANDED
SOCIETY

IN THE NINETEENTH
CENTURY

STUDIES IN SOCIAL HISTORY

edited by

HAROLD PERKIN

Lecturer in Social History, University of Manchester

ENGLISH LANDED SOCIETY

IN THE NINETEENTH CENTURY

by

F. M. L. Thompson

Lecturer in Modern History
University College London

LONDON: Routledge & Kegan Paul
TORONTO: University of Toronto Press

First published 1963
in Great Britain by
Routledge & Kegan Paul Ltd
and in Canada by
University of Toronto Press
Second impression 1963
Third impression 1969
Printed in Great Britain by
Eyre and Spottiswoode Limited
© F. M. L. Thompson 1963
No part of this book may be reproduced
in any form without permission from
the publisher, except for the quotation
of brief passages in criticism
SBN 1700 4558 1

Contents

v

Preface

THE theme of the decline of aristocratic power has often been treated in the political histories of the nineteenth century, and is indeed inescapable. Almost as often the influence of the landed interest has been prematurely dismissed, in eagerness to write nineteenth-century history in terms of the growth of middle-class power, the democratization of institutions, and the increasing importance of radical and working-class movements. While not seeking to re-tell the political history of the period, this book may contribute towards a more just appreciation of the relative importance of the different major social groups in the life of the country. It deals in the main with the economic history of the landed interest, and with its role as a social group. It includes much agrarian and some industrial history as seen from the landowners' point of view, although it is not intended to provide a history of agriculture, still less one of industry or the economy as a whole. It should not be taken as a definitive or exhaustive history of the landed interest: the vast riches of the private archives of landed families are increasingly being made available to historians, and are only just beginning to be tapped. In the present early stage of such research this book is, like all history only more so, an interim report.

The first seven chapters of the book aim to present an analysis and description of the main elements in the institutions and way of life of the landed classes, suggesting their significance for society at large, and emphasizing the forces of change which were at work within an order which in many ways presented a remarkably stable appearance to the outside world. The last five chapters take up the theme of change, and examine the dynamic elements in the economic social and political life of the group, in a sequence of chronological subdivisions of the century and a half with which this book is concerned. The impact of the major changes in the social structure of the country, and

vii

of the industrialization of the economy, is hinted at, but no attempt is made to treat in detail those developments which were external to the landed interest. The main concern of the book in the fortunes of the influential classes is such that, re-inforced by the limitations of space and records, the histories of the smaller landowners, the farmers, and the labourers have been deliberately confined to a very subordinate position—which is not intended to provide a measure of their own intrinsic importance and interest.

It would have been impossible to write a work of this nature without the generous help and co-operation of the owners of private collections of manuscripts, and I am deeply indebted to the following for access to their collections. The Marquess of Ailesbury (the Savernake Papers); Lord Barnard (the Raby Papers); the Marquess of Bath (the Longleat Papers); H. Lorenzo Christie (the Jervaulx Papers); R. F. Dickinson (the Dickinson Papers); Earl Fitzwilliam and the Trustees of the Fitzwilliam Settled Estates (the Milton Papers and the Wentworth Woodhouse Papers); Earl Fortescue (the Castle Hill Papers); Hoare's Bank (the Ailesbury Trust Papers and the Bank's records); Sir Stephen Hugh Middleton (the Belsay Papers); the Duke of Northumberland (the Alnwick Papers); the Earl of Pembroke and Montgomery (the Wilton Papers); Viscount Ridley (the Blagdon Papers); the Duke of Rutland (the Belvoir Papers); Sir Richard Sykes (the Sledmere Papers); the Earl of Verulam (the Gorhambury Papers). As the entries in the Bibliography show, I have also enjoyed the help of many County Archivists, and been able to take advantage of the service which many owners have rendered to historians by placing their papers in County Record Offices. To all these I should like to express my thanks.

In the years that have passed since I began the research on which this book rests I have been helped by many people, not least those who make the discussions of the Seminar in Modern English Economic History at the Institute of Historical Research so wide-ranging and stimulating. In particular I should like to thank Dr G. E. Mingay, the author of the companion study of the eighteenth century, who has read most of the draft and made many helpful comments. But I owe most to Professor H. J. Habakkuk, who originated modern work in this field, supervised my post-graduate work, and who read and made valuable comments on a part of my final draft. Without him I would never have embarked on this work. Without the help of my wife the book would never have been written. She has not only spurred a naturally reluctant author to work, but has developed an enthusiasm for a subject she found naturally dull, and has helped the book on its way with an immense amount of typing.

The research has involved much travel and expense, and I would like to conclude by thanking the Trustees of the Houblon-Norman Fund and the Trustees of the Leverhulme Foundation, who awarded me research grants which were invaluable.

Wheathampstead,   F. M. L. THOMPSON
Hertfordshire
March 1962

Note on Abbreviations and Footnotes

The following abbreviations are used in the footnotes:

Agric. Hist. Rev.	*Agricultural History Review*
C.R.O.	County Record Office
Econ. Hist. Rev.	*Economic History Review*
H. of L.	House of Lords
P.R.O.	Public Record Office
R.C.	Royal Commission
S.C.	Select Committee (of House of Commons unless otherwise stated)
V.C.H.	*Victoria County History*

Footnotes have been kept to a minimum, and references have not been given where the source is apparent. In particular, extensive use has been made of the standard works of reference, Burke's *Landed Gentry*, Burke's *Peerage*, and G. E. Cockayne, *The Complete Peerage*, and separate references to these have not been given.

English Landed Society in the Nineteenth Century. Map showing the country seats, and the centres of detached estates, which are chiefly mentioned in this book. A selection of other country seats is marked by numerals. All except the shaded counties are represented by documentary material in the study. The line dividing the predominantly corn counties of the east from the grazing counties of the west is from J. Caird, *English Agriculture in* 1850–51.

Key to the seats marked by numerals.

1. Lambton	24. Euston Hall
2. Wynyard	25. Ragley Hall
3. Lowther	26. Althorp
4. Holker Hall	27. Kimbolton
5. Hornby Castle	28. Garnons
6. Castle Howard	29. Madresfield
7. Harewood	30. Blenheim
8. Knowsley	31. Audley End
9. Brocklesby	32. Badminton
10. Eaton Hall	33. Ashridge
11. Cholmondeley Castle	34. Panshanger
12. Chatsworth	35. Hatfield
13. Welbeck Abbey	36. Cashiobury
14. Clumber	37. Thorndon Hall
15. Thoresby	38. Bowood
16. Alton Towers	39. Strathfieldsaye
17. Trentham	40. Knole
18. Lilleshall	41. Bifrons
19. Beaudesert	42. Powderham
20. Himley Hall	43. Berry Pomeroy
21. Burghley House	44. Petworth
22. Holkham	45. Goodwood
23. Houghton Hall	46. Arundel

Alnwick

Kielder
Belsay
Netherby

Blagdon

Netherhall
Lamplugh

Raby
Stanwick

Jervaulx

Sledmere

Little Crosby
8

Wentworth-
Woodhouse
Burton

Belvoir

Thorney
Milton
Brigstock

22

23

Ercall
Wolverhampton

Minsterley
Higham Ferrers
Overstone
Weobley
Stowe
Hinwick
Ckwellbury
Woburn
Flitwick
Gorhambury
Syon
Albury
Gatton
Savernake
Longleat
Wilton

Cheveley

24

Messing

Boxley
Sharsted
Calehill

Castle Hill

Up Ottery
Canford

Alresford

Werrington
42
43

0   100 miles

I

The Nature
of Landed Society

For as long as the horse and carriage were the symbols of social standing, and possession of stables and grooms the sign of a prosperous competence, the English landed aristocracy retained its predominant place. The power of horse and aristocrat was challenged by the railway, but both learned to recognize an ally as well as a rival in its influence. Both were vanquished by the horseless carriage of the twentieth century. From steam to motor both showed great tenacity in survival, and the power of the aristocracy disappeared no sooner than the last, anachronistic, cavalry charges of the First World War. The landed aristocracy survives into our own times with great social prestige; and the horse survives also, dignified and recreational rather than functional.

The aristocracy was not, of course, dominant in every one of the varied aspects of economic, administrative, social, religious, literary and artistic activity which go to make up the life of the nation, for to that it had never aspired and for that it was never qualified. In politics, church and army, however, and in society as we see it defined in those newspaper columns which deal with the daily lives of the great, England remained, down to 1914, or more precisely until 1922, not merely an aristocratic country, but a country of a landed aristocracy.

1

At the opening of the period covered by this book, in 1790, this order of things, the traditional and established order, made good economic and political sense though intellectually it was by no means unchallenged. Agriculture was still much the largest single occupation of the people. The wealthiest individual landowners were generally regarded as the richest men in society, though individuals with fortunes more precariously based on sugar, Indian operations politely obscure in their details, or City operations of cunning and lucrative simplicity, could already rival them in point of income. Above all, the structure of politics was weighted in favour of the landed interest. And yet by half-way through the period, by about 1850, all these conditions had ceased to exist. Even the most valuable perquisite of landed wealth, the well-endowed leisure provided by its rentier character, could be emulated from other sources well before the twentieth century. The central problem of this book is to discover how it came to pass that the social order based on landed estates survived far into an age in which the initial superiority of the landed classes in possession of the material sinews of power had evaporated.

What did survive was not an unchanging social order. If there had been rigidity, if the landed interest had been ready to take up entrenched positions in unyielding defence of power, privilege and prestige, historians of the nineteenth century would no doubt be analysing violent revolution in this country. The territorial magnates may have remained the apex of the social structure, but it was a constantly changing structure, whose components altered in character and grew or declined in importance under the pressures generated by industrialization. Neither was this apex itself of constant shape and form. The landed classes themselves formed an inner social pyramid within the structure of society at large, and here also the relations between the parts, and the nature of the individual parts, were moulded and re-moulded by the forces of ideas and of economic change. The duchess, her house party and her guests, of 1910 were superficially similar to their counterpart of 1790, but basically different. The leaders whose abdication or surrender was consummated by the First World War bore many of the same names and owned most of the same lands as their predecessors of 1790, but the leadership then relinquished bore only a pale resemblance to the proud and confident superiority assumed in the eighteenth century. The problem, then, is also to unravel some of the complicated interactions which eventually so modified the landed interest that its power came to an end without sudden crisis, revolution, or naked expropriation.

These changes, in social habits, political behaviour and financial standing, did not all stem from a single cause, but at the back of them all lay the interplay of the economics of the estates and the households they supported and the social outlook of the landowners. The problems, then, are best approached through a study of the economic and social history of the landed interest and its dependants, set against the background of those events, actions and opinions of the outside world which impinged on them. It is economic history with a difference: for where economic history in practice concerns itself with production and exchange, this must be a history of the economic affairs of a group which possessed a particular type of property. In the main they did not produce anything. They managed their property and they spent their incomes, and a history of management and of consumption forms the most important part of their economic history. It is also social history with a difference: for in place of the single class, or occupational or regional sub-class, with whom it is customary to deal, we have in the landed interest not one but several classes. Some interests they had in common, but others were in direct and sometimes open conflict. Particularly when the controlling element was acting as the champion of the national interest if necessary against the sectional interests of their own subordinates, the whole order was only held together in the arms of a violent love-hate relationship; just as the landed interest was for long held in its position of pre-eminence by the ambivalent attitude of the non-landed who, while denouncing it as functionless, privileged and parasitic, envied and sought to emulate it as the embodiment of all that was admirable in taste, manners and civilized living.

Opponents of the landed interest, whether they were discussing parliamentary reform, corn laws, the state of agriculture, or housing conditions, habitually reduced it to a set of landlords who possessed peculiar advantages for pursuing the normal human activity of furthering their own interests. Defenders and admirers of the landed interest in turn expanded it until it included not only the whole rural population, idealized as a happy harmonious community, but also every class and group which seemed to them to have any pretence of serving causes above those of private interest and profit. Thus Disraeli in 1843, with his usual flair for extravagance, claimed openly that which the more well-bred left to be assumed. 'When I talk of the preponderance of the landed interest, do not for a moment suppose that I mean merely the preponderance of "squires of high degree". . . . I do not undervalue the mere superiority of the landed classes; on the contrary I think it is a most necessary element of political power and national civilization; but I am looking to the population of our innumerable villages, to the crowds in our rural towns: aye, and I mean something more than that by the landed interest – I mean that estate of the poor . . . I mean by the estate of the poor, the great estate of the Church . . . I mean also by the landed interest that great judicial fabric, that great building up of our laws and manners which is, in fact, the ancient polity of our Realm.'[1] This was in fact less a definition of the landed interest than an adumbration of its claims to represent all that was solid and permanent in the political and social order, claims which it was scarcely necessary to formulate explicitly until the paramountcy of landed property became the subject of dispute.

The landowners headed the landed interest and controlled it, but it undoubtedly contained more than them alone. The traditional eighteenth-century view, when analysing society into those interests which merited consideration and political representation, contrasted the monied or commercial interest with the landed interest, assuming two different but not necessarily conflicting sets of interests. If discussion necessitated more precise sub-division, then an East India interest, a West India interest, a City interest, a shipping interest and a manufacturing interest could be identified. Early nineteenth-century developments added others, such as a cotton interest and a railway interest. This language of classification cut right across the lines of modern class distinctions. Not only did it make for greater terminological ease and clarity in discussing gradations than is afforded by ungainly hyphenated attempts to describe the varied

[1] Disraeli, 9 May 1843 at Shrewsbury, quoted in *The Conservative Tradition* (ed. R. J. White, 1950), pp. 174–5.

ranks who shelter under the labels of the upper, middle and working classes, but also it reflected accurately a society in which vertical divisions by sources of livelihood seemed to be more real and important than horizontal divisions by class.

The landed interest in this sense, at least until 1851, formed the largest group in society. Besides the landowners who formed the nobility and gentry of the country it comprised the great body of the agricultural community, the farmers and labourers who were the producers, and the blacksmiths, wheelwrights and publicans who provided them with services. It provided direct employment for a high proportion of the large class of domestic servants and for the sizeable body of estate workers of varied skills and trades. But it also provided the chief means of livelihood for most of the professional men and retail traders of the country towns.

The processer of agricultural produce who was in a large way of business, the brewer, distiller, tanner, miller, or clothier, probably ranked as a member of a separate interest in spite of his close links with the land. But his brethren who catered only for local needs from a base in the market town were still definitely under the wing of the landed interest at the opening of this period, as were most of those engaged in the marketing of foodstuffs. The parson was clearly a member of the agricultural community. Moreover, he was part of the landed interest by virtue of more than the ties of residence and the location of his flock, for the arm of private property reached far into the possession of livings, benefices, advowsons and preferments, and the ownership of tithes, glebes, episcopal and capitular estates showed a fine confusion of lay and clerical interests. Squire and parson shared kinship, responsibility, local leadership and often membership of the bench. The higher ranks of landed society, as we shall discover, extended their presence and influence into many more spheres than these. But in themselves these elements constituted an interest so wide in its ramifications and so widespread throughout the country that at the close of the eighteenth century it seemed as unnatural as it was impossible to imagine that the landed interest should ever collapse, disintegrate, or cease to be the preponderant interest in the kingdom.

Looked at from one point of view, this whole edifice rested on

5

the efforts of the labourers at the bottom. Looked at from another it rested on the landowners and farmers, who provided landed society with the organization, institutions, moral and social authority that made it into an effective and powerful entity. This book is mainly concerned with the landowners who were the controlling element in this order partly because they were by and large its wealthiest members, but mainly because their position was at the same time territorial and hereditary. Property in land was not merely immovable, and therefore a guarantee that its owner would have an inescapable attachment to the concerns of a particular locality, but it also formed a real, tangible and visible domain, a territory naturally felt to be under the authority of its owner. The lawyers may have got into a tangle with their distinction between real property and personal property, and their language of hereditaments and chattels took them into a world of their own, but in the roots of their concept lay a distinction which seemed plain to ordinary men. The hereditary nature of the property was perhaps even more important, for it was this which conferred stability, permanence and continuity, this which established the landed family with its generations of tradition and its wide cousinhood, distinct from the mere passing single landed individual. It was this which fostered the idea, often honoured in the breach, that the owner of an estate for the time being was steward of a trust for unborn generations and temporary recipient of the fruits of his forbears' endeavours.

We can see how Burke, the philosopher of the landed interest, arrived at his 'partnership not only between those who are living, but between those who are living, those who are dead, and those who are to be born'. The idea could be expanded until the permanence of the state and its constitution was identified with the existence of the landed interest. 'Has not the hereditary possession of a landed estate been proved by experience to generate dispositions equally favourable to loyalty and established freedom?' Coleridge asked in 1800.[1] This took the idea, familiar enough in the eighteenth century, that the House of Lords was the key element in the English constitution, the factor which by balancing between King and Commons ensured the preservation of English liberties, and interpreted it to mean that

[1] Quoted in *ibid.*, p. 178.

hereditary landowners were the source and guarantee of liberty and authority. Some arrogance, and much truth, went to furnish such a view.

Society might be envisaged as a series of vertical interest groups, and the business of politics might be conceived ideally as the reconciliation of these interests in order to arrive at the national interest, but the inner structure of the landed interest was nonetheless hierarchical. Moreover, it was generally assumed that the hierarchy within the landed interest was repeated outside it in less rigid form, for only by the deference of all to the great was social authority and respect established and society held together as an organism, viable as a mere collection of detached interests could never be. Deference and its support, the subordination of the inferior orders, could not for long survive the corrosive influence of new ideas and new economic facts with their insistence that there were essentially but three varieties of subservience and independence, corresponding to the upper, middle and working classes. When this happened the landed aristocracy might be accepted as the leaders of the upper class, and might provide the type to which its non-landed members strove to conform, but it was not an exclusively landed upper class, and a decisive step would have been taken towards the dissolution through transmogrification of landed society.

Certainly the landed aristocrat at the close of the eighteenth century already admitted some others as his social equals, or near equals. But these were admitted as individuals who were made acceptable by their wealth, manners and tendency to invest in landed estates. At the head of the landed order stood these aristocrats, 'the Major Barons, or great Landowners, with or without title,' whose pride and hauteur were at their height in the four decades before the Great Reform Bill. Next to them stood the country gentlemen, in many respects their equals in status though not in possessions. Both ranks supported and were supported by the tenant farmers, who conducted over 80 per cent of the country's farming at this time, although there were some differences between the types of tenantry to be found on the great and lesser estates. The small landowners, cultivating their own land, survivors of the true yeoman stock, fitted somewhat uneasily into the structure of the landed interest and were

7

liable to exhibit both independence and resentment of the power of the great.

Historians comparing the society of England and Continental countries have tended to imagine a greater fluidity in the upper reaches of English society than in fact existed. It is true that the attempt to turn the peerage into a legally exclusive and limited club was never repeated after the failure of the Peerage Bill in 1719, and that it remained theoretically possible for the sovereign to confer titles on whomever he pleased, in whatever numbers. In practice, however, it was not easy to acquire the acceptability and securely independent means which were essential for the grant of an hereditary peerage. It must be admitted nevertheless that the difficulties in the way of the acquisition of sufficient landed estate to satisfy the second condition were purely personal and financial, and not a matter of legal incapacity as in some countries. In any case the size of the English peerage remained roughly constant, at something under 200, from the Revolution until the advent of the Younger Pitt. The English nobility may have been prevented from becoming a caste proper by the rule of primogeniture in the inheritance of titles, but it was certainly simpler and easier to acquire a title, by straightforward cash transaction, in the France of the *ancien régime* than it was in England.[1]

It is also true that it was quite possible for a man of wits, some gentility of manner, no means and humble birth, to win acceptance and even adulation in London society, and reception in the country houses. This was at least equally possible in the Paris salons, and is a sign that the aristocracy were catholic and tolerant in their quest for enlightenment, amusement and diversion, not a proof that they were willing to receive recruits from low stations. The distinguishing mark of the English aristocracy was not readiness to absorb newcomers and syphon off new wealth and talent as it arose, but acceptance and discharge of the authority and responsibility which absence of any apparatus of centralized administration left to them.

It is only superficially a paradox that the caste attitude of the landed aristocracy became more pronounced at the very time

[1] A. S. Turberville, *The House of Lords in the Age of Reform, 1784–1837* (1958), pp. 15, 42.

that Pitt inaugurated the great expansion of the peerage.[1] Three separate considerations have to be borne in mind; the character of the creations, promotions within the peerage and the relationship between the peerage and the landed aristocracy. Although the creations of his great Administration may have increased the volume of the House of Lords by more than a third, they did not noticeably dilute the strength of its contents. The expansion was much criticized, but Disraeli's accusation that Pitt 'created a plebeian aristocracy and blended it with the patrician oligarchy. . . . He caught them in the alleys of Lombard Street and clutched them from the counting-houses of Cornhill' is beside the mark, for the only new British peer from commerce, Robert Smith who became Lord Carrington, had already ceased to be active in his banking business before his elevation, and had acquired vast landed estates in Buckinghamshire and Lincolnshire. The other banking peer of the period, Peter Thellusson, had also acquired vast landed estates, in Suffolk, and in 1806 celebrated his peerage by quitting his London house and selling the greater part of his collection of pictures, 'being much more inclined to a country residence'. His title, Rendlesham, was in any case an Irish barony.[2]

The more cogent and contemporary criticism of the expansion, that it caused discontent among the disappointed, claimed that there were 'few country gentlemen of any tolerable fortune who have not thought themselves qualified for the honour, and felt their envy excited by the promotion of some less meritorious acquaintance.' This admitted that the bulk of the new creations came from the traditional source of the peerage, the substantial landowners. For the rest Pitt turned to sources equally traditional: high service in the navy, army, diplomacy or the law.[3] Most of these were already allied to the landed aristocracy in any case, for unless they had been younger sons, or members of cadet branches, they would have found it difficult to get a good start in their careers. The great wars after 1793 naturally swelled the stream of service peerages, and this was one cause of the expansion. The other, and more important, cause was political: the forced discovery as other forms of government patronage

[1] *Blackwood's Magazine*, XXXVII (1835), 69–78.
[2] J. Greig, ed., *The Farington Diary* (1922–28), IV. 224.
[3] Turberville, *House of Lords*, pp. 45–51.

shrank that honours were a financially inexpensive, even if socially somewhat risky, method of purchasing, rewarding and consolidating political support. Once made, no politician has ever allowed this discovery to be forgotten. It remains doubtful whether any peerage has yet been granted solely for the services an individual has rendered to himself by making his fortune in trade or industry; but those who render political services—in Pitt's time landowners with influence or pocket boroughs—have since become more various in their sources of wealth and claims to political importance.

In the second place, the new peerage technique was not simply a matter of liberality in fresh creations, but also of even greater liberality in the promotion of existing peers. From the constitutional standpoint the conferment of British, or later United Kingdom, peerages on holders of Scottish or Irish titles had the same effect as new creations, since it added fresh members to the House of Lords. In political terms this was perhaps the main explanation of such conferments. But in social terms they were very much the equivalent of promotions within the English peerage. Irish titles were generally regarded as junior to those which carried writs of summons to parliament, they 'constituted an intervening grade of social rank'. It was normal to speak of an Irish peer as being 'advanced' to a peerage of Great Britain, because he enjoyed greater standing in this position. Moreover, a goodly number of Irish peers, with large estates in Ireland, were also large landowners in England, while some owned no Irish land at all. It was a matter of consequence to them to obtain a title which reflected their English interests.

This was a process which had operated throughout the eighteenth century; the Irish Earl Fitzwilliam, for example, had been advanced to the English Earl Fitzwilliam in 1746. It was much accelerated from the closing years of the century. To cite but a few examples, the Irish Earl of Shelburne was also a large Wiltshire proprietor, and in 1784 took his promotion as Marquess of Lansdowne; the Irish Baron Delaval was an important Northumbrian landowner and emerged as British Baron Delaval of Seaton Delaval in 1786; the Irish Viscount Grimston was in reality a purely English landowner and appeared more appropriately as Baron Verulam of Gorhambury in 1790; the banker Robert Smith had started his career in the peerage as the Irish

Baron Carrington, but continued more suitably as British Baron Carrington of Upton from 1797; that the Irish Baron Sheffield was more at home in Sussex was recognized in 1802, as in 1815 was the position of the Irish Viscount Melbourne as owner of Melbourne in Derbyshire and Brocket in Hertfordshire; while the vast Lancashire possessions of the Irish Earl of Sefton were not reflected in his title until 1831. To obtain an English title could be an object of consuming ambition, as we know from Frances Anne, Marchioness of Londonderry, who recorded 'thus my favourite object was attained' when in 1823 her husband the Irish Marquess was created Earl Vane and Viscount Seaham, of Wynyard and Seaham in County Durham, with a special remainder to her own son. On the same occasion the Marquess, never backward in assessing his own proper station in life, claimed that 'one step in the peerage' was the minimum reward which 'has been usual after long diplomatic service', and for himself proceeded to claim two steps, in the English peerage.[1]

The same considerations did not altogether apply to Scottish peers, for Scottish titles were not used for apprentice years in the peerage and it was not common to find a Scottish lord whose principal estates in fact lay in England. Nevertheless, landowner-ship did straddle the border, and some Scottish peers were eager enough to acquire titles appropriate to their English estates. Thus the Earl of Strathmore became Baron Bowes of Streatlam Castle, County Durham in 1815; the Earl of Balcarres became Baron Wigan, Lancashire, in 1826; and Viscount Falkland became Baron Hunsdon, Yorkshire, in 1832. But apart from this minority it was desirable even for Scottish peers whose terri-torial designations remained Scottish to obtain advancement into the British or United Kingdom peerage. This gave them mem-bership of parliament as individuals, saved them from the need to compete for a place among the limited number of Scottish Representative Peers, and thus enhanced their standing. It is perhaps significant that this avenue to membership of the House of Lords was only open after 1782, when the rule of 1711 against the conferment of British titles on Scottish peers was reversed.

If, then, the Scottish and Irish lords who became peers of parliament are added to the English lords who received advance-

---

[1] Edith, Marchioness of Londonderry, *Frances Anne* (1958), pp. 118–20.

ments, we find that the number of promotions consistently exceeded the number of new creations. This was the case not only during Pitt's Ministry of 1784–1801, when there were fifty-one creations and sixty-six promotions, but throughout the time from 1784 to the accession of Queen Victoria, in which there were in all 133 creations and 187 promotions. Indeed, the promotions exceeded the creations in every single year except 1797 and 1814, the years of Camperdown and of final victory, and 1835, a year in which the coming and going of Peel's brief Ministry produced two ministerial lists.[1]

Preoccupation with rank, precedence and dignity was evident among the nobility. Within this circle obsession with the degrees of the peerage was a new phenomenon of the age. Its most striking manifestation was the extraordinary proliferation of marquesses. A rank almost unknown in 1784, there being but two, no less than twenty-three had been created by 1837, though for some of the new marquesses it was simply a halting place, in the case of Wellington a brief halting place, before ascending to a dukedom. Others less illustrious in service had to wait longer, and had to work hard in intrigue and in display of their political wares, before they received their promotion. The Leveson-Gowers achieved a marquessate in 1786, but had to wait until 1833 before reaching the dukedom of Sutherland. The Grenvilles, as ambitious as they were proud, became Marquesses of Buckingham in 1785, but the son hankered after a dukedom in vain until 1822. Creevey in 1831 saw this same 'stately Buckingham going down to the Lords just now. I wonder how he likes the boroughs of Buckingham and St Mawe's being bowled out. He would never have been a duke without them, and can there be a better reason for their destruction?'[2] The Vanes languished for over seventy years as Earls of Darlington, but then promotion came swiftly, Marquess of Cleveland in 1827 and Duke of Cleveland in 1833, signifying both the ambition, importance and the particular brand of Whiggery of Creevey's friends the 'two arrogant rogues' of Raby. Charles Brudenell-Bruce, son of the Earl of Ailesbury, wrote to his father in 1807

---

[1] Calculated from Appendix III to Turberville, *House of Lords*. Royal dukes, successions by special limitations, and eldest sons who received writs of summons in their fathers' baronies have been omitted from the reckoning.
[2] J. Gore, ed., *Creevey* (1948), p. 323; for the hankering in 1815, p. 128.

pressing him to apply 'for the title I have so long wished to have, a Marquessate', and added 'there certainly appears no reason why you should not obtain the rank in the peerage to which your immense estates, long attachment to Government and your party interest entitle you.'[1] The father did not press his case, but the son pursued his desire in person and became Marquess of Ailesbury in 1821.

Other honours might be equally acceptable as rewards for services. 'Lord Hertford owes his blue ribbon to his having purchased *four* seats in Parliament since his father's death, and to his avowed intention of dealing still more largely in the same commodity,' observed Creevey in 1822.[2] It is symptomatic of a change in the aristocratic outlook that these elevations in rank or dignity were effective in eliciting political attachment to ministers, in place of the more familiar eighteenth-century inducements of expectations of offices or sinecures for the nobleman or his relations. Ministers may indeed have had a declining amount of financially valuable patronage at their disposal. But in turning to this alternative method of managing the great they were exploiting a passion for the emblems of prestige which came into existence independently. We may say that with the rising incomes from property from the late eighteenth century the attraction of further accessions of income from sinecures diminished; at the same time the attraction of further accessions of rank increased.

That this was so stemmed in part from the old nobility's desire to see themselves adequately differentiated in style from the newly ennobled. In this they were not entirely successful, since several families who were commoners in 1784 had penetrated as far as earldoms fifty years later, whereas by no means all the older nobility had attained that rank. More important, it seems, was a drive to sort out the nobility into the ranks proper to differing sizes of estates and degrees of general consequence. The 7th Earl of Bridgewater, for example, in 1823 bequeathed property estimated at £2 million to Lord Alford on condition that if he should die without becoming either a marquess or a duke, or should not become one within five years of becoming Lord Brownlow, then the property should go to his brother,

---

[1] Quoted by Earl of Cardigan, *The Wardens of Savernake Forest* (1949), p. 295.
[2] *Creevey*, p. 235.

Charles Henry Cust, on like terms.[1] In other words the nobility was organizing itself into a hierarchy, albeit using haphazard methods and only partially relevant considerations to attain the end. This full extension of the hierarchical principle gave some measure of cohesion and structure to the landed aristocracy. It was made under the broad pressure of subversive and revolutionary ideas and events, and indicates how the fullest formal expression of a whole social order is not reached until its classic days of unchallenged, and therefore unsystematized, supremacy are waning.[2]

At the close of the eighteenth century nobles were above all great landowners, but by no means all great landowners were noblemen. The landed aristocracy has always remained a body wider in membership than the nobility. The new creations undoubtedly inaugurated a tendency towards a greater identity between the two categories than had hitherto existed, and families of such indisputably aristocratic bearings as the Lascelles, Pelhams, Greys or Lambtons began their elevations to the earldoms of Harewood, Yarborough, Grey and Durham. An individual like Thomas Coke of Holkham, 'the greatest commoner', might stoutly resist ennoblement at the hands of the Tories until finally accepting the earldom of Leicester from the unexceptionable young Victoria. But on the whole the number of willing applicants far exceeded the ration of peerages which crown or ministers were prepared to dispense, and a great many who could well consider themselves landed aristocrats remained permanently as commoners.

Just how many one cannot easily tell, but the statistics of the 1870s show that just on half of those who had £10,000 a year or more from landed property in England were outside the ranks of the peerage. If we make the test more severe, about a quarter of those with landed incomes over £30,000 were commoners.[3]

---

[1] J. B. Burke, *The Vicissitudes of Families* (1883 ed.), II. 390. On Lord Alford dying in 1851 without fulfilling the conditions, the inheritance was contested up to the Lords, which held that the Earl of Bridgewater's condition was invalid, since it was not a matter within the devisee's control, and therefore Lord Alford's son, the Earl of Brownlow, inherited.

[2] For caste-conscious views see the debates in the Lords on the Irish Union, 1800, Cobbett's *Parliamentary History*, XXXV, esp. pp. 159–176.

[3] Calculated from J. Bateman, *The Great Landowners of Great Britain and Ireland* (1883 ed.), which in turn derived from *Parliamentary Papers*, 1874, LXXII, Return of Owners of Land, 1872–3.

This last group certainly included a few newly wealthy men of the nineteenth century, such as the Tomlines of Suffolk, but in the main it was composed of old families like the West country Aclands or rather younger families like the Sykes of Sledmere, who remained honourably content with baronetcies, or of county families with respectable ancestry like the Cornish Bassets, the Lancashire Blundells and Cliftons, the Lincolnshire Chaplins and Vyners, and the Wiltshire Wyndhams, who were innocent of all title. If this was the situation in the 1870s, eighty years earlier the peers must have formed a distinct minority of the landed aristocracy.

The landed aristocrats had much in common besides the possession of large landed estates. Their upbringing, way of life, family setting, occupations, avocations, social outlook and political beliefs, though certainly not conforming to any rigid or stereotyped pattern, were all shaped by a readily identifiable mould. They formed a loosely-knit club whose unwritten rules ensured that all members were gentlemen, and it was they above all who formed the standards of gentlemanly conduct. The strength and virtue of the conventions which governed behaviour were that they permitted great diversity and colourful eccentricity, and very rarely produced either that hypocrisy of mere outward conformism or that brand of well-bred inhibition which have sometimes been attributed to the English upper classes. The starchy idolization of etiquette belongs to the aspirants, the new genteel, somewhat uncertain of their position. The landed gentleman could afford to be unconventional without endangering his standing because the solid guarantee of his estate lay behind him. Thus in the revolutionary period when a duke was found among the Jacobin sympathizers, it occasioned criticism of the mischievous folly of his views, but did not impugn the aristocratic status of the Howards.

Nevertheless, individual diversity existed within a framework of behaviour some or all of whose features were generally accepted by landed gentlemen. In politics, for example, differences between factions or parties were normally about personalities, tactics, the requirements of expediency or the scale of priorities. Even parliamentary reformers within the landed groups felt that they were seeking to preserve and strengthen, not overthrow, the fundamental structure of government and distribution of power, to which their opponents also expressed attachment. The quality of a gentleman is elusive and difficult to define, and is perhaps best captured from the atmosphere conveyed by the picture of the landed order as a whole. Certain characteristics, however, may be singled out as illustrating the roots of behaviour in the possession of estates.

Honour, dignity, integrity, considerateness, courtesy and chivalry were all virtues essential to the character of a gentleman, and they all derived in part from the nature of country life. Not only did the stability and permanence of country society foster the subordination of personal whims to these traditional and enduring values. But also the intimate nature of country society, its lack of openings for anonymity, its necessary exposure to the public eye of many of the doings of landowners, called forth these very virtues which made for good feelings, neighbourliness and absence of friction. At the turn of the century such perversions as pride and arrogance were widely commented upon, but there is little reason to think that these were ever typical of the order.

A gentleman's attitude to money is proverbially one of lordly indifference, but while there are many examples at this time of recklessness, ostentation or simple disdain of tradesmen's bills, this is too simple a view of the matter. Normally, value for money was expected; where extortionate charges were made the dignified course was to refrain from haggling but withdraw one's custom for the future. Certainly, where an occasion called for special display or effort, a coming of age, a royal visit, a contested election, it was aristocratic not to count the cost. This, however, was but one aspect of a general subordination of money matters to more important considerations. Indeed, for as long as land was chiefly valued for the social and political consequence which it conferred, and the facilities for founding a family which it presented, the profit motive could hardly be the uppermost consideration in its management. Nonetheless, this did not make prudent management, or careful judgment in the buying and selling of land or horses, unrespectable, even if they were by no means universally practised. In general, concern for the well-being of the propertyless poor, who were directly or indirectly his dependants, was as much a part of the character of the landed gentleman as it was an essential element in the structure of the deference society. Paternalism, which the outside world found it easy to criticize as autocratic, he looked upon as a natural accompaniment of landed wealth, and indeed as one of its prime justifications. It could be practised to best effect from a well-run estate.

In law a gentleman is 'a man who has no occupation'. Envy and denunciation of those 'who toil not neither do they spin' long preceded Joseph Chamberlain. But if they did not have gainful occupations, landed aristocrats filled their days in a great variety of ways, most of them of great benefit to the community. Some were absorbed by the attractions of agricultural improvement at the turn of the century, and devoted a great deal of time to the management of their home farms and estate. Some gave much detailed attention to the business of county administration through quarter sessions. Others were attracted by politics and either assisted in the business of government at Westminster or in the colonies, or at least helped to operate the machinations by which combinations were formed and patronage was secured and dispensed. Some might devote themselves to the arts as practitioners, and not infrequently excel the professionals. Connoisseurship and patronage of painting, sculpture, architecture, music, literature or scholarship was widespread, generally informed by a discriminating taste which left great riches to posterity. For many, participation in the pleasures and engagements of society life was occupation enough in itself. The chief interest of others lay in hunting, racing or shooting. Yet none was able to lead a life which was either wholly private or wholly devoted to the pursuit of his personal inclinations. All refreshed themselves, from time to time, at their country houses with country pursuits. All acknowledged, even if only occasionally, that the privileges of leisure were balanced by the duties and responsibilities of leadership and administration which were attached to landed estates.

Individually gentlemen, collectively the landed aristocrats formed a series of families, so linked by intermarriage that they have been likened to tribes. The family interest and the family reputation were normally superior to the claims of any individual within it. Only rarely does an aristocrat appear who was indifferent to the claims of loyalty to the family, its fair name, its traditions and its future, and was prepared to sacrifice these to present indulgence. The landed family was wide in extent, embracing several generations and degrees of cousinhood, not usually under a single roof so much as under the protection of a single estate. The estate was expected to succour the inner family, and the head of the family was expected to put the influence derived from the estate at the disposal of the more distant members. Certainty of inheritance, which safeguarded the continuity and integrity of the family estates, did not always make for harmonious relations within the family, but it ensured the permanent importance of the landed family as an institution in English life.

Predominantly, landed families revolved round their menfolk. Those gifted ladies who ventured into the man's world of politics, like the Duchess of Devonshire or Lady Melbourne, were careful to conceal their evident power and prowess beneath a veil of deferment to the male politicians. Nevertheless, there was a strong matriarchal undercurrent beneath the surface of male ascendancy and manly virtues. Not only were the dowagers formidable figures in the aristocratic world, but also mothers usually had the arrangement of marriages, the instruments by which families were made and the tribal connections formed. From marriage the landed aristocrat might hope for both love and good fortune. It was the mothers with marriageable daughters who largely determined the field of selection, and contrived suitable combinations of these qualities. George Lamb, younger brother to Lord Melbourne the prime minister, described the process in an unsuccessful comic opera of 1807:

> 'And every candid female here allows
> How hard a Misses life, who seeks a spouse,
> At Operas, plays, and routs we never fail,
> Put up, alas! to everlasting sale.
> . . . . .
> At night again, on us all pleasures pall;
> Bid for by inch of candle at a ball –
> And e'en when fashion's toilsome revels cease,
> For us no pause, no liberty, no peace –
> Then when the Matrons speak of suppers small,
> "A few choice friends besides ourselves – that's all,"
> This language in plain truth they mean to hold
> "A girl by private contract to be sold." '[1]

[1] Quoted by Mabell, Countess of Airlie, *In Whig Society* (1921), pp. 69–70.

Marriage was rightly regarded as a serious matter, with far more at stake than gratification of momentary infatuations. Social compatibility, adequate provision for children and for the bride should she chance to be widowed, the formation of desirable connections and the advancement of the family's standing were the important purposes served by match-making. Those who escaped from the toils and found spouses of humble birth served to emphasize the conventions through the comment which their *mésalliances* regularly excited.

When momentous issues were at stake, and the rescue of an estate from ill-fortune was in question, the conduct of marriages was liable to be taken out of the hands of the matrons. Necessity impelled an impoverished aristocrat to seek a bride of fortune. An heiress to a landed family was the most desirable solution in such a situation, but one who was willing to unite such wealth to foundering gentility could not always be found, unless a large advance in rank was involved. In default, the occasion called for an infusion of mercantile wealth. By marrying his daughters into the established nobility many a man of new wealth smoothed the path to respectability. This sensible arrangement brought much needed succour to some old families, and provided a means of entry into landed society. Thus private necessities helped to preserve the old order from such rigidity and exclusiveness as might have built up explosive resentment against it.

The kind of new wealth which was absorbed in this way was, however, limited. Lord Sefton's adviser, canvassing ways of clearing off a debt of some £40,000, made this tolerably plain. After discussing various other courses he came to the possibility of the heir, Lord Molyneux, marrying. 'To marry a fine brought up Lady with little or no fortune would be to hurt the Estate. By the Estate [which was currently in 1791 worth some £8,500 a year] he has a right to expect a large sum with a Lady, not to look at less than 60,000 . . . *many* a great and rich banker would be glad of the offer to give his daughter that fortune for her advancement and dignity (vide Messrs. Child), or many a rich heiress to a large estate and of good family would also be glad of the offer.'[1]

---

[1] Lancashire C.R.O., Sefton MSS, DDM 11/63, Arrangements for paying Lord Sefton's debts, 1791.

Bankers were among the few sizeable groups which had such sums available for investment in the social advancement of their daughters. But the wealthiest set among them, the London private bankers, had the added advantage of close and confidential contacts with the landed aristocracy whose money affairs they handled and very often alone understood. Alongside the bankers' daughters one should place the daughters of some of the wealthiest lawyers, brewers and West India plantation owners, three other groups possessing either close connections or affinities with the landed magnates, though in their case it was normal for the father to establish himself first as a large landed proprietor, before his daughters became marriageable. This method of social mobility scarcely operated outside these spheres. The age of the American heiresses lay well in the future. The case of the three Caton sisters from America, who had completed their trilogy of marriages to the Marquesses of Carmarthen and Wellesley and Lord Stafford by 1836, was then still unique. 'It is a singular instance,' remarked the gossip Thomas Raikes, 'of three sisters, foreigners, and of a nation hitherto little known in our aristocratical circles, allying themselves to such distinguished families in England.'[1]

In many respects the country gentry and squirearchy resembled those above them, the landed aristocracy, except in the scale of their possessions and style of living. The homogeneity of the two groups, nobility and gentry, magnates and squires, often thought of as forming the single order of the English landed gentry, was however subject to two crucial qualifications, one social and one economic. The gentry were at one and the same time a more fluid class than the aristocracy, permitting easier entry and exit, and as a result of the provincial limits prescribed by their resources and way of life fundamentally a more conservative class. Taken together, these two factors played a substantial part in the prolongation of the aristocratic control of society.

The gentry had wide scope for intermarriage with their own kind, and used their opportunities freely for improving the interconnections of county families. But the gentry also formed connections fairly freely with non-landed families who were

[1] *Journal of Thomas Raikes* (1856–7), II. 383–4.

roughly their equals. In such marriages daughters of the clergy abounded, followed by those of other professional groups, but country bankers, merchants, career officers or servants of the East India Company were also well represented in this way. Families of tradesmen who were akin to shopkeepers were not held to be eligible, and neither were those of manufacturers generally acceptable until they had had a chance to acquire at least second generation respectability. Nevertheless, this provided a fairly broad avenue of recruitment into landed society, one which generally proved of mutual advantage to the parties concerned.

Of greater importance was the facility enjoyed by new wealth for the acquisition of social position through land purchase. This was of course no new phenomenon, and fortunes made in trade, finance or the law had long found their way into landed estates. In the course of the eighteenth century the element of pure investment in this process, the search for a secure home for savings, had diminished. It continued as an act of social investment, the surest way to satisfy the urge to found a family. Because of the price of land, its relative scarcity in the market and the level of social ambition of the new men, it was as landed gentry rather than as landed magnates that they usually emerged. The important point was that while fortunes from trade continued to take this route, they were joined by the newer fortunes from mining and industry. In the early decades of this period, while the Sykes of Sledmere exemplified the old practice in their transformation from Hull merchant to East Riding landowner, the new practice could be seen in the acquisition of estates by the Darbys from iron, Matthew Boulton from engineering, the Peels, Arkwrights, Fieldens and Strutts from cotton, Marshall from flax, the Ridleys, Cooksons and Cuthberts from coal, or Samuel Whitbread from brewing.

By no means all successful businessmen sought to set themselves up as landed gentlemen. But that a good many of the most able and forceful could do so was a source of great strength to the landed interest. Money placed in land could not, of course, always purchase automatic and instantaneous acceptance. Established county society often scorned newcomers as vulgar aspirants, and it might take two generations for humble origins to be forgiven, in the course of which it might become congenial or

21

politic to sever connection with the business on which the fortune was founded. But fresh applicants for land and status were all the time forthcoming, and the fact that this process of absorption into landed society was continually in motion must be accounted a prime reason for the failure of the cleavage between capitalists and landowners ever to become so deep as to be unbridgeable.

Movement out of the landed gentry was also of consequence in preserving contacts with other social groups. Apart from cases of individual misfortune this was a function of the size of gentry estates, for their resources did not allow of large provisions for younger sons. Younger sons of the landed aristocracy were certainly not debarred from having careers, but these were more likely to be dignified than self-supporting, and to require injections of private income supplied by allowances from the family estate. Younger sons of the gentry, on the other hand, were likely to seek careers which would support their independence. Such careers might simply be the less ornamental versions of the careers favoured by the aristocracy, in church, army or civil service. They could also include practice in the law, other professions, or entry into a merchant's business, while younger sons whose fathers or grandfathers had been in industry might well enter the old firm. For instance, in the family of Cumberland squires, the Dickinsons of Lamplugh, around 1800 we find brothers who were an attorney, a liquor merchant, a grocer and a mariner.[1] This flow from landed families into business and the professions was another important factor in preventing the landed gentry from developing the isolation of a caste, and in blurring the distinction between the landed interest and the rest of society.

Against these elements of fluidity in the gentry class, however, we must set the underlying conservatism of the great body of the landed gentry. However much the gentry shared the standards and conventions of the aristocracy, they did not share fully in their metropolitan and cosmopolitan life. The incomes and habits of the gentry made the county the normal sphere of their activity. Even if they entered politics they could not usually contemplate the luxuries of borough-mongering or contested elections, but would appear as county members seated by the

---

[1] Red How, Lamplugh, Cumberland, Dickinson MSS, Will of John Dickinson, 30 Oct. 1802, and connected documents.

consensus of county opinion without expense of contest. County ways and outlook tended to change a good deal more slowly than London habits. Moreover, as industrialization advanced, the gentry in the counties had fewer opportunities and less necessity than the aristocracy for making bargains and compromises with the new thrusting interests which operated at the national level. It was not for nothing that county administration continued in its old unregenerate quarter-session ways until 1888.

Ultimately, of course, not even county society could resist the forces of change. In the late nineteenth century and much of the twentieth century, the gentry have been less favourably placed than the aristocracy in the struggle for economic survival, a return to the situation prevailing in the corresponding period 200 years earlier. This has meant the dilution of county circles by many whose gardens are their only landed property, thus helping in the by no means unsuccessful effort to preserve many of the features of county society, from its hunt balls to its instinctive leadership.

The essential point, however, is that change here came a generation or two after changes at the centre had led the aristocracy either to share power or to accept a lower place for the landed interest in determining the course of government. From their country seats the aristocracy shared the life of county society, and while they were taking part in these central changes they found periodical consolation, reassurance and encouragement in the traditional and unchanging order of the countryside. Indeed, stability in the counties seemed, to the aristocracy, to make possible concessions and compromises on other fronts without incurring mortal risks to the deference society. When, in some heavily industrialized counties, this stability was threatened by insubordination from urban and industrial elements, we find that the aristocracy felt they had reached the edge of the precipice, and that the time had come to abandon compromises and efforts to accommodate the forces of change. Thus in the West Riding in 1848, in the face of a threat from a section of his own party 'to subvert the legitimate influence of the aristocracy of the land', Lord Fitzwilliam felt compelled to advocate 'an union of moderate men of both parties for the common safety'. A friendly critic interpreted this as a desire to put 'all the aristocracy and landed gentry on one side, the democracy and town people on the other.'[1] This attempt to organize politics along the lines of class divisions was abortive, and for the country as a whole it was premature at that time to hold that the fabric of county society was threatened. The incident, however, shows the sensitivity of the landed aristocracy in this sphere, and hence the great importance of the gentry in preserving a stable order in the counties. The reverse side of this coin was the political dependence of the gentry on the aristocracy. By circumstance and tradition the gentry inclined towards a 'country party' position in politics, and could not aspire to form or conduct governments. Unable to provide leadership from within their own ranks, the gentry had perforce to accept the lead of the aristocratic groups, often more flexible and less conservative in policy than themselves. Sometimes recalcitrant, often reluctant, the gentry had to accept reforms, at the hands of Whig and Tory alike, for anything more than token resistance could only lead them into the wilderness. In this fashion the social conservatism of the gentry was prevented from developing its corollary of political intransigence.

The differences between the two key elements in the landed interest, the aristocracy and the gentry, and their interdependence, thus furnished a mechanism by which the peaceful transformation of landed society was accomplished. The landed gentry provided the safety valve through which some of the pressure of new wealth escaped into the relaxing atmosphere of landed proprietorship. The landed aristocracy, through its metropolitan and national responsibilities, was inescapably confronted with the problems of the new England generated by coal, steam and iron. It was eventually prepared to accept the new realities, while the gentry, because they were fundamentally capable only of political obstruction and not of political initiative, were constrained to accept from conservative hands changes which they would have resisted to the death if proposed by middle-class radicals. The end result in the twentieth century was rule by an élite who were no longer a landed aristocracy, and control of the counties by notabilities who were no longer an exclusively landed gentry.

[1] Sheffield Central Library, Wentworth Woodhouse MSS, G.7.d, H. Walker to Lord Fitzwilliam, 6 Nov. 1848; Lord Fitzwilliam to J. H. Scarlett, 29 Nov. 1848; J. G. Marshall to Lord Fitzwilliam, 29 Nov. 1848.

II

◇◇

Aristocratic England

◇◇

WHETHER considered in economic terms, as owners of estates above a certain size, or in social terms, as men who were undoubted powers in the land, the landed aristocracy was to be found in every part of the country, though it definitely favoured some parts more than others. It was a group of rather over 300 landed families which contained wide differences of wealth and resources. These ranged from the grandees who already by 1790 could comfortably dispose of over £50,000 a year, such as the Dukes of Bedford, Bridgewater, Devonshire or Northumberland, down to individuals like the Earl of Clarendon whose income from land at this time was about £3,000 a year, and whose ancient lineage compensated for this modesty of resources and ensured that he was indisputably an aristocrat in the political and social as well as legal senses of the term.

The feature which they all had in common was the ability to support both a country mansion and the establishment which went with it, and a metropolitan life during the London season. This in effect constituted a minimum financial qualification for membership of the aristocracy, and provides a yardstick by which its size and geographical distribution can be measured. It is not, however, a yardstick which permits of precise measurement, for even when the size of individual incomes is accurately known it is notoriously difficult to define a social group in terms of income size. The rough rule for most of the nineteenth century was that

25

'a man who only wanted all the conveniences and comforts that London and the country could give, could have them for 10,000l. a year. To spend more than this, he must go into horse-racing or illegitimate pleasures.'[1] For the closing years of the eighteenth century the minimum annual aristocratic expenditure was substantially less than this, perhaps little more than one half. For although the ensuing rise in the cost of provisions did not by itself make an overwhelming impression on the aristocratic cost of living, the increase in servants' wages and the rise in the cost of London housing, taken with it, did produce a decisive effect. In addition there was a practically continuous tendency for the scale of living expected of an aristocrat to expand and luxuriate, a tendency which had set in during the eighteenth century and was not to be decisively halted and reversed until after 1914. Nevertheless for the early nineteenth century Jane Austen provides some confirmation for the general rule when she says that a £10,000 a year man was as good as a lord.

There were always some cases in which a family's landed income was too small to permit this level of expenditure, and yet it clearly remained part of the aristocracy. Almost invariably in such instances of deficiency in landed estate a peerage was an essential element in the retention of aristocratic status. Very occasionally, as in the cases of de Lisle of Garendon Park, Leicestershire, or Legh of High Legh Park, Cheshire, possession of sound claims to really ancient descent might suffice by themselves, without any title. Sometimes deficiency in landed income was compensated by enjoyment of income from other sources, but the usual compensation was not financial so much as the social weight attached to a title or ancient lineage, or both. It was a method of circumventing the financial canons of aristocracy which, however, had its limits. As Townsend put it in 1865, 'There is no pedigree in England, and very few in Europe, which can vie with that of the Earls of Devon—and, unlike most, it is not of heralds' manufacture – but an additional five thousand acres would represent five times the political influence derived from that descent.'[2]

[1] W. Bence Jones, 'Landowning as a Business', *The Nineteenth Century*, XI (1882), p. 254.
[2] J. L. Sanford and M. Townsend, *The Great Governing Families of England* (1865), I. 9.

On the other hand the landed aristocracy did not consist of the peerage plus all those with incomes of over £10,000 a year from land, but rather of the peerage plus a fraction of these other great landowners. For at any given moment some of those who qualified on bare financial grounds either did not wish to live as aristocrats, or from the rawness of their origins were not yet acceptable as such. The Chaplins of Blankney, Lincolnshire, for example, were a well established family by the end of the seventeenth century, and by the nineteenth century owned an estate of over 20,000 acres; they preferred to remain great squires, and to furnish a dynasty of county members, and did not definitely merge into the aristocracy until the acceptance of a peerage in 1916. If, therefore, the income requirement is translated into possession of an estate of 10,000 acres or more, a reasonably reliable guide is provided for measuring the size and distribution of the landed aristocracy, for while it excludes some who socially and politically formed part of the group, it includes others who did not.

In 1872 Lord Derby managed to procure an official return of the landowners of the United Kingdom, showing the acreage and annual value of their estates, with the object of confounding the popular opinion that landownership was concentrated into the hands of a mere 30,000 individuals, an opinion based on the shifting sands of the Census occupation tables. Thus originated the Return of Owners of Land in 1873, commonly called the New Domesday Survey, the first and last survey of English landownership since 1086. As a weapon in political controversy it proved to be a boomerang, for although it showed that there were over a million individuals who owned some land in the British Isles, even if it was frequently no larger than a cabbage patch, it also showed that four-fifths of the land of the United Kingdom was owned by less than 7,000 persons. As the only solid point of reference in a sea of conjecture the New Domesday Book is indispensable to any discussion of the distribution of land in England, both at the date of compilation, and in the century which preceded and the half-century which followed it, during which changes in landownership were not sweeping enough to render it inapplicable.[1]

[1] Lord Derby's motion Hansard *Parliamentary Debates*, 3rd ser., CCIX, 1872, Feb. 19. *Parliamentary Papers*, 1874, LXXII, Return of Owners of Land 1872–3. The

Just before the New Domesday return was made, Townsend in 1865 produced a map of the great landowners of England, as part of his introduction to the thirty essays which formed the *Great Governing Families of England*. There are some 217 country seats on his map, which allowing for the double appearances of some of the grandees who were great men in more than one county, represented some 202 individuals. These, to Townsend, constituted the aristocracy: 'it is, then, perhaps, worth while to define what the English "Aristocracy" really means. It is, I conceive, only another word for the greater owners of land.'[1] Of his 202 great landowners, thirty-six turned out to have estates of less than 10,000 acres in England. Of these thirty-six, however, nine had estates elsewhere in the United Kingdom which brought their total landed property above 10,000 acres, and a further fourteen had landed incomes of over £10,000 a year even though their estates were relatively small in area. Townsend's aristocracy, therefore, conforms closely to the income and property qualifications already arrived at.

To Townsend, however, not every great landowner qualified for insertion on his map. In 1873 there were some 360 owners of estates of over 10,000 acres in England, and although prior to the appearance of the New Domesday Book Townsend might understandably have been unaware of the existence of some of the less illustrious of these, ignorance alone certainly did not account for the great bulk of omissions from his tally. In effect Townsend applied some unstated criteria of social and political influence to reduce the general body of great landowners to the smaller élite of the landed aristocracy, criteria whose vividness and objectivity were doubtless not seriously impaired by the difficulty of defining the principles on which they were based. Possession of a hereditary title as well as a large estate was clearly one of the main qualifications. Of the 363 owners of

---

errors, defects, and misrepresentations of the New Domesday were widely examined at the time, for example by A. Arnold, *Free Land* (1880); G. C. Brodrick, *English Land and English Landlords* (1881); J. Bateman, an appendix in Brodrick's work, and *The Great Landowners of Great Britain and Ireland* (final ed. 1883). For analysis of estates of over 3,000 acres Bateman's work has been used extensively; for convenience this analysis is referred to the date 1873, although it is in fact drawn from the material of both 1873 and 1883.

[1] Sanford and Townsend, *op. cit.*, I. 9.

estates of over 10,000 acres, 186 were peers, 58 were baronets, and 117 were untitled; whereas of the 202 mapped individuals, 168 were peers, 19 were baronets, and only 15 were without titles.

There were a few commoners, both baronets and gentry, whose exclusion from the map might have been queried or resented. To name but a few, Whitbread of Southill Park, Abel Smith of Woodhall Park, Fermor-Hesketh of Rufford Hall, Thorold of Syston Park, Trevelyan of Wallington, Savile of Rufford Abbey, Bowes of Streatlam Castle, or Sykes of Sledmere, might have a legitimate sense of grievance at not obtaining notice on a map which managed to find room for men who were much inferior to them in property and scarcely their social superiors, such as Radcliffe of Rudding Park, Cotterell of Garnons, Miles of Kingsweston, Miles of Leigh Court, quite apart from Colonel Patten of Bank House, Warrington, whose estate was very modest. But while Townsend's inclusions and exclusions of commoners may appear capricious, his general bias in favour of the nobility remains understandable. In any case, although he included, on account of their local importance, a number of peers whose purely English estates fell below the 10,000 acre limit, there was a very much greater number of peers whose seats might well have been plotted, on account of their possessions and their consequence. These absent nobles ranged from the Duke of Buccleuch, through the Marquess of Headfort, to the Earls of Dysart, Eldon, Harrington, Harrowby, Jersey and Redesdale, and the Lords Carrington, Aveland, Clinton, Howard of Glossop, Bolton, Stanley of Alderley, Walsingham, Waveney, and Willoughby de Broke, to name only some of the more conspicuous.

Without, therefore, accepting all the details of Townsend's map, it does show the general distribution of aristocratic seats. Their density in each county is shown in Table I. These figures are useful in showing the lack of uniformity in the location of seats over the country as a whole, the considerable diversity between neighbouring counties, and the attractiveness of the different counties to the aristocracy. The density of aristocratic settlement ranges from one seat to every 31,000 acres in Rutland, to one to 449,000 acres in Westmorland. The nine most densely settled counties include two, Hertfordshire and Kent, which were attractive for residential purposes because of their proximity to London; but also four, Cheshire, Dorset, Durham, and Staffordshire, which are well removed from the metropolis, and the remaining home counties did not enjoy anything like an equal popularity with the aristocracy. Buckinghamshire, indeed, is to be found among the nine most sparsely seated counties. The

TABLE I

COUNTIES IN ORDER OF DENSITY OF COUNTRY SEATS IN 1865

Number of acres (in thousands) per seat
(The ranking of each county in Table II is noted in brackets)

1.	Rutland	31	(1)	21.	Hereford	129	(36)
2.	Stafford	64	(8)	22.	Bedford	143	(15)
3.	Hertford	65	(18)	23.	Middlesex	145	(39)
4.	Huntingdon	72	(30)	24.	Sussex	149	(19)
5.	Kent	73	(34)	25.	Oxford	150	(33)
6.	Northampton	75	(9)	26.	Norfolk	156	(28)
7.	Cheshire	76	(6)	27.	Hampshire	160	(21)
8.	Dorset	84	(4)	28.	Cambridge	175	(35)
9.	Durham	94	(11)	29.	Devon	177	(23)
10.	Lancashire	101	(16)	30.	Essex	191	(38)
11.	Nottingham	101	(3)	31.	Shropshire	202	(22)
12.	Wiltshire	103	(5)	32.	Northumberland	203	(2)
13.	Leicester	104	(27)	33.	Buckingham	229	(25)
14.	Derby	105	(7)	34.	Somerset	243	(24)
15.	Gloucester	106	(31)	35.	Yorkshire	258	(10)
16.	Berkshire	108	(29)	36.	Cornwall	276	(14)
17.	Warwick	108	(17)	37.	Cumberland	281	(26)
18.	Surrey	109	(37)	38.	Lincoln	403	(12)
19.	Worcester	111	(32)	39.	Westmorland	449	(13)
20.	Suffolk	115	(20)				

Source: J. L. Sanford and M. Townsend, *The Great Governing Families of England* (1865), I, endplate map.

distribution by size of counties, or by prevailing types of agriculture, whether cereal-growing, stock-keeping, or dairying was almost entirely random. If, however, we make the classic Severn-Wash division between highland and lowland England (throwing in the three south-western counties with the North and West), which produces two approximately equal groups of counties, then seven out of the nine most sparsely seated counties were in the North and West. This might reflect the real or supposed scenic or climatic drawbacks of Cumberland, Westmorland and Northumberland, but such discouragements to residence can hardly be held to have applied to Shropshire, Cornwall or Somerset. In fact it would seem that nearness to London was of considerable, though not of decisive, importance in the siting of aristocratic seats.

It must be emphasized that this pattern of distribution was of mansions and was largely influenced by considerations of comfort and convenience. Inasmuch as they were the places of residence, and were all in the heart of at least sizeable portions of the family's estates, the pattern gives a general impression of the way in which the social power of the aristocracy was spread. But the bulk of a family's estates was not necessarily in the same county as the family seat, and many of the largest estates were scattered over several counties. The distribution of great estates was in some respects markedly different from that of aristocratic seats. The proportion of the area of each county occupied by estates of over 10,000 acres, and parts of estates which in aggregate reached that size, is given in Table II. From the point of view of the economic position of the great landowners as such, it is this table which gives a picture of the varying importance of large estates in different counties. Even the great landowning peers' political influence was related to the size of their estates as well as to the location of their seats. Thus the Duke of Northumberland was of much greater importance in his county than was Earl Stanhope in Kent, though Alnwick Castle and Chevening Park each counted as one seat; and the Duke of Cleveland was a power in Shropshire as well as in Durham, where his seat of Raby Castle lay. These points are best allowed for by taking actual estate size into consideration.

The lack of uniformity in the distribution of great estates over the country is at once evident in Table II, and the frequent wide differences between adjoining counties. These great estates, in 1873, occupied nearly a quarter of the area of England as a whole. Three counties, Bedford, Lancashire and Warwick, themselves conformed exactly to this national average, but the spectrum ranged from 53 per cent of the area of Rutland, 50 per cent of Northumberland, and 38 per cent of Nottinghamshire, down to 4 per cent of Middlesex, 9 per cent of Essex, and 10 per cent of Surrey, in the hands of great landowners.

31

Table II
THE GREAT ESTATES

Counties in order of the proportion of total area (excluding waste) occupied by estates which in aggregate exceeded 10,000 acres.

Percentage of total area

1.	Rutland	53	21.	Hampshire	21
2.	Northumberland	50	22.	Shropshire	21
3.	Nottingham	38	23.	Devon	20
4.	Dorset	36	24.	Somerset	20
5.	Wiltshire	36	25.	Buckingham	19
6.	Cheshire	35	26.	Cumberland	19
7.	Derby	31	27.	Leicester	19
8.	Stafford	31	28.	Norfolk	19
9.	Northampton	30	29.	Berkshire	17
10.	Yorkshire	28	30.	Huntingdon	17
11.	Durham	28	31.	Gloucester	16
12.	Lincoln	28	32.	Worcester	16
13.	Westmorland	27	33.	Oxford	15
14.	Cornwall	27	34.	Kent	12
15.	Bedford	24	35.	Cambridge	11
16.	Lancashire	24	36.	Hereford	11
17.	Warwick	24	37.	Surrey	10
18.	Hertford	23	38.	Essex	9
19.	Sussex	23	39.	Middlesex	4
20.	Suffolk	22			

Average for all England: 24 per cent

Source: J. Bateman, *The Great Landowners of Great Britain and Ireland* (1883 ed.)

Regionally the pattern of distribution is again most variegated, with some tendency for the North and West to have a higher proportion of great estates than the South and East. Thus of the fourteen counties which were above the national average, nine were in the North and West, while of the twenty-two counties which were below average, only seven were in that half of England. Stock and dairy counties like Northumberland, Cheshire and Derbyshire were near the top of the table, but so also were arable counties like Dorset, Northamptonshire and Wiltshire. A grass county, Herefordshire, was near the bottom but so also was an arable county, Cambridge. The influence of London made itself felt in the immediate Home Counties, Kent, Surrey, Essex and Middlesex, where the demand for land was such that it was impossible or undesirable to build up or retain very large estates. Outside this immediate vicinity the metropolitan influence against concentration of ownership was not very apparent. A second influence of the recent or past price of land can be detected in the way in which great estates tended to favour those counties which either possessed or had once possessed large tracts of poor, infertile, or barren land, which as in the case of Lincolnshire might at one time have been acquired relatively cheaply. Such influences might reinforce the effects of history, such as proximity to borders which had once been serious military frontiers, but equally they might conflict with other material considerations like the uncongeniality of fen lands or the attractions of good fox-hunting country, so that the 1873 pattern was a patchwork rather than a symmetrical design.

The conclusion must be that although the landed aristocracy and the great estates were not spread evenly over the country, the unevenness of their distribution fails to show any such unmistakeable rhythm or bias as would make their social and economic history specifically typical of any particular geographical or farming regions, and clearly unrepresentative of others. On the contrary, a pronounced aristocratic presence may be thought of as normal for the great majority of counties, either in the form of great estates occupying from a fifth to a half of their area, or in the shape of a network of great country houses dominating their landscape. At the same time, in a few counties, isolated from each other, the aristocratic element was sufficiently weak to allow an unusual degree of prominence and independence to the landed gentry, and even in one or two cases to the yeoman class of small landowners, as the discussion in Chapter V indicates. Without anticipating this discussion a rough measure of this aristocratic presence can be made by blending the two tables. This shows that Rutland was beyond question the most aristocratic county, followed by Staffordshire, Dorset, Cheshire, Nottinghamshire, and Northamptonshire, in that order. Essex was the least aristocratic county, with Cambridge and Cumberland in joint second place, Middlesex third, Buckinghamshire, Oxfordshire, and Somerset sharing fourth place, and Herefordshire fifth. Nevertheless there is only one county, Essex, which appears in the last quarter of both tables, and in general this scattering of aristocratic influence may be regarded as uneven but impartial.

This general picture of aristocratic England applies strictly only to the years immediately around 1873, and the actual figures, especially of the proportion of area held in great estates, cannot be considered to apply to any other period. On the other hand there is reason to believe that the general order of ranking of the different counties revealed by this analysis had remained broadly unaltered since 1790, and was to remain broadly unaffected until 1919. In the case of the country seats of the aristocracy we can be reasonably certain of this. Of those marked on Townsend's map only some four would have been unnoticed on a similar map in 1790, because their owners acquired their estates and their standing after that date. These were Drayton Manor, the seat of Sir Robert Peel, Canford Manor, the seat of Sir John Guest, Alresford Grange, the seat of Lord Ashburton, and Overstone Park, the seat of Lord Overstone. Conversely, there were only a few country seats which might have been shown on a map drawn up in 1790, but were not shown in 1865, on the grounds that not only had they changed hands in the interval, but also the new owner was of less aristocratic potency than his predecessor. Rufford Abbey might be an example of this; owned in 1790 by a nephew of the last Savile baronet, who succeeded to the Earldom of Scarborough in 1807, by 1865 it was in the hands of Henry Savile (Lumley), second illegitimate son of the 8th Earl of Scarborough. On the other hand where the title of one of the grandees of the 1790 period, such as the Duke of Dorset, had subsequently become extinct, the mansion in question, Knole Park, was still entered in 1865, under the name of the descendant then in possession, the Countess Amherst.

It is also true that few if any of the seats recorded in 1865 had ceased to be tenanted with aristocratic vigour before 1919, though the continued occupation of some had by that time become precarious. Equally, it is doubtful whether a man of Townsend's fastidiousness and discrimination would have admitted any newcomers to his list after 1865, although there were a few new landowners on an aristocratic scale, and a rather larger number of new men who sought to infuse an aristocratic style of living into old mansions.

It is less easy to be positive that the estate distribution of 1873 was the same as that of earlier or later periods. The general impression is that the tendency was towards greater concentration of ownership from 1790 and before until a few years after 1873, and that existing great estates tended to expand more by fresh purchases than to shrink by sales of inconveniently situated outlying properties.[1] The aggregation of estates through marriage of heiresses and by inheritance was less prominent among the magnates after 1790 than it had been earlier. The nineteenth century can offer few parallels to the spectacular advancement of the Leveson-Gowers or the Grenvilles, whose skilful marriage policies brought together the vast territories of Bath, Bridgewater and Sutherland for the first family, and of Temple, Nugent and Chandos for the second, and had laid the foundations for the dukedoms of Sutherland and Buckingham. But such accumulation of this kind as did continue may possibly have outweighed the disintegrating effect of failure of heirs male and partition of estates among coheiresses, which did afflict some families. It may be remarked, however, that when for example the large Ancaster properties were so divided, the process still left Lord Willoughby de Eresby with a great estate in Lincolnshire as his share, with Grimsthorpe Castle as its centre.

In this instance we can see at work in the nineteenth century that dissolving and regrouping of estate blocks, through a succession of heiresses and coheiresses, which was more frequent earlier. On the death of the 5th and last Duke of Ancaster in 1809 the property was finally divided between his two nieces who were sisters of the 4th Duke. The elder of these took with her the barony of Willoughby de Eresby and the Lincolnshire and Welsh estates and passed them to the Burrell family through her marriage to Peter Burrell in 1779. Their son married the heiress of James Drummond, Lord Perth, in 1807, and acquired for the family the vast Drummond estates in Perthshire. In turn his two sisters eventually became his coheiresses, in 1870, and again the elder inherited the barony of Willoughby de Eresby and the bulk of the combined estates. She had married, in 1827, Gilbert Heathcote, future 5th baronet and 1st Lord Aveland, a landed magnate in Rutland and Lincolnshire in his own right. On her death, a dowager, in 1888, their son combined in his own person the titles of Aveland and Willoughby de Eresby, and the estates

---

[1] vide F. M. L. Thompson, 'The Land Market in the 19th Century', *Oxford Economic Papers*, New ser., IX (1957).

of the Willoughbys, Drummonds, and Heathcotes. This dynastic union spread over 163,505 acres, a fitting foundation for the earldom of Ancaster created in 1892, and a larger empire than that ruled by the dukes.

In a few cases, just how many we cannot be sure, financial necessity forced sales of sizeable portions of estates which had certainly been in the category of great at the end of the eighteenth century. The effect of such sales, however, although they reflected the straitened circumstances and diminished stature of the individual vendors, was likely to be an increase in the number of great estates and possibly an increase in the area occupied by them. This process developed its fullest impact in the case in which a financially embarrassed landed magnate was obliged to divest himself of large blocks of territory, but at the end was still left with a rump of the family property which in itself formed a great estate. At the same time, some of the purchasers at the receiving end of the process might succeed in upgrading themselves into the ranks of large landowners, by adding several thousand acres to their former possessions. This happened to the second Duke of Buckingham, whose great forced sales between 1844 and 1857 reduced his empire by a good 50,000 acres in England and Ireland, but still left his successor with a compact 10,000 acres or so to command from the vantage point of Stowe. At this feast of land the individual morsels were of considerable size, and to not a few of the purchasers the disintegration of the Buckingham empire was but an opportune step in their own careers of accumulation. Estate-building bankers, on their way towards founding families, were prominent among these. Thus Samuel Jones Loyd, who was created Lord Overstone in 1850, bought the Aston Abbots estate, and Sir Anthony de Rothschild the Aston Clinton estate, both in Buckinghamshire; while Alexander Baring, who had been created Lord Ashburton in 1835, used the occasion to continue the rounding out of his Hampshire territorial base by purchasing the Itchen Abbas estate.[1]

Those new men who set out on the path towards becoming

---

[1] Hampshire C.R.O., Ashburton MSS; J. K. Fowler, *Recollections of Old Country Life* (1894), p. 170. And see F. M. L. Thompson, 'The End of a Great Estate', *Econ. Hist. Rev.*, 2nd ser., VIII (1955). The account which follows of the formation of Alexander Baring's estate in Hampshire is based on the Ashburton MSS.

great landowners in the period after 1790 on the whole preferred to buy their land in large blocks, that is to say in the form of ready made estates. Thus Alexander Baring, who had bought Wiltshire land from Lord Chedworth in 1808 and the Earl of Malmesbury in 1815, began his full entry into the world of landed respectability in 1816 by purchasing from his fellow banker Henry Drummond, of the Charing Cross bank, the estate surrounding The Grange, Alresford, then worth close on £4,000 a year, for which he gave £136,620. Drummond's grandfather had only recently pieced together this estate, by joining two lesser properties, one purchased from Lord Northington in 1787 and the other from a heavily indebted Mr Threlkeld in 1791. Henry Drummond was in 1816 liquidating his Hampshire interests as part of his move to Albury Park in Surrey, which he purchased in the same year from Harriet Wall, a widow. Later in the century Albury passed to the Duke of Northumberland, by the marriage in 1845 of Algernon George Percy, subsequently 6th Duke, to Louisa, the eldest daughter and coheiress of Henry Drummond.

In Hampshire the field was left clear for Alexander Baring, and in 1818 he added a further 1,800 acres by purchasing Abbotstone and Itchen Stoke from a landed magnate, Lord Bolton, for £64,200. Lord Bolton was the successor to the last Powlett Duke of Bolton who died in 1794, and had been granted the title in recognition of his marriage to the only and illegitimate child of Duke Charles, his adoption of the name of Powlett alongside his own Orde, and his acquisition of the Bolton estates. His son, the second Lord Bolton, under the pressure of financial difficulties, was engaged in scaling down his Hampshire interests in the post-war period, and the sale to Baring was followed in 1820 by the sale of the Itchen Abbas estate of some 2,264 acres to the then Marquess of Buckingham, for £60,000; it was part of this estate, rather under half, which Baring in turn agreed to buy from Buckingham in 1844, for £30,000. Lord Bolton nevertheless remained a great landed magnate in both Hampshire and the North Riding after these sales had been completed.

At the time, in 1818, Baring thought of his purchase from Lord Bolton as his final essay in the land market. He wrote of this as 'what will be I trust the last of my follies in the way of land purchases . . . I pay very fully, but the property is very

essential to me, and I am therefore a very willing purchaser . . .
Lord Bolton's family are anxious to move rapidly, and so am I.
They have been making titles to other sales exactly similarly
situated.' The temptations of empire-building, however, proved
too great to resist, and apart altogether from his ventures into
new areas of colonization, such as Essex, Herefordshire or
Wiltshire, Baring continued to build up his main base in Hampshire until it extended over 15,000 acres. One of these further
purchases was also a major one, the fourth of the main pieces
which Baring fitted together to form his domain. This was the
purchase in 1824 from Sir Thomas Freeman Heathcote of an
estate in Brown and Chilton Candover covering 4,200 acres, for
which Baring gave £85,000. The Heathcotes of Horsley Park,
near Winchester, were one of the well-established county
families. Sir Thomas's father had only bought this particular
property in 1809, for £90,000, from Lord Carteret, whose
family had acquired it by inheritance at the beginning of the
eighteenth century. During its brief ownership by the Heathcotes
Sir Thomas had added a small parcel to the estate for £1,900,
so that he sold at a moderate loss in 1824. Yet again, this sale
did not demote the Heathcotes from the ranks of great landowners, for they still retained over 14,000 acres in Hampshire in
1873.

Many of Baring's further purchases were from landowners in
a much smaller line of property, lesser gentry and small freeholders and copyholders. In absorbing such smaller properties
he adopted the logic of ring fences and the rounding out of
boundaries. Administrative convenience, counsels of efficiency
in game preservation and the control of poachers, and territorial
pride combined to make pursuit of this course compulsively
attractive. By 1843 Baring was explaining the need to acquire a
small property on the ground that 'in the middle of my property
at The Grange is a freehold of about 160 acres belonging to a
Mr Brettingham – it is the only speck of alien property in five
adjoining parishes'. He had progressed a long way since 1818
in acquiring the outlook of the landed aristocracy.

Samuel Jones Loyd, of the Manchester bank of William
Jones, Loyd & Co., and the London bank of Jones, Loyd & Co.
which was merged in the London and Westminster Bank, was
furiously active in the land market, especially during the 1840s.

His wealth was enormous, and his disposition to translate it into a landed position was on an equal scale. While the Ashburton branch of the Baring family were ranked 'as among the foremost representatives of the new commercial aristocracy', in an 1865 assessment, 'the chief of that aristocracy is, we suppose, Lord Overstone, one of the wealthiest subjects in the world – his fortune is estimated at five millions.' Between 1823 and 1883, the year of his death, he laid out £1,670,000 in the purchase of estates. Since, in addition to his landed property, he left £2,118,804 in stocks, shares, and personal property, his fortune was perhaps slightly exaggerated.[1] His enormous investment in land eventually procured him an estate of over 30,000 acres, spread over eleven counties, and returning a rent of nearly £60,000 a year. The main effort was concentrated in Northamptonshire, spreading out from the starting point of Overstone Park, which was purchased in 1832, but he established important interests also in Buckinghamshire, Warwickshire, and Cambridge, and also had more than a thousand acres each in Leicestershire and Huntingdonshire.

Overstone's Northamptonshire estate reached almost exactly the same size as Ashburton's Hampshire property, its main formative period coming some twenty years later, and its method of formation being somewhat different. While Loyd also made some purchases from the magnates, as in the Buckinghamshire acquisition from the Duke already noted, or from the Earl of Westmorland in Northamptonshire, the great bulk of his supply of land came from the gentry and smaller landowners, whose connection with the land or at least with the county was often terminated. Thus a large purchase in 1842 from the Tomlin family, that of the Fotheringay estate for over £100,000, which capped an earlier loan by Loyd to Tomlin, eliminated the family from the county, although they continued to be able to keep up the style of landed gentry in their native Thanet. Sizeable purchases from Whitworth of Irthlingborough, Christie of Irchester, or Hill of Great Harrowden House, appear to have finished these as landed families. Quintus Vivian of Knutson Hall, however, remained after his sale of a farm in Irchester to

[1] Sanford and Townsend, *op. cit.*, II. 132. The account is based on the Overstone MSS, Northamptonshire Record Society, Delapre Abbey, Northampton.

Loyd what he had been before, an absentee member of the lesser gentry, resident in Hyde Park Square.

There is here a clear example of a straightforward increase in the proportion of land held in great estates, occurring between 1790 and 1873. In a third case, the purchase of Canford by Sir John Guest in 1845 from Lord De Mauley, we can see the simple replacement of one great landowner by another, with no significant effect on the balance of property.[1] The £354,000 which Guest paid for Canford may have been a speculative venture in a pecuniary way, since it yielded under $2\frac{1}{2}$ per cent on the 1845 rental, but it was a sound social investment for it marked the beginning of the transformation of Dowlais iron into Dorset aristocracy, and laid the foundation for the Wimborne peerage which was granted to his son in 1880. Lord De Mauley no doubt had more pressing calls upon the purchase money than those of maintaining his position by re-investing in lands elsewhere, for his son in 1873 enjoyed only the modest estate of 3,712 acres. In fact Canford was his wife's, which he had acquired in 1814 by marrying Barbara Ashley Cooper, sole heiress of the 5th Earl of Shaftesbury and inheritrix in 1811 of all his estates which did not pass with that title to his brother. Lord De Mauley's title, obtained in 1838, was an acknowledgement of his wife's descent. He sold Canford soon after his wife's death in 1844, and retained for his support the residue of her inheritance.

The preference for keeping estates intact on transference was a sound financial reflection of their social and political value. An estate was more than the farms and cottages which composed it, and was therefore worth more than their sum. It normally included, of course, a house fit for a gentleman's residence, with the requisite appurtenances of garden, kitchen garden, paddocks and parkland. But this could be valued separately, and subject to some difficulty in disposing of it without any accompanying home farm or tenanted land, it could if necessary be sold separately. An estate might include some of the directly proprietary features of landed position, such as an advowson or the nomination of a member of parliament; but again these rights could be, and were, valued and sold separately. Very commonly it would include manorial rights, in general and outside mineral districts valuable only for the rights they gave over game, but

[1] *Diaries of Lady Charlotte Guest* (ed. Earl of Bessborough, 1950), pp. 162–84.

these also could be sold divorced from the land to a limited class of purchaser with an appropriate existing stake in the locality. The one essentially indivisible asset of an estate in being was that it was the functioning centre of influence, the territorial basis of a social entity in which the strands of respect and deference led to the owner, and at one and the same time the source of a landowner's weight in the community and the means by which he exercised it. This quality could not survive the partition of an estate into its constituent properties, and hence the value attached to it would be lost by any such action.

Those who had an estate to dispose of, therefore, tended to seek a purchaser who would take it in one lot, as a going concern. Similarly, the type of purchaser which we have been examining was likely to seize opportunities of buying estate by estate, rather than in small parcels which would need to be laboriously pieced together, since acquisition of social position was an essential object of this investment in land. The Guests, for example, had no predeliction for Dorset as the soil in which to sink their landed roots. They had been talking about the desirability of buying a country place since 1837, and in the years that followed managed to fit in some serious estate-hunting among their business preoccupations and foreign travels, inspecting properties in Herefordshire and the East Riding among others, and having the superior attractions of Northamptonshire strongly pressed upon them. Canford was simply the first suitable property of which they received the offer.

Significantly it was the matter of influence, and the necessity of maintaining it in continuous cultivation, that Lord De Mauley urged as the ground for the Guests' first visit to Canford, by which time negotiations for the purchase were far advanced, sight unseen. Lord De Mauley 'appeared very anxious we should go down and stay at Canford, talked of the indiscretion of leaving Poole not looked after in these troublous political times, and of the hardship to himself of having the expense of keeping up the place.' When they made this visit a few weeks later in January 1846 the serious talk between the two men on the evening of their arrival was of politics. 'We talked formally enough, though very courteously, till 10, . . . and I went to bed,' wrote Lady Charlotte. 'When Merthyr [Sir John Guest] came up he said he had had a long talk with Ld. De Mauley,

41

who seemed to wish to put him in communication with the political leaders at Poole, and suggested his going there in the morning.' Instead the chief agent called at Canford next morning, and between them 'they appear to have arranged for Merthyr to stand himself for Poole at the next election.'

The transference of borough influence at Poole, something much more shadowy and delicate than secure proprietary control, as an integral part of the ownership of Canford, did not work out quite so smoothly as this. Although Lord De Mauley's eldest son, who had been Member for Poole since 1837, dutifully retired from the borough at the next election in 1847, Guest preferred to continue to represent his first love, Merthyr Tydvil, but he talked confidently of how 'it seemed almost necessary that he should bring Edward [Hutchins, their nephew] forward as the Canford Member for Poole.' But in the course of canvassing it was found that 'a great feeling appears to have sprung up against any dictation or nomineeship on the part of the Canford Estate', and no Canford Member for Poole was returned in 1847. A by-election in 1850, however, saw the Canford influence once more effective in Poole, and through all the subsequent vicissitudes of boundary and franchise changes the Guest family influence remained prominent, if not always triumphant, in the representation of this part of Dorset, until well into the present century. In 1874, for example, Lady Charlotte's son, Sir Ivor, by then the owner of Canford, failed to get returned. But in 1880 Lady Charlotte's second husband, Charles Schreiber, former tutor to the Guest children, was safely elected for Poole. There could be no clearer illustration of the real, though imprecise and somewhat intangible and unreliable influence which could be handed over with a great estate. The presumption of bald nomination might be resented, but with tactful management and manipulation a new owner could be every bit as influential as any well-born aristocratic predecessor.

From all these considerations it is clear that the tide was in favour of a rising concentration of landownership and a growth in the relative importance of great estates in the period between 1790 and 1873–83. While individual families might come and go, the process of accumulation itself proved irreversible under the social and political conditions of the time. The landed aristocracy perpetuated itself as an order in a variety of ways.

Not the least important of these was the conservation of major territorial units when misfortune and extravagance obliged older-established landed families to scale down the range of their possessions. *Morcellement* of landed property, as will be seen in later chapters, did not become a noticeable consequence of sales of great estates until about 1910, and did not begin to operate on an important scale until 1919.

While we may conclude that the proportion of the country which was held in great estates was appreciably smaller at the close of the eighteenth century than it was eighty to ninety years later, the illustrations given provide only a slender indication of any changes in the balance of property as between different counties or different parts of the country. The assembly of the Overstone estate may, for example, have made Northamptonshire a more aristocratic county than it had been previously; the Baring operations in Hampshire did not alter the complexion of that county in this respect, nor did those of Guest in Dorset; while the dispersal of some 25 to 30,000 acres of the Grenville property in Buckinghamshire, although it occurred in large lots of 3,000 or 4,000 acres apiece, probably produced a decline in the proportion of that county held in great estates of over 10,000 acres each. There may well have been, therefore, some changes since 1790 in the placings of counties as they appear in Table II. A further and more important inference may be drawn, that these changes in aristocratic ranking were likely to have affected particularly only those counties in which either landed magnates, or landed gentry, or both, were already established as numerous and fairly typical in the eighteenth century. For it was a necessary consequence of the processes described, that areas in which ready formed estates did not already exist in quantity did not form favourable fields for empire-building, either economically or socially. A low density of estates, whether of the great or of the gentry, in any particular area in the eighteenth century, probably signified that in any event the climate, topography or general situation of that area was uncongenial to a flourishing landed society. As a result there was during the nineteenth century a widening of the gulf between the aristocratically preferred counties and the handful of ill-favoured areas, among which Middlesex, Cambridge, Essex, Cumberland and Surrey stand out.

The nobility, as the next chapter shows, was also becoming more, and not less, representative of the landed class in the period down to the 1880s. On the assumption that the grant of a peerage, coupled with possession of landed estate worth over £3,000 a year, transformed what would otherwise have been a member of the landed gentry into a member of the landed aristocracy, then the landed aristocracy was a body which was growing faster than the group of great landowners alone, and a body much removed from the essentially static set of magnates which Townsend depicts. Moreover, inasmuch as peerages were essentially awarded for political services, it was a group which as time went on was increasingly representative of the politically important and active elements in the landowning classes. This gathering in of the influential gentry to join the band of lords was an important element in an increasingly formalized differentiation between landed aristocracy and landed gentry, which played its part in the process of transforming the basic social and political structure of England.

We have then the seeming paradox of a landed aristocracy which was increasing in material strength, in terms of the balance of property, and in social cohesion, in terms of the expansion of the nobility, in the period from 1790 to the 1880s. For this was the period in which the relative importance of agriculture, and the wealth of the landed class in relation to other classes, were in sharp decline. It was also the period in which fundamental changes in the political structure took place, and at the end of it the coming of a fully democratic franchise was clearly in sight. The paradox was, however, part of the machinery of change. For the points of growth, within the general context of a relatively declining importance, gave to the landed aristocracy a sense of security in the possession of positions of strength which made concessions and compromises on other fronts seem on the whole acceptable as well as inevitable.

III

◇◇

The Institutions
of the Landed Aristocracy

◇◇

IT was the general opinion at the close of the eighteenth century that all peers ought to be great landowners, and although the converse was not necessarily true, the peerage was certainly the most conspicuous and powerful institution of the landed aristocracy. The House of Lords was the direct institutional expression of the political power of the nobility, but by no means the only one, for in addition a sizeable fraction of the nobility exercised a considerable degree of direct control over the composition of the House of Commons through proprietary rights of nomination and virtually irresistible influence. A still wider control is revealed if we add to this variety of patronage the hereditary leadership of constituencies which depended for its effectiveness on the co-operation of other independent landowners. The nobility, moreover, provided a formidably overwhelming proportion of the political élite, the men who wielded power, made decisions and conducted the business of government, if this can be measured by membership of the cabinet. In society, granted certain attributes of wealth and aptitude for the life of the great world, the sentiments of tradition, respect and snobbery marked out the noblemen and their ladies as inevitable leaders.

The power of the House of Lords, especially its power to fight delaying actions in defence of established practices or vested interests, at least until the Parliament Act of 1911, is too well known to merit further description. Power of direct control over the structure of the House of Commons through nomination and commanding influence, at the time of the accession of George III, has been placed in proper perspective by Sir Lewis Namier, whose list shows for England 111 borough patrons determining or influencing the election for 205 seats, rather less than half the total representation of England. Of these 111 patrons, 55 were peers who had the return of 111 Members, and 56 were commoners, returning 94 Members.[1] The distinction between peers and commoners would not appear, in this context, to have had any significance. It should be remembered, however, that the expansion of the peerage between 1761 and the first Reform Act had a tendency to validate this distinction, since borough-mongering was one of the leading qualifications for ennoblement. In the second place, Namier deliberately omitted from his classification all those numerous instances in which personal influence was less than commanding, because he wished to compute only those cases in which control of a seat could in the last resort be enforced by compulsion.

For the present purpose, however, this second kind of electoral influence is of great significance. It was one which theoretically, and occasionally in practice, could be successfully defied by the electorate. Conversely, it included personal influence which was in normal times predominant, influence which could be expected to prevail, given reasonable tact in the management of the constituency and a certain amount of care in avoiding offence to the susceptibilities of the electors. It also differed widely in intensity. It embraced both the seat in which a single individual was preponderant, and could generally rely on nominating one Member out of two, and the seat in which on the one hand there was a body of rudderless independent voters, and on the other a handful of men with some interest at their disposal, where no candidate could normally expect to stand a chance without enlisting the support of some of this select band. The variety and imprecision makes this sort of influence difficult to evaluate, but contemporaries were not backward in attempting the exercise. Thus of the county representation of Buckinghamshire in

[1] Sir Lewis Namier, *The Structure of Politics at the Accession of George III* (1957 ed.), pp. 143–50.

1808 we are told, for example, that 'The Duke of Portland and the Marquess of Buckingham are the two greatest landed proprietors, . . . and the junior branches of their families experience no opposition whatever.' At the other extreme we can find Berkshire, where 'The family of Craven was once able to seat a junior branch as knight of the shire, but the influence of late years has been greatly divided, and that on account of the influx of new families, chiefly Asiatics.'[1]

The individuals to whom political importance was attributed in this fashion sometimes owed this influence to the fact that they were socially powerful in the localities in question, itself an expression of inherited leadership of men and opinions. They were invariably men with considerable landed property. The fact that such individuals did in practice determine the election of Members, even though their direction might in principle have been repudiated, was in itself eloquent of the habits of deference and obedience to the wishes of a few great men. By taking this into account we obtain a clearer picture of the practical political power of the select band of key property owners, than we can do by counting only those with proprietary rights of electoral patronage. Given the subjective nature of the term 'influence' in its wider sense, contemporary estimates of its extent naturally differed in detail. The best opinion seems to be, however, that in the final decade of the unreformed Commons 177 individuals influenced the return of 355 Members, just over two-thirds of the representatives of England and Wales. Within this total, 87 peers were credited with the return of 213 Members, and 90 commoners with that of 137 Members.[2]

Taken in this light, the control over the structure of the House of Commons exercised by peers appears to have been of considerably greater importance than the control possessed by influential commoners. Since they also possessed their own chamber, the concentration of political power in the hands of the nobility was indeed formidable. The eight leading peers in this respect, Devonshire, Newcastle, Norfolk, Rutland, Hertford, Darlington, Fitzwilliam and Lonsdale, could between them

---

[1] Joshua Wilson, *A Biographical Index to the present House of Commons* (1808), pp. 96, 61.
[2] *The Black Book* (1820), p. 423, quoting T. B. Oldfield, *The Representative History of Great Britain and Ireland* (1816), VI. 295–9.

muster about fifty Members. The nobility, however, did not act in politics as a united class: rivalries between families were too strong, differences of opinion too deep-seated, and the power at their disposal too abundant, to have made this conceivable. Only when the power had contracted almost to vanishing point did it appear that the indulgence of their differences had become a luxury which the nobility could no longer afford. Earlier, the fact that the political machine was to a great extent run by the nobility did not mean that it was necessarily used to promote their sectional interests.

The Great Reform Bill undoubtedly marked the end of the great days of borough proprietors, but 1832 brought about neither the total destruction of the nomination system, nor the elimination of interest and influence as essential ingredients in the electoral process. One of the purposes of the framers of the Bill, indeed, was to preserve and fortify the legitimate influence of rank, position and property, while undermining that which, by acting through close boroughs and bribery, was held to be illegitimate, or too much at the disposal of Ministers. As it was, a not inconsiderable contingent of pocket boroughs escaped destruction, some of them undergoing a change of patron as a result of the boundary extensions which were the price of survival. Between the first and second Reform Acts it would seem that some 54 individuals controlled the return of 72 Members sitting for proprietary boroughs in England; 44 of these were peers, with power over 59 seats.[1] Within a diminished band of outright patrons, therefore, the relative importance of the nobility had made a striking advance. This predominance becomes even more marked if we also include those English county seats which were generally considered to have a single all-powerful patron whose wishes were almost invariably reflected in their representation. There were at least 23 such county seats after 1832, effectively patronized by 20 peers and 3 commoners.[2]

As before 1832, so also after, there existed beyond this world of parliamentary seats dominated by single individuals a wide reach of the electoral stream whose course was much affected, though not determined, by the presence of influential

[1] N. Gash, *Politics in the Age of Peel* (1953), pp. 438–9.
[2] Based on C. R. Dod, *Electoral Facts, 1832–52* (1852).

individuals of rank and property. There were a further 200 English seats in which the personal influence or interest of outstanding people carried weight which could not be ignored by candidates or party organizers. In these seats some 250 peers and 150 commoners were singled out for mention by name, though all these were far from being equal in political importance.[1] Between 1868 and 1885, under the Second Reform Act, it appears that 16 English county seats still acknowledged an individual patron, in whose ranks were to be found 13 peers and 1 commoner; while 23 peers still survived as borough patrons with 25 seats at their command, alongside 19 commoners controlling 14 borough seats. 'After 1885 a number of predominant interests could still be maintained, but the hold of patrons was precarious, and by 1900 very few of them looked upon any seat as if it were absolutely in their gift.' In this last age of patronage 12 seats, all of them divisions of counties, have been accounted in the gift of patrons, amongst whom there was only a single commoner.[2]

It is of some significance that as the political power of patronage and influence in general dwindled after successive Reform Acts, the proportion of the remnant in the hands of the nobility showed a tendency to increase. This was some solace for loss of power, some offset to fears that the House of Lords politically and the lords socially were increasingly being made hostages to popular and democratic forces. The nobility was a continuously expanding order in this period, the number of hereditary peers in the House of Lords rising from some 350 in 1832 to over 400 by 1870, nearly 450 by 1885, and over 570 by 1914. Peers with great political importance were never more than a fraction of their order, but such peers were not exclusively members of the ancient nobility. Out of the eleven peers who were county patrons in the last age of control, for example, three were of post-1832 vintage, two of these being created after 1885, which was roughly proportionate to the balance between 'old' and 'new' peers within the peerage as a whole. Moreover the new peers, down to 1885, remained essentially as representative of the landed interest as the older nobility, and

---

[1] *Ibid.*

[2] H. J. Hanham, *Elections and Party Management* (1959), pp. 405–11.

the entire order in effect continued to be the political embodiment of the landed aristocracy.

It had always been held that an estate was indispensable for the support of the dignity of an hereditary title, and by this was meant land, the most permanent, transmittable and socially acceptable form of property. In spite of economic growth, and the multiplication of large personal fortunes made in business, this principle was by and large enforced until after 1885. When Bateman made his analysis of landowners in 1883 he listed some seventy peers who owned some land but had less than 3,000 acres apiece; only eleven of these had been created since 1832. There were in addition some sixty peers, in the whole of the United Kingdom, who appear to have been completely landless; nine of these had been created since 1832.[1] The landless and poorly landed nobility probably owed their fate largely to accidents of inheritance, or disinheritance, which despite the devices of entailing had succeeded in divorcing estate from title. Attainders subsequently reversed without recovery of forfeited estates made some contribution, but personal ruin through debts and forced sales of every acre of property probably made little.

Responsibility for succouring destitute nobles and ensuring that they could live in a fitting manner was for long recognized. The case of Lord Falkland is one in point, noticed by Farington in 1805. 'Lord and Lady Falkland went . . . home to Lynn. Lord Falkland is stationed there, being second in command over the Sea Fencibles. He is a post captain in the Navy, and without fortune. His present employ brings in about £700 a year. He has lodgings at Lynn. The fortunes of his family have been long reduced and in succession those who have borne the title have received a pension or some employ from government. His wife had no fortune.' His pension from the crown apparently amounted to £200 a year.[2] This was continued to his son, who however successfully revived the family fortunes by marrying Amelia Fitzclarence, illegitimate daughter of William IV, on the strength of which match he had a successful career as a

---

[1] In 1883 there were 443 hereditary members of the House of Lords, 7 peeresses in their own right, 38 Scottish peers and 97 Irish peers who had no U.K. titles; a total of 585 individual peers. 525 peers were listed as owning land to some extent.

[2] *Farington Diary*, III. 112 (1805). *The Black Book* (1820), p. 39. *The Extraordinary Black Book* (1831), p. 441.

colonial governor, and at his death left a comfortable estate of just over 3,000 acres at Scutterskelfe, near Yarm, Yorkshire. Direct subvention of the destitute by civil list pensions was probably on the decline after 1830, but we may be sure that authority continued to take responsibility for avoiding the scandal of a starving nobility forced into degrading occupations, by smoothing the path to careers in the public service.

It was a different matter to avoid creating new nobles whose successors might become destitute, in the sense that they might be without the means to support the dignity of the title save by recourse to gainful occupations, to which they might be unsuited personally, or which might be unsuitable for peers. Great care was taken here, as may be seen from the large grants made in honour of men of great naval and military eminence, who were thus provided with landed estates to accompany their titles. In general terms the notion that only wealthy men could be made peers, and that if a man deserved a peerage because of the eminence of his service to the state he must if necessary be made wealthy, prevailed until well into the twentieth century. As late as 1919 Field Marshal Haig informed the Prime Minister that 'unless an adequate grant was made to enable a suitable position to be maintained', he must decline any offer of a peerage, and he eventually settled for an earldom and a grant of £100,000.[1] The more specific notion, that this wealth ought to be in the form of landed estate, prevailed until 1885, after which the Marquess of Salisbury's Administrations began its erosion.

In one special field a conflict was long felt between the requirement of an adequate estate and the need for peers of particular abilities and experience. In order to discharge its functions as a court of law the House of Lords needed to recruit a steady stream of able and eminent lawyers. Besides the Lord Chancellor there was a strong convention by the early nineteenth century that the Lord Chief Justice of the King's Bench should be made a peer. These two, together with such of their immediate predecessors in office as chanced to survive, formed the pool of legal talent available to the Lords. In Chancellor Eldon's time a combination of his lack of dispatch and the growing press of legal business produced a feeling in legal circles that this pool was not

[1] P. A. Bromhead, *The House of Lords in Contemporary Politics, 1911-1957,* (1958), p. 25.

51

adequate, and required reinforcement especially by lawyers versed in equity and Scottish law. The doubt whether lawyers could be found possessed both of the requisite talents and of adequate estate, as distinct from their professional and therefore precarious incomes, gave rise, in 1830, to the first proposals to create life peerages.[1] In any case the selection of the two normally ennobled lawyers sometimes occasioned difficulties with the estate rule, and the problem was of regular recurrence, for the sons of ennobled lawyers were seldom as industrious or illustrious as their fathers, so that noble hereditary lawyers were rare. The eldest son of Charles Abbot, first Lord Tenterden, did indeed become a barrister, but this was before his father's elevation in 1827, and there is no record that the second baron achieved distinction in his profession. The first clear case of the eldest son of a lawyer-peer himself becoming a distinguished lawyer did not occur until the 1890s, when the second Lord Coleridge became a judge, his father having been Lord Chief Justice from 1873.

The issue of the existence and legality of any prerogative to create life peers was put to the test in 1856, when the government attempted to raise James Parke, a Baron of the Court of Exchequer since 1834, to the barony of Wensleydale for his life only. The Tory Peers, following the strong lead of Lyndhurst, and supported by the Liberal law-lords Brougham and Campbell, successfully contended that no such prerogative existed. Viewed as a matter of constitutional law it was no doubt inevitable that a majority of the lay lords should accept the opinion of the expert Lyndhurst, even if this was in fact somewhat shakily based on the argument of long desuetude. Nevertheless the debate in the Lords made it clear that considerations of political expediency weighed at least equally heavily, and that some were merely anxious to find respectable constitutional grounds to cover their resistance to what they took to be a threat to swamp the House with a flood of life peers subservient to the Ministers for the time being.

The Earl of Derby, 'as the organ of the Conservative Party', felt compelled to resist encroachment on the constitution, whether this was threatened by the crown or the people. He

[1] Sir Nicholas Harris Nicolas, *A Letter to the Duke of Wellington on the Propriety and Legality of creating Peers for Life* (1830).

embroidered on the dangers of swamping by arguing that the House was threatened also with an invasion of men of distinction from the army and navy, 'men of science too for aught I know', who laboured under the impediment of poverty. This, he felt, would destroy the hereditary character of the House, and thus its ability to oppose the wishes of the Commons; 'you will have signed the doom of the House of Lords', and the country would degenerate into a republic. Campbell argued in a snobbish way for the sectional interests of lawyers in not having a life-peerage system, since it would take away from them the opportunity of founding a family. 'The change is an injustice to the middling and humbler ranks of society, to whom a prospect has hitherto been held out of rising with the ancient nobility through the profession of the law.' If lawyers had always been confined to life peerages he estimated that about one-third of their present lordships would have been degraded, and he added 'I would act a sordid part . . . if I assisted to kick down the ladder by which I myself have risen.' Lord St Leonards, a former Conservative Chancellor, also asserted that a body of life peers could never stand against the Commons elected by the popular voice, blithely disregarding the fact that a goodly proportion of the Commons was in fact elected still by the noble voice. He also voiced the dislike of the successful lawyers who had already arrived for any proposal which would introduce a class division into the nobility. He could only answer in the negative the question 'whether a lawyer without sufficient fortune for a peerage, but whose services are required in the House, should be created a peer for life', since life peers would become known as those of great ability but insufficient wealth, and hereditary peers as those of great wealth and little merit.[1]

The Government speakers very properly demolished that part of the opposition argument which rested on fears of swamping and approaching republicanism, by pointing out that it was only the restraining forces of tradition, custom and propriety which preserved the House from swamping by hereditary peers, and that these forces would continue to operate. In fact, as Earl Grey put it, 'there are two things which this House has to fear. One is, that its benches may become overcrowded by peers not

---

[1] *Hansard, Parliamentary Debates*, 3rd ser. CXL (1856), 280–375, for the whole of this debate.

possessing adequate means for the maintenance of their rank; the other, that it may sometimes want among its members a sufficient proportion of those who have raised themselves to the dignity of the peerage by their own talent and industry.' The issue was whether lawyers, generals and admirals should 'be precluded from coming here unless they have what may be called a proper endowment for the support of their dignity and rank', because Parliament could not be expected to treat every deserving prospective recipient of a peerage, who had not amassed sufficient fortune, as though he were a Marlborough, Wellington or Nelson. The Government case was, therefore, that 'any man must be a fool to wish for' an hereditary peerage unless possessed of fortune enough to sustain it, and that in order to have every description of talent represented in the Lords there should be life peers, who would not encumber the House with unprovided heirs who would degrade the peerage.

In the course of presenting this case Earl Granville quoted a letter from Eldon to Lord Kenyon, himself also a law-lord, written in 1818 on the occasion of Abbott's appointment as Chief Justice, which illustrates the difficulties presented by the estate rule. Eldon wrote, 'I agree that the Chief Justice of the King's Bench should be a peer; and no one is fitter than Abbott. But see the effect. Lord Mansfield had had a long practice in lucrative situations at the bar – he was of a noble family – he was not likely to have descendants. Your father had been, at the bar, the most eminent lawyer of our times, he had made by his practice, independently of the law offices, a larger fortune than any professional man of his time . . . Lord Ellenborough had likewise made some fortune, much less certainly, at the bar; but if he had died before Mr Way I doubt whether the peerage would have been either convenient to the family or useful to the public . . . Lord Loughborough had no children . . . his peerage could not descend and his office would support him during his life. What he meant, when he left the Chancellorship, by getting an unendowed earldom for his nephew, I cannot pretend to say. When I came to the Common Pleas I had made some fortune in successful practice at the bar, and in the great law offices, which I held nearly 12 years. Mr. Pitt was unwilling to give me an office which would take me out of Parliament; I could not be in it unless in the Lords, . . . and if I had survived the acceptance of the peerage but a short time, I had accepted what would have been a nuisance to my family and no benefit to the public. Of our dear friend Lord A., can anybody now say that it was a wise measure . . . to accept a peerage? Now, as to Abbott, his practice has been behind the bar. He never had any office . . . he enters therefore upon the office in very moderate circumstances, with a considerable family. The permanent offices of profit in the gift of the Chief Justice as I understand, without exception are not any of them likely to be vacant while he is likely to live or to hold his office; what he can save out of the other emoluments of the office he did not, and indeed he could not, think would enable him to transmit with a peerage a fully competent fortune to support it,' but without a peerage he was quite willing to accept the post.

Abbott in fact became Lord Chief Justice in 1818, but was not advanced to the peerage until 1827, when he became Lord Tenterden. Eldon's letter is a beautiful demonstration of the vital part played by the perquisites of office, as distinct from the very high professional income of the top men at the bar, in enabling lawyers to found families in the aristocratic style. The emoluments of the Chancellorship in unreformed days, which Eldon held with a gap of one year from 1801 to 1827, were reckoned at £35,000 a year, and in addition the Chancellor had immense legal, educational and ecclesiastical patronage in his gift, the legal part of which at least was saleable. The means by which this coal factor's son amassed landed estate which by 1873 had a rent-roll of over £28,000 a year are thus readily apparent. Eldon's elder brother, created Lord Stowell in 1821, was a judge of the Admiralty Court for over twenty years before his retirement in 1828, including much of the war period when the prize business of his court was brisk. Since he left no surviving son he did not succeed in founding a family, but he followed his brother's path in acquiring landed estate in the grand manner. Some time before 1817 he, as Sir William Scott, 'having abundance of money, purchased the estates which Lord Chedworth left to [Thomas] Penrice, the apothecary of Yarmouth. This speculation which cost Sir William, it is said, £300,000, at present does not produce him more than 2 pr. cent for his money.' At his death in 1836 Stowell left land with a gross rental of some £8,000, part of which had however been acquired by marriage to a coheiress, and nearly a quarter of a million in the Funds; about half of this property passed to Lord Sidmouth, through his second marriage, to Marianne, widow of Thomas Townsend and only daughter of Lord Stowell.[1]

In the 1810 Report on Saleable Offices in the Courts of Law four principal offices were enumerated as saleable in the King's Bench, at the disposal of the Chief Justice. The emoluments of these offices totalled nearly £13,000 a year net of deputies' salaries, and it was said that on occasion as much as 70,000 guineas had been offered and refused for one of them. It was this source of livelihood which was barred to Abbott in 1818, since none of the saleable offices was likely to fall in during his tenure.[2] As the spirit of financial reform penetrated into the courts and the law departments, and judges as well as Chancellors settled down to live on their salaries, this type of rather unreliable perquisite became increasingly a matter of history after 1830, and opportunities of founding landed families inevitably receded from the grasp of lawyer-peers. Thus of the twenty-six new peers created between 1832 and 1885, whose landed estates in 1883 fell below the 3,000-acre limit, fourteen were law officers or judges. Lord Chancellor Campbell, who was thought by Bateman and the *Complete Peerage* which follows him to have fallen into this class, was in fact an example of a law-lord who continued to figure in the ranks of great landowners. Of him it was said that it is 'impossible to be unaware he enjoyed a large and lucrative practice; that he possesses very extensive estates in Ireland; that he enjoys the advantage of having one of the few large houses in this town [London] which has the aristocratic appendages of a court and a garden.' Besides the extensive but poor Irish property in Galway, he acquired a valuable estate at Hartrigge, near Jedburgh, and his Irish and Scottish land totalled 9,720 acres worth £4,063 a year in 1873.

A few other post-Reform law-lords climbed into the ranks of substantial landowners, such as Lords Abinger, Cottenham and St Leonards. Lord Brougham fell only just below this class, with some £2,500 a year from land in Cumberland and Westmor-

---

[1] *Farington Diary*, VIII. 119 (1817). Devon C.R.O., Sidmouth MSS, Bagnall estate papers.

[2] *Parliamentary Papers*, 1810, IX, Report of Committee on Saleable Offices in Courts of Law, p. 4. *The Black Book* (1820), p. 12.

land, and Lord Denman had much the same from land in Derbyshire, while Lord Selborne had £1,755 a year from land mainly in Hampshire. But six of the eleven Chancellors who held office between 1832 and 1885 appear to have possessed virtually no land at all. As far as lawyers provided recruits for the hereditary peerage, they came to violate the estate rule much more frequently than in Eldon's day.

In an age when the great lawyers were accustomed to becoming territorial magnates, an age of Mansfield, Camden, Bathurst, Thurlow and Redesdale, as well as Eldon and Stowell, the exceptions had appeared particularly galling and unseemly. They had in fact, however, scarcely offended heinously against the dignity of the peerage. 'Our dear friend Lord A.' whose peerage Eldon regretted, was Richard Pepper Arden, Master of the Rolls from 1788, and appointed Lord Chief Justice of the Common Pleas in 1801, when he was created Lord Alvanley. Though he worked his way up, through Manchester Grammar School and the law, his father was a landed gentleman of Hawarden, Cheshire, and his mother the heiress of Preston Pepper of Pepper Hall, Yorkshire. He was a prosperous lawyer-politician, holding the offices of Solicitor and Attorney-General, married a sister of Lord Skelmersdale, and probably left a comfortable landed estate at his death in 1804. It was his son, 'well known as a wit and spendthrift', in other words a Regency rake, and one of the Oatlands set, who created the scandal. He ran through his patrimony in style, and was apparently obliged to sell up in 1825; some 400 acres of the Cheshire land, at Tarporley, Alpraham and Alvanley, were purchased for the great Tollemache estate, with which it intermingled, and more besides was probably sold.[1] In spite of this disaster, however, an estate worth £2,668 a year belonged in 1873 to the Hon. Miss Arden of Arden Hall, Tarporley, the surviving representative after the peerage became extinct in 1857.

When Eldon reproved Loughborough for obtaining 'an unendowed earldom' for his nephew to inherit, he was referring to the earldom of Rosslyn, conferred in 1801. The lack of endowment was highly relative, and Eldon's view throws an interesting light on the scale of provision considered suitable, not to say

[1] C. Stella Davies, *The Agricultural History of Cheshire, 1750-1850*, Chetham Society, 3rd ser. X (1960), p. 13.

indispensable, for the support of a peerage. For Rosslyn's descendant in 1873 was still happily installed in Dysart House, Kirkcaldy, with over 3,000 acres in Fife and a bit more besides in Midlothian, with a rental of £9,186 and mineral rights worth a further £1,224 a year. The land had no doubt appreciated markedly since 1818, when Eldon was writing, but even then must have afforded a moderate subsistence. A much plainer instance of an unendowed title was yet to occur during Eldon's Chancellorship, when in 1824 Robert Gifford was created Lord Gifford of St Leonards in Devon, on his appointment in close succession as Lord Chief Justice of the Common Pleas and Master of the Rolls. His title commemorated his father, a grocer and linendraper of Exeter, but did not reflect his territorial interest, for he apparently had none in that county or any other. The lack of endowment obliged his son to pursue a moderately active regimental life for fifteen years after his succession, and his grandson to seek his fortune in the army and the colonial service for an equal period after his own succession in 1872.

Charles Abbott's title, as baron Tenterden (Kent) of Hendon, Middlesex, did honour to his father, a hairdresser and wigmaker of Canterbury, and to his own modest estate of 20 acres in Middlesex. Although he left £120,000 on his death in 1832, he had not endowed his title in the accepted fashion, and his heirs were obliged to support themselves by their own exertions to some extent. His grandson, the third baron, was a Foreign Office official of some distinction, and reached the top of his profession, as Permanent Under-Secretary, some time after he had inherited the title. Finally the unreformed era closed with the elevation in 1829 as Lord Wynford of William Draper Best, who had been Lord Chief Justice of the Common Pleas after Gifford's brief tenure in 1824, and who was apparently as innocent of landed possessions.

The pre-Reform exceptions to the estate rule among the nobility were indeed few, and perhaps because of their scarcity the fate of the heirs to the successful and personally affluent lawyers of the first creations did not bear out the implied dread, that hereditary nobles without landed incomes would be forced into unbecoming positions and unbecoming occupations. For the number of such unprovided heirs was small enough for the rest of the order, and the established institutions offering respectable careers in the public service, to see that they were absorbed and provided for without scandal, at least without scandal to any except Radicals who were always protesting against 'the gigantic system of outdoor relief for the aristocracy'. The Great Reform Bill produced the greatest opportunity for the creation of new peers which had ever occurred. The occasion was only to be repeated, and similarly passed by, in 1911. Although in the event the mass creations were not required in 1832, from the lists of prospective Reform peers it is abundantly plain that Grey had no intention of diluting the peerage by disregarding the estate rule. Further than this, Brougham makes it clear that Grey intended to muster the requisite majority for the Bill in the Lords by means which would scarcely add to the body of permanent peers at all, even though an abundance of applicants adequately qualified in birth and estate stood ready and eager to hand. The trick was to be turned by calling up peers' eldest sons in their fathers' baronies, by promoting Scottish and Irish peers, and by ennobling some carefully selected elderly and childless landed gentlemen.[1]

Even an aspirant who felt himself to be so deserving and appropriate as Sir William Eliott, baronet, of Stobs Castle, Hawick, failed in his efforts through his intermediary, Earl Fitzwilliam, to procure a peerage. Grey's generally fastidious standards were shown at their best when he told Creevey in 1833 that 'he should have liked very much to have recommended Sir Thomas Baring for a peerage as the head of that family, and as an additional mortification to Alec [his brother], but his having sons to succeed him put that quite out of the question. Western being a single man, and at his time of life, added to his service of two and forty years in the field, made it quite another thing.'[2] Squire Western, with a 10,000-acre estate in Essex, was thus allowed on sufferance to make the grade to hold the first 'consolation' honour granted to a long-service M.P. after defeat at a general election: in due course the title died with him. Sir Thomas Baring, the Whiggish foil in the banking firm to the violently diehard anti-Reform Alexander, in spite of his

---

[1] *Life and Times of Henry Brougham, by Himself,* (1871), III. 206.
[2] Northants. R.O., Fitzwilliam MSS, Lord Milton's Letter Book 732, Sept. 1831. Gore ed., *Creevey,* p. 339.

assiduous acquisition of the position of a landed magnate at Micheldever, Hampshire, and his own long service in the Commons, never did attain a peerage. His son, however, after being an M.P. for forty years and holding in 1839–41 the office of Chancellor of the Exchequer, reached the peerage as Lord Northbrook in 1865. Meanwhile the less rigorous Tories had admitted his uncle, Alexander, into the preserves in 1835.

From 1833 until the fall of Gladstone's Ministry in 1885 some 176 peerages were conferred, and there were 139 new recruits to the Lords, an annual rate precisely half of that achieved by the younger Pitt, and well below that attained by Lord Liverpool. It could scarcely be argued from this that the Age of Reform led Prime Ministers to more frequent recourse to the honours list or to debasement of the nobility. In one respect indeed a change of substance is noticeable. There were in this period only thirty-seven promotions, either within the peerage or of Scottish or Irish peers, but this perhaps indicated only that the great and powerful ancient nobles had already been largely saturated with promotion before 1833.[1] The time was approaching when the Garter was the only carrot which a political manager could offer as a reward for the support of the really great.

The great majority of these recruits were politicians, who owed their titles to service in ministerial office, or more commonly simply to their membership of the Commons. Over three-quarters of the new creations fell into this class.[2] It is an interesting comment on the age which is supposed to have witnessed the advent of democracy, and certainly did witness a vast growth of non-landed wealth, that no more than twenty-six, or one-fifth, of all the new peers possessed less than 3,000 acres of land yielding at least £3,000 a year in rents. Of these twenty-six only five were politicians, three Liberal and two Conserva-

[1] See above p. 12.
[2] See H. R. G. Greaves, 'Personal Origins and Interrelations of the Houses of Parliament', *Economica*, IX (1929), 184. His analyses, however, break at the years 1864 and 1896; and they do not, apparently, distinguish between peerage promotions and fresh creations, so that they show a slightly lower proportion of 'political' origins. Though it is stated that the number of 'origins' counted exceeds the actual total of peers created, because some individuals had more than one 'origin' or service to which the title is attributable, the point is somewhat obscure since the number of peerages created, 1833–96, including promotions and titles which became extinct with the first holder before 1896, in fact was larger than the totals in the table, being 218 against Greaves's total of 188 'origins'.

tive creations. Nevertheless, all five did have landed estates, and Disraeli, although not quite the least landed, was certainly the least wealthy. The Hughenden estate, purchased for him with money borrowed from the Duke of Portland in order to give him some semblance of suitability as a Tory leader, was only a modest thousand acres. George Carr Glyn had indeed a smaller estate, 712 acres equally divided between Middlesex and Dorset, but it was a more valuable one, producing £2,126 in rents against Hughenden's £1,494. Carr Glyn might in any case perhaps be more properly regarded as a railway and banking peer than as a political one, although he was a Liberal M.P. for twenty-one years. He chose the title Lord Wolverton, after the railway town on his line, the L.N.W.R. and he was a partner in Glyn, Mills bank. He made no serious attempt to translate his fortune into land, and leaving nearly 2 million pounds at his death was easily the wealthiest of the five men under consideration.

The second of the Conservatives, Lord Cottesloe, was both a politician and a civil servant, holding office in the Peel Administration and then retiring from politics to be Chairman of the Customs Board from 1846 to 1873; also a Buckinghamshire landed gentleman, he drew £5,675 a year from his 2,683 acres. The first of the Whig-Liberal creations was Lord Ebury, a Grosvenor, an M.P., and third son of the Marquess of Westminster, who became a peer in his own right in 1857; he was also a landowner in his own right, with 2,723 acres in Hertfordshire and Middlesex, centred on Rickmansworth, yielding him £5,803 a year. The last of the Liberal trio was Monsell, Postmaster-General in 1871–3, who became Lord Emly on the resignation of the Ministry in 1874; he was an Irish landowner, with 2,246 acres in Limerick which brought in £2,683 a year. Thus none of these political peers, with the possible exception of Beaconsfield, broke the estate rule in any grievous fashion.

Fourteen of this band of twenty-six as has been noted, were lawyers.[1] The balance was made up of three generals, Raglan, Napier of Magdala, and Wolseley; two Governors-General of India, Hardinge and Lawrence; one diplomat, Ampthill; and the Poet Laureate, Tennyson. In this collection Napier, Wolseley, and Ampthill seem to have been totally without landed estate;

[1] See above p. 56.

the others had modest properties, ranging from Raglan's ninety-five acres in Monmouth to Lawrence's 923 acres in Hampshire. Raglan, however, besides being eighth son of the Duke of Beaufort, was voted an annuity of £1,000 for his widow and £2,000 for his son and his next heir. Napier was voted £2,000 a year for himself and his next heir when his exploits in the Abyssinian campaign of 1867 were rewarded; and Garnet Wolseley, besides the thanks of Parliament received a total of £55,000 in recognition of his services. Lord Odo Russell, for long British Ambassador in Berlin, and created Lord Ampthill in 1881, was as the nephew of the Duke of Bedford essentially aristocratic in any case. Lord Lawrence's estate was as stated in 1873, but his son, who succeeded in 1879, claimed that he owned 10,000 acres in Hampshire.[1] This would appear to leave Alfred Lord Tennyson, solitary representative of the arts, as the only new peer who was both virtually landless and lacking in close aristocratic connexions or parliamentary provision, to set alongside the ten landless lawyer-peers, and the poorly provided Beaconsfield.

The standard of landed competence assumed in this discussion might have appeared somewhat inadequate to Eldon. It is, however, one which accords well with the notions of the genealogist Burke. Writing in 1861 he said; 'But for the immense difficulty of rendering, even by legislative enactment, real property perpetually inalienable, it might be well that the crown made it a condition of conferring an hereditary title that the recipient endow the title with a landed estate which could never be separated from it. A baronet's qualification might be fixed at £500 a year, a peer's at £2,000.'[2] This was Burke's view of the absolute minimum of landed estate, below which a peer or baronet would find himself in disgracefully reduced circumstances.

The fact that less than one-tenth of the new peers were unable to show clearly visible means of support for their heirs indicates that, down to 1885, the concept of an essentially landed nobility had been upheld very nearly as effectively as in the days of Pitt. The slight relaxation of standards in practice was almost exclusively due to the reforms in the administration of justice,

[1] *Who was Who, 1897-1916* (1920), p. 416.
[2] J. B. Burke, *The Vicissitudes of Families* (2nd ser. 1861), p. 6.

which made it difficult for lawyers to become as rich as formerly. The nobility being still the leaders in society, the prolongation of the dominance of landowners is plain. Whether there had been any relaxation at all in the standards of gentility, as measured by birth and background, is most doubtful. Lawyer-peers had for long risen in one generation from very humble tradesmen's origins, as earlier discussion showed, and no new departure was involved in their case. Wolseley was indeed a new portent in the line of noble generals, and it is well known that his whole military career was slowed down by his lack of aristocratic connexions and the prejudice against genuine career officers, but it was only a single portent.

For others the steps of the social ladder had long been clearly marked. 'They were trade, a fortune, the acquisition of an estate, a baronetcy, membership of Parliament, and finally a peerage.'[1] In the late eighteenth century the process had usually taken at least two generations, and there is no sign that the nineteenth century easily permitted any greater speed. Fortunes made in banking, and transmuted into land, definitely played a larger role in founding peerages after 1832 than they had done before, but even so they could not begin to rival in number the peerages won by families which were already well established on the land by the end of the eighteenth century; the Cokes, Batemans and Leighs, the Pakingtons, Palks and Sturts, were the solid landed backbone of the new peerage. Most significant of all, fortunes directly derived from industry were not represented until Home Secretary Bruce became Lord Aberdare in 1873, and Guest became Lord Wimborne in 1880; the landed estate of both was provided by the great Dowlais ironworks. The new departure was foreshadowed in 1856 when the grandson of Jedediah Strutt became Lord Belper, though in this case the cotton fortune had been mellowed by generations on the land. The advent of the 'plebeian aristocracy', which Disraeli professed to believe was Pitt's creation, was in fact delayed until after 1885.[2]

The technique used on Squire Western, of conferring a title on an old man with no sons, was exhibited in other instances either by design or happy coincidence. The Beaconsfield earldom was a case in point, as was the Wensleydale peerage. A life

[1] Greaves, *op. cit.*, p. 181.
[2] The later developments are discussed in Chap. XI.

peerage in form having been deemed illegal a life peerage in fact was nonetheless given to Parke, since the limitation to the heirs male of a man aged 74 whose three sons had all died in infancy was obviously a legal fiction. Lawyers naturally leant themselves to this treatment, since they were unlikely to have reached peer-worthy eminence until of sufficient age for their chances of leaving male heirs to be judged to a nicety. In this way the evil, such as it was, of unprovided peerages was further mitigated, to the extent of six titles which died with the first holders. The plain intention behind hereditary titles, however, was that they should normally be inherited, and the second main institution of the landed aristocracy concerned the formal organization of family arrangements in such a way that heirs should be guaranteed succession to the family estates.

Sir Nicholas Harris Nicolas had argued in 1830 that the only group whose ennoblement was unobjectionable was the landed gentry, since their estates were usually settled upon their eldest sons, who were thus assured of the means of supporting their rank. He suggested that in future no hereditary peerage should be granted unless the new peer was both possessed of estate in keeping with his rank and undertook to settle it strictly upon his male heirs. The legal instrument by which this could be done was known as a strict settlement, and was frequently executed at the time of the marriage of the eldest son, and hence is more commonly, but loosely, referred to as a marriage settlement. In its main feature it differed from the perpetual entail on heirs male which was known to Scottish law from 1685, since English law 'abhorred a perpetuity' and allowed land to be tied up for three generations only, in the typical case a father, his eldest son, and his (unborn) eldest grandson until he was 21 years of age. Normally, however, a settlement was not allowed to run its full course, which would have left the final unspecified heir the opportunity of breaking the entail and gaining unfettered possession of the family estate, with the complete powers of selling, alienating, bequeathing, enjoyed by a freeholder, but on the contrary the property was re-settled in each generation. Provided this was done, which depended on sufficient agreement subsisting between father and eldest son for them to concur in new conditions of settlement, a regular succession of these deeds had the same practical effect as a perpetual entail in implement-

ing the principle of primogeniture without some of its disadvantages. For the opportunity of a rearrangement of family
affairs in each generation meant that the maintenance of widows
and younger children could be provided for, on a scale attuned
to the particular fortune of individual brides, and it meant also
that some latitude existed for varying the precise areas of the
family estate which were subject to settlement, since at times it
might be expedient on commercial or personal grounds for
parts of it to be free from restraints on their use. The eldest son
generally carried out the resettlement willingly enough, since it
was this which provided him with an independent income during
his father's lifetime. The close structure of the family both produced these arrangements and was reinforced by them. The head
of the family was given responsibilities especially for promoting
the welfare of his younger brothers and younger sons, and the
landed family was preserved as a powerful institution in running
the whole machinery of the country's administration.

As Nicolas's remarks implied, the habit of settling their
landed estates was by no means confined to the nobility. There
was nevertheless a feeling that the powers of settlement were
particularly adapted to the needs of the aristocracy. James
Humphreys, for example, the first of the nineteenth-century
conveyancing barristers to present systematic proposals for
land law reform, argued in 1826 that primogeniture and the
strict settlements which were its manifestation had 'a peculiar
value . . . in preserving the independence of the aristocratic
branch of the constitution'. Brougham, in moving successfully in
1828 for the appointment of a Royal Commission to investigate
the absurdities and anomalies revealed by Humphrey's proposals, claimed that 'I do not by any means wish to interfere
with the power of making or of barring entails; I consider the
English law as hitting very happily the just medium between
too great strictness and too great latitude in the disposition of
landed property . . . as much power is given of annexing estates
to families as may prevent a minute division of property, and
preserve the aristocratic branch of the government.' Edward
Sugden, the later Lord St Leonards, and first of the nineteenth-
century conveyancing lawyers to present a systematic opposition
to all proposals to touch the land laws, also voiced the same view.
In rebuttal of Humphreys he argued, of the proposed changes in

the law of settlements, 'it would not be advisable to make real estate liable to all debts; such a provision would lead to an extension of credit ruinous to young men and spendthrifts, and have a strong tendency to weaken the aristocracy, by lessening, through improvidence, those possessions without which their dignities would be a burden to themselves and a heavy calamity to the country . . . and [would] leave many peerages without an estate to support their honours.'[1]

One main purpose of the settlement was indeed to protect the family estate from the worst depredations of spendthrift heads of family. The head for the time being was only life-tenant of the settled estate, unable in general to do anything with it whose effects might run beyond his own lifetime, and therefore in theory unable to do any lasting damage to the inheritance of generations yet to come. This was of interest to others besides the peerage, and the habit of settling their estates was typical of the entire order of landowners, aristocracy and gentry. Thus Robert Greaves, head of the old gentry family of Ingleby Hall, Derbyshire and Mayfield Hall, Staffordshire, had his estates of about 1,300 acres under settlement in 1803, as did Humphrey Senhouse his estate of about a thousand acres at Netherhall, Cumberland. This was also the case in the late eighteenth century with the Blundells of Little Crosby, Lancashire, whose estate was some 1,700 acres; and in Bedfordshire the Brooks of Flitwick settled their estate of some 900 acres in 1816. Other examples of very small settled estates include the 500-odd acres of John Tasker of Horton Kirby, Kent, the 700 acres of Edmund Barrell Faunce of Sharsted, also in Kent, and the single farm of James Young at Catwick in the East Riding.[2]

'Can you form any estimate of what is the proportion of property in the country held under marriage settlements?' a barrister was asked by a select committee in 1848, and he answered, 'I should say, speaking at a very rough guess, more than two-thirds.' A year before, Lord Fitzwilliam's faithful

---

[1] James Humphreys, *Observations on the Actual State of the English Laws of Real Property: with the Outlines of a Code* (1826), p. 207. Brougham's speech, *Hansard*, new ser. XVIII (1828), 128–247. Edward B. Sugden, *Letter to James Humphreys* (1826), p. 25–27.

[2] Cumberland C.R.O., Senhouse MSS, 19/12. Lancashire C.R.O., Blundell MSS, 55/105. Bedfordshire C.R.O., Brooks Lyall MSS, LL. 17/11, 12. Kent C.R.O. Faunce Delaune MSS, U. 145, T. 89/8, T. 89/13 and T. 89/5.

correspondent and adviser, Evelyn Denison, himself a considerable landowner, had thought that 'speaking generally . . . half or two-thirds of the land of England' was in encumbered estates, which may be roughly equated with settled estates. Such figures were only guesses, based on no certain information, though they were guesses made by men with relevant experience. In 1874, before the publication of the New Domesday Book, Lord Dacre's heir was of opinion that 'seventy per cent of the land in this country is held by men whose power over it is limited by modern settlement.' On the basis of the New Domesday Book, and on the assumption that all estates of more than 1,000 acres were under settlement, the reformer Arthur Arnold concluded 'that four-fifths of the land of the United Kingdom are strictly settled'. On the same assumption the proportion for England alone was only just over a half.[1]

Arnold thought that the number and extent of estates under 1,000 acres which were settled probably balanced the area of larger estates or portions of them which were kept out of settlement. There was substance in this point, but neither Arnold nor other critics of the landed order were inclined to make sufficient allowance for the area of larger estates unsettled. Great landowners, whether by accident or design, might well find themselves in unfettered possession of their entire estates. Such, for example, was the case with the consolidated Hawarden estate, which Gladstone deliberately made over to his son in fee simple in 1875, so that he might have the untrammelled powers and responsibilities of a real owner of the land. It was also the case, though this was the result of the extreme necessity of having power to sell the bulk of the estates, with the Buckingham property after 1847; and it apparently applied to the Howick estate in the time of Earl Grey and his son.[2]

Apart from entire great estates which at any given time, and sometimes for long periods, were unsettled, it seems to have

[1] *Parliamentary Papers*, 1847/8, VII, S.C. on Agricultural Customs, Q.1004–5, (Chandos Wren-Hoskyns). Wentworth Woodhouse MSS, G. 20, J. E. Denison to Lord Fitzwilliam, 18 Aug. 1847. H. R. Brand, 'Free Land', *Fortnightly Review*, new ser. XVI (1874), 624. Arthur Arnold, *Free Land* (1880), p. 26.

[2] J. Morley, *Life of Gladstone* (1903), III. 345. F. M. L. Thompson, 'The End of a Great Estate', *Econ. Hist. Rev.*, 2nd ser., VIII (1955), 49. Other instances are noted by D. Spring 'English Landownership in the Nineteenth century: a critical note', *ibid.*, 2nd ser., IX (1957), 482.

been a fairly normal practice to retain part of a great estate out of settlement. This might be done either on grounds of policy, because the commercial or industrial development of particular areas made it expedient, or on family grounds, in order to be able to vary provisions for wives and younger children either in money or land, or simply from reluctance to transfer into settlement land freshly acquired by purchase or inheritance. It might well have been a practice chiefly confined to the great estates, whose total size made it possible to retain this room for manoeuvre, and not one much used by the gentry who needed to commit their maximum landed resources to supporting the purposes of their settlements. It may not have been universally true on the great estates, but since portions varying from a tenth to a half of the estates of Bedford, Cleveland, Fitzwilliam, Northumberland, Portland, Rutland and Westminster, to name a few, were kept out of settlement in the nineteenth century, it was clearly a widespread practice among the magnates. Any generalization on the matter is hazardous. In a sample covering one-eighth of the total area in great estates in England, however, and including some estates which were wholly settled, some wholly unsettled, and some which were split, it appears that on average nearly a quarter of the land was out of settlement. On the assumption that this sample was representative, and on the slightly more questionable assumption that virtually all estates of 1,000 to 10,000 acres were wholly settled, but including nothing for estates of less than 1,000 acres, just under half the area of England was subject to settlement. Although no more than a provisional estimate, this is probably a great deal nearer the truth than the view expressed by an experienced firm of estate agents in 1889, that 'it may . . . be assumed that all estates of over 6,000 acres in any one county are entailed; these amount to about 8 million of acres, and being entailed do not often come into the market', which confined settled land to less than a quarter of the area of England and Wales under reference.[1]

The capital purpose of the strict settlement was, no doubt, to keep the family estates intact, and from the lawyer's point of view the element of strictness was precisely that device, the

[1] Norton, Trist and Gilbert, 'A Century of Land Values', *The Times*, 20 Apr. 1889.

trustees to preserve contingent remainders, which had been introduced to defeat any unscrupulous life-tenant who might scheme to deprive his unborn son of his inheritance. In point of fact, however, in view of the occasional non-settlement of entire estates, and of the more frequent practice of reserving powers of sale and disposal to a father and son acting jointly, it was the deeply held convictions of the landowners, quite as much as the parchments, which protected the integrity of their estates. The passionate emotional attachment to the principle of primogeniture was, after all, frequently demonstrated in the debates on the modest proposal to make the law on intestacy relating to real estate the same as that which already provided for equal division in the case of personal property. Bills for this purpose were introduced almost annually from 1836 until the 1870s, and were always violently and successfully resisted by the landed interest, on the grounds that any tampering with primogeniture must, by leading to the division of estates, destroy 'that fair and reasonable influence which the property and aristocracy of the country was (*sic*) allowed to possess.' As Palmerston put it in 1859, such a bill was incompatible with the existence of a landed gentry and 'tended to republicanism'. Two violently clashing views of the national character were seen to be involved: the territorial view that 'the law of primogeniture is inherent in the character, customs and feelings of Englishmen' put forward by Lord William Graham; and the liberal view that 'the middle classes of the country were almost to a man against the system of leaving the entire of a father's real property to one child.'[1] If the character, customs and feelings of landowners inclined so strongly to the conservation of undivided estates, this was in itself enough to attain that object. It is perhaps no cause for wonder that equity and justice, as understood by the non-landed, did not triumph in this field until 1925.

The second purpose of the strict settlement, to make provision for members of the family other than the eldest son, was perhaps after all the purpose which produced the greater effects in practice. There were wives to be supported, requiring while a

[1] *Hansard*, 3rd ser., XXII (1836), 12 Apr., 900–13 (Tooke). *ibid.*, 3rd ser., CLII (1859), 2 March, 1120 (Lord William Graham), 1122 (Mellor), 1155 (Palmerston).

husband was alive pin money which was often overspent, and in widowhood a jointure which was an income intended to keep them in the style to which they had become accustomed. There were all the daughters to be provided with portions, which it was hoped would enable them to marry well, and which at the worst would afford an income to mitigate spinsterhood. Finally there were the younger sons, generally furnished also with capital sums equal to their sisters' portions, sometimes supported by annuities. It was generally true that the fortune of a younger brother was but a minute fraction, either in capital value or in income, of the inheritance of the eldest. But these family charges tended to accumulate over the generations, and the head of a family, life-tenant of a great estate, might find that his gross income was severely depleted by payments to his brothers and sisters, and perhaps his aunts and uncles, as well as to his own children; and if he was very unfortunate it was not unknown for there to be as many as three or four dowagers all drawing their jointures from the estate simultaneously.

These family charges were the price paid by the landed classes for primogeniture, a price imposed by the strict settlement as much as by the dictates of family affection. The size of the price varied greatly according to individual circumstances, but invariably the whole income of an estate was not available for the purposes of the immediate family of the current head. It could happen that the titular head and apparent owner of a great estate had command over the spending of only a tithe of its revenues. What was kept intact, therefore, was essentially the land itself, the territorial unit, and it did not necessarily follow that its wealth was preserved mainly at the disposal of a single individual. To the outside world, however, the unbroken shell of a landed estate, even if in reality it was empty within, was the object which conferred position, authority and responsibility on the owner for the time being. If it had been broken up, to correspond to the claims which different members of the family had upon it, this position would in many cases have evaporated altogether.

The fortunes of younger sons were seldom sufficient to enable them to lead the lives of independent gentlemen who could afford to dispense with all thoughts of pecuniary rewards when selecting a career. This was the preserve of the few sons of grandees who, like Lord John Russell, could depend upon parental backing for a political career. At the same time younger sons generally had private incomes large enough for them to indulge a preference for the more honorific and less arduous types of career, which could be happily combined with continued pursuit of the sort of sporting and social interests for which their upbringing had created an appetite. The family structure which preserved all power and influence in the hands of the head provided the means for fulfilling such preferences. Colonel Thomas Perronet Thompson, author of the famous *Catechism on the Corn Laws*, concluded that 'this is clearly the end and aim of the law of primogeniture, that £10,000 a year is to be concentrated in the hands of the eldest son, that it may act as a battering ram for procuring a thousand for each of the others, or as much of it as may be found practicable, by entry into the public pantry, and appropriation of the victuals that is (*sic*) therein'.[1] Influence and patronage could place men to advantage in the church, the army and navy, and the more lucrative sections of the civil service, and in these careers the progress of men without such backing was handicapped indeed.

There were close institutional links with the church, for it was reckoned that 7,268 out of a total of 11,342 livings in England and Wales, were in the gift of private patrons, that is in the hands of the aristocracy and gentry.[2] The aristocracy may not have made excessive use of their powers of presentation to further the interests of their own families, since it seems that only about one-eighth of the 400-odd clerical pluralists listed by the same source came from aristocratic families. The matter is, however, uncertain, since in another place 2,886 of the 7,191 individual incumbents who shared out all the livings are referred to as 'aristocratic pluralists, mostly non-resident, and holding two, three, four, or more livings, in all 7,037 livings'; the term 'aristocratic' may well have been used here simply in a generally pejorative and abusive sense. More usually, perhaps, the aristocracy made use of their church patronage to advance their friends and gratify the requests of men whom it was important to propitiate for county or other reasons, and also to reward their

[1] Quoted by James Beal, *Free Trade in Land* (1855), p. 36.
[2] *Extraordinary Black Book* (1831), pp. 41, 54, 502-35.

children's tutors. In extreme necessity an advowson was used simply to raise funds by selling the next presentation.

Influence and means were probably of greatest use in a military career, perhaps the favourite haven of younger sons. 'The 3,000 commissions in the army are specially reserved for the connections of this class of society', it was stated.[1] Money was vital, not merely in securing a start by the purchase of a commission, but also in ensuring progress by purchasing promotion. It was quite usual for part of a younger son's portion to be paid over before he was strictly entitled to it, which was when he was 21, in order to secure his 'advancement' in this fashion. In obtaining entry into the fashionable regiments, and in arranging transfers to avoid Indian service, aristocratic connexions were supremely valuable; while in order to live as an officer in such a regiment private means, such as a younger son's portion afforded, were indispensable. Success in naval careers, though doubtless assisted by influential connexions as in the case of Lord Prudhoe, second son of the Duke of Northumberland, would seem to have demanded far more genuine application, competence and experience.

In a rarefied and limited field, that of the most picturesque and lucrative sinecures in the gift of government, progress was possible only for those with high influence with ministers or at court. Many of the most glittering prizes were reserved by the heads of families for their own or their eldest son's enjoyment. Thus among the eleven commissioners for the affairs of India worth £1,500 a year apiece, 'very snug and profitable places', we find in 1820 Lord Apsley, Earl Bathurst, Lord Binning, Viscount Castlereagh, Viscount Cranborne, the Earl of Liverpool, Viscount Lowther, Viscount Sidmouth, Lord Teignmouth, and Lord Walpole, none of whom were younger sons. A short list of some of the most profitable and least onerous places would certainly include Earl Bathurst, who was also a teller of the Exchequer at £23,117 a year gross; the Marquess Camden, another of the tellers; Viscount Cathcart, lord vice-admiral of Scotland at £14,000 a year; Lord Grenville, auditor of the Exchequer at £4,000 a year; the Hon R. D. Kenyon, filazer and exigenter at £4,986 a year; the Earl of Liverpool, who as

[1] James Beal, *loc. cit.*, quoting J. J. Macintyre.

well as being Prime Minister was constable of Dover Castle at £4,100 a year and clerk of the Rolls in Ireland at another £3,500; Lord Stewart who had £3,700 a year as a lord of the bed-chamber as well as being ambassador at Vienna; the Marquess of Wellesley who was one of the joint remembrancers of the court of Exchequer in Ireland at £4,852 a year as well as being ambassador at Madrid; and the Earl and Countess of Westmeath who aggregated £4,460 a year from their posts as auditor of imprest accounts and clerk of the hanaper. These also were all heads of families or eldest sons.[1]

Younger sons, nevertheless, were not wholly exluded from these rich pastures by their elders, and some of those with the most highly placed relatives were able to obtain a modest competence in this way. Thus Thomas Grenville, one of the younger brothers of the first Marquess of Buckingham, was chief justice in Eyre south of the Trent, at £2,316 a year,[2] while Charles Villiers, one younger brother of the Earl of Clarendon, was chief justice in Eyre north of the Trent, George the other brother being paymaster of the marines and groom of the bed-chamber receiving £3,300 a year. The Duke of Manchester's brother, Lord Montagu, was collector outwards of the customs at London; the sisters of the Earl of Northington were jointly clerk of the hanaper; Wellesley Pole, brother of the Duke of Wellington, was master and worker of the Mint and joint remembrancer of the court of Exchequer in Ireland at £12,450 in all; one brother of the Earl of Harrowby was accomptant-general of salt duties and register to the commissioners of excise, the other being Bishop of Gloucester; the three brothers of the Marquess of Hertford between them held the jobs of prothono-tary in the court of King's Bench in Ireland, and keeper of declarations there, one was a commissioner of excise and one was a craner and wharfinger in the port of Dublin, the combined emoluments being £17,473. And so the list could be continued.

This was a field for the parking out of younger sons which

---

[1] Information on places and sinecures taken from *The Black Book* (1820), pp. 12–91.

[2] On his death in 1846 Lord Grenville made handsome amends, stating in his will that 'a great part of my library has been purchased from the profits of a sinecure office given to me by the public, and I feel it to be a debt and a duty that I should acknowledge this obligation by giving that library so acquired to the British Museum for the use of the public'.

largely disappeared in the generation after Reform. It was in any case one which had never been available to more than a handful of the most highly privileged. The radical M.P. Ewart depicted the normal situation when, in 1836, he countered the argument that primogeniture was socially useful because it ensured that younger sons were merged 'in the people again from whom they had sprung', by claiming that in the professions where merit and toil were needed there were no younger sons to be found, and that they only went into those professions where patronage was essential, the church, the army, and the navy.[1] Naturally it was far from true that merit and toil were never shown in these professions. Within them there may have been a significant difference between the career patterns of younger sons of the aristocracy and those of the gentry. It was not only a case of the gentry not having patronage levers of equal power at their disposal, but also a question of the effect of the smaller scale of portions which the gentry could afford. This meant that their younger sons could not contemplate those careers in which considerable private means were necessary for the support of obligatory styles of living. In the choice of regiments, for example, the 'best' or most expensive were ruled out, and service in mere line regiments and long tours in the working army in India, had to be accepted. Further than this, their comparative poverty might well oblige younger sons of the gentry to 'merge again in the people', at least to the extent of pursuing practical working careers in the law, the administration, or commerce.

Patronage and purchase as methods of selection of public servants did not really break down until after 1870, and even then in the case of the civil service it was arguable that the change to competitive examinations merely replaced the patronage of ministers by the patronage of the older universities; hence it was perhaps the intellectual rather than the social quality of the entrants which was changed. In any case, the effect of this change, and of the abolition of the purchase of commissions in 1871, on the prospects of younger sons of the aristocracy should not be exaggerated. Perhaps even more without purchase, since openings for men of mere wealth and little other recommendation were now minimized, the 'best' regiments were havens for young men of good birth and breeding, and private means. The

[1] *Hansard*, 3rd ser., XXXII (1836), 12 Apr., 897–900.

professionalization of the army did not reach very far until just before 1914, and indeed the earlier professionalization of other services with its demand for ability and efficiency in church and civil service, may have produced an even greater concentration of younger sons in the army. Above all there was a great multiplication of jobs requiring men of good education and background, a multiplication caused by the needs of administering an ever more complicated society in an ever more complicated way, and quite unmatched of course by any comparable increase in the number of aristocratic career-seekers. In the shadow of this process the younger sons in fact remained well provided, but no longer conspicuous. Unable any longer to run the country from the resources of their own families and dependants, the landed aristocracy found that the process of producing this larger supply of rulers had merged them with a wider élite, and deprived them of their unique position of command.

IV

The Life of a Landed Aristocrat

T H E ordinary events of life, birth, majority, marriage and death were marked in aristocratic circles by a publicity which served to emphasize and enhance the standing of the family. Church bells were rung on these occasions, in the parish certainly and quite often throughout the whole county. The tenantry of the estate expressed their joy or sympathy, as was appropriate, and the neighbouring gentry joined with them in honouring a leader and enjoying his hospitality, in the rejoicings or sorrowings of ceremonies lavish and magnificent suitable to his degree, while the rest of the local public looked on at the doings of their superiors. Something of all this of course still survives, great ceremonies and large receptions are still held, the publicity of *The Times'* announcement columns reaches further than the church bells, and public interest in the private lives of selected aristocrats is cultivated by the popular press. The general public, however, is in this largely gratifying its curiosity and its desire to share vicariously in the lives of the great, while the throngs of guests are not a little gratified by the pleasant savour of friend-ship or acquaintance with notabilities openly demonstrated. The sense of paying homage to a local dynasty has entirely vanished. This essential part of the atmosphere of these earlier proceedings survives today only at the national level, where it informs royal occasions. Elsewhere, the popping of champagne corks is no substitute for the roasting of oxen.

76

The birth of an heir was matter for much rejoicing in the neighbourhood of a great house; if this chanced to be a castle, such as Alnwick, guns might be fired to salute the news that the succession was assured. A great dinner would be given for the tenantry, and the senior tenant, the steward and the owner would all make speeches; this would happen again at weddings, with separate provision for the gentry, the substantial tenant farmers, and the lesser tenants and estate workers, with three different menus. In the family circle births were occasions for a gathering of the clan, the sequel of baptism and christening often being taken in two stages sometimes separated by as much as five months from each other, both ceremonies usually being performed by a clerical relative or friend in the private house, and being crowned by a large christening dinner for which it might be necessary to import a special cook. Births also could be a source of private embarrassment where a family threatened to become over large, and at least one noble lord who confided his monthly anxiety to his diary would have welcomed birth-control knowledge in the 1820s. Birthdays, accompanied in the Regency period as now by the giving of presents within the family, were often celebrated by a ball for the servants. But the greatest birthday of all was the eldest son's twenty-first.[1]

The end of a minority produced the summit in such celebrations, for it called for something special to mark the close of a period during which the potency of a great family had been somewhat in abeyance. When the Duke of Rutland came of age early in 1799 weeks of preparations culminated in three days of feasting and display, which must have marked indelibly on the minds of the revellers a vivid impression of the magnificence, munificence and grandeur of the owner of Belvoir, now entering into his full inheritance. A range of temporary buildings was erected for the festivities, and it being winter and Rutland being a duke these were substantial structures with brick fireplaces and chimneys. More than 18,000 bricks were used, and the special workmen included 'plasterers, glaziers, painters, upholsterers, carpenters, bellhangers, tailors, stovefluemakers, and other men for the birthday preparations' for whom board had to

---

[1] This chapter is largely based on the MSS of the landed aristocracy mentioned in the Preface and Bibliography, and individual references are only given where specific events are mentioned in the text or where individual documents are quoted.

be provided. Within the house too, much preparation was needed for the reception of the castle guests, and quantities of feather beds and carpets were bought in. When they came these house guests brought with them grooms whose board cost over £54; at a time when servants' board wages were around ten shillings a week this conjures up a picture of a noble company of grooms in attendance on their masters. It took eleven days to set up the extra beds in the castle, and a baker had baked for eighteen days in the kitchens before the celebrations began.

The feasting, naturally enough, was notable for the large quantities of food and drink consumed. There were six whole oxen, twelve sheep and twenty-one pigs to keep the turn-spits busy, and the equivalent of at least another hundred sheep came dressed from butchers. Beside this the fish and fowl, twenty-three turkeys, one hundredweight of cream cheese, and the solitary stuffed peacock for the high table seem unimportant. The quality drank two pipes of port and forty-six and a quarter gallons of brandy; they also shared with the more superior tenants twenty-three gallons of rum and four hogsheads of Lisbon wine. There is no tally of the beer drunk on the occasion, but one brewer had brewed for thirty-four weeks in order to provide sufficient and had used over thirty quarters of malt, enough for several thousand gallons. Replete, surrounded by flags and bunting, the guests of all degrees listened to the music of the Grantham Infantry and several other bands and no doubt marvelled at the wealth and openhandedness of a man who could command such entertainment. By repute, so much did legend like to emphasize the port of a great nobleman by putting an inflated monetary figure on his liberality, all this had cost the duke £60,000. In more sober fact the accounts indicate a total expenditure of under £5,500, though this does not include all that the large house party consumed during their stay. It was still a very large sum of money, though it was nearly matched by the £4,500 which the duke spent at the tailor, hatter, breechesmaker, whipmaker, saddler, shoemaker, coachmaker, hosier, perfumer, jeweller and gunsmith in procuring his own birthday presents.[1] On Lord Milton's coming of age in 1808, by

[1] T. F. Dale, *The History of the Belvoir Hunt* (1899), p. 84. The account in the text is based on the Belvoir Castle Accounts, and the Minority Accounts of the 5th Duke.

way of contrast, the cost of the celebrations at Milton House was only £393 10s. 4d.[1]

In death the dignity and rank of the great were accorded respect in the elaborate and stylized ritual of impressive public ceremonies. The etiquette of mourning embraced a wide circle of the family as well as the household servants both indoor and outdoor, and extended over many months with its rules of abstention from entertainment and its prescription of muted social intercourse, and this of course remained in observance until the present century. The most public expression of the dignity of the departed, however, was in the cortège itself, the carriage procession of hearse, mourners and hired mutes, the length of which varied with the consequence of the family. Sometimes great distances had to be covered between the place of death and the family vault or burial ground, and it was on these journeys that the dead man's personal carriage, or if a husband was mourning his wife his empty carriage emblazoned with his coat of arms, informed the world at large of the passing of a great person. Thus in 1807 the Countess of Darlington died at Cleveland House in London, and was transported by road to Raby Castle for burial in Staindrop churchyard. The Earl's agent gave precise instructions to the undertaker for the conduct of the funeral 'in which all unnecessary parade and show was avoided, but a desire shown that proper attention should be paid to her ladyship's rank', but it nevertheless occasioned what were considered 'tremendous charges' which totalled over £1,400. The undertaker provided a hearse with six horses, a mourning coach with six horses, and nine mounted outriders, who spent nineteen days on the journey out and home. A full procession went up Bond Street, Oxford Street and Tottenham Court Road to Highgate, where all the extra people turned back at the bottom of the hill. The hearse, coach and nine horsemen proceeded on the journey, accompanied by a caravan of the Earl's own horses and servants, until met by the Raby servants at Piercebridge when a full procession re-formed. The undertaker's men were to proceed one stage on their homeward journey on the afternoon of the burial, and were allowed eight days afterwards to

[1] Northants R.O., Fitzwilliam MSS, Milton Accounts 1808/9.

reach London.[1] By way of comparison, the state funeral of Nelson in 1806 is said to have cost £14,000.

The coming of the railway and the adoption by the aristocracy of the facility of the special hearse coach and the special mourning train, removed from the social scene this slow-moving and very public demonstration of deceased grandeur and made mourning and funerals into more intimate family and local affairs. The body of the third Duke of Northumberland, for instance, went by road from Alnwick Castle where he died in February 1847 to Gateshead station, and then by special train to London for burial in the Abbey. His death, however, still brought wide notice in his own locality, notwithstanding the fact that he was expressly described as 'a man whose intellect and attainments procured for him a very moderate degree of respect . . . of the House of Lords he was by no means a distinguished member.' On the news of his death all the tradesmen of Alnwick at once partially closed their shops, and when his funeral procession passed through Newcastle a week later the streets were lined and all shops closed. In this procession we can see the county and the Northumbrian tenantry bidding farewell to their feudal chief. A mile outside Alnwick on the southward road the column halted and the townspeople and household staff on foot dismissed; two miles further on the mounted tenantry fell away. The reduced party of notabilities from the estate staff and the comptroller of the household passed streets lined with people at Felton and Morpeth on their way, and seven hours later reached the Town Moor at Newcastle where a full procession was again formed. This now included the Mayor and Corporation and many other gentlemen on horseback, and more still on foot, including the committees of various charities which the Duke had supported. The tenantry of the southern parts of his estates were marshalled in military fashion according to their bailiwicks, each mounted column under the command of its own bailiff, and the whole accompanied the coffin to Gateshead station. There could be no mistaking the ducal style of this. An inner coffin of french-polished figured mahogany lined with padded white silk and lace was encased in a lead coffin; over this was an outer coffin of oak covered with rich crimson Genoa silk

[1] Raby MSS, Muniment Room, Account of the Funeral Expenses of the Countess of Darlington, 1807.

velvet, emblazoned with the Percy arms in gold plate, and provided with eight coroneted handles and coffin nails all also in gold plate.[1]

Movement by rail may also have brought economies to the funerals of the great. When the third Earl Fitzwilliam died in 1857 a special train was run from Peterborough to Rotherham for the burial at Wentworth Woodhouse, and the total cost including servants' mourning and the tolling of passing bells was about a thousand pounds. A great nobleman who won the admiration and love of his countrymen by his qualities as an individual continued to receive the public respect of his neighbourhood. 'The Duke of Northumberland is dead', wrote the *Newcastle Journal* in 1865; 'it will spread a gloom and sorrow in the north, whose dark shadow will fall upon a generation to come', and the entire issue of the paper was black bordered. The dead duke was Algernon the Benevolent, 'the greatest of all the Percies', whose practical efforts for the poor and for the welfare of his county had earned him the love of the humblest cottagers, some 7,000 of whom filed past his coffin during the two days it lay in state at Alnwick. For his special train the platforms at Newcastle, Darlington and Durham were crowded, and the Minster bells tolled as it passed through York.[2] Great public demonstrations of respect simply for the titles and wealth of the dead, as distinct from feelings genuinely evoked by the character of an individual, were however distinctly on the wane by this time and vanished along with the feudal attitude in the last quarter of the nineteenth century.

In death all were ultimately equal even though the undertaker's arts might seek to prolong the illusion that they were not. In life inequality began at birth and was indelibly stamped by education and upbringing. At the opening of the nineteenth century an aristocrat's education was most likely to be completed by a spell at Oxford or Cambridge, and by a year or more on the Grand Tour which, however, was subject to irritating interference by the wars. As a preparation for this it was very likely but not by any means certain that he would have been at

---

[1] *The Times*, 13 Feb. 1847. *Newcastle Courant*, 12 Feb. 1847; 26 Feb. 1847.

[2] Wentworth Woodhouse MSS, Accounts of the Executors of Charles William Earl Fitzwilliam. He was 3rd earl in the U.K. title but 5th earl in the Irish peerage. *Newcastle Journal*, 13 Feb. 1865; 21 Feb. 1865; 22 Feb. 1865.

one of the great public schools, and in that case generally speaking it would have been either Eton or Harrow, the latter under first Drury and then Butler enjoying its first great vogue in the later eighteenth century. The rest of the nine old public schools, Winchester, Rugby, Shrewsbury, Charterhouse, Merchant Taylors', St Paul's and Westminster, did not enjoy anything like the same degree of aristocratic patronage. Of Rugby indeed it was said in 1806 that 'in it are many of the sons of gentlemen, but more of those who are sons of manufacturers at Birmingham, Wolverhampton, etc., who having little sentiment of the disgrace of anything dishonourable, act as their inclinations lead them'.[1]

In any case the public schools of the time were not so remarkable as seats of learning or so attractive as examples of well-mannered or obedient communities that it was considered obligatory for a gentleman's son to attend them. The same source of 1806, a successful and respectable private school proprietor, said that 'the bane of the public schools is that the parents of many of the boys fill their pockets with bank notes, and opportunity is allowed for the expenditure of it viciously. He described the characters of three great schools by saying that the youth at Eaton (*sic*) are dissipated gentlemen; those at Westminster dissipated with a little of the black guard; and those at St Pauls the most depraved of all.' At Harrow alone did he allow that the boys were recognizably gentlemen. For the boys who went to public school as well as those who did not, continuity of instruction was probably provided by a private tutor, on whom also was placed the chief reliance in the training of character. In essence therefore the only distinctive contribution which the public school had to offer was the opportunity for making advantageous acquaintances and for gaining knowledge of the ways of the world. Where such facilities were already provided in abundance by the ordinary social life of a great nobleman there was thus no pressing cause for him to give his sons anything beyond private tuition before they went up to university.

The position of the private tutor was thus one of great responsibility and influence over the personalities of his charges. He might begin his duties when the eldest boy was six or seven; or he might not be taken on until the boy was 12 or 13, after

[1] *Farington Diary*, IV. 6.

spending the earlier years at a private school which was frequently run by a local parson, like Mr Faithful's at Hatfield
which all the Grimston boys attended in turn in the 1820s. The
tutor might be dismissed when the boys had finished at public
school, as was Henderson when the two eldest Grimstons moved
on from Harrow to Oxford; or he might accompany his charge
throughout his university career and on a Grand Tour afterwards, as King accompanied the Duke of Rutland in the late
1790s. The tutor was usually in holy orders, as befitted his
prime task of moulding the character, principles and manners of
a Christian gentleman, and he normally lived as a member of
the family in accordance with his role of intimate companion to
the sons of the house. His rewards could be great, for it was
usual to honour good service by presentation to a living in his
employer's gift, and this with continued patronage in later life
launched not a few eminent ecclesiastical careers. William Pitt
made his old tutor, George Pretyman, bishop of Lincoln in 1787
and later translated him to Winchester; Addington's tutor
Huntingford was rewarded with the see of Gloucester in 1802;
and Bethell, the Duke of Northumberland's tutor, became bishop
of Bangor in 1830.

In 1815 Lord Liverpool explained how the great men competed over the advancement of their former tutors. 'The bishop
of St Asaph is dead,' he informed Lord Sidmouth, 'I want to
talk with you before I see the Regent, knowing the deep interest
you naturally take in the bishop of Gloucester [Huntingford].
The situation is that on the formation of this Administration the
see of Ely was vacant, and the competition was between the
Duke of Rutland for Dr Sparke [one of his old tutors] and the
Duke of Buccleuch for Dr Luxmore [his tutor]. I decided for the
former, but I informed the Duke of Buccleuch that I did so
because of the connection between the Duke of Rutland and the
county of Cambridge, but that his wishes should be attended to
on the first opportunity. The Duke of Buccleuch did not expect
to have his wishes gratified when the see of London fell vacant,
acknowledging that that appointment must be on public grounds.
Therefore I am very anxious to offer St Asaph to Dr Luxmore.
The bishopric of Hereford is worth at least double Gloucester,
and the Bishop might retain with it the Wardenship of Winchester, and continue to reside there as at present. Hence I

doubt whether the difference between St Asaph and Hereford would compensate him for giving up Winchester, though it might do so in point of income. Alternatively you may wish to wait for Bath and Wells for the bishop of Gloucester.'[1] And so it fell out, Luxmore to St Asaph and Huntingford to Hereford.

Rewards might also come in another direction. In 1795 Farington reported 'the Duchess of Leinster, sister of the Duke of Richmond, is about 65 years of age. Mr Ogilvie to whom she is now married, is a Scotchman, and was placed as an usher for £12 a year at a very small school in Ireland. After the death of the duke, the duchess requiring a tutor for her young children, Ogilvie had the luck to be recommended; and being domesticated in the family, the duchess conceived a passion for him which ended in marriage. They have three children, daughters. The duchess has about £4,000 a year jointure, and by savings it is supposed Mr Ogilvie has about £20,000 which will be divided among them.'[2] The widowed Lady Charlotte Guest did much the same when in 1855 she married Charles Schreiber, her son's tutor.

To employ a private tutor could be expensive in a more straightforward way. The salary of the Duke of Rutland's tutor was £300 a year in the 1790s, and in the 1820s Lord Verulam was paying £150 a year to Henderson. Public school bills alone might be felt to be heavy, ranging between £175 and £250 a year for board and tuition at Eton and Harrow in the early nineteenth century. For such as could afford neither the one nor the other, private boarding schools were available and were considered suitable for well-born boys before going up to university. From 1838 to 1846 Lord Monson's two older sons were at Mr Malden's school in Brighton, there receiving for £120 a year the bulk of their schooling; for the eldest son did not leave until he was 17, and then spent some six months at Mr Bull's select cramming establishment at Sowerby near Halifax before going up to Christ Church. The third son, however, more conventionally went to Eton in 1848.

The essentially personal and individual quality of education, even when attending one of the great public schools, is well brought out in the scheme which Huntingford, then Warden

[1] Sidmouth MSS, Liverpool to Sidmouth, 15 May 1815.
[2] *Farington Diary*, I. 103–4.

of Winchester, outlined in 1790 for 'the liberal and virtuous education' of Addington's eldest son. 'My new plan for your son would be for him to become a member of my family as soon as you please, and there to learn his first elements under Mr Brereton, make progress with Mr Richards, and then enter the College School, but still be in my house out of school hours. During these early years there would be little occasion for a person whose sole business it might be to attend him. But at twelve years of age, I should recommend you allowing me to look out for a gentleman and a scholar to be with him as much as possible. I know the evils arising to young men of that age from associating with servants in their hours of recreation. My province in the meantime shall be to superintend, assist, and direct the whole plan.'[1]

With this emphasis on the vital importance of the personal tutor, and given the variety of institutional ways in which education might be furnished, there was no uniform type to which their schooldays might impel the aristocracy to conform. The lack of standardization meant that there was full scope for variety, the flowering of individual idiosyncrasies and the development of independence of mind, as well as for the self-assertion of strong-willed, dull or indolent boys. It also tended to perpetuate aristocratic exclusiveness, for in the absence of a uniform mould which could press the sons of the new wealthy and of the older nobility alike into the amalgam of a common public school type, the means of such social fusion remained unorganized and hence slow and haphazard in their operation. In one essential matter, however, uniformity was the aim of the landed aristocracy long before the days of public school reform, the uniformity of accent which has since become perhaps the most sensitive instrument of class. In comparison with the precision attained in this field in the later nineteenth century, in diction, vocabulary and form as well as in pronunciation, the earlier attention to this matter was rudimentary, a question of ruling out unacceptable forms of speech rather than of instilling conformity to a standard. 'The person who has hitherto had the instruction of my children,' Christopher Sykes of Sledmere wrote to a friend at Oxford, 'is going into another line of life, indeed he is no loss as he has done them all the good he is capable of,

[1] Sidmouth MSS, Huntingford to Addington, 14 Feb. 1790.

which was to teach them to read English though but ill. If you know of any young man you think fit to succeed him, who can correct their Yorkshire tone and instruct them to your wishes . . . I wish you would let me know, to continue with them till you and he think they are fit for school.'[1] The feeling that local dialects were lower class had arrived.

Attendance at university did indeed impose something of a pattern as a counterweight to the individualism of schooling, but it was largely a pattern devised by the aristocratic undergraduate sets themselves, its shape owed little to college authority, and it had virtually no intellectual content. 'I am quite surprised at your account of lectures and themes,' Lord Monson wrote to his son at Christ Church in 1847, 'we had nothing of that kind in my day.' In 1805 Farington had breakfasted with a friend who was a fellow of King's College, Cambridge, who unburdened himself about the tedium of a fellow's life of waiting idly until he could hope to go off to a College living at the age of about 45: 'On College life he said members look forward to other situations. In a College life the society of women is wanting, men grow splenetick; positive occupation is also wanting.' The purpose of college life for an undergraduate, Lord Monson told his son, was to 'make a select acquaintance, as much in your own rank as possible', and he approved of him 'becoming a subscriber to the concerts. The musical set, though I did not belong to it, I will own as the most gentlemanlike in my time at Christ Church.'[2] At university, then, the sons of the nobility got to know their peers, made the friendships and contacts which would form the structure of their later social life and assist them in political groupings if inclined to that life, and tried out their paces in the ways of the great world away from parental supervision. They proceeded to degrees without qualification or examination, purely on the basis of satisfying the terms of residence. A very few, and these perhaps younger sons more often than not, might join a 'reading set' and equip themselves seriously from the store of learning and scholarship which could be discovered by any who were interested. For the general run the university was a finishing school, more effective

[1] Sledmere MSS, Sir Christopher Sykes's Letter Book, 1775–90, Sykes to Revd. W. Cleaver, 15 Sept. 1778.
[2] *Farington Diary*, III. 106–7. Monson MSS, 25/10/2/1, especially nos. 2, 16.

and lasting in its impress, even if its course was less paved with the visible emblems of culture, than the Grand Tour.

The real element of uniformity was imparted by upbringing in the atmosphere of life in an aristocratic household. This influenced the minds, habits and attitudes of youth while at an impressionable age, and in spite of the diversity of individual tastes and interests in the aristocratic world there was a wide similarity in the main structure of this life. This factor also was a powerful influence in maintaining the landed aristocracy as a closed circle, since the conditions were not easily reproduced except in the country house surrounded by its park and estates, and the affinities of those brought up in such surroundings were naturally with their own kind, while with outsiders there was lack of common interests as well as suspicion of alien ways.

The majority of the great country houses had already been built before our period opens in 1790, but the motives of emulation and competitive architectural ostentation which had played such a part in inspiring the great eighteenth-century activity in aristocratic building continued to operate for many decades thereafter. In an age sufficiently removed from the sometimes stark realities of the originals to take delight in romanticizing the past, admiration for the Gothic, both medieval fortified baronial and ecclesiastical, was starting its long reign over taste at the close of the century, for some decades running in uneasy harness with the final fruits of stucco classicism which we know as the Regency style. There were always some among the great and wealthy who felt the urge to keep up with the times in order to give a proper demonstration of their standing, while for those who aspired to found a family the building of a new house continued to be an almost essential step.

Christopher Sykes, for example, consolidated the family's withdrawal from trade and banking at Hull in the recognized fashion. He added largely to the estate at Sledmere which he inherited from his father, entered Parliament, obtained a baronetcy for his pioneering improvements of the Yorkshire Wolds, and built a fine new mansion. Begun in 1788, it was some seven years in the building, completely encasing the old manor house in the best classical Georgian executed in Clumber stone, and providing one of the most handsome libraries in the country, its exterior decorated with a frieze in which were incorporated scenes depicting Agriculture, to symbolize the family's new interests and fame, and the Woollen Manufactory to acknowledge one of its origins. The house is sometimes ascribed to Joseph Rose of London, but Sykes's first letter to Rose makes it clear that he was called in at a late stage. 'I am building a large house,' he wrote in 1789, 'and through the recommendation of Sir Thomas Frankland and your general fame wish you to undertake the plaistering . . . I intend to finish very slowly as I wish the work to be well done, neat and simple rather in the old than new style, nothing rich or gaudy, but suiting to a plain Country Gentleman.'[1] In fact no architect is ever mentioned in all the correspondence relating to the building, and from the way in which Sykes emerges as personally managing all the business of ordering and procuring the stone, glass, timber, artificial stone ornaments, fireplaces and doors, all with exact specifications, it is possible that he was his own architect as well as his own clerk of works. 'I propose but to go to the top of the facia between the lower and upper story this season,' he told his main quarryman in August 1788, 'but we cannot get there till we have the last of the eight columns . . . and not being far from the sea our climate in autumn naturally moist, which fills me with the greatest anxiety to get on as fast as possible, for the house which we are obliged to live in, having no other, is laid open on every side and will be till the facia is put on, as my additions entirely surround my old house. When you read this, which I wish you would do every Monday morning, and consider my situation with a large family, you must not be of human materials if you do not employ all hands to get me stone for one vessel not to wait an hour, and two vessels if possible, and I assure you we have not stone here for 14 days work without turning away the hands we have employed all summer.'[2]

Owner-architects were something of a rarity, large-scale building projects by new families were rather more frequent, although there was at least one wife-architect, Lady Frances Henrietta Jermingham, who planned the rebuilding of Costessy Hall near Norwich in castle fashion at ruinous cost. From the late 1790s Beckford with the aid of James Wyatt was engaged on the stupendous enterprise of building Fonthill Abbey, the ill-

[1] Sledmere MSS, Letter Book, 1775–90, Sykes to Rose, 26 July 1789.
[2] *Ibid.*, Sykes to Marson (at Clumber), 20 Aug. 1788.

starred cathedral of a mansion on which perhaps £400,000 was lavished and whose tower collapsed so soon after its completion. On a more prudent and typical scale Sir Francis Baring, the first baronet, having bought a large estate in Hampshire from the Duke of Bedford, employed George Dance in 1803–6 to extend and improve the house of Stratton Park at a cost of £25,000. Every now and again there would arise from the ranks of the older established families an owner anxious to build himself a new house or give his old one a radical remodelling, and this was a much more frequent source of employment for the architects. Eaton Hall in Cheshire, built for Lord Grosvenor between 1804 and 1812 by William Porden at a cost of some £40,000, was one of the earliest noble mansions in the Gothic style, complete with cast-iron pinnacles. Grosvenor's father 'had always been a dupe upon the turf, and expended in that way vast sums of money. His debts, when he died, amounted to £180,000', and his son was somewhat cramped. The discovery of a very productive copper mine on the estate, which yielded over £40,000 a year, was most opportune in assisting the son's resolve to make Eaton into 'a compleat dwelling'. As the Grosvenor, subsequently Westminster, fortunes and titles mounted, wings were added to Eaton in 1823–5, considerable alterations were carried out in 1845–53, and the entire house was remodelled in 1870.[1]

Steps in the peerage, only too often unaccompanied by steps in the family fortune, were a not uncommon spur to building in keeping with the dignity and with the scale of entertainment expected of higher rank. When Charles Brudenell-Bruce achieved his ambition and became Marquess of Ailesbury in 1821 he at once began to cast around for suitable designs for enlarging Tottenham House, Wiltshire, and rendering it more convenient to his station. In the end he built to the grand classical plans of Thomas Cundy, and his outlay was perhaps £250,000.[2] James Grimston received a smaller step than Ailesbury when he

---

[1] *Farington Diary*, II. 128, 270; III. 261. *Correspondence of William Beckford*, ed. Boyd Alexander (1957), pp. 9–15, 326–8. H. M. Colvin, *Biographical Dictionary of English Architects, 1666–1840* (1954), p. 468, from whom all the following details of building are taken except where separately noted.

[2] F. M. L. Thompson, 'English Landownership: the Ailesbury Trust, 1832–56', *Econ. Hist. Rev.*, 2nd ser. XI (1958), 121. There is some reason to doubt the figure of £250,000, which also chances to be the rough total of the Marquess's debts, in which building costs were by no means the only ingredient.

became the Earl of Verulam in 1815, but he had in six sons and four daughters a much larger family, and he had an equal desire for accommodation adequate to the reception of the royal dukes and fashionable house parties. He and William Atkinson destroyed the symmetry of Gorhambury House as built by Sir Robert Taylor in the 1780s by adding on new wings in 1816–17 and 1826–8, but prudence and an economical severity of style doubled the size of the house for an expense of some £11,000.[1]

Gothic was, however, becoming the dominant fashion in country house building by the time of the Regency, and several architects contrived to demonstrate considerable virtuosity in meeting the demands for versatility in style imposed by their patrons. Atkinson, for example, specialized in the Gothic, between 1803 and 1828 executing the major works of Scone Castle for the Earl of Mansfield, Mulgrave Castle for the Earl of Mulgrave, Rosebery for Lord Rosebery, Himley Hall for Lord Dudley and Ward and, perhaps his largest Gothic achievement, Panshanger for Earl Cowper, where Lord Verulam greatly admired the appearance and internal arrangements. But apart from his work at Gorhambury, Atkinson also fitted in the addition of Ionic wings to Broughton Hall for Stephen Tempest. George Dance managed the Tudor style for Lord Ashburnham at Ashburnham Place, as well as Gothic and regulation classic for the Marquess of Camden's Wilderness Park. James Wyatt, who died in 1813, worked almost entirely in the Gothic, with large works at Goodwood House for the Duke of Richmond, Wilton House for the Earl of Pembroke, Wycombe Abbey for Lord Carrington, Elvaston Hall for the Earl of Harrington, Alton Towers for the Earl of Shrewsbury, Bulstrode Park for the Duke of Portland, Powderham Castle for Viscount Courtenay, and Sheffield Place for the Earl of Sheffield. His main achievements besides Fonthill, however, were probably Belvoir Castle which was entirely remodelled for the Duke of Rutland between 1801 and 1813 to form a genuine fairy-tale castle, and Ashridge Park for the Earl of Bridgewater which he began in 1808. Belvoir was badly damaged by fire in 1816 and subsequently restored by Sir J. Thoroton. Ashridge was not finished until 1817, under the direction of Jeffry Wyatt; while it was building

---

[1] J. C. Rogers, 'The Manor and Houses of Gorhambury', *Trans. St. Albans and Herts. Architectural and Archaeological Soc.* (1933), pp. 105–6.

and while the park was being landscaped by Repton it was a great object for expeditions and criticism by noble tourists. 'Went to Ashridge and looked over the new house which promises to be a magnificent building,' Lady Grimston recorded in 1810. 'The architecture Gothic. Some faults are to be observed, the library will be dark, and the drawing room 50 feet in length has but one fireplace and that at the end.' 'To Ashridge to meet Lady Salisbury,' Lord Verulam noted in 1820, 'Giles and I had a pleasant ride and took the liberty of criticizing Lord Bridgewater's new approach, not yet finished. It is not usual for roads to be turned up hills merely for the purpose of going down them again.'[1]

Jeffry Wyatt, who became Wyattville after his great restoration work at Windsor Castle, employed the Gothic and Tudor collegiate at will. For example he did baronial work on Chillingham Castle for the Earl of Tankerville, and a Gothic house at Lilleshall Hall in 1829 for Earl Gower, but also carried out considerable reconstructions and additions at Longleat for the Marquess of Bath, Wollaton Hall for Lord Middleton, and Chatsworth for the Duke of Devonshire during the period 1804–40 in keeping with the sixteenth-century styles of those houses. At Endsleigh in Devonshire he built a modest 'cottage ornée' for the Duke of Bedford in 1810, which apparently 'cost between £70,000 and £80,000, and the grounds, laid out with inimitable taste, must have cost thousands more. There are sixty miles of grass rides and gravel walks.'[2] Wyattville's successor as master of the castellated was Anthony Salvin, 1799–1881, who worked in Nash's office in the 1820s. Starting with commissions for country gentlemen, in 1830 he designed Methley Hall for the Earl of Mexborough; he followed this with Peckforton Castle for Lord Tollemache, and Thoresby Hall which was eleven years in the building for Earl Manvers after 1864. He was a notable restorer, and among his large operations were Petworth for Lord Leconfield, Longford Castle for the Earl of Radnor, Encombe Hall for the Earl of Eldon, Birdsall House for Lord Middleton, and Dunster Castle for G. T. Luttrell. By far his largest work, however, in the grandest baronial manner with

[1] Gorhambury MSS, Lady Charlotte Grimston's Diary, 15 Aug. 1810. Lord Verulam's Diary, 30 Nov. 1820.
[2] *The Greville Memoirs* (1888), VI. 211, visit in July 1848.

Italian cinquecento interior, was the enormous reconstruction of Alnwick Castle for the Duke of Northumberland between 1852 and 1866. This, in the words of enthusiastic contemporaries, made Alnwick into the Windsor of the North, as imposing a medieval fortress as the imagination could wish to behold, complete in every detail down to the fortified estate offices and stables.[1]

This great work, which was said to have made Alnwick the largest and noblest baronial structure in the possession of a private subject, cost in all some £320,000, of which the architect received £14,000 and the Italian artists and carvers under Commendatore Canina £17,000. The main building contractors received £225,000, but the mechanical equipment was not inexpensive, some £20,000 going on steam closets, hydraulic lifts and gas fittings. At the peak of activity over 800 workmen were employed; they were entertained at a works dinner every November at a cost of 4s. 6d. per head, and at the opening of the new kitchens in 1859 this dinner occasioned a graphic account of the engineering marvels which could be blended with Gothic splendour. 'The new kitchens are probably in point of architectural grandeur and adaptation to the several processes of the culinary art the finest in the world,' the local paper reported. 'They are planned in the Gothic style. . . . It surprises the beholder that so grand a piece of architecture could be designed in these degenerate days. A huge baron of beef . . . weighing three hundredweight . . . and numerous other joints were before the principal range all on spits turned by a water wheel. . . . The screen before the fire is of a size, and possesses culinary contrivances and architectural features, alone sufficient to confer celebrity upon any ordinary architect. . . . Not only is water power applied to the rotation of the spits, but mechanical contrivances are used in various other ways. Hydraulic presses hoist with steady power the coals from the vaults below, and lift the viands from the kitchen to the galleries which lead to the banqueting hall. . . . Communicating with the main kitchen are separate pantries for the reception of butcher meat, fish, game, cold meat, stock, pastry and other edibles. Last but not least we notice the studio of Mr Reed, His Grace's cook. The

---

[1] *The Builder*, obituary notice of A. Salvin, 31 Dec. 1881, 809.

guests made their exit by a stone staircase which it would have done the heart of William of Wykeham good to have seen.'[1] Contrivances and gadgets adapted from the technology of industry and mining were indeed one of the features of aristocratic houses in the nineteenth century. As early as 1825 Knole was warmed by steam, in 1835 some of the rooms at least at Tottenham Park were heated by hot air ducts, and Raby Castle seems to have been provided with some central heating in 1843; the chilliness which Lady Diana Cooper recollects in late nineteenth-century Belvoir was not the universal lot of the great mansions. A miniature indoor railway was not unknown, to convey the hot muffins round the guests at their stations in the drawing room; and in the application of mining techniques to subterranean domestic architecture the 5th Duke of Portland was unrivalled in the 1860s.[2] All in all it would not seem that the passion for building and for the improvement of country houses had spent itself before 1870. Possibly the passion came to be pursued with greater moderation and prudence in relation to available wealth, for the Marquess of Ailesbury seems to have been the last of the great men to over-build himself to the point of serious financial difficulties, though he was far from being the last of the grievously indebted aristocrats. At any rate modest provision tuned to modest resources was not incompatible with the diginity of a nobleman, for in 1845 the 2nd Lord Sidmouth provided himself with a mansion at Up Ottery for £6,440.[3]

Many of the greater magnates possessed more than one country house and kept up something of the old medieval practice of peregrinating with their households from one part of the country to another. The purpose of these annual migrations had of course altered, and instead of eating one estate out of provisions before moving on to the next the nineteenth-century baron might well have the duration of his visits fixed by the supply of game. To open the secondary houses for residence for

[1] Alnwick MSS, Castle Building Ledger, 1854–66. Alnwick MSS, cutting from *Newcastle Journal* in Business Minutes XXV, 28 Nov. 1859.

[2] Gorhambury MSS, Lord Verulam's Diary, 22 Feb. 1825. Savernake MSS, Trustees' Memoranda Book, June 1835. Raby MSS, Household Accounts 1843. A. S. Turberville, *Welbeck Abbey and its Owners* (1939), II. 436–40. L. Jewitt, *The Stately Homes of England* (n.d.) II. 349.

[3] Sidmouth MSS, contract for building a mansion house, 31 May 1845. The political 1st Lord had not resided on the Devon estate, and prior to 1845 there was no house suitable for a gentleman's residence.

a few weeks in the year was a way of showing the flag in out-lying territories, seeing that influence was kept bright and ready for use through the refreshment of periodic visible presence, and settling any local estate affairs which needed personal inspection or interviews. The local agent could generally store these matters up until the autumn when all could be happily combined with the fortnight or month's supply of pheasants which the estate was gauged capable of furnishing.

Thus the Duke of Cleveland would generally pay a visit to his Shropshire estate in the autumn and live for a while in Ercall House. His normal routine was to come up to Raby in good time for the opening of grouse shooting, and perhaps go onto his moors for a week or two at his shooting lodge of High Force in upper Teesdale; then he would fit in his Shropshire visit, and return to Raby for some pheasants and some hunting, departing in the early winter for Battle Abbey in Sussex, where the winter was milder and which was convenient for moving up to Cleveland House for the next London season. Similarly the Marquess of Ailesbury generally made a point of visiting his Yorkshire estates for the grouse season in August, and his house at Jervaulx Abbey, convenient for the moors, was briefly opened up for the accommodation of himself and his family. Not all of these moves were so closely tied to the shooting calendar. The Duke of Rutland used Cheveley primarily for its convenience for Newmarket racing; one Duke of Devonshire sometimes retired to Hardwicke because he could enjoy a more private life there than at Chatsworth, and a later duke lived for part of the year at Holker Hall mainly in order to look after his business interests which were centred on Barrow-in-Furness. The 4th Duke of Northumberland and his duchess preferred Stanwick to Alnwick, because they could lead a less stately life there. Sometimes they went to their house at Werrington in Devon for a few weeks, but one of their greatest pleasures was to pass a couple of months at Kielder in the remote border reaches of the North Tyne, 'with never more than two friends, the house being so small that the dinner-room is also the sitting room'.[1] Earl Fitzwilliam divided the country part of his year fairly evenly between Milton House and Wentworth Woodhouse because these were residences of equal rank. He did not manage to visit

[1] G. Ticknor, *Life of William Hickling Prescott* (1863), p. 307.

his vast Irish property so regularly, and his house of Coollatin Park in Wicklow was in fact the residence of his agent, with rooms kept for his lordship's occasional use. Those who were in terms of property fundamentally Irish landlords with small English estates, perhaps normally behaved like the Earl of Caledon who resided for most of the year at Tyttenhanger near St Albans, and found it most congenial to visit Caledon House in Tyrone for relaxation in the summer.

Life in the country houses rested on the great structure of domestic servants, but for the owners and their families it revolved round five main activities: the pleasure and interest to be derived from the gardens and park, the pleasure and excitement of country sports, the pleasure and duty of dispensing and receiving hospitality, the duty often but lightly observed of supervising the steward and agents who managed estate and household affairs, and the duty of attending to the local and county affairs of magistracy, yeomanry, churches, charities and schools. These might form only the skeleton of the structure of country life, in the interstices of which an individual might develop his bent for agricultural, philosophical, literary or scientific pursuits, or they might comprise the full armoury of weapons for warding off country boredom. An individual brought up in a spacious and graceful house, conversant with the latest in taste and style even if his own home chanced to remain unredeemed and old-fashioned, imbibed from this life in which he was at first an onlooker and then a participant, a subtle blend of authority and obedience, freedom and restraint, leisureliness and obligation. The master in his own house was subject to the discipline of his own butler, valet and household timetable. Even in the purest pleasures obligation to others was considered in the making up of shooting parties. The owner of thousands of acres and the inevitable authority whose approbation was sought in local causes might himself defer to the judgment of his steward in estate matters, and would certainly consult the wishes, in matters of public concern, of those of his less wealthy neighbours whom he chose to regard as gentlemen. The nobleman who was received with condescension and familiarity by royalty would in turn himself entertain the local gentry as his equals, and in the hunting field might accept without question the leadership of one who was keener though less expensively mounted than himself. What was owing to rank, what to wealth, to age and experience, to good family, to good taste, and to intelligence, all this was taught in the school of the country house. Institutionalized and made a matter of formal instruction in the reformed public schools its teaching reached a wider public but the content narrowed and hardened.

It was an essential characteristic of much of this country life and a source of its strength, that it formed part of the lifeblood of county society in which aristocracy and gentry mingled freely together. Nevertheless certain elements which derived from the superior scale of their establishments served to emphasize aristocratic prominence. The aristocrat was more often giver than receiver. Pineapples were one of the status symbols of the nobility, and the great kitchen gardens besides furnishing the house with fresh supplies and fruits out of season, held in their pine-pits a useful social product. At Burton Hall the pines were listed and numbered for Lord Monson long before maturity so that they could be despatched with all haste to relatives, friends and others whom it was desired to impress. If this custom was a casualty of the cheap imports by refrigerated steamship after the 1880s, the equally carefully regulated distribution of haunches of venison among the elect continued with the deer parks at least until 1914.

This was one of the social functions of the great parks, whose maintenance was part of the imposing fabric of the aristocratic presence, and which were never intended to be economic propositions in themselves whatever secondary economic arguments might be advanced as to their utility in deriving pleasurable service from inferior quality land. Parks did indeed provide some cash returns from casual sales of timber and bark and more regular receipts from pasturing of beasts, while by the 1830s it was becoming respectable to sell venison to the public, which had been abhorrent to eighteenth-century sensibilities. Nevertheless the real returns on the several hundred pounds which were spent on the annual upkeep of a park were not visible in monetary terms. The aesthetic delight of the owner was a most important consideration, especially when he had been instructed by the school of landscapers on the directions in which this was to be sought. The main enjoyment was the family's, who could savour their own piece of countryside in privacy and deploy the elaborately casual carriage picnics of the kind which often wound their way through Hulne Park from Alnwick. A second wider social purpose was fulfilled, however, through the facility which the aristocrat enjoyed of bestowing the favour of visiting his grounds and house upon selected members of the general public. Visiting country houses and parks is by no means a twentieth-century innovation, it has merely become motorized and indiscriminate. Farington in his travels made a habit of visiting famous houses, at which he was a complete stranger. In 1801, for example, he went round Blenheim: 'We were three quarters of an hour in the house, and five companies arrived to see it before we left.' Holkham Hall was open every Tuesday, and at Wentworth Farington apparently joined in the regular public dinner which Lord Fitzwilliam gave to such local notabilities as chose to apply. In the 1840s it was the practice of the Duke of Cleveland to allow the run of Raby Park in approved cases. By the late 1860s, however, at least at Wilton House, the attractions of the house were already being commercialized, and a small item for receipts from visitors on show days made its appearance in the accounts; it was never very large, some £50 in the early years, tailing off to £20 a year or less in the late 1870s when the novelty had worn off.[1]

The aristocracy led also in the scale of their expenditure on game preservation, on hunting where not uncommonly a nobleman might maintain a pack at his own sole charge, and on riding horses generally, while in racing it was hard for any others to compete. At the very start of the nineteenth century, for example, Lord Fitzwilliam was spending between £2,000 and £2,500 every year on his ordinary riding horses, some £500 or more on his kennels, and from £1,500 to £3,000 a year on his racing stables at Wentworth, and these sums were to increase considerably in the course of the century.[2]

In the scale and composition of their house parties no one could rival the entertainment afforded by the aristocracy. Lord Verulam, who with his gross income of around £15,000 in the second and third decades of the century was not one of the wealthy magnates, regularly entertained the royal dukes York

[1] *Farington Diary*, I. 311; III. 125. Raby MSS, Letter Book, 1843–65. Wilton MSS, Estate Accounts, 1869 *et seq.*

[2] Fitzwilliam MSS, General Accounts, 1803–10.

and Gloucester, Princes Leopold and Esterhazy, as well as the political friends of his wife's brother the Prime Minister Liverpool, the Duke of Wellington and his followers the Arbuthnots, the Londonderrys, the Peels and the Robinsons. The penalties of this high society were the *ennui* of playing interminable games of commerce with the Duchess of Gloucester in the evenings and the mortification of witnessing the Duke of York's poor shooting; the rewards were the invitations to Frogmore or Oatlands, where the compliment was returned by the Duke of York playing whist in a way which afforded Verulam no amusement, though at Frogmore he might have 'an excellent party' for the Ascot meeting comprising Grafton, Rutland, Portland, Darlington, Exeter, Foley, Verulam, Alvanley and Bentinck.[1]

It was at Oatlands in the Regency period that the Duchess of York introduced the habit of giving Christmas presents to high society. 'Another custom, likewise of German origin, was annually kept up by the duchess at Oatlands on Christmas Day,' Raikes later recollected. 'The great dining room was converted into a German fair, and booths were erected round the sides, stored with various commodities; in the centre was placed a tree, or *mat de Cocagne*, the branches of which were garnished with oranges, cakes, gingerbread, etc. On one table at the end of the room were displayed all the presents which we the guests had brought from town to lay at the feet of H.R.H.; on the other side were placed those which H.R.H. presented to us as keepsakes. . . . All the servants were admitted in their best attire . . . and also the charity children supported by the bounty of the duchess, who at a given signal flew upon the *mat de Cocagne* and in a few minutes stripped it of its gingerbread blossoms.'[2] In the course of time the custom would percolate down through the layers of society. In the meantime not even the gentry could compete in these preserves of aristocratic society.

Sometimes the country house parties were used for matchmaking, perennial preoccupation of womankind. At Gorhambury Lord Cranborne the Cecil heir came 'per special request' to stay at the same time as the heiress Miss Gascoygne in January 1820; by October, back again at Gorhambury, the

[1] Gorhambury MSS, Lord Verulam's Diary, esp. 21 Jan. 1822, 3 June 1822, 31 Jan., 1823, 10 June 1823.
[2] *Journal of Thomas Raikes*, I. 145–56.

couple were 'making love quite as they ought', and by the next February they were married. Lord Monson commented on his son's stay at Four Oaks in Warwickshire 'I suppose the dash will be continued until the three young ladies are married, after which the necessity for entertaining will not be so great.'[1] This, however, was in September, well after the end of the London season. It was more usual, and generally more productive of results, to play the marriage market during the five or six months of the London season between January and July. Lord Monson, who succeeded to the title in 1841, was always urging his son to find a girl with a fortune to rescue the house of Monson from its predicaments, which were mainly caused by the prolonged burden of two dowagers until 1851 and one survivor until 1891. His son, he hoped, could fend for himself in London, and follow up some of his aunt's helpful suggestions. 'She should like to see you married to a nice girl with a good fortune,' she was reported as saying in 1850, 'and she says Miss Clara Thornhill who is about just coming out promised to be a very nice girl and has nine thousand a year (that would do, eh!) . . . there are two younger daughters of £40,000 each, not bad but the first is the large prize. I should be very sorry for you to marry for money but a nice wife with it would not be bad.' Three days later he added 'I understated it, Miss Thornhill has £15,000 a year.'

Next year he was reproving his son because the aunt had recommended many rich wives to him and he had let one slip through his fingers: 'Lord have mercy on you if she does ferret out a young heiress.' For his own daughters, however, he was resigned to the necessity of a town life which he felt ill able to afford. 'I was . . . anxious to avoid laying out money on our own selves for domestic luxuries and to devote it while we had no daughter in the world where it might benefit the property,' he wrote to his son in 1854. 'You can have no conception of the increase in expense in seeing company. . . . Now only just imagine what would be the increase if we went into the London life – first we must either have a house or what is worse go to an hotel. Then I must have another carriage, horses and coachman. Then people care little for you and will not entertain you unless

[1] Gorhambury MSS, Lord Verulam's Diary, 17 Jan., 5 Oct. 1820. Monson MSS, 25/10/3/2 no: 32.

you entertain them . . . and must be kept up yearly or it has been to no use. I am convinced that this would be £2,000 per an. and I have it not of my income . . . I am perfectly convinced my dear Monson, if you desired it you would not only easily get into London society, but you would be sought for. I thought you avoided it. It is different I own with a girl, but with a man it does not depend at all on having entertaining parents.'[1]

From Lord Sefton in the 1790s through Lord Verulam in the 1820s to Lord Monson in the 1850s and beyond hopes ran high that an eldest son's marriage to a fortune would solve present difficulties and free the family from future anxieties. The only material difference in the later nineteenth century was that eyes might see a solution across the Altlantic. An heiress whose fortune could be reckoned in thousands of income rather than in thousands of capital was of course the mirage which fathers, who had themselves failed to find such a creature, dreamt of their sons discovering. Even on the most cynical calculation she was likely to be an unrepeatable bargain, for her jointure as a potential dowager was unlikely to be fixed at more than 1 per cent on the capital value of her inheritance. Heiresses, though, were scarce, and it was more realistic to value brides in terms of their portions. In the late eighteenth and early nineteenth centuries it seems that a girl who was marrying somewhat above her station, a daughter of a banker or new landed family marrying into the older nobility, or a daughter of the lower aristocracy marrying into the ducal class, would be provided with a marriage portion of the order of £50,000 or £60,000. In an ambitious family resources would be mobilized behind the daughters, the instruments of family advance, while younger sons might be less generously portioned and left to make their own way in the world.

When Alexander Baring's daughter Harriet married Lord Henry Thynne, one of the Marquess of Bath's younger sons, in 1830, the disparity between the families was made plain by the fact that into the marriage pool Lord Henry put £10,000 to match Harriet's £50,000. This formed the entire sum for the portioning of their own children, and moreover Harriet's maximum jointure was fixed at £2,500, that is 5 per cent on her own

---

[1] Monson MSS, 25/10/2/4 nos: 9, 8. 25/10/3/1 no: 16. 25/10/3/4 no: 56.

fortune. In the same way on the marriage of Sir Matthew White
Ridley's eldest son in 1803 to Laura Hawkins of Hampton Court,
that lady's fortune of some £20,000 in the funds was to form
the fund for portioning, and her jointure of £1,000 was also
5 per cent of her own fortune.[1] In marriages between equals in
aristocratic circles portions of £10,000 to £30,000 were
perhaps normal, and the bride would expect a jointure of 10 per
cent at least on her fortune. When the next Sir Matthew White
married in 1841 he was already in possession of his estates. In
return for Cecilia Parke's fortune of £10,000 he proposed to
charge his estates with £300 a year pin money for her, a jointure of £1,000, and a scale of portions to be divided among their
younger children if one, two, three, or four and more, of £4,000,
£10,000, £15,000 and £20,000 respectively. In commenting
on this Cecilia's father Baron Parke remarked that 'the proposed
jointure is what is very common in settlements, being ten per
cent on the lady's fortune, yet [my solicitor] does not think it
enough for the widow of a baronet of considerable property; it
would not enable her to live with a separate establishment, with
decent comfort, in a manner proportioned to what she will have
done. But Lady Parke and I are content to leave this to you to
provide for in your will. Also I am not sure you allow enough
for younger children. I am not an advocate for very considerable
fortunes though, for the boys especially!'[2]

In fact the tariff laid down at the time of marriage, both in
respect of jointure and of portions for younger children whose
numbers were unpredictable, was a minimum which was quite
often augmented by will as circumstances and affection allowed.
There turned out to be ten younger children of the 1803 Ridley
marriage, and they were all stepped up by their father's will to
portions of £10,000 each, save for one son in the church who
was limited to £8,000; they were not actually paid for some
time, not until 1861 in the case of the son who by then was
Major-General Charles William Ridley, though he had received
£2,500 on account to launch his army career. In negotiating
his daughters' marriages Sir Matthew White sought for better

---

[1] Ashburton MSS, Marriage Settlement, 17 April 1830. Blagdon MSS, Marriage
Settlement, 12 Aug. 1803.
[2] Blagdon MSS, Proposed settlement, 1841; Baron Parke to Sir Matthew White
Ridley, 4 Aug. 1841.

terms than his son was willing to accord Cecilia. In 1835 his daughter Laura married the eldest son of Sir Charles Monck of Belsay, and in return for her £10,000 her father insisted that a jointure of £1,500 should be charged on the Belsay estate and one of £800 should Atticus Monck pre-decease his father, which last he still considered inadequate 'considering she takes £500 per annum into the family.'[1] In an alliance between Blagdon and Belsay it is by no means clear that there was a disparity great enough to justify a 15 per cent jointure rate on the bride's fortune. A change in expectations between the generations may have been at work: the old Sir Matthew White died in 1836, and when Laura's sister Sarah married in 1837 it was her brother who had charge of negotiations. Though her alliance with the eldest son of Isaac Cookson of Meldon Park was certainly most respectable, and although the fortunes of the Ridleys and the Cooksons were coevally based on the coal trade, it was nonetheless unmistakable by this date that the Ridleys with their baronetcy and their greater property were the superior family. Nevertheless Sarah's brother was well content that her £10,000 should simply be matched by Isaac putting his son in possession of a share in his business valued at £10,000, and that the jointure should be limited to the interest on the £20,000 fund thus formed.[2]

As well as consideration of that relation between jointure and marriage portion which properly reflected the answer to the question which family was honouring the other in an alliance, the framing of a marriage treaty would normally take into account the absolute size of jointure felt to be appropriate to different stations in life. In 1850 it was felt that £600 a year was a woefully small jointure for a Countess of Guilford, yet this was all Lord Guilford proposed for the match between his eldest son Lord North and Charlotte Eden. In 1847 the Marquess of Ailesbury felt that £2,500 a year was the least which ought to go to his second wife Maria; his own eldest son had in fact settled a jointure of £3,000 a year on Caroline Herbert in 1847, should she chance to become the dowager Marchioness, but this was a normal 10 per cent return on her fortune. Also

[1] Blagdon MSS, Sir Matthew White Ridley to Sir C. M. L. Monck, 10 Dec. 1834; Marriage Settlement, 1 May 1835; Indre. of Release, 9 Dec. 1861.
[2] Blagdon MSS, Proposals for marriage, 10 Jan. 1837.

in 1847 £3,500 was a respectable figure for the contractual jointure of a dowager Duchess of Northumberland, though the actual dowager of this time, widow of the 3rd Duke, received £12,500 a year. For the widow of an untitled magnate, William Vernon-Wentworth of Wentworth Castle, £1,400 a year was sufficient, even though his wife was a Marquess's daughter and brought £15,000 with her. A hundred years earlier £2,500 was the jointure received by the dowager Duchess of Somerset, ancestress of the Northumberlands, and £2,000 that of the Countess of Ailesbury, so that high-ranking dowagers only doubtfully kept pace with the growth of their husbands' incomes.[1]

It was thus a complicated matter to arrive at the going rates of the marriage market and negotiations of some delicacy might be called for, with the family solicitor in reserve to say what was normal in any given case. But while fathers might propose it was generally the sons who disposed. Fathers could and did impose a veto on their children's choice, as when Lord Verulam prevented his eldest daughter Katty, future wife of the 4th Earl of Clarendon, from marrying one of the Coutts Trotters because his father 'came most unwillingly to the post and the alliance is so very moderate.' This was an affair of May in London, when Katty was just 19 and all the world was coming and going at her father's house in Grosvenor Square.[2] Positive parental injunctions, however, were not necessarily obeyed. In spite of proddings neither the Verulam nor Monson heirs did in fact make wealthy matches, but followed their own inclinations. Lord Grimston married Elizabeth Weyland, daughter of a well-established Norfolk and Oxfordshire squire with a fortune of £10,000; William Monson did not marry until seven years after his father's death, waiting until 1869 for the hand of Maria Adelaide, widow of the Earl of Yarborough. Choice, indeed, was made by the sons or possibly by the mothers with marriageable daughters; the arranging in an arranged marriage was largely a matter of fixing terms which fitted an engagement already made. Choice, nevertheless, was understood to be limited to the circle of the acceptable; when a friend married a

---

[1] Monson MSS, 25/10/2/4 no: 31. Savernake MSS, Marriage Settlement, 10 April 1825; Marriage Settlement, 10 May 1837; Will, 23 March 1847. Hoare's Bank MSS, Ledgers U, 1750–2, and A, B, C and G, 1847–77.
[2] Gorhambury MSS, Lord Verulam's Diary, 9–12 May 1829.

farmer's daughter in 1850 the Monsons were horrified at the *mésalliance.*

This circle was gathered together in one place, and the choice was therefore widest and easiest, in the London season, but it would be misleading to accept George Lamb's as a complete account of life in the town houses. This was the world of politics and high society, of attendance at the House and gaming in the clubs, the place where wagers were laid and race meetings arranged, the source of fashion in dress and taste in art, the place where portraits were painted and galleries visited, as well as being the world of drawing rooms and levees, glittering entertainments and extravaganzas, soirées, balls and operas. For those who entered the town life for a few seasons in the hope of disposing of their daughters, and then withdrew again, the unrivalled opportunities for marriage were its great attraction, and the outlay of a few thousands a year was counted as the expense of finding a husband. For those who were permanently committed to the life, however, and returned year after year to open their houses at the start of each session, the round of town life was its own object and justification.

The town houses or palaces of the magnates were objects of great luxury and magnificence, and at least from the second half of the eighteenth century onwards their building, embellishment and furnishing was one of the principal fields for the competition in grandeur and rivalry in conspicuous consumption and investment which was such a powerful stimulus to aristocratic expenditure. By the early nineteenth century it is likely that this arena, in which the contestants' achievements jostled one another physically, had supplanted the scattered country houses as the most fashionable and agreeable location for the contest in wealth, display and extravagant ingenuity. The Lambs spent £100,000 in building, decorating and furnishing Melbourne House, subsequently Albany, in the late 1770s, and it was then the last word in luxury. In 1821 the Londonderrys bought Holdernesse House in Park Lane for £43,000, and by the time this shabby house had been made fit to receive them and the great world in 1825 they had spent another £200,000 in altering and equipping it. Even then it was not universally accepted as being the finest or most resplendent town house of its time; Lord Verulam thought that the Marquess of Stafford's or the

Duke of Northumberland's houses were more imposing and magnificent. When Northumberland House in the Strand was acquired by the Metropolitan Board of Works in 1874 for demolition and street widening, the duke received £497,000 in compensation; only five years earlier a new ballroom had been built, so that improvement was kept up until the end. Other town palaces which were built or much improved in the early years of the nineteenth century, for example Breadalbane House, Cleveland House, Grosvenor House or Hertford House, cannot have come far behind these leaders in the spectrum of splendour.[1]

More modest town establishments than these were of course entirely possible. The Duke of Leed's house in St James's Square, which had cost him about £38,000 to build, was sold in 1803 for £11,500; and Lord Verulam built his house in Grosvenor Square in 1815 for £12,902, while at this time and later an adequate town house in the West End could be rented for a thousand a year.[2] These of course were adequate only for the smaller class of entertaining where dinner parties might reach a couple of dozen and evening receptions approach a few scores, and were no exact substitute for the first flight of houses in which guests and servants might be counted in fifties and the grand receptions in hundreds. The cost of a town life therefore naturally varied widely, but it showed a distinct tendency to rise, during the war period because the prices of provisions, wines, coals, horses, carriages, servants and liveries all increased substantially, and after 1815 because rising standards more than compensated for falling prices. In any case not all luxury goods moved in step with the general price level: a pipe of Madeira, which cost £40 in 1796, went up to £91 in 1803 and £115 in 1813, and was still £100 in 1822, while a pipe of port which could be had for £42 in 1803, soared to £137 in 1819 and in 1826 still cost £78. Lord Verulam's town expenses in the early 1790s were about a thousand a year, while Earl Fitzwilliam's were double this; by the later stages of the war, in the period

[1] Sheila Birkenhead, *Peace in Piccadilly* (1958), p. 9. Edith, Marchioness of Londonderry, *Frances Anne* (1958), pp. 74, 136. H. B. Wheatley and P. Cunningham, *London Past and Present* (1891), II. 603.
[2] *Farington Diary*, II. 80. J. C. Rogers, 'The Manor and Houses of Gorhambury', p. 105.

1810–14, they had risen to £2,000 and £3,000 on an average, and in the 1820s were about £2,500 and £3,500. About half Fitzwilliam's expenditure was on food and wine, and about one-sixth each on servants and on horses and carriages; his Milton household was rather more expensive than Grosvenor Square, his Wentworth one rather less. In the ducal reaches Northumberland had seemingly attained town expenses of £10,000 a year by 1808–10, and under the 3rd Duke who succeeded in 1817 these mounted to £15,000 in the 1820s and £20,000 or more in the 1840s.[1]

Those who launched the great extravaganzas of the season might lay out larger sums. The wife of a West India planter was said to spend five or six thousand pounds a night on the great routs which made her a distinguished figure in London society. The expense of the Marquess of Hertford's great water party in 1823 is not recorded, but it must have been very great; Lord Verulam found the journey up the Thames in a chartered steam boat and the feasting at the Richmond house brilliant and sumptuous beyond description.[2] The normal intercourse of society was less spectacular, but more fruitful in the formation of friendships and contacts and more successful in promoting a species of both political and social mobility. The circles in which London society moved had a tendency to follow political grooves, and the great houses tended to attract party labels, as Holland House for the Whigs and Cecil House for the Tories; but the reigning London hostesses always mixed the political complexions of their parties, and the friendships which bound the habitual sets cut across party divisions, while before the 1830s the London clubs were united by the ties of conviviality not of party interest. It was with a sense of unexpected relief, in his deep anguish at finding Ministers propounding Catholic Emancipation in 1829, that Lord Verulam attended a magnificent dinner at Lady Hertford's where the whole party were anti-Catholic and another where Lord John Manners had carefully gathered an exclusively Protestant party to meet the Duke of Cumberland.

---

[1] Herts C.R.O., Verulam MSS, General Accounts, xi, 74, 81, 92. Fitzwilliam MSS, General Accounts. Hoare's Bank MSS, Ledgers Q, W, Y and Z, 1808–47. The figures do not include the personal expenditure of the owner and his family.

[2] *Farington Diary*, II. 267. Gorhambury MSS, Lord Verulam's Diary, 3 July 1823.

This foreshadowed the disastrous season of 1832, when Raikes had never seen 'so little gaiety, so few dinners, balls and fetes. The political dissensions have undermined society, and produced coolnesses between so many of the highest families, and between even near relations, who have taken opposite views of the question'.[1] Within a year or two this temporary stratification had melted away, leaving the Carlton and Reform Clubs as its deposit.

In London society the aristocracy dined frequently with one another, but they also met as equals men from other walks of life, who were well endowed with wealth, wit, elegance, politics or art, but not with land. Just as in the counties they mingled with the gentry and refreshed their contacts with a wider fox-hunting and farming world, so in town they mingled with and patronized a *beau monde* which propagated new ideas and values, either trivial or profound. It was in London that Brummell was first noticed, that Creevey the Liverpool merchant's son and Raikes the City merchant's son made their entry, and Disraeli made his mark, making the contacts which put them on the invitation lists for the country house parties and the road to social success or political influence and power. It was to London that the artists came, and there that the portrait painters established their reputations, moving from obscurity through patronage to full membership of the élite. Here a Reynolds, Hoppner or Swinton could find fortune as well as fame in the portraiture of the great, and a Stubbs in the portraiture of their animals. It might be very hard work: Lawrence reckoned on painting a half-length picture per week, at 60 guineas a time. The fruits were appreciated by contemporaries, and more often than not highly treasured by posterity. Only a few of the nobility were like the Earl of Egremont, who launched Turner on his career by providing him with a studio at Petworth, and was also a generous friend to Constable, Flaxman, Nollekens and others. But very many commissioned portraits of their wives, children and themselves, for this was a virtually inescapable incident of aristocratic life. Besides patronizing living artists not a few were interested in the old masters, and like Bridgewater or Grosvenor

---

[1] Gorhambury MSS, Lord Verulam's Diary, 29 March, 14 April, 1829. *Journal of Thomas Raikes*, I. 49.

spent fortunes in assembling collections of pictures and arranging their proper display. The interest in art might be shared with the public at large, the private galleries of Grosvenor, Stafford or Northumberland, for example, being open to visitors.

The family portraits, the picture collections, a very few of the town houses, and many of the country houses and parks, are perhaps the surviving monuments of aristocratic life most widely known and appreciated in the mid-twentieth century. But while the social and political order which was enshrined in this life no longer survives, it did in itself through its blend of exclusiveness and catholicity help to give birth to new social forms, which survive as witness to the capacity of the stately aristocratic life to germinate the seeds of change.

V

<hr>

The Landed Gentry
and County Society

<hr>

T H E landed gentry came in a bewildering variety of shapes and
sizes, but contemporaries were confident that they formed a
reasonably homogeneous group, the solid core of the landed
interest, mainstay of the hunting field and backbone of the
resident magistracy which managed the country. To the genealogist and lawyer it was a simple enough matter to define them:
they were the untitled aristocracy, and since for them the nobility
of the land consisted of peers, baronets and landed gentlemen
entitled to hereditary arms, it was easy to presume that all those
with arms were also with land. In the nineteenth century, however, the assumption did not always hold and by the time of his
fifth edition in 1871 Burke was beginning to drop from the
Landed Gentry families which had become separated from their
land though not from their arms. The founders of new families,
it is true, in general took care to furnish themselves with a coat
of arms, and quite often with a pedigree to match, even though
the compiler of a work of reference almost necessarily did not
admit them to the social register quite as rapidly as they rose in
landed wealth and position. Simply to be armigerous was not
enough for old or new; the quantity of landed estate requisite for
acceptance into the landed gentry remained essentially a matter
of social judgment.

If one could define the tests applied for admissions to the commission of the peace, by lords lieutenant and those on whose recommendations they acted, a fairly close approximation might perhaps be obtained to the contemporary notion of what constituted a landed gentleman. This sieve was designed to ensure a bench staffed by men who were resident in the county and of independent means and judgment, which until after the middle of the nineteenth century was taken to exclude those with any close connexions with trade or business. It did, however, allow through a goodly number of clerical magistrates, and even if the country parson was often merely 'a squire who was obliged to wear a black-coat and say his prayers', he was equally often only a landowner *ex officio* in virtue of his life tenancy of tithes and glebe land.[1] On the other hand the statutory requirement of possession of an income of £100 a year from land was far from being sufficient qualification in itself. Thus in 1831 in response to a request from Lord Lonsdale, the lord lieutenant of Cumberland, for information on the chances of supplying the large district round Keswick with a resident magistrate, Humphrey Senhouse stated: 'There is not a single permanent resident either in Keswick or its vicinity whom I think properly qualified for the office of acting magistrate.' This was in spite of the fact that the district abounded in small freeholders with estates of more than £100 a year, for these of course were working farmers.

The suggestions which Senhouse did feel able to make are revealing. 'Of those who spend a considerable portion of the year [at Keswick], I may name Joseph Pocklington of Barrow, James Stanger of Dovecote, and Thomas Spedding of Mirehouse. Mr Pocklington of course in rank and station is a very fit person for the Commission of Peace. Mr Stanger was brought up to business, from which however he has lately retired (a linen draper of Cheapside). Mr Spedding is a lawyer.'[2] Pocklington in fact was the descendant of a sixteenth-century family, owner of the estate and house of Barrow Hall at Crosthwaite in the county, and of the estate and house of North Muskham in Nottinghamshire, and in 1835 was to marry the Senhouse heiress. Stanger had acquired an estate of more than a thousand acres with a rental of as many pounds, and Spedding had about as

---

[1] *Hansard*, 3rd ser., CCXXIII, 13 April 1875, 770-1 (Bishop of Peterborough).
[2] Senhouse MSS, 19/88, H. Senhouse to Lord Lonsdale, 8 Dec. 1831.

much land, yielding slightly less. Retired men of sufficient landed wealth, professional men, and men of old families, these were the preferred categories for J.P.s. Even at the time of its enactment in 1745 the qualification of £100 landed income fell far short of defining the subsistence level of a landed gentleman. It and its companion qualification of entitlement to the reversion of land worth £300 a year were useful means of admitting sons to the bench, and other gentlemen who did not primarily depend on rents for their support, but shared many of the habits of thought and life of the landed gentry. The qualities looked for in a J.P., therefore, were a position of respect in local society and a life of gentlemanly leisure, and since these were most often found in a landed gentleman it was a matter of courtesy to refer to all country magistrates as being members of the landed gentry, as indeed in social terms they all were. In more strict economic terms, however, the landowners who were in a position to live as leisured rentiers did not have a complete monopoly of the bench, and it was such landowners who constituted the properly landed gentry.

As we have seen, Burke in 1861 suggested that a landed income of £500 a year might be enforced as the minimum qualification for a baronet. Yet by this date this was almost certainly not more than half the income required to support a landed gentleman. When Bateman, twenty years later, defined the squires as those with estates between 1,000 and 3,000 acres he may have set the lower limit on the high side, inasmuch as many of these smaller estates were rented at more than a pound an acre, but it was as accurate a definition in terms of acres as could well be devised. Before 1800 rather less than £1,000 a year should have sufficed, though it is perhaps more than a coincidence that out of the dozen or so gentry families whose records have been examined, only one had an income from land in the 1790s which was below £1,000. This one, Alured Pincke of Great Sharsted in Kent, was clearly a gentleman with his port and madeira and hundred-windowed old mansion, and his 600-odd acres producing some £400 a year. He was also in farming seriously as a business, with the speciality of growing vegetable seeds for the London market, and although in 1795 he noted that he had mislaid his accounts for the early 1790s he computed his annual farming profit at £200. Moreover he owned a small

111

property at Newington on the southern fringe of London, and the first building lease on it had been granted in 1788. By 1790 leases for ten houses had been issued, and £44 was received from ground rents; rapid development between 1790 and 1795 was soon to carry these to £500, with further development to follow. Meanwhile the 25 acres of unbuilt pasture land was advantageously let to men in the meat trade for keeping beasts overnight, at £190 a year in all. Thus pieced together Pincke's income in 1790 was £634 as a property owner, and £200 as a farmer, and with this he just managed to maintain the style of a gentleman.[1]

For most of the nineteenth century it would be reasonable to adopt a landed income of £1,000 a year as the lower limit for the gentry, and from previous discussion £10,000 a year formed the upper limit; for purposes of analysis of the structure of landowner-ship these incomes may be very roughly equated with estates of 1,000 to 10,000 acres. Such a range of wealth obviously embraced a variety of types, and these included not only the local village squire as well as the figure of commanding county importance, but also the pure rentier, the man with a secondary occupation alongside that of landowner, and the man whose landownership was quite subsidiary to his main profession. There is no means, apart from the study of every individual case, of distinguishing between those who were straightforward landowners and those who combined ownership of estates with other activities, although something of the extent to which this last occurred in the families with lesser estates will emerge in later discussion. It is useful, nevertheless, to distinguish between the greater and lesser gentry, and Bateman's classification is followed here, even though it is somewhat of an over-simplification to force all of England into the same strait-jacket. The squires are therefore taken to be those with estates of 1,000 to 3,000 acres, or with larger estates whose rentals were less than £3,000 in 1873; and the greater gentry are those with estates of over 3,000 acres yielding more than £3,000 a year, and under 10,000 acres.

In 1873 there were in England about 1,000 members of the greater gentry and about 2,000 squires, which gives a close numerical accord with the 4,000-odd entries in Burke's *Landed*

---

[1] Kent C.R.O., Faunce MSS, U 145 nos. E 29, A 11 and A 12, F 12.

Gentry and *Baronetage* for similar date, embracing the whole United Kingdom. The two groups, however, were not identical in membership, about one-fifth of the qualified landowners not being recognized by Burke, and at least an equal proportion of those listed in Burke not possessing adequate landed estate. The estates of the greater gentry covered about 17 per cent of the area of England, and those of the squirearchy 12½ per cent, so that in aggregate the gentry estates were slightly more extensive than the great estates. This territorial power was, however, comparatively so diffused as well as being unevenly spread over the country that it could not in general rival the aristocracy. In thirteen counties, indeed, which were mainly in the north and west, the great estates occupied a larger area than the gentry and were thus unmistakably predominant. Elsewhere, as we shall see later, both aristocratic and gentry elements might be

TABLE III

THE GENTRY ESTATES

Counties in order of the proportion of total area (excluding waste) occupied by estates of 1,000 to 10,000 acres

Percentage of total area

1.	Shropshire	44	21.	Bedford	30
2.	Hereford	41	22.	Worcester	29
3.	Oxford	40	23.	Devon	29
4.	Hampshire	38	24.	Suffolk	29
5.	Berkshire	37	25.	Warwick	28
6.	Norfolk	37	26.	Cheshire	27
7.	Sussex	36	27.	Rutland	26
8.	Northumberland	35	28.	Northampton	26
9.	Dorset	35	29.	Stafford	26
10.	Kent	34	30.	Cornwall	26
11.	Essex	34	31.	Derby	26
12.	Hertford	34	32.	Lancashire	26
13.	Surrey	34	33.	Nottingham	24
14.	Gloucester	33	34.	Durham	24
15.	Huntingdon	32	35.	Lincoln	23
16.	Buckingham	32	36.	Cambridge	23
17.	Leicester	30	37.	Cumberland	22
18.	Somerset	30	38.	Westmorland	20
19.	Wiltshire	30	39.	Middlesex	17
20.	Yorkshire	30			

Average for all England: 29·5 per cent

weak, yielding predominance to smaller landowners. But also where the aristocratic element was weak the gentry might be exceptionally strong, and in another thirteen counties they in fact owned more than twice as much as the aristocracy, and these may be considered the most gentrified parts of England.

The areas occupied by the gentry ranged from 44 per cent of Shropshire down to 17 per cent of Middlesex and 20 per cent of Westmorland, as shown in Table III. In the main the thirteen counties in which the gentry were most likely to outweigh the aristocracy lay in eastern England, but they included Shropshire and Herefordshire, which were the most gentrified of all, as well as Gloucestershire and Oxfordshire; and in two of this thirteen, Cambridgeshire and Middlesex, neither gentry nor aristocracy were dominant, both being heavily outweighed by lesser free-

TABLE IV

THE ESTATES OF THE GREATER GENTRY

Counties in order of the proportion of total area (excluding waste)
occupied by estates of 3,000 to 10,000 acres
Percentage of total area
(The ranking of each county in Table V is noted in brackets)

1.	Shropshire	31	(14)	21.	Yorkshire	18	(21)
2.	Huntingdon	27	(39)	22.	Northampton	17	(34)
3.	Hereford	25	(5)	23.	Devon	17	(16)
4.	Oxford	25	(10)	24.	Hertford	17	(3)
5.	Hampshire	24	(11)	25.	Nottingham	17	(37)
6.	Berkshire	22	(6)	26.	Stafford	17	(35)
7.	Norfolk	22	(7)	27.	Suffolk	17	(18)
8.	Buckingham	21	(24)	28.	Cheshire	16	(26)
9.	Gloucester	21	(17)	29.	Cornwall	16	(28)
10.	Kent	21	(15)	30.	Derby	16	(29)
11.	Northumberland	21	(13)	31.	Surrey	16	(1)
12.	Worcester	20	(33)	32.	Bedford	15	(8)
13.	Essex	19	(9)	33.	Durham	13	(27)
14.	Sussex	19	(4)	34.	Lincoln	13	(30)
15.	Leicester	18	(19)	35.	Cambridge	12	(25)
16.	Warwick	18	(16)	36.	Lancashire	12	(12)
17.	Dorest	18	(2)	37.	Middlesex	11	(38)
18.	Rutland	18	(36)	38.	Westmorland	11	(32)
19.	Somerset	18	(23)	39.	Cumberland	10	(22)
20.	Wiltshire	18	(20)				

Average for all England: 17 per cent

holders, products of the fens in the one case and the great wen in the other. There were some striking differences between the distribution of the estates of the greater gentry and those of the squires, which are given in Tables IV and V. Huntingdonshire, for instance, came second in the country for the greater gentry, and had virtually no squirearchy at all, while in Shropshire it was the greater gentry who predominated although neighbouring Herefordshire had a reasonable supply of both types. Cumberland on the other hand had very few of the greater gentry, but an average supply of squires, a projection into the upper reaches of landed society of its traditional 'statesman' class of smaller landowners. In Surrey and Lancashire also the squires outweighed the greater gentry, and the two groups owned equal

TABLE V

THE ESTATES OF THE SQUIREARCHY

Counties in order of the proportion of total area (excluding waste) occupied by estates of 1,000 to 3,000 acres

Percentage of total area

1. Surrey	18	21. Yorkshire	12
2. Dorset	17	22. Cumberland	12
3. Hertford	17	23. Somerset	12
4. Sussex	17	24. Buckingham	11
5. Hereford	16	25. Cambridge	11
6. Berkshire	15	26. Cheshire	11
7. Norfolk	15	27. Durham	11
8. Bedford	15	28. Cornwall	10
9. Essex	15	29. Derby	10
10. Oxford	15	30. Lincoln	10
11. Hampshire	14	31. Warwick	10
12. Lancashire	14	32. Westmorland	9
13. Northumberland	14	33. Worcester	9
14. Shropshire	13	34. Northampton	9
15. Kent	13	35. Stafford	9
16. Devon	12	36. Rutland	8
17. Gloucester	12	37. Nottingham	7
18. Suffolk	12	38. Middlesex	6
19. Leicester	12	39. Huntingdon	5
20. Wiltshire	12		

Average for all England: 12·4 per cent

Source: J. Bateman. *The Great Landowners of Great Britain and Ireland* (1883 ed.)

areas in Bedfordshire and Hertfordshire, in which perhaps one can detect the influence of commercial and industrial wealth seeking squire status. This influence was not, however, decisive, since Buckinghamshire appears alongside Shropshire, Worcestershire, Rutland, Nottinghamshire and Huntingdonshire in the group of counties in which greater gentry estates were more than twice as extensive as those of the squires.

Below the squires Bateman recognized three categories of landowners: the small proprietors with estates of more than 1 acre and under 100 acres; the lesser yeomen with between 100 and 300 acres; and the greater yeomen with between 300 and 1,000 acres. Their distribution is given in Table VI. Together these three groups owned some 39 per cent of the area of England, but only a minority within them were yeomen in the farming sense, since at this date only just over 10 per cent of the land was farmed by owner-occupiers.[1] The majority then were small landlords holding land as an investment – yielding a sense of social status or security rather than a remunerative income – either actively made out of savings, or passively retained out of a mixture of calculation and inertia from the time when a family had moved from a smallholding into the world of towns and business. In the upper reaches of Bateman's 'greater yeomen' group there were undoubtedly many who were close to the squires in status, with estates of not much under 1,000 acres which might comprise three or four tenanted farms and a country residence. Such owners, if endowed with other sources of income besides their farms, could well lead the lives of country gentlemen. It would be surprising if their ranks did not contain a goodly array of men with commercial and manufacturing origins, who had purchased small landed properties while retaining much of their assets in other forms. The land-purchasing activities of such men may, indeed, have been the prime factor in the disappearance of the older race of small landowners.[2]

In ten counties the estates of aristocracy and gentry occupied less than half the area, but if the land owned by institutions – crown, church and colleges chiefly – is subtracted, then Somerset and Gloucestershire, as well as Essex, Kent and Surrey, dis-

[1] Sir John Clapham, *An Economic History of Modern Britain* (Cambridge, 1952 ed.), II. 260–1.
[2] See also below p. 233.

appear from this list. These three home counties had a very similar pattern of landownership. In all three the two 'yeomen' groups were well above average and the 'small proprietors' well below, indicating perhaps that the more wealthy retired business men had a good start over their brethren in heading out into the country; in all three also the gentry estates were well above average, the greater gentry favouring Kent and Essex more than Surrey. 'There are very few yeomen now in Essex, as

TABLE VI

THE ESTATES OF THE SMALLER LANDOWNERS

Proportion of the total area (excluding waste) of each county
occupied by three categories of smaller estates

Column 1. Estates of 300 to 1,000 acres
Column 2. Estates of 100 to 300 acres
Column 3. Estates of 1 to 100 acres
Percentage of total area

	1.	2.	3.		1.	2.	3.
Bedford	13	11	14	Lincoln	15	12	14
Berkshire	18	9	10	Middlesex	15	19	24
Buckingham	14	13	8	Norfolk	13	11	12
Cambridge	19	16	16	Northampton	13	12	11
Cheshire	10	9	13	Northumberland	7	4	3
Cornwall	15	16	14	Nottingham	10	9	12
Cumberland	16	22	16	Oxford	14	12	10
Derby	11	10	15	Rutland	5	5	7
Devon	16	17	13	Shropshire	14	9	7
Dorset	11	7	7	Somerset	14	15	18
Durham	13	11	11	Stafford	10	10	16
Essex	20	17	10	Suffolk	16	14	11
Gloucester	17	14	13	Surrey	22	13	12
Hereford	17	15	10	Sussex	16	10	9
Hampshire	16	8	9	Warwick	13	15	11
Hertford	17	10	8	Westmorland	16	18	16
Huntingdon	14	13	12	Wiltshire	12	7	6
Kent	18	13	12	Worcester	14	18	15
Lancashire	13	12	18	Yorkshire	12	11	10
Leicester	16	16	13				

England   14   12·5   12

Source: J. Bateman, *The Great Landowners of Great Britain and Ireland* (1883 ed.)

compared with what they were formerly', it was stated in 1846.[1] The observer was thinking of the owner-farmers and their decline, for there were still 6,816 owners in 1873 in Bateman's groups of 'yeomen' and 'small proprietors', owning 47 per cent of the area of the county. In Middlesex, as might be expected, the two 'yeomen' groups were equally strong, but the outstanding feature was the group of 'small proprietors', the strongest in the country, owning nearly a quarter of the area of the county. Of the remaining four counties, Cumberland and Westmorland formed a region in which the more genuinely agricultural yeomen groups were strong, although in Westmorland their independence of the higher orders was limited by the presence of an above average quota of great estates; Cambridgeshire was marked by its large contingent of greater yeomen, the independent fenmen, and Worcestershire by the size of its body of lesser yeomen, the plum-growers perhaps.

Political observers had always been interested in the balance between gentry and aristocratic forces in order to assess electoral influence in the counties, and it is apparent from their remarks that the map of gentry England was in its essentials of long standing. At the same time it should be remembered that this sort of assessment was affected by the sheer size of constituencies as well as by the balance of forces, so that for example the reputation of Yorkshire or Devon for electoral independence based on numerous gentry and freeholders was a product of size more than of abnormalities in estate distribution. The relatively numerous gentry of Berkshire, Norfolk and Worcestershire, for example, were noted by Joshua Wilson in 1808 when discussing the state of the counties, as was the scarcity of resident gentry in Cambridgeshire. In terms of power, however, this latter circumstance did not open the way for domination by the peasantry, but since they were unorganized and largely indifferent to politics it rather left the field clear for two magnates, the Duke of Rutland and the Earl of Hardwicke, to share the county representation. In remarking of Oxfordshire also that the gentry were not numerous Wilson appears, however, to have been attempting an explanation for the absence of county contests, which in fact was sufficiently explained by the ruinous

[1] *Parliamentary Papers*, 1846, VI, pt. i, Q. 512.

expense of the mid-eighteenth-century contests and the ensuing reluctance to repeat that experience. In 1873 Oxfordshire was the third most gentrified of all English counties, well furnished with both greater gentry and squires, and it does not seem that this was wholly a nineteenth-century development. Out of the 100 possibly gentry families with landed incomes of over £1,000 in 1873, the origins of sixty can be identified; sixteen of these appear to have been new families of the nineteenth century, and this includes four who were only technically new, since they had become established in Oxfordshire by marriage to heiresses. It is of course possible that the forty unidentifiable families, which never reached the social register, were all nineteenth-century newcomers, but even so it would be unwise to assume that none of them had replaced older gentry families.

Although the Oxfordshire example indicates that there were no revolutionary upheavals in gentry circles in the three quarters of a century before 1873, it also illustrates the ever-continuing process of the rise of the new gentry. Matthew Piers Watt Boulton of Haseley Court and Tew Park, although not yet recognized by Burke as being in the landed gentry, represented in his name and his 8,000 acres some of the profits and position derived from the engineering works. Albert Brassey of Heythrop House, Chipping Norton, also not yet included in the social register, had transformed part of the fruits of the great railway contracting enterprise into a substantial landed position. Another successful civil engineer, Edward Mackenzie, had purchased his Fawley Court estate at Henley in 1853, and also acquired vast sporting estates in Norfolk and Suffolk, as well as in Dumfries and Kirkcudbright; while George Glen, a Liverpool merchant, was more modest in his purchase in 1858 of the 1,647-acre estate of Stratton Audley Park. Thomas Taylor of Aston Rowant was an industrialist from Wigan, and Isabella Crawshay of Caversham Park was the widow of William Crawshay the great ironmaster of Cyfarthfa. It is noticeable that when industrial fortunes were invested in social position the new families were generally entering the gentry or squire groups. This was inevitable, since to break into the circle of magnates and great estates required the much larger resources and profits of the world of finance, but it was nonetheless important in making the gentry the principal vehicle for this form of social mobility.

The first Sir Robert Peel alone of the early industrial magnates entered the landed aristocracy though Richard Arkwright could have done so if he had so chosen. Instead of concentrating his resources, however, he founded a clan of landed families, and four of his five surviving grandsons emerged in the early nineteenth century as Arkwright of Sutton Scarsdale in Derby, Arkwright of Willersley also in Derby, Arkwright of Mark Hall in Essex and Normanton Turville in Leicester, and Arkwright of Hampton Court in Hereford; the crests of all these families bore a hank of cotton, argent. The banking sons of Abel Smith of Nottingham were if anything even more successful in the planting of landed families. Robert Smith, Pitt's financial adviser, became Lord Carrington; his brother Samuel purchased Woodhall Park in Hertfordshire in 1801 and established a redoubtable county dynasty of Abel Smiths; and another brother George purchased the Selsdon Park estate in Surrey. Within a few years each of these two last had again multiplied, the first producing the Smiths of Sacombe Park, also in Hertfordshire, and the second the Smiths of Ferriby in the East Riding. A similar disinclination to follow the rules of primogeniture was shown by John Marshall, the great flax-spinner of Leeds, who purchased land extensively in Cumberland and Lancashire in the early nineteenth century, and to a lesser extent in the North Riding, and set up four of his sons as squires, of Patterdale Hall, Monk Coniston Park, Cookridge Hall, and Weetwood Hall, each with more than £1,000 a year from land.

Any widespread projection of such peasant or middle-class habits of equal partibility into the world of the landed gentry would in itself have produced a great acceleration in the rate of growth of the gentry classes in the nineteenth century. There is not, however, any convincing evidence of such a development though the same practice of producing two landed sons can be seen in the cases of Samuel Walker of Rotherham and Joshua Fielden of Todmorden, notable figures in the early iron and cotton industries respectively. It is in any case difficult to establish that there was any acceleration in the rise of the gentry. On the one hand it is clear that industrialization generated a growing number of large personal fortunes, a proportion of which were always seeking outlets in landed positions, and it is perhaps mainly to this form of demand that the very high land prices of the land market boom of the late 1860s and early 1870s in particular should be attributed.[1] On the other hand, at least from the end of the 1820s, the movement of rents and taxation in relation to the gentry's living costs was such that the conditions of survival for established gentry became easier, so that in general terms the new rich would find fewer ready-made estates on the market than had been usual in the eighteenth century, and would thus be forced back on the more laborious and increasingly difficult task of gentrifying themselves at the expense of an ever-contracting supply of smaller properties.

It has long been recognized that the rise of new gentry is a permanent feature of the English social scene, the rise probably being more rapid in some centuries than in others. The corresponding perennial feature of the fall of old gentry has not obtained such general recognition, except for the early eighteenth century when it apparently operated in favour of the aristocracy.[2] It seems possible, however, that during much of the eighteenth century when an old landed family was obliged to part with its estate it was replaced by a new gentry family rather than being swallowed up by a neighbouring great estate. For a large number of new families were founded during the eighteenth century, some by marriage but most by purchase, and this formation certainly did not take place exclusively at the expense of the peasantry, if only because the new gentry so frequently attained their object of possessing a manor house, not a normal emblem of peasant status. 'It is impossible to be at ease and quiet in the country without manorial property', Sir Christopher Sykes wrote in 1792 to a Londoner who wished to purchase property in the East Riding with a view to 'future retirement with ease and the command of country amusements.'[3] In the nineteenth century, it is suggested, the rate of formation of new gentry families may have slackened, but since the rate of wastage of old families also slowed down the total size of the gentry and squire groups may have grown faster than formerly, at the expense of the smaller properties.

It certainly became much more expensive to enter the gentry

[1] F. M. L. Thompson, 'The Land Market in the Nineteenth Century', p. 294.
[2] H. J. Habakkuk, 'English Landownership, 1680–1740', *Econ. Hist. Rev.*, X (1940).
[3] Sledmere MSS, C. Sykes to E. Topsham, 1 March 1792.

group, for with rents per acre settling down at about double the pre-1790 figure by the end of the 1820s and the number of years purchase tending to climb above thirty, the capital cost of a typical 1,000 acre estate might have grown from some £12,000 to over £30,000. In the 1860s a further rise in years purchase carried the cost of a landed income of £1,000 to £40,000 or more.[1] The costs of acquiring a given income from land or from Consols had remained roughly in step from 1790 to the 1840s, apart from the period of the French Wars and the special influence of war finance in depressing the price of Consols. In the 1850s and 1860s, however, the cost of a landed income clearly outpaced the cost of a funded income. This increasing relative expense of land, due to the high pressure of demand and the somewhat inelastic supply of land for sale, was obviously matched by a growth in the size of some of the individual mercantile fortunes seeking outlets in land purchase, since it was this type of demand probably more than that from established landowners which pushed land prices up.

Nevertheless the rising price of land might well induce some of the mercantile and industrial wealth to lower its sights and aim at the lesser properties of 'yeoman' size, which in itself would produce a change of social habits, since instead of endowing a family with a self-supporting estate this process would produce a comfortable country house and pleasure grounds suitable for retirement, or at most an estate of a few hundred acres whose rents might supplement the income of some more leisured occupation than that of the founder. On financial grounds as well as on grounds of availability of property in the market, it was in any case simpler to become a squire than a member of the greater gentry group. In Essex, very much within the orbit of new wealth, changes in ownership in the generation between tithe commutation and the New Domesday Survey illustrate this process. At the time of the New Domesday Survey 38 per cent of the owners of 'lesser yeoman' sized estates were newcomers since the 1840s, 23 per cent of the 'greater yeomen', 15 per cent of the squires and 10 per cent of the greater gentry. The differing degrees of fluidity in the landed structure of Essex are also

[1] F. M. L. Thompson, 'The Economic and Social Background of the English Landed Interest, 1840–70' (unpublished D. Phil. thesis, Oxford University, 1956), pp. 297–316.

illustrated by the fact that over three-quarters of those who had owned estates of over 1,000 acres in the 1840s were still present in 1873, though not necessarily with the same sized properties, while only 60 per cent of owners in the two 'yeoman' groups still survived as owners of some landed property. These 'yeomen' who came and went, people like Sir F. Agar, Sir T. G. Apreece, Major Shitty, or the Rev. W. Y. Smythies, we may be sure were in the main rentiers and not farmers.[1]

The increasing expense and frustration meeting those aspiring to become landed gentry may well have found vent in the attacks on landed society and the land laws which are discussed in Chapter X. At the same time, though, it is important to remember that all that is in question is a slowing down of a previously higher growth rate of new gentry, not a halt in the process. Moreover it is entirely possible that an increasing number of new men from industry and trade succeeded in acquiring some land, though their acquisitions were below the 1,000 acre limit and generally beneath the notice of Burke. Burke, in commenting in 1861 on the long-standing tendency of merchants' or manufacturers' gold to displace the ancient proprietary, remarked that 'its action is most generally felt within a limited circle round the metropolis or the great city wherein its accumulation has been made. The aim of the prosperous trader is to fix himself on some estate in his own immediate neighbourhood.' Hence he concluded, few old families were to be found in Middlesex, Surrey or Essex, and many in Northumberland, Cheshire, Devon, Cornwall and Shropshire.[2] The reasoning was sound up to a point, but it was probably already a little out of date in the eighteenth century, since it applied essentially to the time when merchants sought land as the only secure lodgment for their savings, meaning to carry on with their businesses, and not to the time when they sought land with a view primarily to social elevation and withdrawal from business. In the nineteenth century at any rate the greater ease of travel meant that it was

---

[1] The Essex figures are based on analysis of the 397 Tithe Awards in the Tithe Redemption Commission, Finsbury Square, which cover 97·5 per cent of the area of Essex. They are of various dates subsequent to the Tithe Commutation Act of 1836; the last award in Essex was not made until 1853, but the great majority were completed by 1844.

[2] J. B. Burke, *The Vicissitudes of Families*, (1st ser. 1861), p. 4.

simple to seek out a landed foothold in any attractive area, and there were in any case few regions which remained remote from centres of commercial or industrial wealth. Northumberland, for example, was notable long before Burke's day for landed families founded out of the coal trade, and in the nineteenth century the profits of the pits raised the Joiceys of Newton Hall, the Strakers of Benwell House, and the Taylors of Chipchase Castle, to name some of the more eminent who sprang from the ranks of colliery lessees and colliery viewers.

In nineteenth-century Shropshire, it is perfectly true, there was a strikingly high proportion of ancient gentry families whose lineages ran unbroken from Norman or Plantagenet times, but they probably owed their survival largely to the fact that they had been sufficiently remote to escape the full force of the sixteenth- and seventeenth-century upheavals in landowner-ship. In Shropshire in 1873 there were 160 gentry and squires with landed incomes of more than £1,000, and the origins of 106 of these can be identified; of these one-sixth were families founded in the nineteenth century and nearly a quarter were founded in the eighteenth century, the remaining three-fifths being of older ancestry. Among the newcomers were such direct representatives of Coalbrookdale's part in creating the iron industry of the county as Rebecca Darby of Stanley House and John Pritchard of Broseley, who married Ann Cranage, daughter of one of the inventors of the puddling process. Nineteenth-century infiltration into the landed society of Shropshire was therefore on a significant scale, but was somewhat less than had occurred in the previous century. This was true also of Oxford-shire, where as we have seen about a quarter of the gentry of 1873 had originated in the nineteenth century, but a third were of eighteenth-century date. In Essex as well a quarter of the 102 identifiable families were of nineteenth-century origins, but nearly half had made their appearance in the eighteenth century. The differences between the three counties in this respect are a fair indication of their different degrees of accessibility to new wealth, but the uniformly higher proportion of eighteenth-century foundations which ultimately made their mark on Burke's social register is striking.

There are several indications that in the nineteenth century the rise of new gentry was roughly balanced by the fall of older gentry. In a 10 per cent sample of the entries in Burke's *Landed Gentry* about a quarter of the families entered in 1846 had disappeared by the time of the 1871 edition, and also about a quarter of the entries of 1871 related to new families which were both newcomers to the social register and had acquired their country seats since 1790. In terms of numbers this was not an exact balance of rise and decline, since the total number who were accorded the rank of landed gentry by Burke expanded as the work became more accurate and more complete in successive editions. The sample in fact shows the disappearance of 108 families and the arrival of 121 new men. In Essex a complete count can be made of those who owned estates of more than 1,000 acres at the time of tithe commutation and at the time of the New Domesday Book. This shows that there were 29 owners in the greater gentry group at both dates, and in the group of squires 111 in the 1840s and 115 in 1873. This appearance of stability was, however, something of a façade. Among the greater gentry 4 of the families represented in the 1840s owned no land at all in Essex by 1873, and 3 of the families of 1873 had not been Essex landowners in the 1840s; among the squires the comparable figures were 21 and 16.[1]

This ebb and flow within the gentry set up a complicated pattern of movement which defies the simplicity of any explanation which seeks to relate the antiquity of a family to a likelihood of decay. Thus among the 108 decayed families from Burke there were 38 which dated from before 1700, 25 which had been founded in the eighteenth century, and no less than 45 which, in 1846, had been represented by the initial or second generation of owners. The fallen therefore included a high proportion of birds of passage, as well as a substantial number of ancient families which at last, for demographic or financial reasons, stumbled into extinction. It would be surprising if there were any great economic or social forces which were responsible for such a result. Some families, no doubt, disappeared through failure of heirs, or through improvidence and debt, and these

[1] In determining the number of families which disappeared from the *Landed Gentry* those which were promoted into the baronetage or peerage have not been included. In 1871 Burke deliberately omitted some extant gentlemanly families whose connections with landed estates had been severed. It is impossible to determine how many of these had already lost their estates before the 1846 edition.

might afflict old and new alike. Among the new men some may not have aspired to found families in the accepted sense, but instead may have sought to provide each of several sons with an equal landed inheritance; that such men had sought the paraphernalia of acceptability, family arms and crests, does mean, however, that they had some dynastic intent, and did not contemplate a merely fleeting flirtation with the possession of landed estate. There was a state of flux in the gentry body. It is more likely to have been the product of a number of individual family circumstances and necessities than of any impersonal factors such as taxation burdens or uncertainty over the economic viability of gentry properties as agricultural estates, though the whole of the nineteenth century, like most other centuries, was punctuated by complaints of the unfair and disproportionate burden of taxes on land.

The state of near balance between the rising and falling gentry might give rise to the supposition that the gentry estates were the medium for a giant game of general post, that the coming and going of gentry families passed, if not unnoticed by the rest of the community, at least without producing more than a ripple on the surface of the property structure of a county. Quite often, of course, this was indeed the case, for a new man sought a ready-made estate, and nothing could be more convenient than to be able to step neatly into the shoes of some departing or departed squire. But the Essex example suggests also that some of the new gentry spread their rise over a number of years, and that some of the falling gentry dwindled gradually away. One of the greater gentry and nearly one-third of the squires of the 1870s had owned substantially less land in the 1840s. Arthur Pryor of Hylands, for example, increasing his estate from 840 to 3,255 acres in that interval. On the other hand one of the greater gentry and nearly one-quarter of the squires of the 1840s were still present as landowners thirty years later only with much diminished estates, Lady Olivia Sparrow's 3,321 acres having shrunk to 13, for example, and Baril Danbuz's 1,624 acres being reduced to 361. The future squires of 1873 in fact numbered 25 'greater yeomen', 6 'lesser yeomen' and 3 'small proprietors' in the 1840s; while the 'lesser yeomen' of 1873, for example, included 5 or 6 who had been substantial squires thirty years earlier.

There was thus an expansion and contraction of estates always under way, which cannot have failed to produce its effects on other landowning groups. Thus we may imagine that a declining family might part with its property farm by farm, and in this way add to the ranks of small landowners; while a new man might start his rise with the acquisition of a single farm or existing gentleman's seat, and continue his ascent either piecemeal by further absorption of small properties, or in a single leap by acquisition of an estate. In this manner, while the smaller landowners were undoubtedly continually disappearing in certain parishes, across the boundary in another parish new ones might be almost as continually emerging, though it must be emphasized that this traffic in smaller properties in the main did not concern owner-farmers but small rentiers. The end result of this complex activity in Essex, in terms of the balance of property expressed in estate-sizes, seems to have been a small increase from 40 to 43 per cent in the proportion of the county occupied by estates of over 1,000 acres, an increase which masked a small decline in the area owned by both squires and nobility and a larger rise in the area owned by the greater gentry. Apart from these internal movements, the slight shift in favour of the upper sections of the landed interest appears to have taken place equally at the expense of the small proprietors and the greater yeomen. The number of separate owners in the greater yeomen range of properties, however, seems to have remained static, while the number in the lesser yeomen range increased, so that the average size of a property in these two groups diminished.

Entry into the social circle of the landed gentry, the prime object of the new men who laid out their savings in land purchase, was achieved with ease provided that the newcomer adopted the conventions of gentry behaviour in his style of living and pursuit of country interests. In Essex, which was experienced in the absorption of new blood, five out of the sixteen who entered the squirearchy after the 1840s were already recognized as being county families by 1860 by one authority, although they were not accepted by Burke.[1] James St George Burke, who had purchased the estate of Auberies in 1857, was too recent for recognition by this social arbiter, and his cousin Sir John Bernard Burke had not

[1] E. Walford, *The County Families of the U.K.: The Titled and Untitled Aristocracy, A Dictionary of the Upper Ten Thousand* (1860), p. 820. This social directory

included him in his own compilation by 1871; nevertheless his
sons went in the usual way to Eton, Harrow, Christ Church, or
Trinity College, entered the army, and became J.P.s, marking
their position as sons of a landed gentleman. The only unconventional feature, perhaps, was that the seventh son finished his education by proceeding from Cheltenham College to the École des
Beaux Arts in Paris, and in due course became Vice-President of
the Royal Society of British Artists. To serve in the magistracy,
and to form marriage alliances with established county families,
these were the twin symbols of the merger of a new family into
the general life of county society. Most frequently, perhaps, these
were accomplished simultaneously, after the lapse of a generation, in the persons of the sons of the founders, but it was not
uncommon for the first owner himself to go on to the bench. In
Essex, where Arthur Pryor the first owner of Hylands became
a J.P., this rapid acceptance is not surprising. In Northumberland, renowned for its social conservatism, it is some indication
of the increased pace of life in the nineteenth century that Joseph
Straker, the first owner of Benwell Old House, became a J.P.,
and that John Joicey, who purchased Newton Hall, Stocksfield,
in 1860, not only became a J.P. but served as sheriff of the county
in 1878.

Shropshire, with its great weight of family pride in medieval
lineages, might perhaps have been expected to take but slowly
to newcomers, but the treatment of the Barkers of Albrighton
Hall shows that it was in fact normally receptive. John Barker,
the founder, from Horton in Cheshire, was a large-scale ironmaster in Staffordshire, Shropshire and South Wales in the early
nineteenth century. He purchased Albrighton Hall in the 1830's,
and himself served as sheriff of Staffordshire in 1851. Out of his
thirteen children two sons became Deputy Lieutenants and
J.P.s in Staffordshire, one became a Shropshire J.P., one became
rector of Henstead in Suffolk, one served in the army, and one
crowned an army career by becoming Chief Constable of Birkenhead. In Oxfordshire also, with the Boultons of Tew Park, it
was the son of the purchaser and grandson of the first Matthew
Boulton of the Soho Works, who became a Deputy Lieutenant

---

includes a substantial minority who were honorary landed gentry in virtue of
being younger sons of the nobility, clergymen, or gentlemen of independent non-
landed means, but not in virtue of possession of sizeable landed incomes.

and J.P., served as sheriff in 1848, and married a daughter of the old Northamptonshire family of Cartwright of Aynhoe. But the family of John Marshall of Leeds probably showed the most comprehensive array of the signs of social conquest. The great flax-spinner himself served as M.P. for Yorkshire from 1826 to 1830. Of his five sons, three in their turn were M.P.s, two served as Deputy Lieutenants and J.P.s in Cumberland and one in Yorkshire, the last being sheriff in 1860. One son married into an old Hertfordshire family, another into a still older Cumberland family, and two married daughters of the first Lord Monteagle; of his six daughters, two married clergymen, one married the Master of Trinity College, Cambridge, one married the second son of Sir Grenville Temple, 9th baronet, and one became the second wife of the first Lord Monteagle. In such manner was a new family firmly tied into the fabric of established society.

It usually took two generations also, or the passage of about half a century, for a new family to withdraw from the scenes of its commercial success and settle entirely in the life of country gentlemen. Clogs to clogs in three generations was matched as a piece of folk-lore by the saying that the third generation makes the gentleman. Irrespective of the origins of a fortune there was a regular pattern of development, in which the sons of the founders continued to take some part, probably increasingly intermittent, in the original business, and the grandsons severed themselves from it altogether. It happened in commerce, where in the second generation of the Sykes of Sledmere Sir Christopher built the great mansion, became a famous agricultural improver, and gradually liquidated his banking and trading concerns, and in the third generation Sir Mark Masterman Sykes was a hunting and racing man almost as dedicated as his brother the incorrigibly countrified and horse-worshipping Sir Tatton. In engineering the Boultons went through this cycle, in linen the Marshalls, and in cotton the descendants of Jedediah Strutt.

In brewing the same process can be observed, though with the Bests of Boxley, Kent, it was somewhat more drawn out. In the third generation of this family of Chatham brewers to live in the country seat of Park House, Boxley, the eldest son, Thomas, did inherit the landed estate divorced from the business. Moreover the second son, James, was thinking seriously of selling out the whole brewery in 1809 to the current manager of the concern, as the only solution to the financial tangle and threatened disaster into which partnership with his profligate nephew Richard Best was steering the family. In the event, however, James bought out his nephew's share in the brewery and continued as sole owner of the concern. Nevertheless it is plain that both James and Richard had the tastes and inclinations of gentlemen of leisure, though Richard woefully lacked the sense of financial discretion present in his equally high-living uncle. Though remaining the owner, James did not concern himself greatly with the control of the brewery, and dying without issue in 1828 ownership reverted to the senior branch of the family in the person of his nephew James. In the old age of this second James negotiations were on foot for converting the existing arrangements into a formal lease of the business to the manager at a fixed annual rent, and these were completed soon after his death in the 1851 lease of the Chatham brewery to Messrs Winch at £5,500 a year. It was largely the neglect bred of family indifference which had run down the value of the brewery property from £120,000 in 1809 to a supposed £50,000 in 1851, mainly because by then 'the public and beer houses are for the most part of the worst description, two-thirds of them old and ill-adapted to business of publicans as now carried on, the greater part of the tenants of a very low class, so that there is constant disorderly conduct in the houses.' Still it was not for another forty years that James's son Mawdistly Gaussen Best in 1894 finally sold the brewery and its eighty public houses outright to Messrs Winch, for £150,000.[1]

In this instance the complete withdrawal from business took nearly a century to accomplish from inception of the idea to final execution. Nevertheless for nearly all this time the Bests were very much sleeping partners or simple lessors, and the principal distinction between them and other country gentlemen was that they enjoyed considerable income from investments outside their landed estate. In this, however, a significant minority of the older gentry kept them company. There was Pincke, later

---

[1] Kent C.R.O., Best MSS, U 480 nos. C 20, Woodgate to James Best, 7 Feb. 1809; C. 21, Dendy to James Best 15 Dec. 1848, Rickards to Mrs James Best, 25 March 1851, and 10 April 1851; B 536, Agreement for sale of Chatham Brewery 5 Dec. 1894.

Faunce, of Sharsted, with the income from Newington and Kennington ground rents grown to £1,300 by 1840; there was Sir Thomas Maryon Wilson with his estates in Essex and Sussex and his infinitely greater ground rents from Hampstead and Blackheath; there were the Wallaces of Featherstone Castle with their few hundred a year from their Penrith property in the early nineteenth century, the Dickinsons of Red How with a small income from Lamplugh collieries in the middle of the century, or the Senhouses of Netherhall with a thousand or more from Maryport collieries. A majority of the landed gentry, no doubt, were mere gentry, dependent on their agricultural rents and without other resources apart from any savings out of rents or from the proceeds of marriage portions which might have been invested in the funds; but the newer families were far from unique in being endowed with the extra advantages of non-landed assets.

Withdrawal from an active business life undoubtedly owed much to the attractions of a rentier's position, for even in brewing, the most gentlemanly and least demanding of all businesses, attention to affairs might interfere with the full enjoyment of country life. The growth in the nineteenth century of a class of managers and wealthy entrepreneurs willing to become lessees of businesses clearly facilitated this withdrawal by making it much easier to separate ownership from management. But fundamentally, perhaps, the whole process was determined by the operations of the mechanism of family life. Even though the founder of a fortune might himself purchase a country place to celebrate his success, his sons were likely to have been born at an early stage in his rise, to have been brought up in the old house in an atmosphere of daily contact with the affairs of business, and to have been educated in the way that a plain and rising businessman could afford. Thus although a son might inherit a country estate the formative experiences of his youth might well dispose him to take a continuing interest in his father's firm. The grandsons, the third generation, would be the first to be born and brought up in the country seat, the first to be educated as gentlemen's sons, and were thus most likely to be the first to prefer conventional gentlemen's lives for themselves: the eldest would gravitate to the position of squire pure and simple, the others to the military, ecclesiastical or legal professions which were considered most fitting. It was perhaps not so much that this generation conceived the desire to live down its origins, as that this generation was so bred that it did not acquire the taste, nor possibly the aptitude, for the world of business.

What was acquired instead was a taste for the life of an independent country gentleman, and this was perfectly expressed by John Thomas Brooks of Flitwick Manor, Bedfordshire. His father George was a London banker, who married the Flitwick heiress in 1789, but continued to live in Twickenham and let the manor house. John Thomas, after a brief spell in the dragoons at the end of the Napoleonic War, was put in possession of the mansion and estate during his father's lifetime, as he recorded in 1846 'a most unusual instance of generous devotion, giving up to me their estate and a handsome fortune during their lives, thus enabling me to marry – in comfort would be too slight a word for it – in happiness as soon as I came of age; and moreover (against their own inclination) permitting me to become a member of the noblest of professions, (gladly would I, as far as my own personal feelings go, do the same by my own son and give up to him now my estates. But having four children instead of one, I could not do it without great injustice to the whole family). . . . My position in life too, is perhaps the most enviable in this glorious country, being high enough to satisfy every reasonable wish, without being so exalted as to require a sacrifice to ardent political duty.'[1]

Brooks gave thanks to God and his parents for 'the good and very beautiful estate on which I have so long resided'. It was beautiful but modest, just under a thousand acres, and the task of managing it was not too exacting; in any case it was undertaken by an agent. Brooks's life in fact was dominated by his interest in his small deer park and his passionate attachment to the Flitwick gardens, which extended over thirteen acres. He enumerated with loving care, in 1838, the virtues of a kitchen garden which was a passable substitute for wintering abroad. 'The forced vegetables start here with seakale and mushrooms in November,' he recorded, 'and continue with radish, lettuce and salads throughout the winter, and conclude with asparagus, peas and french beans in early spring, at which time cucumbers

---

[1] Bedford C.R.O., Lyall (Brooks) MSS, LL. 17/280, Journal of J. T. Brooks, 16 Dec. 1846.

come in. Young potatoes at Christmas are supplied by the system of box layers. The forcing season commences here with the vine, the earliest being introduced into the stove in December, which produces fruit by the end of April, followed in succession in the other houses until the grape season ends in the following January. The fire of the peach house is lighted at the end of January, which produces fruit by the end of May. The fig house is heated at the same time, securing crops in succession from June to December. These houses also supply strawberries . . . the variety of pine grown here is chiefly Queen for its superior flavour. From early May to the end of September melons in great variety are supplied.'[1] The flower garden was so arranged that there were separate gardens for each of the four seasons, and in addition an American garden, rose garden, summer bulb garden, botanic garden, exotic flower garden, and a labyrinth. He obtained rare specimens from the Chatsworth gardener, Paxton, one appropriately named *Musa Cavendishii*; and when this enthusiast could spare time from his own garden he went on a summer garden tour through Hendon Rectory, Highgate Mausoleum, Redleaf, Knowle, Windsor, and Eton to end at Dropmore.

For every horticulturalist among the landed gentry there were probably ten keen sportsmen, but apart from their special interests their lives were all filled in much the same way. Attendance at quarter sessions in the county town was generally a social as well as an administrative and judicial occasion, and in the intervals the magistrates acted either singly or in pairs as the local bench for their home district. After 1834 they were likely to be members of a Board of Guardians, often active in the interests of keeping the rates down and adept in obstructing the will of the central authority whose requirements always seemed to involve extra expense. They might take part as officers in the annual turnout and exercises of the county's military force, whether militia, yeomanry or volunteers. Though 'a sacrifice to ardent political duty' might not be exacted from many, all would take an intermittent part in political life, and some played an active and sustained role. They or their wives were certain to be interested in the running of a village school or a clothing club

---

[1] Lyall (Brooks) MSS, LL. 17/284.

for the village poor, and wives would devote much time to charitable works and visiting the sick. Above all there was the great round of social entertainments, the winter season of hunt balls, subscription balls, and private dances, and the year-round visiting and dining at each other's houses. Most of these activities took place within the framework of the county. In mountainous parts the watersheds marked out the boundaries of the social area, since it was hard to ask the horses to cross them. Elsewhere a stranger might find it hard to tell whether the county formed the basis of society and friendship because quarter sessions, race meetings, and by the mid-century agricultural shows, were held for the county, or whether these were held for the county because it was an established social entity.

The county families moved with ease on terms of equality with the magnates, and generally took for granted as part of the inevitable and pre-ordained natural harmony of society the leadership of the aristocracy in government, sport and pleasure. There might, from time to time, be signs of schizophrenia in their attitude. The gentry might pride themselves on their independence of the aristocracy, draw attention to the superiority of their plainer and simpler mode of living over the hollow elaboration of London ways, and emphasize the closer identification with county interests which was theirs by right of permanent residence and closer contacts with the soil and the farmers and labourers who lived by it. Not only might the supposed wholesomeness of country life contrasted with town and aristocratic decadence be in question, but also there might be open mutiny against aristocratic leadership, as when several Whig gentry of Northamptonshire and of the West Riding informed Lord Fitzwilliam that they placed the maintenance of protection before their party loyalties and traditions. Repeal occasioned what was perhaps the last revolt of the gentry; 'for in 1846', Clarendon told Fitzwilliam in answer to an allegation that Lord Russell had given totally insufficient weight to land in his cabinet, 'the landed gentry were in a state of rabies, they thought themselves both plundered and betrayed, and nothing could have satisfied them but retracing our steps. . . . If half the Cabinet had consisted of men of large landed property it would neither have inspired confidence nor brought support . . . I fear the time [1850] is not come when he can expect any regular support from the landed interest'.[1] Revolt, although it laid bare the feeling of division between the gentry and the aristocracy, between those maddened by regard of their immediate personal interests and those who shouldered responsibility for the good governance of a whole nation, was perhaps less of a mutiny than a defection to the other side, for one of the virtues of aristocratic leadership was that it always tried to lead in at least two different directions.

Such episodes, however, were aberrations from the normally harmonious relations between gentry and aristocracy. In time they proved open to persuasion or conviction that they had no alternative but to accept the lead of their superiors, and even the arch-exploiter of the sense of betrayal, Disraeli, could lead in unexpected directions. Disaffected gentry might obstruct and embarrass a government, but in the mid-nineteenth century they could scarcely hope to run a government themselves, a chimera which had bemused the gentry at moments of great stress ever since the seventeenth century. 1846 was the last gentry revolt because by then the railway was fast making country isolation a thing of the past. For squire and duke to meet in the country houses, or if not there in the great parks or in the hunting field, was of course not exactly a novelty. Brooks, strolling in the enormous park and gardens of Woburn which almost overshadowed his own, was flattered to shake hands with the Duke of Bedford: the first Lord Verulam, when not busy with the entertainment of royal dukes and high society, was busy entertaining his Hertfordshire neighbours, Sebrights, Gapes, and Lawes. Such contacts, however, could be infrequent and deferential, rather than close. Any lingering suspicions of the aristocratic way of life as something mysteriously superior, alien, or foppish, were blown away as the gentry welcomed the chance of trips to London, and incorporated membership of London clubs or possession of a modest town residence into their standards of life. Life at railroad pace was more than the cloistered individuality of provincial towns with provincial seasons could stand; the sons of the gentry, too, could ride the rails to Rugby, and a single world of manners emerged. By the 1850s old Sir Tatton Sykes, arriving booted and spurred at his London house, hating

[1] Northants. C.R.O., Fitzwilliam MSS, Lord Clarendon to Lord Fitzwilliam, 14 Dec. 1850.

the smart world but impressed in spite of himself that his son 'knoa's oo t'hond leadies in curriage', was unmistakably antediluvian.[1]

The squire who could not abide the aristocrat, and who felt that there was something faintly improper and unmanly about his elaborately cultivated mannerliness, had in any case never been more than a rarity. The two groups were thrown together on too many occasions for the points of difference between them ever to outweigh the shared outlook and common interests in the normal course. This was readily observable at the dining tables of the country houses or on the floors of the new Assembly Rooms in the county towns, which were springing up in the late eighteenth and the first half of the nineteenth century, largely financed by the aristocracy and gentry, and largely designed to meet their social needs. It was apparent in county administration, where lords lieutenant and chairmen of quarter sessions were figures of key importance, dependent on the co-operation of the county gentry, conscientious in consulting their opinions, and scrupulous to avoid giving any appearance of offence. For manning and running each petty sessional division of a county the lord lieutenant relied on the judgment and advice of a senior locally resident magistrate, and it was vital that mutual confidence should subsist between them. It was from this source that recommendations came of new men suitable for inclusion on the bench. It was to the local magistrates, for example, that Lord Fitzwilliam felt obliged to explain his action in dismissing a clerk to the magistrates in petty session because he had become a common brewer: the act was strictly beyond his competence as *custos rotulorum*, but he felt that immediate action had been necessary in order to protect the fair repute of the county magistracy as a whole.[2] Harmony between the upper ranks of landed society was clearly expected, where the structure of official county life was so much more federative than hierarchical.

Acting together to enforce the game laws the aristocracy and gentry had a great and growing common interest, one which linked official capacities with the favourite recreations of county society, and one in which there were shared facilities as well as shared outlooks since in sports which flourished best on large

---

[1] Christopher Sykes, *Four Studies in Loyalty* (1946), p. 18.
[2] Fitzwilliam MSS, Letter Book 733, 11 Jan. 1844.

areas and long purses it naturally fell to the magnates to set the pace. Strict preservation of game, begun in the eighteenth century on some estates, became very much more widespread and highly organized in the early nineteenth century, forming one of the most noticeable effects on the living standards of the landed interest produced by agricultural progress and increased incomes. Technically, the spread of root-crop husbandry and the cultivation of grain crops two years in four instead of one year in three provided a farming environment increasingly palatable to the pheasant and partridge. Financially, the elaboration of permanent gamekeeping staffs, the running of hatcheries, and the provision of winter feed for the game birds, were products of buoyant landed incomes. Preservation itself was made feasible and enforceable by the compactness of estates in ring-fences, and to perfect its arrangements was a common motive for buying out small intermingling properties; enclosure therefore made a great contribution to the practicability of strict preservation where it sorted out open-field country into the manageable pattern of fields and compact farms.

The pleasures of shooting were of course of very long standing; it was the steps taken to foster and safeguard the means for gratifying those pleasures which were more novel. Game books, in which were entered each day's shooting party and each day's bag, seem to have made their appearance towards the end of the eighteenth century, a sign of growing organization of the sport. Strict preservation, in the sense of formally notifying all tenants and the general public that all game birds were reserved exclusively for the owner, and employing sufficient keepers and assistants to enforce the rule, was started by the first Lord Verulam on his estates, and this was apparently part of a general movement in his generation. The height of organization in execution, the grand battue in which carefully nurtured birds slothful from too good living were methodically slaughtered in droves, was reached in the decade after 1815; the remaining excitement in this branch of the sport seemed to lie in the establishment of national records for the largest single day's bag, which was put at 525 pheasants in 1823, shot at Ashridge by twelve guns.[1]

Growing interest was reflected on many great estates by the

[1] Gorhambury MSS, 1st Lord Verulam's Diary 17 Jan. 1823.

formation of a separate game department in the managerial structure, and an immense growth in outlay on the sport. At Longleat, for example, the expenditure on the pheasantry in 1790 was £264, and there was no separate game account; by 1810 there was a separate department under a head-keeper and the annual outlay had grown to about £400; by 1856 the cost was £2,555, and in the 1880s and 1890s there was no single year in which it fell below £3,000. At Belvoir the £90 a year spent on game in the early 1790s had grown to £500 by 1800. At Savernake the game expenses in the 1820s fluctuated between £30 and £500 a year; in the 1830s they settled down at around £700 a year, and were held there by many decades of economy, but by the 1890s the annual expenditure was about £1,500. At Raby the game expenses in the 1790s do not seem to have reached far beyond the retention of a keeper at Middleton-in-Teesdale to look after the moors, at five guineas a year, and it was indeed not until the 1860s that a separate game entry emerged from the general welter of household accounting, when it was running at about a thousand a year.

Increased expenditure clearly meant increased numbers of gamekeepers, but it is unfortunately impossible to trace this movement at the national level. The sport was first tapped for revenue in 1784, when game licence duties were imposed, but until 1812 figures of the receipts were not kept separately. In that year there were some 40,647 game licences in Great Britain, a number which grew to a peak of 51,375 in 1827. Thereafter there was a steady decline to 42,398 in 1839, at which point an increase in the rates of duty precipitated an apparently steep decline in the popularity of shooting until a turning point was reached in 1853. From 1836 the number of licensed gamekeepers can be distinguished from the licensed gentleman shooters; there were then 2,857 of them in England, and a decline had already set in before it was accelerated by the rise in the rate of duty. This pushed the number of licensed keepers strongly downward until in 1853 there were only 1,452; after this there was recovery, assisted by a reduction of duty in 1861, so that by 1868 there were 3,241 such keepers. The varying temptations to evade the duty probably meant that the number of real keepers in England did not fluctuate so widely as the number of fiscal keepers, but if that is so then the great strength of the movement in favour of the Scottish moors becomes apparent, for the 608 gamekeepers in Scotland of 1836 grew to 774 in 1853, and to 1,050 in 1868.[1] For England the figures would suggest a first peak in the popularity of shooting in the 1820s, followed by a genuine setback on account of poor game seasons and political and social fears felt by the landed interest, whose scale however is exaggerated by fiscal changes. A second, and greater, wave of popularity got under way in the late 1850s, and received no serious check until 1914.

The game record at Gorhambury registers this cycle in terms of numbers of birds killed, the pheasants being a more sensitive indicator than the partridges. The 1820s saw the best seasons since the start of preservation, with 1,767 pheasants in the season of 1822 and 1,726 in 1827, and any year with under a thousand being deemed poor. This fell away after 1832, until by the end of the 1830s it was abnormal to bag more than 200 pheasants in a year. Revival started in 1848 and built up to the 1,000 a year mark once more in the 1850s; the season of 1900, with 2,319 pheasants, showed the largest bag in the whole series from 1821 to 1923. The elements, of course, made their mark on the the sport, particularly excessively wet breeding seasons such as 1829. But it was political and social factors which produced the long term movements. 'The worst season I ever recollect,' Lord Verulam recorded of 1830–1, 'the birds were scarce, the cover bad, poaching became more prevalent and less easy of detection; another such season and farewell to preservation. It would be far better to have no care for game than to incur the expence of so much mortification.' The next year, naturally, brought no relief: 'So ends the season of 1831–2,' he minuted in February 1832, 'during which we were taken much from Gorhambury by the odious Bill for Reform proposed by H.M. William IVs Whig Administration, which if carried we expect will do away with the amusement of shooting and the pleasure of continuing this book. We have other fears respecting it which induce us to set at naught any inconvenience so that we may give it our most hearty opposition.' He stuck to his belief that Reform brought the end of shooting in sight, and two years later was ready to throw in his hand: 'New Game Bill giving security to poachers,

[1] *Parliamentary Papers*, 1870, XX, pt. ii, 13th Rep. of Commrs. of Inland Revenue, pp. 82–3.

agricultural distress making farmers grumble, rising generation satiated with the slaughter of battues, expences on the rise, rents declining, preserving given up, book finished.'[1] Convinced of the gloomy prospects for the landed interest, game establishments were curtailed and pheasant-rearing abandoned, and the first heyday of the sport was over. The Corn Law controversy and agitation against the game laws prolonged the gloom in the 1840s, and confidence in a secure future for the insecurity of pheasants only returned in the 1850s.

In very slight degree the great outlays on game were recouped by sales to game and poultry dealers, a traffic which was still illicit in the 1820s. The real reward, of course, was in the enjoyment of the sportsmen, and the wider social reward lay in the sharing of this pleasure. Quite often a gentleman's estate was not large enough to afford sustained shooting throughout the season, and although the magnates might reserve their greatest set-pieces for battues in each other's company, it was customary for the great men to invite the neighbouring gentry for a day's shooting from time to time. In return the gentry were expected to co-operate in the work of preservation on the great estate, as when the Duke of Cleveland enlisted the aid of squires as well as colliery owners in his perennial attempt to stamp out the suspicious practices of colliers with lurcher dogs who liked to go coursing within sight of his coverts. A severe rebuke was administered to a neighbouring squire, one of whose tenants was deliberately trying to destroy all his hares: 'The Duke of Cleveland never interferes with any man's sporting as a sportsman, but such a case as this is unprecedented in a civilized country.'[2]

The farmers were generally excluded from the sport, though on a very large estate it was sometimes the practice to allow the tenants on distant outlying farms to shoot their flying game. Running game might be differently treated, and the Gorhambury arrangement was not uncommon: during the season ground game was restricted to the keepers, but the farmers were allowed the run of the woods for rabbit- and hare-shooting once the close season for birds began. In law this was not possible until 1831, when the restriction of the right of shooting to owners of land

[1] Gorhambury MSS, Game Books 1821–1923.
[2] Raby MSS, Letter Book I, W. T. Scarth to R. Addison, 17 April 1854.

worth at least £100 a year was repealed, and it became possible for anyone to purchase a game licence. In practice, even after 1831, it would be a mistake to suppose that the normal tenant farmer was allowed any shooting by his landlord.

Game preservation gave rise to a real conflict of interests between landlord and tenant. Since the eighteenth century many farmers and stewards had held that excessive preservation was damaging to agriculture and its progress. Pheasants, although they were corn-eaters, were on the whole granted a grudging tolerance: 'no appreciable proportion of such damage can be ascribed to feathered game' John Bright's Committee on the Game Laws reported in 1846. Rabbits and hares were the great ravagers of crops, sometimes destroying a quarter or more of a field of corn. Hares in particular had a rare taste for the key crops of the improved husbandry: they would travel miles to a field of turnips, Lord Hatherton observed, and still further to carrots. Such damage furnished fuel for complaints against over-preservation, swelling into considerable agitation in the 1840s and 1870s. 'Nearly all the practical agriculturalists examined' in 1846 spoke 'of game as being . . . the principal source of the unpleasant feelings which sometimes exist between landlords and tenants.'[1] The grievance was not removed until the Ground Game Act of 1881, which authorized tenants to destroy rabbits and hares on their farms without seeking their landlord's permission.

There is some reason to believe that the scale of this grievance was exaggerated through the publicity devoted to the issue by radical politicians, delighted to find such discord in the ranks of the agricultural interest. In the first place, in spite of the roving hares, damage from game was on the whole confined to the fields adjoining the great game preserves, and therefore was far from affecting all farmers equally, and perhaps did not affect the generality of farmers at all. In the second place most of the great game preservers were not indifferent to their tenants' complaints, and did something to mitigate the evil. Such action might take the Gorhambury form of allowing tenants to shoot the running game at certain seasons, or it might take the form of occasional

[1] *Parliamentary Papers*, 1846, IX, pt. i and ii, S.C. on Game Laws, Report, pt. ii, v, xxix, Evidence, Q. 7417. Cf. *Parliamentary Papers*, 1828, VIII, S.C. on Game Laws, Evidence, p. 51.

wars on over-population conducted by special rabbit-catchers employed by the landowner. More commonly, perhaps, where owners accepted the gamekeepers' view that it was impossible to destroy rabbits without interfering with the breeding of pheasants, tenants were paid compensation in money for damage done by game. John Bright's Committee reported that such compensation was generally given, and estate accounts bear out the conclusion.[1] There was, of course, always room for disputes between landlord and tenant over the valuation of the damages, and room for objections in the national interest that agricultural output suffered even if the farmer's pocket did not. It may be supposed, however, that many farmers welcomed restriction of output provided they did not have to bear the cost.

In spite of these palliatives, and the quite general custom of giving presents of game to the tenantry as well as to the gentry and the local parsons, it remained rare to find a farmer who was sympathetic towards game preservation. The labouring classes saw game as a fair prize for anyone who could take it, saw nothing wrong in poaching, and were antagonized by the unspeakable severity of the early nineteenth-century game laws. This severity, and recognition of the spice of adventure in poaching, prevented many respectable citizens from accepting the landowners' view that poaching was simply a form of theft, often a form of robbery with violence. Increasing viciousness of the laws against poaching and mounting ruthlessness in the methods used to protect game preserves were features of the first quarter of the nineteenth century. But it would be wrong to assume that the use of spring-guns and the penalties of transportation for night poaching or hanging for killing of gamekeepers placed the protection of game on a level of legalized barbarity wholly different in kind from the laws and practices used to protect other forms of property. The decade which produced a humane tempering of the criminal law in general in fact also witnessed the prohibition of spring-guns in 1827 and the relaxation of the penalties on poaching in 1828.[2]

The game laws had been tightened in step with the great increase in the number of game preserves, and the associated

---

[1] S. C. on Game Laws, 1846, Report, iv.
[2] J. L. and Barbara Hammond, *The Village Labourer* (Guild Books ed. 1948), I. 184–96.

growth in the amount of game and the costs of rearing. Land-owners were anxious to protect their increasingly costly birds, both by employing greater numbers of keepers and watchers and by trying to increase the deterrent effect of the law. At the same time the concentration of large numbers of birds in readily recognized preserves, in place of the previous scattering of naturally bred birds over wide stretches of countryside, increased both the temptation to poach and the chance of taking a large bag in a single foray. The stage was thus set for the increase in poaching offences, the appearance of organized poaching gangs, and the waging of savage battles between them and bands of keepers, quite apart from the intrusion of aggravating factors. In fact it was generally agreed that many agricultural labourers were driven to poaching by their acute distress after 1815. This affected those southern counties where wages were lowest, unemployment was considerable and poor relief inadequate in scale and demoralizing in its effects. Within this context poaching offences in such counties as Bedford and Dorset tended to be highest in years of especially severe agricultural distress such as 1821–3, and tended to fall away in years of comparative prosperity like 1825–6. In manufacturing districts a contrary influence operated, and prosperity stimulated poaching in the surrounding country. In Lancashire, it was said, commercialized poaching was a response to the demand of opulent Manchester merchants and manufacturers for game, a demand which grew as they came to give more dinner parties and lead a more active social life. As long as the sale of game remained illegal this demand was largely satisfied by the poachers who supplied the poulterers.[1]

It is therefore highly likely that the game laws would have earned notoriety at this time, through the growth in poaching, even if they had remained unaltered. That they were made more savage may be understandable, but still remains a stain on the record of the landed interest as legislators. In may also be argued that the incentive to one type of poaching was lessened by the legalization of the sale of game in 1831, and that in its efforts to

---

[1] *Parliamentary Papers*, 1826/27, VI, S.C. on Criminal Commitments and Convictions, Report, pp. 4–5, Evidence, p. 31; *Parliamentary Papers*, 1828, VI, S.C. on Criminal Commitments and Convictions, Report, pp. 7–8, Evidence, pp. 54–65; S.C. on Game Laws, 1828, Evidence pp. 51, 80.

protect agriculture, and hence agricultural employment, the landed interest was incidentally trying to reduce the motives for the other type. Nevertheless game preservation continued to make few friends outside landowners' circles, and undoubtedly made many enemies. As a sport shooting emphasized the solidarity of aristocracy and gentry, sitting together as magistrates trying poaching offences, and standing together at the butts. It also stirred the resentment of farmers and labourers and was a notable hindrance to rural harmony.

Fishing, enjoyed in solitude, attracted outsiders rather than the landowners as far as organization and expense were concerned. It is notable that the magnates regarded fishing as a suitable indulgence for their young boys rather than as meriting their own serious attention, and that they were generous in granting fishing permits to all manner of local residents. With hunting, the last of the classic trio to be considered, the case was far different. A sport eminently suited to the mounted and leisured aristocracy and gentry, fox-hunting engaged the passions also of a cross section of the whole rural community, and the fashionable hunts attracted the entire world of high society. In the nineteenth century, moreover, it was an increasingly organized activity, with a growing body of conventions and etiquette, which gave the hunting community a mystique and cohesion of its own. An expensive activity, the major part of the expense was frequently carried by a member of the aristocracy, whose enthusiasm for the chase was in this way the means of cementing his leadership of all branches of county society. The hunting interest, based on a common excitement at the thrill of the run, sharing common memories of frustration, disappointment and exhaustion as well as achievement, informed by respect and admiration for a great Master, was perhaps the most real and fundamentally influential element in county society. The brotherhood reached far beyond the loyalties bred by estates, and embraced men from a great many stations in life, for alongside the lord, the squire and the parson, the farmer, the doctor, the solicitor and even the village sweep could all be seen at the meet; the labourer alone perhaps had no representative there. As loyalties founded on emotions outrun the calculus of economic interests, so the fox did more for the unity and strength of the landed interest than rent rolls, and barbed wire did more to destroy the ties of county society than death duties.[1] It was during the eighteenth century that the fox replaced the stag or the hare as the favourite object of pursuit, and simultaneously the formation of the first famous packs like the Belvoir or the Beaufort got under way. In these the indispensable specialized instrument, the foxhound, was first evolved by selective breeding, most notably in the Belvoir, a lasting contribution by the ducal owners. The systematic organization of foxhunting did not, however, at first proceed very far beyond the maintenance of a pack and liveried huntsmen, and a hunt would roam enthusiastically, somewhat indiscriminately, and without assured continuity beyond the lifetime of an individual master. It was in the later eighteenth century, and above all in the first third of the nineteenth century, that the hunting countryside was quartered out between regular hunts, their 'countries' or territories receiving defined and well understood boundaries, and their meets becoming sufficiently ordered and controlled to provide for thorough hunting of the whole of their country. Thus in the 1780s and the 1790s the country round Sledmere might be hunted from Castle Howard or Driffield or not at all, as packs formed and dispersed, with the steadfast refusal of Sir Christopher Sykes to permit any hunting invasion of his immediate estate as the only fixed point. 'You will excuse me for being extremely desirous to enjoy them [the estates adjoining Sledmere] as I received them, not subject to foxhunters' law,' Sir Christopher told the Earl of Carlisle in 1788. The next year he told the Hon H. Willoughby that apart from the neighbourhood of Sledmere 'I shall have the greatest pleasure in sanctioning the preservation of foxes on my other estates . . . I hope the fox will live to give you a good occupation.'[2] In Wiltshire it was not until 1826 that the county emerged roughly divided between four hunts, and their countries were still too large for thoroughly effective treatment, so that subdivisions took place in the 1830s, and again later in the century. And so the movement towards regularity, permanence, and

[1] Barbed wire is said to have been introduced about 1880 from the U.S.A. by an ardent foxhunter, the 5th Earl Spencer, to protect his fox coverts: *V.C.H. Leicestershire*, III (1955), 279.
[2] Sledmere MSS, Letter Book 1775–90, Sir C. Sykes to Earl of Carlisle, 9 Oct. 1788; do. to Hon. H. Willoughby, 27 Dec. 1789.

thoroughness proceeded. The number of packs of hounds in Britain, including an unknown proportion of non-foxhounds, grew from sixty-nine in 1812 to ninety-one in 1835, after which there was a slight decline until 1850. From then on there was a steady increase to a total of 125 packs in 1866. The number of these kept in Scotland was fairly stable at a dozen.[1]

This organized thoroughness consumed a great deal of time, hunting six days a week throughout the season for the Beaufort, for example, with the duke himself hunting on 102 days in 1853, and his children rationed to no more than three days a week until they were five. It also consumed a great deal of money, and when this was provided by the private fortune of a single aristocrat the country was much beholden to him. At Belvoir during the minority of the 5th Duke the pack was farmed out and the guardians' commitment was limited to a subscription of £300 a year, but when the young duke took the pack into his own hands in 1798 the annual hunting outlay at once bounded towards the £2,000 mark. The pack itself was a valuable investment, worth anything up to 3,000 guineas in the early nineteenth century according to quality and size. Its maintenance involved large operations, the Belvoir hounds consuming 34 tons of oatmeal in 1798–9, as well as quantities of horseflesh, and the kennels burning 48 tons of coal. There were the hunt servants to be provided, the two whippers-in at this time receiving £21 a year each, and the huntsman £80, with board and liveries in addition. The convenience of the hunters had to be consulted, with proper attention to the maintenance of hunting gates and hunting bridges and perhaps the cutting of fresh rides through the coverts.[2] Beyond all this there was the fox to be considered and nursed until the appropriate moment for his pursuit might have arrived. Land had to be set aside for coverts, or rented from other landowners, so that every part of a hunt's country might have a fair share of foxes; as in the Raby country, this might involve the expense of ploughing, draining, and sowing with whin in order to produce a gorse patch which a fox might accept as furnishing habitable quarters. His Grace's Earth

---

[1] *V.C.H. Wiltshire*, IV (1959), 369; for the Beaufort, *ibid.* 370–2. Division of single-county hunts also occurred in the early nineteenth century in Leicestershire and Lincolnshire for example. *13th Rep. Inland Rev.*, p. 81.

[2] Belvoir MSS, Guardians' Accounts 1787–99; Estate Accounts 1788–1804.

Stopper was a figure of key importance, responsible for ensuring destruction in the course of a hunt should a fox go to earth, and in between times carrying the even greater responsibility of protecting and nurturing the unsuspecting quarry so that too much might not be left to chance when it was desired to meet with the right number of foxes in the right places. In the late spring the earth stopper took an annual census of the numbers and locations of fox litters, and throughout the summer it was his duty 'to look after the foxes, visit their haunts and see that they are all right – objection can hardly be taken to this by watchers, farmers or owner.'[1]

The expense to the great hunting Vanes, the first and second Dukes of Cleveland, was of the order of £1,000 to £1,500 a year until in 1861 the pack, hunt servants and coverts were made over to the Durham County Hunt, and the hunting outlay of later dukes was limited to some £50 a year on the maintenance of hunting gates and bridges, and a subscription to the hunt probably of £50 or £100. At Milton the upkeep of the pack cost about a £1,000 a year from 1803 onwards, falling away for a decade in the middle of the century when the hounds were farmed out, but rising to £2,300 in 1870 when the pack was once more in Fitzwilliam hands. Hunt establishments, moreover, were meaningless without the mounts to accompany them, and the provision of a reasonable string of hunters cost at least as much again as the apparatus of kennels and hunt servants. As a general rule accounting arrangements did not distinguish between carriage horses and hunters, but grouped both under the single establishment of the stables; but where the stable expenses of a hunting enthusiast were on a considerable scale it is a fair assumption that the great part of the total was devoted to the hunters. At Belvoir in 1802 the stables absorbed £1,421; at Raby they cost £919 in 1819, and moved up to £1,407 by 1854; at Milton they moved up from about £700 in 1803 to over a £1,000 a year in the 1830s, and about £2,000 a year net of horse sales in the early 1870s. The string of hunters, which might number up to thirty or forty in a large establishment, was itself a precious possession: a good five-year-old

---

[1] Raby MSS, Letter Book I, esp. W. T. Scarth to Duke of Cleveland, 12 Aug. 1846; do. to G. Armstrong (owner of Anniscliffe estate), 6 July 1858.

might fetch 75 guineas in the later 1790s, and 120 or more from the 1830s onwards.[1]

It was not often, of course, that investment in foxhunting on this sort of scale was within the means of a single individual, and it was more common for a hunt to be supported by subscriptions levied on the principal foxhunting gentry, with a few of the leading men guaranteeing a minimum annual income to the Master for the upkeep of the pack. Thus the series of impermanent arrangements for hunting the East Riding in the later eighteenth century were generally on a subscription basis, and Sir Christopher Sykes strongly preferred this system since 'a general subscription of small sums on a permanent footing' would be proof that it really was 'the general wish of the Riding to have a pack of foxhounds.' When something like a settled arrangement was made in 1806 the agreement hammered out at Beverley Races was that Sir Mark Masterman Sykes and Mr Watt should hunt the country jointly for five years certain, and the hounds were to be kept at Edelthorpe Grange, Digby Legard agreeing to farm them at £3,000 a year, which in the main was to be found out of subscriptions.[2]

Whether hunted by subscription or not, the whole of a hunting country was expected to promote the interests of the sport. By the 1840s, if not sooner, the somewhat reserved attitude towards complete protection of foxes and towards the claims of a hunt to enjoy leave of access to every piece of property, which Sir Christopher Sykes had displayed in the 1780s, was considered unpardonably lukewarm or even outrageously bad form in any ingrained hunting country. When a farmer threatened to kill a fox which had been worrying his chickens, the Duke of Cleveland's agent could only assume that the threat was uttered in jest, and coolly point out that such damage 'most frequently arises from neglect on the part of those in charge of poultry. The same assumption of universal participation in the preservation of foxes was more persuasively put to an absentee clerical landowner: 'Though you are not a foxhunter yourself,' the letter

[1] Raby MSS, Muniment Room, Household Accounts 1819–93. Fitzwilliam MSS, General Accounts 1803–24, Milton Accounts 1792–1886. Belvoir MSS, Guardians' Accounts 1787–99, Estate Accounts 1788–1804. Blagdon MSS, Diary 20 Oct. 1845.

[2] Sledmere MSS, Letters and Papers 1780–1852, Sir Christopher Sykes to P. Langdale, 9 Feb. 1784; Letter Book 1795–1806, Sir M. M. Sykes to Lord Middleton, 16 June 1806.

ran, 'I feel quite sure you will not allow a tenant of yours to damage the sport of others. Your estate is a resort of foxes in the breeding season, which in a foxhunting district makes it most desirable they should meet with fair play or a whole country may be spoilt. Last season three dead foxes were found near the boundary of your land, which completely destroyed the Duke of Cleveland's hunting in that district.' There was no mincing of words to an absentee lay landowner: 'There has been foul play with foxes . . . an unlooked for and shameful outrage that has taken place in a foxhunting country . . . a tenant of yours has made it his business to destroy foxes on Anniscliffe Moor.'[1]

Such sentiments could only be uttered on behalf of a duke, whether politely or brusquely, because they were indeed the prevailing sentiments of the landed interest, farmers included, towards the rights of foxes. The great hunting passion, especially when from the early nineteenth century it evolved an organized structure of considerable costliness for its better satisfaction, was a prime field for the display of aristocratic leadership, for the development of aristocratic partnership with the gentry, and for the perpetuation of the whole of county society on the footing of deference willingly accorded to the gentlemen in pink. The social value of the sport was explicitly recognized: 'When the pleasures of the chase can be made the means of calling the gentlemen of the country together,' Sir Christopher Sykes wrote in 1792, 'they become really useful and beneficial to society. They give opportunities of wearing off shynesses, dispelling temporary differences, forming new friendships and cementing old, and draw the gentlemen of the country into one closer bond of society.'[2] The bond, at least in the nineteenth century, certainly embraced the farmers as well. In the early years of the century the prosperous graziers of Leicestershire, 'the Bluecoats', were keen followers of the Quorn, and in Lincolnshire one of the fruits of the great agricultural improvements of the Wolds was that 'the number of smartly turned out tenant farmers who hunted with the Brocklesby exceeded that

[1] Raby MSS, Letter Book I, W. T. Scarth to W. Bowman, Gainford, 1 Aug. 1853; do. to Rev. W. Poole, Hereford, 19 Apr. 1857; do. to G. Armstrong, 29 June 1858.
[2] Sledmere MSS, Letter Book 1790–5, Sir C. Sykes to T. Grimston, Driffield, 5 Dec. 1792.

in any other country. At one time 60 or 70 farmers followed hounds, all clad in scarlet and all beautifully mounted.'[1]

The intellectuals and aesthetes have frequently derided the particular means by which this bond was formed. It is, nevertheless, difficult if not invidious to seek to place all the different pleasures of all the different sorts of men in an order of merit, and to the social historian this one stands out as a great social fact. With this curious mixture of a desire to love and cherish the fox and a desire to chase and kill it, most of those who could command the use of a riding horse found that one of the aims of life was fulfilled in the exhilaration of riding to hounds. It was a fact which, perhaps more than any other, gave vitality, cohesion and stability to county society – a fact, also, which epitomized the virtues and limitations of enjoyment of that leisure which it was the prime purpose of the structure of the landed interest to provide.

[1] *V.C.H. Leicestershire*, III. 271; *V.C.H. Lincolnshire*, I (1906), 494.

VI

<div align="center">~~~~~~</div>

The Management
of the Landed Estates

<div align="center">~~~~~~</div>

A life of leisure with freedom to pursue occupations that were not dictated by the compulsions of economic necessity was the great object of estate management. But while landowners might be either zealous, perfunctory or indifferent towards the management of their resources, it would be wrong to conclude that they confined themselves exclusively to the proper expenditure of their incomes, and were content to leave the procuring of their spending money entirely in the hands of their agents and servants. It would be equally misleading, on the other hand, to suppose that agents did no more than execute orders, and that all the main decisions in the running and development of estates were taken by the owners. Management in its higher reaches was very much a co-operative enterprise, in which even the most sybaritic owner would concern himself in matters of great consequence, and the most enterprising owner might feel himself hemmed in by his agents, prisoner of his steward on estate affairs and of his lawyer on family arrangements. In the decisions of high policy, which might have profound effects on farming, or on the development of coal mining, or on the growth of towns, it is hard to disentangle the parts of owner and of agent in the framing of an initiative. What is certain is that through its managerial structure ownership of estates was translated into a way of life, and the landed interest exerted its most direct influence on the economy of the country as a whole.

As seen through the pages of estate account books it is inevitable that the large landowner should wear the look of a remittance man, recipient of the 'neat surplus' as it was termed after others had deducted all outgoings from the gross receipts. In the books it was the accountant, that is the steward who rendered the account, who authorized and paid all the estate expenses, who remitted the remaining balance of the receipts to his employer's London bank, and who expressed his regrets if the remittance chanced to fall short of expectations because of some unforeseen contingencies. From experience the owner came to rely on a given level of remittances, and framed his whole expenditure pattern accordingly, generally knowing to a nicety by how much his bank account would be refreshed after the next half-yearly rent day. Sometimes an owner literally carried his own remittances, Lord Verulam in the 1820s and 1830s making regular appearances at Snow's, his City bankers, to lodge the net proceeds of his Hertfordshire and Essex account days, which he brought with him in coin and paper in a bag. Nevertheless this window onto reality does not command a view of the whole of real life, and no landowner ever attained the passivity and irresponsibility of the true remittance man with his steady annuity, paid in quarterly instalments. The problems of the trustworthiness of servants, of large capital outlays, and of cultivation of political interest were in themselves enough to involve any owner in active supervision of management, and very many of them of course had other motives besides for taking a positive interest in the business of their estates.

Although the steward was a person of growing importance during the eighteenth century, and although good management was recognized to be both increasingly necessary and profitable in an age of agricultural change, at the close of the century the triumph of any one single pattern of estate organization was not yet definitely assured. For the great estates the model structure had long existed, of the single full-time salaried agent who was wholly responsible for the administration of the economic affairs of all lands in single ownership which were grouped together in one geographically compact estate, with clearly defined authority over a number of subordinate officials. The estates which did not function according to this model, however, were still fairly numerous. In terms of organization, divided responsibility was by no means uncommon, either with a rent-collector and an estate bailiff running in parallel, or more frequently with a series of district agents each of whom was directly responsible to the owner and not subordinated to a steward-overlord. In terms of methods of remuneration, the fixed and adequate salary that betokened the hiring of the undivided attention of a properly qualified man had not yet ousted payment by a percentage on the amount of rents collected, the badge of the agent working on commission for a multiplicity of clients, nor part-payment by tenancy of a farm gratis or at a nominal rent, the sign of the part-time steward who was also in business on his own account as a farmer. As this last circumstance suggests, in terms of personal qualifications and status the steward who was in any sense a professional land agent worked in a field whose possession he was still disputing with others, principally attorneys and farmers, to whom estate management was a secondary occupation. Finally, in terms of accounting procedure the apparatus of journals, ledgers and double entry, segregation of estate, household and personal expenditure, and separation of capital and income accounts, co-existed at the end of the eighteenth century with direct descendants of medieval practice. These were still employing the terminology of charge and discharge accounts, and confusing the consumption of oats by race-horses with the payment of wages to coal-miners in one single tally, which effectively concealed his real financial situation from the owner even if it served to square the accounts of the steward.[1]

The lack of uniformity in administrative arrangements, and the absence of a business-like approach on many estates, was in part a reflection of the persistent idea that an estate was primarily a unit of consumption rather than a unit of management. The old idea that the function of an estate was to furnish surplus crops which the owner and his household consumed on the spot had, of course, long since passed away in its primitive form. Something of its spirit nevertheless survived in the attitude which saw an estate simply as a unit of ownership, and the function of a

---

[1] The house steward at Wentworth Woodhouse, for example, continued to account in this indiscriminate fashion until well into the nineteenth century, long after his principal duties had become those of a colliery viewer.

steward simply as guardian of routine processes against dishonesty and embezzlement in order to hand over an accustomed
surplus income to the owner for his personal spending. The
spirit of improvement, the favourite eighteenth-century phrase
for the awareness of the possibilities of change, development
and growth, on the other hand meant, for landowners, that the
estate was given a positive role as a unit of management.
Through investment and supervision of farming practices the
task of managers under such a system was to encourage technical
and economic efficiency, and to promote the growth of income
from purely estate operations without paying much attention to
what was happening to the expenditure pattern under household
and personal demands. For a variety of reasons the standards of
such estate managers tended to be those of maximum physical
output from the land rather than those of businessmen concerned
with maximum financial return from outlay, but at least they
were obliged to be business-like in their administrative methods
and paper-work. In so far as the spirit of improvement had not
yet infected all estates by the close of the eighteenth century
archaic methods of management still survived, and in the subsequent course of events the further breaking down of the comparative insulation of landowners from market forces hastened
the decline of diversity.

Divided or parallel responsibilities, however, also derived
from the perennial doubts about the trustworthiness of servants.
Horror stories about the deceitfulness, rapacity and dishonesty
of stewards were one of the staples of gossip in eighteenth-
century landed circles. Although instances of grand peculation
may have been infrequent, every large landowner could not
avoid being uncomfortably aware that his prolonged absences
and his inevitable detachment from the details of affairs placed
great opportunities for surreptitious profit in the way of his
servants. Sometimes, indeed, one has the impression that every
servant from the valet, butler or cook up to the land steward was
under suspicion of lining his own pocket at the expense of his
master's property and interests, and hence arose elaborate
systems of checks and supervision of one servant by another
intended to plug the loopholes for embezzlement. Any complete
structure of supervision, however, depended on the confidence
that could be placed in the top levels of management, and hesita-

tions about this impeded the full development of a hierarchical estate bureaucracy. Instead, one method of limiting the temptations and the scope for profiteering presented to higher management was to share out its duties. Thus one man might arrange the terms of tenancies and another be responsible for collecting the rents, as on Lord Verulam's estate; or a number of distinct collectorships might be retained, without geographical separation of their territories and without any subordination to a head agent, as on the Duke of Rutland's estate; or the head agency might be put in commission, as on the Duke of Northumberland's estate where three co-equal commissioners ruled from Alnwick until 1847, sharing their responsibilities territorially to a certain extent but also keeping a check on one another in their joint discharge of all central estate business.

In extreme cases a peculiarly shattering experience might drive a great landowner into becoming his own chief agent, dispensing altogether with the services of a steward. Thomas Coke of Norfolk, while sitting for his portrait in 1807 mentioned to Lawrence that 'he had no land steward, but did all that business himself and has done it during many years. There had been a strong lesson in his own family to induce him to undertake it. A boy of the name of Caldwell was recommended by a person at Norwich to the late Earl of Leicester, for some family purpose, and came to Holkham with half a guinea in his pocket. He was gradually advanced by the Earl, and at last became steward, in which capacity he amassed £100,000. The following instance showed how he carried matters on. A tenant of Lord Leicester being desirous to have his lease renewed sent Caldwell a goose pie, and with it a letter in which he mentioned that Mr Caldwell would find an egg, which he desired him to look to. It contained £2,000 with which Caldwell was so well satisfied that the lease was soon granted'. Coke had to take Caldwell to Chancery before he could dismiss him, and then managed to do all the steward's business between seven and ten o'clock every morning, after which 'he is at leisure to shoot or for any other amusement'.[1] Coke of Norfolk obviously had the personal taste for agricultural pursuits which made the regular habits of estate office work congenial to him. It was more usual, when the

---

[1] *Farington Diary*, IV. 138–9. The offending steward is referred to as Cauldwell in Chancery proceedings.

delinquencies of a steward came to light, simply to dismiss the offender and replace him by another whose references seemed sound and promising.

Even to Coke of Norfolk the delights of such a light office routine were not indispensable, and it was only shortly after this time that he appointed his famous steward, Francis Blaikie, whose regime lasted until 1832, during which many of the agricultural practices for which Holkham was famous were put on to a regular and systematic footing.[1] Blaikie was an unmistakably professional land agent; neither a successful farmer, nor a solicitor, nor a retired army officer, nor a younger son of a gentleman with good connexions and claims to patronage, he was the plain son of a Scottish tenant farmer, coming to England as a very young man and working his way up in the business of management until he became agent to the Earl of Chesterfield before moving on to Holkham. It was his type of professionalism, endowing the practice of land agency with the standards and standing of a profession, which relieved owners of their burden of mistrust at the potential rascality of stewards, and in laying the foundations of complete confidence between owner and agent made possible the full development of the structure of estate administration and the emergence of head agents to whom many of the powers of owners were virtually delegated.

Professionalization was in part the product of those forces which were making improvement, efficiency in administration and in management of resources, both more attractive and less avoidable, and which were thus creating careers for expert land agents. It was also in part reliant on the diffusion of relevant knowledge and experience, and its progress was inevitably determined to a considerable extent by training facilities and the supply of qualified land agents as well as by the demand for their services. Enclosures provided widespread practical experience, touching very many estates, in the reorganization of estate resources and in the provision of new capital equipment for farming on a large scale, experience which was paralleled in a less obvious way by the simultaneous changes in farming practices in general. A generation after the final phase of rapid enclosure, field drainage faced management with similarly widespread

[1] R. A. C. Parker, 'Coke of Norfolk and the Agrarian Revolution', *Econ. Hist. Rev.*, 2nd ser., VIII (1955), 161–2. *Gentleman's Mag.* (1857) pt. ii, 572

problems of decision, organization and finance. Canal schemes to some extent, and railway schemes to a much greater extent, presented estates with the problems and opportunities of development and radical departure from traditional practices, while the wide fluctuations of farming fortunes in war and peace and in a rapidly changing economy from the later eighteenth century called for resilience in questions of rent and informed judgment about forms of tenure. It was in this environment of change that land agency grew to maturity, earlier on some estates and in some regions than others, and that the older view of management as something primarily concerned with law, the legal relations of landlord and tenant and the punctilious enforcement of legal obligations, seemed increasingly inappropriate, along with the lawyers who had played such a large part in running that system.

The school of experience was the main source of land agents. Many agents on great estates in the early nineteenth century may have started in other careers, but they found that a proper performance of their duties required a full-time concentration on management. It was not long before the great estate offices, such as Holkham, Woburn, Welbeck or Alnwick, became recognized training grounds for a career in land agency, and young men would serve in them as clerks and juniors in roughly the same way as men were articled to solicitors. The products of these schools were sometimes criticized for having acquired habits of needless extravagance, and for pursuing technical perfection without due regard to cost and profit. Thus Henry Parr Jones who came to Longleat in 1859 from Holkham where he was one of the many pupils trained by Lord Leicester's agent Carey, was felt to have erected buildings at Longleat of quite unwarranted magnificence. But this was excused when on inquiry it was found that Lord Leicester put up most extravagant farm buildings: 'his pride has been to make them as fine as possible. He now begins to see the mistake, and said the other day, of some workshops he had erected, that the pulling them down would be a better deed than the building them.'[1] Nevertheless, these training grounds produced land agents who made up in their professional pride and competence for their deficiencies in cost-consciousness.

[1] Longleat MSS, Revd. Whitwell Elwin to Lord Bath, 6 Feb. 1861.

As long as there was not a sufficiency of experienced land agents it made good sense to employ as stewards persons with other than technical qualifications. The landowner needed above all assurance of the probity of his chief agents, who would have the handling of large sums of money and the negotiation of weighty affairs in which there were undoubted opportunities for defalcation. In the absence of any recognized source of men with both the relevant experience and unimpeachable character it was natural that the second quality should be the essential qualification, and that knowledge of agricultural matters should be regarded as of secondary importance, something that anyone could pick up in the course of doing the job. Personal friends of a landowner, respectable local solicitors, and retired army officers who could be assumed to bear the characters of gentlemen, these were the favourite sources for recruits who had to be fitted to work in a close personal relationship with their employer, and often had to deputize for the owner socially as well as administratively. In Ireland, where the absences of owners might be prolonged into years instead of months as in England, it was not uncommon to take the logical step of employing as agent for a great estate some member of an Irish landed family, perfectly qualified to act as proxy for the absentee. Robert Chaloner at Coollattin and John Stewart Trench at Carrickmacross were cases in point in the mid-nineteenth century, on terms of easy familiarity and equality with their employers Earl Fitzwilliam and the Marquess of Bath, aware that they were landed gentry in their own right as well as agents with the high degree of autonomy which their situations afforded.

The professional and managerial revolution on estates was proceeding at about the same time as similar movements in the legal and medical professions and in the managerial structure of manufacturing firms, and derived from the broadly similar circumstances of increasing complexity in the economy and increasing demands for expert services. The revolution was felt to have proceeded sufficiently far by the 1840s and 1850s for land agency to claim to be regarded as a distinct profession. 'The land agency business, in the true sense of the name, is of comparatively recent origin', a technical treatise stated in 1858. 'In England it has become a regular profession: but in Scotland, where every proprietor . . . gets his rental and other accounts audited by a law agent . . . there is comparatively little employment for men of this class.'[1] By this time, in the works of Morton, Low, Cross and others a textbook literature on the management of estates was growing up, of which William Marshall's work a generation earlier had been the forerunner. In its organized treatment of the subject, its sense of business expertise and its emphasis on calculated economic planning of the use of resources, this marked a great departure from the eighteenth-century works describing the routine duties of stewards, the broad general advice of Kent's *Hints to Landed Gentlemen*, or the line of descriptive legal handbooks for stewards and tenants which culminated in Kennedy and Grainger's *Present State of Tenancy* in 1828.[2]

Nevertheless it was a long time before land agency acquired the institutional organization of a profession, and individual land agents were much more conscious of sharing the outlook and interests of the landed gentry than of possessing any interests in common with other professions or other types of managers. Among themselves land agents were certainly aware that they had some common interests, and they corresponded with one another on many questions, and in particular tried to co-ordinate the timing and scale of general rent reductions when these were necessary. But the nature of their employment was so personal and its duration so long that they felt no call to act together as a profession with a professional body to protect their interests and regularize the terms and conditions on which clients could obtain their services. The Land Agents Society was not founded until 1902, and professional qualifying examinations were not introduced until the 1920s, with actual experience of the full-time management of an estate of not less than 2,000 acres remaining the primary qualification for membership. Land agents, however, were quite frequently recruited from the ranks of surveyors, for those surveyors who dealt extensively in the valuation of land

---

[1] J. L. Morton, *The Resources of Estates: being a Treatise on Agricultural Improvement and General Management of Landed Property* (1858), p. 96.
[2] J. L. Morton, *op. cit.* D. Low, *Landed Property and the Economy of Estates* (1844). F. Cross, *Landed Property: its Sale, Purchase, Improvement, and Management* (1857). W. Marshall, *On the Landed Property of England* (1804). W. Marshall, *On the Management of Landed Estates* (1806). J. Mordant, *The Complete Steward* . . . (2 vols., 1761). N. Kent, *Hints to Landed Gentlemen* (1793). L. Kennedy and T. B. Grainger, *Present State of Tenancy of Land in G.B.* (1828).

were well prepared to take over its management. Enclosures, tithe commutation, railway land purchase and spreading tenant-right practices created an expanding demand for land valuers, and since their work was in the form of a number of separate specific jobs for different owners they naturally lived on professional fees and not salaries. This fact was probably the driving force towards organization of the profession, and in 1834 a Land Surveyors' Club was formed by six London surveyors. It developed, however, into a dining club, and it was not until a generation later, in 1868, that the effort at organization was successfully repeated with the foundation of the Institution of Surveyors.

In 1868 the surveyors counted 'the management of landed estates' and 'the improvement of landed estates' as two of the four main branches of their profession. John Clutton, perhaps the most eminent surveyor-land agent of the century and first president of the Institution, remarked with some surprise that 'a considerable number of the men in country districts called "Land Agents" are, in fact, not surveyors at all. Many most respectable gentlemen are entrusted with the management of land, whose education and early pursuits were directed to entirely different objects. Gentlemen learned in the law and physic, officers of the army and navy, and members of other classes of professional men, think themselves competent to manage and deal with land.' A fellow surveyor, pleading for the proper education of the profession, took a view both more gloomy and less charitable. 'By far the greater part, probably, of the landed property of England is under the management of solicitors, who are usually little more than receivers, without much knowledge of the details of management. . . . Military men are great favourites, though in what respect their previous habits have fitted them for estate management it is hard to understand.'[1] In this he was echoing Morton's opinion of ten years before, that 'as a general rule law agents make bad land agents', and at least of the great estates it was certainly not true that as late as 1868 the solicitors still had the bulk of the management.

By 1877 the Institution of Surveyors was 'understood to represent the management of something like three-fifths of the

[1] *Trans. Institution of Surveyors*, I (1868–9), 10 (Clutton); 56 (Sturge).

landed property of England', and this penetration by surveyor-land agents was certainly not an achievement merely of the preceding decade.[1] Most of the more gentlemanly professional land agents in any case kept aloof from the Surveyors' Institution, feeling that the majority of its members were 'devoted to urban and suburban properties', and for this reason formed their own independent Society in 1902.[2] Bearing this in mind, it seems likely that by the 1870s the two groups between them dominated the field of estate management, and that the long-drawn-out movement towards professionalism which started in the eighteenth century, and quickened from the 1840s, was by then virtually complete.

The growing importance of the stewards was mirrored in their salaries. Already by 1790 there were a few posts on the largest estates carrying a salary of as much as £1,000, but £300 to £400 was the more usual figure on great estates, and less where the steward was still in reality a farmer-bailiff. During the period of the wars there was a fairly general revision of salaries, which on the whole seems to have comfortably outpaced the rise in the cost of living and established new levels which persisted after 1815. Thus at Raby the steward received £150 in 1790, £200 in 1800, £300 in 1804, £750 in 1806, £1,000 in 1807, and £1,200 in 1810, at which level the salary remained unchanged for over a century. At Belvoir the salary of the most important of the land stewards moved from £300 to £500 between 1790 and 1804; at Longleat also the salary moved from £300 in 1790 to £500 in 1809, and then after a gap in the accounts reappears at over £900 in 1839; at Wentworth the steward's salary was raised from £400 to £1,200 in 1811, although this fell back to £800 in the 1830s, while at Milton the £200 of 1792 became £500 from 1813 onwards. At Alnwick, on the other hand, salaries remained stable until 1839, during which time there were three commissioners receiving £500 a year each; between 1839 and 1847 there were two commissioners with £700 each; and the sole commissioner appointed in 1847 received £1,000, his successors in the post reaching a maximum of £1,850 after 1878. The posts clearly varied considerably in their responsibilities, even if these are

[1] *Ibid.*, X. 317.
[2] Sir A. M. Carr Saunders and P. A. Wilson, *The Professions* (1933), p. 200.

measured solely in terms of the gross incomes which were handled. There could also be important variations in the significance of the salaries, for on a few estates it remained the practice until the 1850s for the agent to find his riding horse and perhaps his clerk out of his own salary, while on the majority this was not so. Generalization about salary levels is therefore difficult, but it is not unreasonable to suppose that the career prospects which were held out to land agents in 1929, of a number of posts carrying £1,000 a year with £600 as a medium figure, in fact also reflected or even slightly understated the levels which had ruled since 1815.[1]

These salary increases, and particularly the sudden large steps in salary, indicated the rising status of the managers. Sometimes they occurred on a new appointment, and the occasion was taken to introduce a significant alteration in occupational terminology: the 'steward' of £150 to £300 a year became the 'agent' of £750 to £1,000 a year. The terminological change was by no means completed within the period of the war-time increases, and took at least another generation to work itself into normal usage, but the debasement of the currency of 'steward' had definitely begun. Apart from a few special and largely honorific posts, such as the stewards of manors, the term 'steward' came to refer to the subordinate estate officials who might be competent and experienced, but were not educated gentlemen, or to the house stewards who normally were highly trusted and intelligent domestics. 'Agent', on the other hand, came to describe the superiors, the professional men of education, who moved in the same circles as the landed gentlemen and who carried the chief weight of financial and administrative responsibility. Similarly the term 'sub-agent' was introduced to describe juniors who were in the top managerial career stream, even though their actual duties of responsibility for a subordinate or detached district under the head agent might not differ markedly from those of sub-district stewards or bailiffs.

As one would suspect from their incomes, and from the respect which attached to them as the supervisors of large properties, the agents were often men of considerable eminence in county society, not infrequently more widely known and more widely

---

[1] *Choice of Career Series*, No. 4, (1929), quoted in *The Professions*, p. 461.

heeded in their opinions than many of the lesser squires. Hugh Taylor, for example, who was the Duke of Northumberland's chief agent between 1847 and 1865, was a greatly respected and authoritative figure in his county, earning a full and appreciative entry in the contemporary dictionary of Northumbrian biography.[1] Socially they established close and confidential relations with their employers, and in a measure partook of their way of life. Farington thought it worthy of remark that Lord Lonsdale 'directs to his steward, Richardson, Esqr., but never invites him to his table'.[2] Others certainly were so invited from time to time, though in itself this was no more of an honour than that regularly accorded to private tutors and chaplains. It was of more significance that an agent might expect to have three days' hunting a week with his master's pack, or that he might be one of the county magistrates. Above all, perhaps, the agent was generally looked upon as the permanent representative on the spot of the great landowner, discharging some of the owner's functions which fell outside the sphere of strictly estate business. These might be small matters, such as attendance at the weddings of principal tenants, or great matters like the cultivation and control of his employer's political interest. In this way the Raby agent, T. F. Scarth, was the natural choice for campaign organizer, election agent and accountant in the Vane interest in the Durham county election of 1820, and again at the next contest, for South Durham, in 1841.[3]

It was often impossible for an agent to devote his full time to estate business, and in addition it was not uncommon for him to have other concerns altogether outside the range of the multifarious interests of a single landowner. Sometimes an agent who was principally concerned with one great estate might find it possible to undertake the agency of one or two smaller estates as well. In colliery districts men like Hugh Taylor were not unusual, who combined the management of the Duke of Northumberland's estate with colliery proprietorship on his own account. Again we may find men like William Allen at Malton, Earl Fitzwilliam's political and estate agent, who found

[1] R. Welford, *Men of Mark 'twixt Tyne and Tweed* (3 vols., 1895), III. 494–7.
[2] *Farington Diary*, V. 67.
[3] Raby MSS, Memoranda made during the Canvass of Co. Durham with Mr Powlett in 1820; Canvass Book of S. Durham elections, 1841.

that his local standing and contacts, and no doubt his advantage in handling in transit the Earl's money from Malton property and the Derwent Navigation, furnished an opening into the country banking business at Malton. In the circumstances of the early 1820s Allen found this experience distinctly chastening.[1] It was therefore not uncommon to find that the principal agent did not reside on the spot, but exercised his supervision by paying more or less frequent visits to the estate office and by periodic tours of inspection of the farms and property in his charge, the detailed routine of daily office work being left to subordinates. This was indeed regarded as the normal pattern by Morton in his discussion of administrative arrangements in 1858, the chief land agent being specifically referred to as non-resident, and being encouraged to visit his estate at least every two or three weeks.[2] By this date, however, there were also many principal agents who were resident, and with the majority attendance was in any case more frequent than this.

In this way the managerial structure of the mid-nineteenth century might not appear, at first sight, to have differed greatly from the general practice of the days of the lawyer-stewards. The reasons advanced in 1811 by Charles Bowns, Earl Fitzwilliam's chief land steward, in support of his request for a salary increase, afford a good picture of these arrangements, which combined the particular oversight of the Yorkshire estate with financial control over the other Fitzwilliam estates. 'The agencies I hold has necessarily occupied so much of my time', Bowns wrote, 'that it has not been in my power to pursue the profession of solicitor to that extent which is sufficient to enable me to answer the growing expenses which I experience . . . on which account I have been obliged to request an increase of salary from Col Beaumont and Mr Fullerton, which they have granted, and must unavoidably have made the same application to your Lordship four years since had I not been favoured with your Lordship's professional employment. . . . The salary which Col Beaumont allows me is 4 pr. cent upon the amount of the rents,

[1] Wentworth Woodhouse MSS, F. 107 k, W. Allen to Lord Fitzwilliam, April 1821. Receipts of about £20,000 a year passed through Allen's hands at this time. It is indicative of an agent's opportunities for delaying part of the owner's receipts in transit that Allen's predecessor Copperthwaite was found to owe £6,000 to the Earl when he died in 1817.

[2] J. L. Morton, *op. cit.*, pp. 93, 99.

etc., which includes the auditing the accounts of the house steward at Bretton, and of the principal Lead Agent at Newcastle, where I go to annually at his expence. . . . The annual amount of the rents and produce of your Lordship's farms, tithes, mines, woods and canal under my collection is very little if any short of £40,000, and the quantity of land exceeds 15,000 acres, the cultivation and cropping of every close of which, as well as the state of the buildings thereupon, must necessarily be attended to every year. . . . To which must be added the auditing of Mr Biram's accounts, the accounts of Law Wood and Elsicar Collieries, and likewise those of the Irish, Malton, Higham Ferrers and Harrowden estates'. The Earl referred this application to his London adviser, who consulted Masters in Chancery, stewards of other noblemen, and others well versed in such affairs, and recommended that since Bowns had 867 tenants directly in his receipt, on 17,522 acres of land, the farm rents amounting to £28,000 and the mines, canals, woods and tithes to £12,000 a year, along with the auditing of other accounts covering full £40,000 a year more, he ought to have a salary of £1,200. 'I conclude that he must necessarily keep one principal person and a horse in continual employ. . . . He has been remiss in not stating these matters sooner to your Lordship, and he has suffered for it as I do verily believe that by his £400 p.a. he has not been much benefited'.[1]

A similar arrangement for the general oversight of a great estate which consisted of a number of distinct territorial units was to be found at this time on the Marquess of Bath's property. Here there was not only a steward of the principal estate surrounding Longleat, who had a house steward under him, but stewards also of each of the detached Irish, Herefordshire and Shropshire estates, and a bailiff of the small Gloucestershire property. Over all these stewards was a receiver-general, who received their annual surpluses, audited their accounts, and dealt with the central family expenditure. In the Duke of Rutland's affairs the superstructure was less centralized. There were, in the 1790s, separate stewards for the Derbyshire, Leicestershire, Lincolnshire, Cambridgeshire and Wiltshire estates, but they were under two different auditors. These two had salaries of

[1] Wentworth Woodhouse MSS, F.106 a, C. Bowns to Lord Fitzwilliam, W. Baldwin to do., June 1811.

£800 and £300, and since it was the lower paid who was stated to have 'correspondence with all the stewards' and to have 'general superintendence of the Duke's affairs', we may surmise that any central direction was rather shadowy. Indeed, apart from the period of the minority, it does not seem that any central, consolidated, account was kept of all the Duke's properties.[1]

Any contrast between this type of structure and that found on great estates under nineteenth-century land agents is, superficially, difficult to discern. In the Vane family we find that from 1803 when T. F. Scarth was appointed agent he managed the principal Durham estate of Raby himself, and overlooked the accounts of the separate agents for the detached Teesdale estate, also in Durham, and the Northamptonshire, Shropshire and Wolverhampton estates. The Marquess of Bath's receiver-general disappeared after 1810, and in his place we find during the tenure of Robert Robertson and H. Parr Jones that these agents managed the Longleat estate, and supervised the accounts of the Herefordshire, Shropshire and Gloucestershire properties. There was, however, the basic difference that these land agents exercised management as well as audit control over the subsidiary agents of detached estates within their province. Thus for all the Duke of Cleveland's estates which have been specified general policy on such matters as tenancies, landlord's improvements, farm repair programmes, game preservation, or town building development, as well as on such philanthropic issues as the amount and kind of support to be given to local schools, was centrally determined at Raby, and Scarth had a regular annual schedule of visitations to the out-Durham estates, whose managers were thus fitted into a bureaucratic hierarchy as sub-agents.

Something of the import of this substitution of direct supervision for remote audit is revealed in the third Duke of Northumberland's ideas for reorganizing the administration of his Cornish estate in 1834. 'The local agency should continue with a common agricultural bailiff under the agent', he wrote, 'and instead of a professional law agent in London, I should be inclined to have him residing upon the spot.'[2] This case, however, also illustrates

[1] Belvoir MSS, Minority Accounts of 5th Duke, 1787 Statement.
[2] Alnwick MSS, Third Duke's Letter Book 1831–44, Duke to J. K. Lethbridge, July 1834.

the limits of the co-ordination of policy and administration over a range of estates, for neither the Duke of Northumberland's Cornish estate, nor his Yorkshire estate of Stanwick, nor his Middlesex estate of Syon, nor his later Surrey estate of Albury, were ever brought within the purview of the chief commissioner at Alnwick. Similarly Scarth never had any dealings with the Duke of Cleveland's estates in Cornwall, Devon, Somerset, Wiltshire and Sussex. There were, of course, auditors for all accounts, but the magnates did not necessarily employ the same man to undertake this independent check of all their different accounts, and in any case the very growth of the land agents' powers was acting to diminish the auditors' supervisory role and confine their functions to the technical tasks of seeing that the books did in fact balance and that the vouchers did indeed support the ledger entries.

Earl Fitzwilliam's friend Henry Drummond was therefore right to argue in 1854 that auditors, in the sense of general managers, did not exist, though he was behind the times in maintaining that the attorney's predominance still persisted in ordinary estate management. 'With respect to Auditors to private property, I never heard but of one, and that was Abercrombie for the Duke of Devonshire: but the circumstances were peculiar: his father and mother who had both neglected it were just dead: old Heaton who had managed there and the Duke of Portland's was become imbecile, and so the Duke got Abercrombie to undertake the whole. But in general each estate has its own manager, in general a local attorney. For example, the Duke of Portland's London property is in Boodle's hands but Boodle has nothing to do with the Nottinghamshire or the Scotch Estate. So the Duke of Buccleuch: his factor in Scotland has nothing to do with the Northamptonshire property, nor the Middlesex: and so of all the others I know, and Abercrombie did but keep his appointment until the Duke of Devonshire's estates were put in order. I fear your Noblemen with Auditors are only heard of in Utopia, but not in Great Britain. There is something like it in Scotland, but they are all Scotch lawyers.'[1]

The absence of any complete managerial superstructure for the greatest estates was scarcely surprising, for their geography

---

[1] Wentworth Woodhouse MSS, G. 52, H. Drummond to C. Sturgeon, 11 Aug. 1854.

would have made it a most exhausting task to exercise effective unitary supervision over the great scattered empires of the dukes who have been mentioned. Unitary financial control which could be exercised from a London office by experts who combined the techniques of accountants and land agents, and whose analytical approach attempted to impose some of the mystique of cost control on to estate expenditure, was not available until the last quarter of the nineteenth century, and even then was not widely used. In the meantime the largest estates were either not managed as a whole, or this function had to be performed by the owner himself. When the owner was a minor his guardians exercised this general supervision, frequently with much benefit to the well-being of the estate. Otherwise only heavy indebtedness could expect to emulate a minority in producing organized supreme control, for there were some instances in which the pressure of debt induced an owner to relinquish his responsibilities to special trustees, who co-ordinated administration, enforced economy, and reduced the debts.

The family solicitors, normally a London firm, certainly had one kind of synoptic view of a great landowner's affairs, but this was an angle of vision focused on the aggregate assets and their distribution among different trusteeships and different beneficiaries, and was no substitute for central direction of estate management. Similarly the London banker who normally received into one account all the remittances from the different estates and investments of a great landowner was in a position to see his current financial affairs as a whole, but naturally enough the only legitimate use to which a banker could put this knowledge was to put a curb on excessive borrowing from himself. Nevertheless although the owner might remain his own supreme managing director it is apparent that within limits imposed by distance there was a movement towards unification and extension of the area under the control of a single principal agent.

It might be thought that all these developments served to relieve owners of personal burdens and anxieties connected with the management of their affairs, and enabled the great landowners to become an even more completely leisured class than formerly. The same argument, however, might be applied equally well to the agents themselves in relation to the growing range of subordinate officials and auxiliary professional services which they could draw upon in the discharge of their own managerial functions. In the estate sphere and in that of the household as well, it is indeed possible that increasingly systematic organization produced a civil service which was capable of the smooth and well-oiled running of the machine without further supervision. On the other hand it was perhaps more likely that the administrative machine was called forth by the increasing complexity of affairs, a complexity which in turn called for increasingly frequent intervention by the ultimate decision-maker, who needed to be more informed, not less, and in closer contact with his estates, not more remote from them, in order to act wisely.

On an efficiently organized great estate by the mid-nineteenth century the estate staff consisted of a great deal more than a principal agent and the sub-district bailiffs under him. The fourth Duke of Northumberland and Hugh Taylor between them created such efficiency, and made the Alnwick estate office the centre of the most advanced practice in administration. The Northumberland estate was divided into two regions, northern and southern, each of which was provided with one drainage and one building superintendent, who were responsible for drawing up detailed annual work programmes in their departments, the drainage men also having a permanent labour force of about 100 under their control. When in due course technical fashion made it suitable, the post of 'His Grace's Manager of the Steam Plough' was created, a dignitary who held the appropriate implements and labour available to undertake work for the tenants at fixed piece-rates. Both a surveyor and a valuer were permanently retained, though not employed full-time, and a regular machinery existed through which any tenant could have his farm revalued and a new rent fixed. It was more traditional that the office should contain a head cashier as well as clerks; that there was a clerk of works with a staff of craftsmen and labourers and a stock of materials, mainly employed about the Castle, home farm and other lands in hand, but also available for some repair work on farms in the home district; and that there was a head forester, a head keeper, a head gardener and a bailiff managing the home farm, each in charge of a separate department and of a separate labour force.

169

On the Northumberland estate this structure of specialist services still left the ordinary routine administration in the hands of the bailiffs. These collected the rents, supervised the observance of husbandry covenants by the tenants, prodded them about neglected hedges or broken gates, received their complaints and passed on their requests for building or drainage work, and often acted as the preliminary sieve in the process of selecting new tenants. Traditionally there were a dozen of these bailiffs, in charge of bailiwicks which ranged from 3,000 acres to the mammoth 57,000 acres of the wild moors of Redesdale, with rentals varying from £5,000 to £14,000 in the 1840s. The bailiffs, with salaries of £50 to £100 according to their experience and responsibilities, were local tenant farmers, with great practical knowledge of local conditions and farming practice but little education. After 1850 the system was gradually changed by the grouping of bailiwicks to form five larger sub-districts under sub-agents who were offered £300 a year. For this salary men of better education could be obtained, not indeed with the knowledge of practical farmers, but with business habits and the ability to bring up-to-date knowledge to bear on farming practice. In this way professionalization reached down to the basic level of management.[1]

It was not every great estate which could rival this degree of elaboration, either because the will towards system and efficiency was weaker, or because few could approach the £100,000 rent roll on which this particular subdivision of managerial functions was based. Nevertheless many of the chief features were to be found not only on estates of comparable size such as the Duke of Cleveland's, but also on estates with a quarter or a third of the Northumberland rental like the Marquess of Bath's or the Earl of Pembroke's. Here the full-time employment of specialists, particularly drainage superintendents, was a marked development from the later 1840s onwards, while the usual departments of estate administration each had their overseer, all of whom were responsible to the principal agent. In some particulars, indeed, even Alnwick was not the foremost estate organization in the country. It was not unusual to find a clerk of the works in charge of a considerable enterprise which undertook all stages

[1] Alnwick MSS, Business Minutes, II, 29 June 1849, 172–8.

of construction from preparation of estate-produced materials, principally timber, to the finishing touches of interior plastering, and was engaged in erecting new buildings as well as in repair work for all the farms and cottages of the home estate in addition to its work at the mansion and on the lands in hand. There were more than sixty men on the strength of the Longleat building yard in the 1860s, for example, and the yearly wage bill, including the clerk's salary of £130, came to £2,200.[1] It was quite usual also to find an active estate operating lime kilns, very occasionally a brick kiln, and again fairly commonly a number of tileries producing earthenware drain pipes, for estate needs and not for commercial sale, for the production of all these requisites of agricultural improvement was comparatively simple and cost was kept down by eliminating freight charges.[2]

As a unit of management, therefore, a great estate might provide certain physical services for its farms, as well as financial and administrative co-ordination, and this was not without its effect on agricultural production. In the exploitation of non-agricultural resources it was quite possible that the great estate would furnish the actual unit of production, mining and selling coal or ironstone, quarrying stone, or building houses for letting in growing towns. Already by 1790, however, it is probable that the more normal course was for the great land-owner to act the part of rentier and lease out his mineral rights or his building sites to entrepreneurs. Nevertheless, whether the landowner's own capital was committed or not, the protection of his interests in collieries, mines or building estates required constant and expert supervision. In these specialized fields of management the employment of specialist managers proceeded closely in step with the scale of operations, and in concerns of any magnitude or complexity owners hesitated to act without expert advice. On the Northumberland estate, for example, Hugh Taylor became the Duke's colliery agent about 1810, just at the time that the Duke's mineral interests outgrew the inland district of Newburn of which Taylor had previously been bailiff.

[1] Longleat MSS, The Longleat Building Yard estimate by H. P. Jones 5 Nov. 1867.
[2] See Ailesbury Trust MSS, Hoare's Bank, Memo. of Oddie's visit to Yorks. Estate Oct. 1840, for an example of estate lime kilns and estate tileries; see Alnwick MSS, Third Duke's Letter Book, vi, J. C. Blackden to Duke May 1843, for a decision to rely on commercial tileries wherever feasible, on grounds of cheapness.

Hugh Taylor was a self-taught mining engineer. His experience in acting on the Duke's behalf in the negotiation of leases, the assessment of dead rents and tentales appropriate to different qualities of coal seams, or the evaluation of colliery lessees' difficulties with water flooding the workings or surplus coal flooding the markets, furnished a store of colliery wisdom which served him well when he also became a colliery proprietor on his own account. His nephew and successor, Thomas John Taylor, was a graduate of Edinburgh and one of the first professional mining engineers, being one of the founders in 1852 of the North of England Institute of Mining Engineers; his value as the Duke's colliery agent was reflected in his salary of £450, very nearly half as much as the chief commissioner himself received.

It was not every estate that retained the services of such eminent mineral agents, although many other examples might be cited of agents equally notable, like Benjamin Biram at Wentworth, who not only made important contributions to the development of mining technique particularly in ventilation, but also was an influential figure in the Yorkshire Coalowners' Association in the mid-century. Other estates, such as Raby, might employ a humble colliery viewer at £30 or £40 a year to look after their relatively minor coal interests. In such a case, however, the permanent official was not a competent professional man able to act as consultant and adviser, but was rather a clerk acting as a check-viewer, and when any new piece of major development was in prospect an outside expert was called in to survey the mineral resources and advise on methods and terms of working them.[1] In any event, as can be seen in the case of the Staffordshire coal interests of the Sidmouth estate or the Cumberland ventures of the Dickinsons, it was unlikely that an owner would embark on the hazardous path of mining ventures without seeking expert guidance.

A distinction might lie, however, in the source of initiative in mining developments. When there was felt to be a likelihood of profitable mineral working on a hitherto unworked estate the first move would probably be made by the owner himself. Not infrequently counsels of caution and common-sense were

---

[1] The colliery viewer for the Durham part of the Raby estates was raised to £40 a year from 1863, and then received half as much as the estate drainage bailiff.

thrown to the winds, and venturesome owners would eagerly search in the most unlikely places. Thus John Harvey of Ickwell Bury sold a farm near Malmesbury in Wiltshire reserving to himself a power to sink pits for coal, and in 1816 his son seriously proposed to make a trial boring there. He was only frustrated in his enterprise because he proposed to import some Yorkshire miners for the job and the owners of the surface at Malmesbury, being Dissenters, objected on religious grounds, 'thinking that your Yorkshire men's habits and manners of life may tend to a corruption of those morals which they are endeavouring to inculcate among the people of this neighbourhood'.[1] This sensitivity no doubt saved Harvey from disappointment and loss, but the present point is that he decided to try the venture after a personal inspection of the site, and that his second step was to carry off some rock specimens to knowledgeable friends in Yorkshire, with whose encouragement he endeavoured to embark on a trial. On the other hand where mineral working was already successfully established on an individual estate or in a particular district, it was likely that the initiative for further workings would come either from speculative capitalists making applications for new concessions, or from the colliery agent proposing expansion. In either case it was the colliery agent who handled proposals for development, and his recommendations, based as they were on knowledge of both technical and market conditions, were generally decisive. The functions of the owner, except in the rare cases of personal intervention to protect the amenities of country life, were generally confined to the receipt of the best income which his agent could procure.

This distinction in the source of initiative reflects differing attitudes towards risk-taking. Some owners provided the capital and management for industrial undertakings on their estates, while many more simply acted as landlords leasing out resources to others. It was natural that the first type should be more conspicuous in mining enterprises in new territories or frontier regions, for no one but the royalty owner himself might be willing to hazard his capital in sinking into untried and unproven

[1] Beds. C.R.O., Harvey MSS, HY 701, 702/1, 702/2, 702/3, esp. J. Harvey to R. Robins 8 June 1816 and R. Robins to J. Harvey 13 July 1816.

depths. At the same time, however, not a few great landowners remained great mining capitalists long after the pioneer stages on their coalfields had been left behind, and in such cases there was no automatic association of owner-initiative and owner-provision of capital. In these cases the distinction lay between routine operations on the one hand and novel or unexpected situations on the other. In this way the suggestions for the increased capitalization of the Ridley collieries near Blyth in the first three decades of the nineteenth century came from the agent, while the final decision to withdraw from the enterprises altogether in 1838 was made by Ridley personally. With the larger scale South Yorkshire colliery investments of Earl Fitzwilliam, which were marked up from a nominal value of £65,000 in 1830 to £100,000 in the 1840s, it seems that the suggestions for expansion were made by Biram and that Fitzwilliam's approval continued to hide a considerable uncertainty as to the real value of his investment. On the other hand Fitzwilliam was closely concerned in the details of management of the adjoining Elsecar Iron Works, to which he had committed some £30,000 in the 1830s, simply because this for long remained a problem child apparently incapable of showing any profit.

A variety of reasons, personal, technical and commercial, determined whether a landowner became, and remained, an industrial entrepreneur. It would be a mistake to suppose, however, that those landowners who remained in business, in a financial sense, were necessarily more akin to industrialists or more attuned to their interests than owners who were simply lessors. Men of both types might be much or little interested in the state of the markets on which part of their incomes depended, assiduous or slothful in mastering the details of their affairs, and enthusiastic or indifferent over the opportunities of industrial growth. It was Lord Granville, an ironmaster, who complained of the tedium of having to go down to the country to look after his iron works, 'a necessary but tiresome operation', and the second Earl of Durham, a colliery owner, who spent his early years in possession in gay unbusiness-like recklessness. The fourth Duke of Northumberland, on the other hand, who read attentively the highly detailed reports and recommendations of his colliery agent, and who fought strenuously and effectively to promote the interests of his section of the Tyne against the threat of competition from other districts, was a royalty and wayleave lessor.[1]

Where great matters were at stake the ultimate decision always rested with the owner, and no agent was ever authorized to embark on a great project without the express sanction of his employer. But the idea of building a harbour, sinking a new pit, laying out a new housing estate, or granting a lease of a new royalty tract might well come from an agent, and it is certain that in many matters of lesser moment the owner's final approval was little more than a formality. The large measure of practical autonomy enjoyed by colliery agents and their equivalents derived from the specialized nature of their managerial and technical skills, for a Duke of Bridgewater with his engineering qualifications was something of a rarity in the aristocratic world. It was otherwise with the land agents, for the one business which a landowner assumed that he understood by nature was farming, and a land agent might well find himself subject to constant interference as well as effective control by his employer. The second Earl of Verulam, for example, generally inspected farm buildings himself before allowing his agent to start any considerable repair work; the fourth Duke of Northumberland personally proposed farming covenants for inclusion; in agreements with tenants, as did the second Lord Ashburton and the sixth Lord Monson personally selected fields for draining. More commonly a landlord might concern himself directly in the choice of tenants, for here considerations of the political suitability of applicants were likely to be involved, as well as appraisal of their knowledge, skill, financial standing and general probity.

When a landowner might intervene in the details of management of his agricultural estate it is clear that in questions of high policy involving large outlays or major changes in estate practice the grand strategy was likely to be his also. Great improving landlords such as Coke or Bedford rightly deserved their reputations, for the broad design of improvement was conceived by them, and their agents were in the main skilled executants of these ideas. The study of the Netherby estate has shown an active

[1] A. L. Kennedy, ed., *My Dear Duchess: Social and Political Letters to the Duchess of Manchester, 1858–69* (1956), p. 69. D. Spring, 'The Earls of Durham and the Great Northern Coalfield, 1830–80', *Canadian Hist. Rev.*, XXXIII (1952). Alnwick MSS, Business Minutes, esp. 1849–54.

collaboration between the owner, Sir James Graham, and his agent Yule in a programme of reform, improvement and investment, in which the main initiative came from Sir James.[1] On the Northumberland estate, undergoing a vast improvement programme, Hugh Taylor acknowledged in a public speech in 1857 that his part as agent was to implement policy which was decidedly the duke's own. 'They were aware that there was no undertaking of any magnitude which the Duke of Northumberland did not himself consider and decide upon, much to the relief of a man like himself, who had been an agent on the Estate for nearly 50 years, and was no way anxious to take greater responsibility than pertained to his position. . . . Still there was an executive part remaining, which belonged again to the agents.'[2]

Nevertheless it remains difficult to generalize about the division of managerial functions between landowners and their agents. On an efficient and improving estate it was certainly normal to find an active owner, as well as an efficient agent, engaged in a joint enterprise, but it was not always so. At Raby, which like many other estates emerged in the 1850s from a period of stagnation and indifference into a bustle of activity, all the evidence seems to point to the fact that the agent, Scarth, made the running, albeit showing every deference to the sporting duke. On the Ailesbury estates, steeped in debts and neglect, the Yorkshire property at least had a conscientious agent who tried to make headway towards rehabilitation in the face of the marquess's indifference. Even though the Wiltshire part of this estate demonstrated the rule that an indifferent owner attracted an indifferent and dishonest agent, it still remained true that an agent could develop loyalty to an estate and zeal for the promotion of its welfare without necessarily having the encouragement of an employer who shared these sentiments. On the other hand it was not necessarily the case that an actively interested owner was only to be found on a vigorously active estate. Lord Monson, who was perpetually dreaming of the revival of his family fortunes and always regretting that the dowagers did not permit him to save and invest on an adequate scale, clearly

---

[1] D. Spring, 'A Great Agricultural Estate: Netherby under Sir James Graham, 1820–45', *Agric. Hist.*, XXIX (1955).

[2] Quoted by C. H. Hartshorne, 'Houses for Working Men', *Trans. Nat. Assoc. for Promotion of Social Science* (1858), p. 445.

looked to the improvement of his Lincolnshire farms as part of the regenerative process. Lack of means may have meant that little was done which involved much expense, but Lord Monson nonetheless combined a lively interest in the supervision of his estate with an equally lively distaste for the endless grumbling of farmers.[1]

Many landowners remained who were desultory and perfunctory in the supervision of their estates, and if these were not neglected and poorly managed it was due to the rare combination of an agent who was both zealous and independent, and an income which was so ample that a considerable ploughing back into the estate passed almost unnoticed. The growing complexity of management, however, by no means meant that opportunities for an enterprising landowner to exercise initiative and direction were curtailed. If anything the openings for effective control by landowners increased in the half-century after 1820, as greater skill and capital came to be needed to meet the difficulties and opportunities of the agricultural situation, and financial decisions grew in magnitude and complexity in comparison with the straightforward days when enclosure had filled the improver's horizon. The second Earl of Verulam in the 1850s spent more than twice as much time on his estate affairs as his father had done in the 1820s, and the time spent on management by an energetic improver like the fourth Duke of Northumberland was vastly greater than that spared by his father, content to let things take their course in the 1800s. The tendency, indeed, was for the great landowners' part in management to increase, and the general impression is that a growing proportion of them did in fact behave as directors of their estates.

In contrast there may have been an opposite tendency among the gentry, for although the smaller size of their estates meant that they always had been, and remained, more intimately concerned in management than the aristocrats, development in the professional facilities available to them perhaps served to relieve them of part of their former personal burden of supervision. In the competition for managerial talents the smaller estates were at a permanent disadvantage in being unable to match the attractions held out by the greater, and therefore tended to have

[1] See below, Chap. IX, for the activity in the 1850s.

less skilled administration. In any case estates of less than £5,000 or £6,000 a year could not afford to retain the services of a full-time steward or agent, and the lesser gentry could only hope for the intermittent oversight of a professional gentleman with a multiplicity of clients. At best such management probably lacked the quality and drive which could be procured by engaging the undivided attention of a full-time agent, but when this oversight was largely in the hands of local attorneys without much agricultural knowledge, who combined the administration of several estates with the conduct of other legal practice, the standards of management on smaller estates were particularly low, and could only be compensated by great attention on the part of the owner. Nicholas Blundell urged his heir in the eighteenth century to show 'diligence in taking some care of his own concerns, for when concerns of moment are left to stewards, and especially to attorneys, they grow rich by their master's poverty.'[1] The development of local firms of surveyors and land agents, often formed by men who had had extensive experience in enclosure and tithe cases, provided an alternative means for running multiple agencies and a standard of competence which did much to diminish the disparity between small and great estates in quality of management. Such firms, becoming fairly general by the 1830s at least, also did much to relieve the gentry of the cares of detailed personal supervision.

As befitted their great difference in size, the gentry estates enjoyed a wide variety of administrative arrangements, and probably never approximated to any single standard pattern. The larger of them, such as Middleton in Northumberland or Mildmay in Essex, merging almost imperceptibly into the ranks of the great estates, supported a similar though less elaborate administration. On the smallest of them, scarcely worth £1,000 a year at the beginning of the period, not only did the owners act as their own stewards, but frequently also they were farming for profit and not simply for their own tables. In between came various combinations of bailiffs, farmer-bailiffs, owner-agents, and part-time solicitor superintendents, with perhaps some more professionally qualified assistance called in at highly irregular intervals when a survey or valuation was required. Through the

[1] Lancs. C.R.O., Blundell MSS, BL 54/42, Tenants Book, 1728–1806.

variations, however, a certain broad tendency may be observed, towards system and towards delegation of responsibility by the owners.

Henry Darell of Calehill, Kent, was a farmer in the late eighteenth and early nineteenth century particularly interested in improving his breed of sheep. He was also his own agent, taking farms into hand in turn, raising the quality of their cultivation, and letting them again at advanced rents to more intelligent tenants, in the meantime occasionally making rough notes which served as accounts. In the 1820s his son was still acting as agent, dealing with tenants who sought indulgence from the strict observance of articles in leases, but by the 1840s a bailiff had taken over much of the routine work and the farming appears to have been given up. Finally by the 1880s estate accounts in regular form drawn by a land agent made their appearance.[1] Richard Orlebar of Hinwick Hall, Bedfordshire, was also a farmer in the closing years of the eighteenth century, but with joy and relief gave it up in 1802. Having sold off all his live and dead stock he departed with his family to winter in Bath: 'so there ends my history of farming. So much the better!' His son returned to farming in 1832, but gave up half his land to tenants in 1847, and the rest in 1852, scarcely the obvious moments to choose for such a switch unless the social and economic pressures against direct farming had been strong. The Orlebar estate meanwhile had all along used one of the tenants as a bailiff, at £20 a year, but the great change in the quality of the accounts after 1843 speaks of the arrival of more thorough supervision.[2]

The Blundells of Little Crosby, Lancashire, with a rental of over £4,000 after 1815, retained a full-time steward at £150 a year, but he was a general factotum in charge of household, home farm and estate, and his total inability, at least down to the 1850s, to distinguish between the different classes of expenditure for which he accounted does not inspire much confidence in the quality as distinct from the honesty of his management.[3] The estate of the Harveys of Ickwell Bury was in two halves, the home estate in Bedfordshire which was under the superintendence of a local solicitor in the early nineteenth century, and the

[1] Kent C.R.O., Darell MSS, U 386/E 20, E 10, A 12, A 6, C 6, C 7, C 4.
[2] Bedford C.R.O., Orlebar MSS, OR 1701, 1372–4, 1709.
[3] Blundell MSS, BL 54/13–23.

Finningley estate in Nottinghamshire and Yorkshire, worth about £3,000 a year and under the management of an untutored steward whose lack of education may be judged from his report to John Harvey in 1803. 'I have been very porley ever since I parted with you', he wrote, 'some of the tenants for they dow give me such a character as if I was the bigest villiam that ever existed. In evrey compney thay come in thay say I have onley stoped in your sarvist wile I have ruind them all with geting thare rent rased, and if it had not bean for me Robinson said thay would have been satled as you promised him when he was at Ickwell Bury. Charles Gibin . . . said to me that he could shoot me as soon as shoot a crow and thear would be no moe sin.' Thirty years later, after a period during which the Ickwell steward had exercised a general control over the northern estate, there was a competent agent in charge at Finningley, capable of presenting a clear and properly analysed account.[1]

Great estates formed from scattered accumulations might suffer from inattention and drift because of laziness in administration, produced by the relative smallness of the component parts and infrequent supervision by the owner. Lord Sidmouth's Devon estate, worth between £3,000 and £3,500 a year, was seldom visited by its owner in the time of the first viscount, who perhaps spent a month at Up Ottery in one summer out of three on average during his lifetime, his lady frequently going off in an opposite direction during these visits to pass her summer at Walton-on-the-Naze. The supervision of the estate was left almost entirely in the hands of Flood and Mules, solicitors in Honiton, who collected the rents and left everything else to the principal tenant who acted as bailiff. Not surprisingly the second viscount found that he had inherited a sadly neglected estate in 1844, on which all had continued to run on traditional lines with never a thought of reform, and where no one had even realized that it might be desirable to take a first step towards administrative and economic efficiency by trying to sort out some of the scattered holdings into compact farms. In his father's last years the son had arranged to supplant Flood and Mules in the stewardship by another firm of local solicitors, but although these made a show of activity on the legal side in trying to get the various conditions of occupancy reduced to writing for the first time,

[1] Harvey MSS, HY 907, 900.

180

they were not equal to appreciating the agricultural requirements of the estate. The second viscount, furnished with a residence at Up Ottery from 1845, in 1850 called in a surveyor-land agent Frederick Thynne, who operated from a Great George Street address, the London centre of the leading professionals. Thynne was shocked by what he discovered: 'There could have been no sound nor valid reason for permitting a property like this to continue in so sadly neglected a state.' He reported on what needed to be done to introduce efficiency and improvement, and was at once put in charge as agent, with a resident bailiff who was not one of the tenants.[1]

The dramatic transformation in the quality of management at Up Ottery certainly illustrates the stirring consequences which might flow from an owner's entry into residence, as well as the superiority of the expert agent over the country solicitor. But while the gentry on the whole were more likely to be found on their estates for more of the time than were the aristocrats, the virtues of residence and the evils of absenteeism were too loudly sung by contemporaries, who were fond of contrasting absentee grandees and resident squires, and who confused the advantages of local employment for servants and tradesmen furnished by local households with the supposed benefits of resident supervision of tenant farmers. As in the case of Lord Sidmouth in 1850 it required an owner to realize that all was not well with the running of his estate, for if he did not dismiss incompetent agents and choose efficient ones there was no one else who would. To do this, however, an owner had to show interest in his estate, rather than prolonged residence on it. In any case resident management was to be found on the great estates with their full-time agents, and not on the smaller properties with their absentee stewards no closer than the nearest market town, and this difference more than outweighed the advantages which might arise from gentry owners living on the spot. Whether the gentry did even this very much more continuously than the magnates might be called in question, for already in the later eighteenth century it was subject for remark, by a reproving conservative, that the country was being deserted by its gentlemen. 'Since the increase of luxury, and turnpike

[1] Devon C.R.O., Sidmouth MSS, stewards' correspondence, Lady Sidmouth's scrap book 1800–40, Thynne's report on Up Ottery Estate 1850.

roads, and that all gentlemen have the gout, and all ladies the bile, it has been found necessary to fly to the bath, and to sea-bathing for relief: there the gaiety, and neat houses make them resolve upon fixing on these spots; whilst the old mansion being deserted, and no longer the seat of hospitality, and the resort of sportsmen, is left to tumble down: and, with it, the strength, the glory, and, I may add, the religion of the country.'[1] An overdrawn picture: but the railway certainly did increase the nineteenth-century squire's mobility far more than the turnpike had done, and he was likely to be away from home for consider-able stretches visiting London, the resorts, his friends or the Continent.

Management was a function vital to the state of agriculture no less than to the state of the landowner's bank balance, yet the records often reveal little about its quality, and it would be rash to base any conclusions on their silence, since so much might be carried in the owner's head or settled verbally. It was certainly not every gentleman's estate which underwent radical alterations in its administrative arrangements in the course of the nineteenth century, judging from the unchanging form of the surviving records in some cases, nor did every estate emerge from the anarchy of rentals casually drawn on loose sheets of paper and accounts roughly jotted on the backs of envelopes into the orderliness of neat ledgers. The country solicitors, in parti-cular, were never ousted altogether from their stewardships of estates. Their share of the business, however, undoubtedly con-tracted, and the signs of traditionalism and symptoms of inert and haphazard management existed alongside a tendency towards greater efficiency. The economic pressures for change were present in the shape of increasing competition in farming and increasing difficulty in maintaining rent levels, which called for greater attention and discrimination in management as well as properly directed landlords' investment, and these were rein-forced by the social pressures which made it unfashionable for a landowner to farm for profit or conduct his own bargaining with tenants. The broad movement tended to blur the distinctions in managerial structure between the estates of the gentry and aristocracy, even if inequalities persisted in the relative standards

---

[1] C. Bruyn Andrews and Fanny Andrews, ed., *The Torrington Diaries* (1954 ed.), A Tour in the Midlands 1790, pp. 272-3.

achieved. The landed gentry became more like the magnates, in their degree of detachment from the cares of their estates. But this greater identity of the landed classes was won at the cost of helping forward the disintegration of rural society. The more formal and frequent interposition of an agent between owner and tenant loosened some of the close ties between farmer and squire, and although deference to the gentry might remain, the roots of deference in a personally administered paternalism were being sapped.

VII

Landowners and
the Local Community

Tʜᴇ essence of the deference society was the habitual respect
which the upper classes, in particular the landed classes, were
accustomed to receive from the community at large. This respect
was the natural attitude of a world in which each man knew
his place and acknowledged his superiors, who were superior by
reason of their style, authoritative manner and air of gentility
and who were acknowledged as such because they claimed the
rights of their social position with self-assurance. Unthinking
respect for rank and title still survives, but in an attenuated
form which no longer carries much political significance, and the
real heart went out of deference with the passing of the age of
Trollope. The principle of inherited authority, which had been
on trial throughout the nineteenth century, was at last found
wanting by the educated public. At the same time, however,
deference had its roots in the relation of a gentleman with his
own immediate subordinates, and its weakening was much
affected, though not caused, by slow changes in these.

Deference to the landed classes had a general social basis in
habitual acceptance of aristocratic authority and a particular
economic basis in the dependence of farmers, servants and the
labouring poor on the patronage or benevolence of individual
landowners. Viewed over the long period it seems that the

184

general social basis was subjected to steady erosion from the later eighteenth century onwards, under the impact of ideas of equality refurbished from the Commonwealth and recharged by the French Revolution, and under the growing weight of economic expansion which steadily curtailed the aristocratic monopoly of wealth, education and widely travelled experience. England moved inexorably from veneration of coronets to honouring of millionaires, from nomination boroughs to universal suffrage, from tuft-hunting at Oxbridge to job-hunting at redbrick. In contrast to the steady transformation of the great world it might seem that the little world of the country house continued serenely in its patriarchal ways until in the twentieth century it was abruptly shattered by death duties, surtax, servant shortage, unionized farmers, and the break-up of estates.

A closer look, however, must blur the sharpness of such a contrast. On the one hand there has been no steady movement towards repudiation of aristocratic leadership, but an ebb and flow between the idea that the landed aristocracy constitutes a privileged vested interest and the notion that it embodies the best traditions of public service. On the other hand country house paternalism was not immune from change during the nineteenth century, and as well as fluctuations in its intensity brought about by changing market conditions it was subject to general contraction before the days of high taxation had dawned.

It can be argued, for instance, that the initial effects of industrialization, in conjunction with the fear of revolution in the early part of this period, were to strengthen the bonds of deference, as new capitalists looked to traditional authority as the only reliable guardian of order and property in a sea of unrest. Certainly the close and sympathetic relations which Earl Fitzwilliam was able to establish with a first-generation industrialist such as John Marshall in the early decades of the nineteenth century derived from a mutual interest in the preservation of rule by men of influence and high local standing. Then between 1830 and 1850 the structure of deference seemed to be on the verge of disintegration, perhaps more seriously threatened by the Corn Law controversy than by the struggle for the Reform Bill, for the persistence of purposeful businessmen in challenging the aristocratic monopoly seemed more deeply revolutionary than the violence of window-smashers in 1831 and 1832. In spite of the great advance which democratic insubordination was felt to have made in 1846, however, there followed a further twenty years of renewed social stability and revived deference, during which not even the scandals of military and administrative incompetence uncovered by the Crimean War seriously disturbed a complacent acceptance of aristocratic leadership.[1]

Bagehot in 1867 portrayed the English as essentially a 'deferential community' in which the 'rude classes at the bottom' 'defer to what we may call the theatrical show of society', and by their deference acquiesced in and welcomed the rule of the aristocratical classes. When, in 1872, he discussed the effects of the Second Reform Act Bagehot conceded that 'the middle class element has gained greatly . . . and the aristocratic element has lost greatly', but he believed that the aristocracy still had it in their power to lead the plutocracy of new wealth by skilful exploitation of deference. 'I doubt if there has ever been any [country] in which all old families and all titled families received more ready observance from those who were their equals, perhaps their superiors, in wealth, their equals in culture, and their inferiors only in descent and rank.'[2] Yet within little more than a decade of this it seemed that the habits of deference must finally fall before the voice of Birmingham demanding that the rich pay ransom for their privileges. The troubles of the 1880s, economic as well as political, did indeed deal a mortal blow to the old ideas, for what emerged at the end of the century was not the old pattern in which the plutocracy was mesmerized by the self-assurance of the aristocracy, but a partnership of wealth and title to which the rest of the world paid homage, a homage which by 1914 possessed more social reality than political utility.

In contrast to the varying respect paid to the old landed classes, the latter's relations with their immediate dependants and retainers moved in a more stately and orderly fashion, isolated from political squalls almost as much as from the corrosive influences of industrial city life, safe within a self-

---

[1] Wentworth Woodhouse MSS, G.20, Denison to Lord Fitzwilliam, 10 Aug. 1847, for a comment on the effects of 'the manner of the Triumph' of the Anti-Corn Law League.

[2] W. Bagehot, *The English Constitution* (1929 ed.), pp. 266–9, and Introduction to the Second Edition (1872) pp. xxvi, xxx.

contained traditional world. Relations with the servant class probably changed least of all, for servants on the whole were a group withdrawn from the general mass of the common people and committed to lifelong service, and were decisively influenced only by changes in the ability to recruit them or pay them. The subversive idea that service was degrading was unlikely to make any appeal to servants themselves until the long reign of abundant cheap labour had clearly ended. Relations with tenant farmers altered most frequently, for here the political effectiveness of deference was directly involved, and methods of giving it effect veered from compulsion to persuasion as ideas of what was respectable and legitimate were modified. Such changes were complicated and overlaid by a long-term rise in the social status of farmers, by short-term movements in the fortunes of agriculture which affected the relative bargaining position of tenants and landlords, and by the contrary pulls of commercial farming and semi-hereditary occupation under paternal landlords. Finally the range of landlord benevolence through charities, schools and churches perhaps underwent the most steady contraction, at first only a relative contraction as outside organizations played a growing part in these activities, and then an outright decline as both the motives and the resources for benevolence weakened.

A life of aristocratic ease no doubt depended on an adequate supply of servants, but although every member of an elaborate establishment may have had a full day's work to perform, from the butler to the groom of the chamber's boy, and from the lady's maid to the third laundry maid, it would be a mistake to suppose that the whole array was strictly functional. A great house required its forty or fifty servants not so much because this was the minimum staff requisite for comfort and convenience as because this was the maximum establishment which the owner could afford, a maximum which he was impelled to attain in order to assert his proper social standing. Servants of course were by definition deferential, and provided a constant reminder that their master was a person of consequence. They also played an important part in exacting deference from others, for through their numbers their master impressed the world with the grandeur of his style of living.

The exclusiveness of a class is strictly relative to the distance which separates it from those next below and next above, so that when in the eighteenth century more and more of the new wealthy began to imitate their superiors in keeping sizeable establishments the nobility and gentry were obliged to seek to increase the size of their own retinues in order to ward off the challenge.[1] This was only part of a general movement to make houses and households more sumptuous and expensive, and defence of status was only one of the motives for the trend towards more conspicuous consumption. The Grand Tour with its aftermath of Continental ideas was one influence, and rivalry among the great themselves another, which together acted as spurs to extravagance. The rise in the scale of living, measured by the number of servants retained, was damped down or even halted during the Napoleonic Wars, under the concurrent influences of patriotism, increases in the assessed taxes on such key items as men-servants, horses and carriages, and some diversion of resources to the lucrative business of lending to government. This of course did not mean that the household bills did not rise, for wage and price increases ensured that a static level of consumption cost more. Farington was informed in 1806 that the cost of keeping a 'genteel establishment' had about doubled in the previous twenty-eight years, but household accounts like those of Earl Fitzwilliam indicate a much smaller rise of between a quarter and a third in costs between 1790 and 1815. Wage bills which in this case moved from about £1,800 to £2,300 indicate if anything a slightly contracting establishment, since the rates of both wages and board wages increased by more than a quarter in this period.[2]

After the wars those with long purses resumed the race in the favourable climate of lower wages and prices, and the period down to the 1830s may be regarded as witnessing the final effort to outdistance the new wealthy. At Gorhambury the domestic establishment had grown by the middle 1820s from about thirty to about forty servants, and the complement of a magnate of the first rank like Fitzwilliam was at least twice as large. Wage rates were cut back by 5 to 15 per cent at the beginning of

[1] J. J. Hecht, *The Domestic Servant Class in Eighteenth-Century England* (1956), p.2.
[2] *Farington Diary*, III. 280. Northants. C.R.O., Fitzwilliam MSS, General Accounts 1788–1829. Similar results are obtainable from the Raby accounts. Although the totals of different years are comparable, it is not clear in either case whether they record all the servants employed.

the 1820s, one butler for example falling from £50 a year to £43 15s. in 1822, and footmen having pounds substituted for guineas. Nevertheless Lord Fitzwilliam's wage bills moved up to a peak of over £3,000 in 1825, and at Raby the Earl of Darlington's wage bills similarly moved up from about £2,500 to the £3,000 level in 1823–5.[1] Such was the background below stairs to the great social entertainments and the grand battues of the 1820s.

The race was won by the grandees, it might be thought, since only in the spacious setting of the great country houses could establishments of fifty or a hundred be fitted in, so that the new wealthy had perforce either to become landed magnates themselves or give up the contest. It is certainly true that from the 1830s onwards the expansion of aristocratic establishments was generally halted, but the reason was not that the middle-class challenge had been warded off, for this challenge was in fact increasing all the time. At Gorhambury for example the number of servants fell to about thirty-five in the 1830s, was sharply cut down to a little over twenty for a few years after the second earl's succession in 1846, in a fit of economy, and then settled down from the early 1850s at between thirty-three and thirty-seven, at which level it continued until the 1880s. At Raby the cost of servants was cut back to around £2,000 by the middle of the 1840s, more by drastic savings on board wages and liveries than by any reduction in the straightforward wage bill, and it was held at this level until in the early 1870s the establishment was reduced to a little over one-third of its former size.[2]

The halt came for a variety of reasons. For many, no doubt, a limit had been reached and finance would stand no more. The second Earl of Verulam certainly felt this, anxiously making his money calculations in his diary, commending frugality and looking for openings for economies, resolved not to follow his father's habit of borrowing in order to maintain a grand style.

[1] Herts. C.R.O., Verulam MSS, XI. 81, Assessments to Assessed Taxes, and Gorhambury MSS, 1st Earl's Diary, allowing that female servants were proportionate to the taxed male servants. Fitzwilliam MSS, General Accounts 1788–1829. Raby MSS, Household accounts 1790–1830. Castle Hill MSS, personal accounts of Lord Fortescue 1790–1828.
[2] Verulam MSS, XI. 115 and XI. 121, Consumption Registers 1847–86, and Gorhambury MSS, 1st Earl's Diary and Attendance Register 1870–86. Raby MSS, Household Accounts 1830–80.

Not quite everyone, however, had reached the limit of his resources: the very rich, like the Bentincks, Grosvenors or Percies, could have afforded to go on expanding their outlay on servants, but for them the point of decreasing returns, either in the form of personal comfort or of social enhancement, had been well passed. These, who could scarcely prevent their surplus incomes from growing faster than their spending habits, turned instead either to the ultimate paradox in conspicuous investment, the expensively concealed excavations of Welbeck, or to the successfully balanced personal, agricultural and social investments of the fourth Duke of Northumberland. For many more, perhaps, it seemed wisest after the finery of the 1820s and the shocks of the Reform crisis that the aristocracy should not call too much attention to itself. There was a marked decline, for instance, in the profusion of servants' liveries; Raby, where the outlay fell from £636 in 1822 to an average £50 a year in the 1840s and 1850s, is a case in point. The indoor servants of course remained in liveries, such as the gorgeous blue, white and gold of the Percy footmen which made a deep impression on Prescott when he stayed at Alnwick in 1850.[1] But with the advance of railway travel there was much less occasion for the display of the gay liveries of postilions.

Railway travel was a convenience to the aristocracy, who could move their plate and servants back and forth between the country and London, with ease, as much as to the rest of the population. It even incorporated the marks of deference into the new system, the special treatment which stationmasters reserved for the great, or the special halts which companies sometimes undertook to make, as with the 'two up first class trains and two down first class trains' which the G.W.R. agreed to stop at a special station at Great Bedwyn 'at such times as the Marquess of Ailesbury or his heirs shall select from each fresh timetable.'[2] But railway travel also had a tendency to cut the aristocracy down to life size: 'the last Duke of St David's used to cover the north road with his carriages; landladies and waiters bowed before him. The present Duke sneaks away from a railway

---

[1] G. Ticknor, *Life of William Hickling Prescott* (1863), p. 304.
[2] Savernake MSS, Misc. Deeds, Marquess of Ailesbury and the G.W.R. 15 April 1846.

station, smoking a cigar, in a brougham.'[1] It may also have tended to curtail establishments, as families travelled with three or four servants and left grooms, coachmen and postilions behind. To the more serious the railway epitomized the quickening challenge from industrial growth and the middle classes, and helped to persuade them that both opportunity and necessity pointed to the careful management and increase of their resources as the first line of defence of their order. But in turning from pomp and circumstance to investment and income as the bulwarks of status such aristocrats were already moving towards conceding that it was wealth pure and simple which counted, not birth and tradition. That was the way to welcome the plutocracy within the gates.

Not every aristocrat kept an imposing establishment, for prudence sometimes overrode convention. The sixth Lord Monson was always regretting his impoverished inheritance. Because he had succeeded a cousin in 1841 he had inherited the family estates but not his cousin's personal fortune, and he found it very hard to make ends meet on the rents alone, which were reduced by jointures and debts to about £6,000 or £7,000 a year. One expedient was the utmost frugality in the household, and although he might muster an attendance of about forty at the annual servants' ball this number included his servants' friends, and he managed with a domestic staff of little more than ten. One of the most startling economies was in the stable department. In 1855 Lord Monson wrote regretfully to his eldest son, 'I would help you more if I could, but we are obliged to keep up so many servants in these large houses – housekeeping is quite doubled in cost since I first returned to England in 1845 – and yet you know I keep no horses – I doubt if there is another peer in England without.' A little later he repeated 'what a pity it is the Dowager runs away with so much of our income – two thousand a year more (less income tax) would make all the difference with us of comfort or pinching. I even think after a few extra comforts that we ought to have such as carriage horses and coachman, and a few other things I could not only help you on better but might at least for a few years lay by a few hundreds . . .'. Some not very smart form of

---

[1] Quoted by Bagehot, *The English Constitution*, p. 94.

transport was of course kept at Burton, but visitors were often met with hired carriages, or they might be unluckier still, like Lord and Lady Denman who 'have just trudged on foot from Lincoln.'[1]

The Monsons were very much aware that their reduced circumstances had withdrawn them from the authentically aristocratic way of living, but although a stroke of good fortune like the dowager's death might be earmarked in the imagination as the remedy, it is interesting that any actual surplus in the 1850s was carefully directed into farm improvements. Social pressures were not irresistible, and the Monsons gave every indication of managing happily with a domestic establishment of about the size that a plain country gentleman might keep. The Harveys of Ickwell Bury, indeed, kept about a dozen servants in the 1820s, but only four of them were men since money went a good deal further on women servants. This staff was under the general control of a steward receiving £40 a year, who supervized the house, stables, gardens and home farm, and the immediate management of a house-keeper who was paid £26 5s. a year and had her own private sitting room. The Harveys were running a fair-sized house with a dozen principal bedrooms, and on the other side of the country in Lancashire a similarly situated family also with about £5,000 a year, the Blundells of Little Crosby, likewise kept an establishment of a dozen to fourteen servants, with a wage bill running at £260 to £290 a year, somewhat ahead of the Harveys'. In Cumberland in the 1840s the Senhouses of Netherhall, not so well off with barely £3,000 a year but still running a house with nine best beds and eleven servants' beds, kept a domestic staff of eight, including however only two men-servants, besides a gardener and boy, at a wage bill of £160 a year. This was almost precisely matched by the Orlebars in Bedfordshire, with the same gross income and a servants' wage bill of £150 to £200 a year, settling down at around £160 in the 1850s. At about the same time a member of the lesser gentry such as Brooks of Flitwick, with a gross income of £1,630 a year in the

---

[1] Lincs. C.R.O., Monson MSS, Correspondence, 25/10/2/3 no. 79, 27 Jan. 1849; 25/10/4/1 no. 115, 15 Feb. 1855; no. 14, 26 Nov. 1855; 25/10/4/4 no. 23. 17 Oct. 1858.

1830s, kept a house with seven principal bedrooms and three servants' bedrooms with a domestic staff of six, who were paid £118 a year.[1]

Although there was thus clearly a correlation between income, status and size of establishment, it was not by any means a direct one: the Duke of Northumberland whose income was eighty times larger than Brooks's did not keep anywhere near eighty times as many servants. Staff, of which a gentleman needed five or six at the least, was therefore likely to be a relatively heavier burden on the less wealthy. There were various ways, however, by which the cost per servant worked out lower for the gentry than for the aristocracy. One cardinal point was the more regular residence of the gentry, which not only reduced wastefulness and dishonesty, but also meant that servants were not so frequently put on board wages, which were thought to be extravagant and open to abuse. A very general saving resulted from the lower proportion of men which it was usual to find in gentry households. Male servants were not only more expensive and impressive than women, but were inevitably more numerous in the larger establishments to service the stables and carriages of the great. In one particular the discrepancy between the sexes was most marked. It was fashionable for the great to employ a male cook, preferably French, and he was often by far the highest paid member of the staff, with a salary which properly recognized his professional status. At Belvoir in the early nineteenth century, for example, while the house steward received a steady £84 a year, Marcham the cook was raised from £147 in 1810 to £161 14s. in 1814. The Duke of Portland, by his will in 1809, 'has left £100 a year for life to his French cook, exclusive of income tax, who has since been taken into the service of the Prince of Wales, at a salary of £200 a year'. Those who were content with the less talented services of a female cook could have one for 16 guineas a year, like the Harveys in 1820, or for

---

[1] Beds. C.R.O., Harvey MSS, HY 877, Servants' Wages 1819–20; HY 636, lease of Ickwell Bury House 8 Nov. 1823. Lancs. C.R.O., Blundell MSS, BL 54/16, 54/18, 54/21, steward's accounts 1832–45. Cumberland C.R.O., Senhouse MSS, 19/165, statement of income and expenditure 1847. Beds. C.R.O., Orlebar MSS, OR 1376, and OR 1377, household and estate accounts 1838–62. Lyall (Brooks) MSS, LL 17/234, statement of income and expenditure 1836; LL 17/284, a description of Flitwick House and grounds 1838.

the £21 which the Brooks paid in 1836, rising only to £22 a year in 1890.[1]

Service in the very great houses was considered more distinguished, and was more sought after, than service with the plain gentry, and one reason was the higher pay. A nobleman's butler, indeed, with his £40 or £60 a year, was paid considerably more than a gentleman's butler with £25 to £35 in the early nineteenth century. But for the lower servants the greater attractions and better prospects for advancement of the greater houses might well mean the acceptance of a lower differential. When he was asked to pay six guineas a year for a housemaid in 1800 Christopher Blundell thought it 'a very great wage for a girl so young and only knows a farmer's place. I never gave more than £4 10s. till Mary came, and I was not pleased when Molly had engaged her at £5.' Humphrey Senhouse in 1810 imported a woman from Newcastle to be a ladies' maid at 14 guineas a year. These rates were not far below the 1810 Belvoir rates of £8 to 9 guineas for housemaids and kitchenmaids, and 20 guineas for 'Her Grace's Woman'. The Flitwick kitchen and housemaids at £8 and £12 in 1836 were not paid noticeably less than the Gorhambury maids who received from £10 to 14 guineas in 1847.[2]

Service in general was valued for the security which it offered, the usually good living conditions – the meat allowance at Gorhambury being 1½ lbs per head per day – the left-overs of food and clothes, and the chance to enjoy some of the reflected glory of the employer's social position. These were advantages which continued to attract the children of farmers, labourers and country tradesmen into service throughout the nineteenth century. Wages it is plain were not the sole attraction, but neither were they the only monetary reward, since some of the perquisites came in cash. There may have been a determined effort by the gentry in the late eighteenth century to stamp out the practice of exacting vails, the fees extracted from departing

[1] Belvoir MSS, House Steward's accounts 1810–15. *Farington Diary*, V. 297. Harvey MSS, HY 877. Lyall (Brooks) MSS, LL 17/234, LL 17/278, account book 1888–93.

[2] Blundell MSS, BL 12/1, C. Blundell to J. Spencer 27 March 1800. Senhouse MSS, 19/34, W. Elliott to H. Senhouse, 19 Nov. 1810. Belvoir MSS, House Steward's accounts 1810. Lyall (Brooks) MSS, LL 17/234. Gorhambury MSS, 2nd Earl of Verulam's Diary, 1847.

guests by each servant according to his degree, but tipping most certainly continued to flourish. As with vails, the more peremptory methods of demanding admission fees from callers as of right may have died out. Lord Verulam was surprised as well as annoyed when he had to give 5 guineas in 1809 because 'having been presented yesterday the following persons requested presents, Yeomen of the Guard, eight Marshals, Porters at St James's, Porters at Queen's House, twelve Footmen. I should not like my servants to go regularly about asking others to pay their wages.' In 1811 he again angrily recorded paying 2 guineas to 'Carlton House servants not paid by their own master.' Nevertheless a porter's situation remained enviable, and in general tips, swelling servants' incomes to an unknown amount, were bound to be more plentiful the greater the house and the more elevated the station of the owner.[1]

Servants' wages varied a great deal with the situation, skill and length of service of the individual, but after the generally marked rise of the period 1795–1815 and the slight fall in the early 1820s a period of stability seems to have followed. This appears to have been broken in the 1860s, when rates generally began to move upwards again, perhaps more under the influence of intensified competition for good servants than because of multiplication of opportunities for alternative employment. Lord Verulam hired a butler for 60 guineas a year in 1847; in 1864 he had to offer 80 guineas, and in 1868 £90. The Flitwick housemaid's rate, which was £12 a year in the 1830s, had grown to £16 in the 1880s, and in the same period the rate for the ladies' maid doubled from £12 to £24, though the butler only moved up from £35 to £40. By the end of the 1880s rising wages and falling rentals were obliging some landowners, though not by any means all, to cut their establishments, and one could see the halcyon days of abundant service beginning to draw to their close.[2]

It was also in the 1880s that a number of circumstances combined to give a decisive push to the growth of farmers'

<hr />

[1] Hecht, *Domestic Servant Class*, pp. 158–168. Verulam MSS, XI. 81, General Accounts 1809–11.
[2] Gorhambury MSS, 2nd Earl's Diary 1847, 1856, 1868, 1889. Lyall (Brooks) MSS, LL 17/234, 17/278, Account book 1888–93.

independence and to the decay of that essential pillar of landed society, the deferential tenant. Gladstonian legislation on Ground Game and Agricultural Holdings marked for the first time the compulsory intervention of the law in the supposedly voluntary bargains made between tenants and landlords, and set in motion the process which culminated in the state declaring that the tenant farmer had a species of proprietary interest in his farm as well as the owner. The Third Reform Act, by flooding the electorates of rural constituencies with agricultural labourers, destroyed any special numerical importance which the farmers' votes had enjoyed, and somewhat weakened the landowners' political motives for wishing to exercise a strong influence over the farmers. Finally, and most important of all, the economic climate was definitely one of grave depression for cereal farmers and of varying degrees of difficulty for most farmers. Survival, if it could be won at all, depended on great resourcefulness and willingness to adapt old methods, but very often old hereditary tenant families were swept away in the first onrush of falling prices, and newcomers arrived without any traditional ties to an estate. One effect of the altered balance between landlord and tenant was that the instruments of landlord control over farming practices lost their force as tenants simply ignored their husbandry covenants. In more general terms, many landowners were only too thankful to keep their farms tenanted at almost any price, and the market had swung full circle from the days when tenants eagerly competed for farms to the days when farms were begging for tenants.

As always, farmers were attached to the familiar ways and were reluctant to face the fact of their greater independence. In a sense they had to be forced to be free by harsh economic facts, as the shelter traditionally provided by landlords through rent reductions and investment in farm equipment turned out to be inadequate, as well as being beyond the capacity of some owners to provide. An early reaction, for example, was the attempt in 1892 to organize the farming interest on a national scale on the old model of an association patronized by the great landowners and incorporating representatives of the farmers and labourers. This, the National Agricultural Union led by Lord Winchilsea, was markedly less successful in promoting the interests of farmers than less ambitious associations such as the Central

Chamber of Agriculture.[1] Well over another decade was to elapse before farmers generally realized that they had to fend for themselves, and at last abandoning their attachment to the landowners which had for so long kept them in the 'house union' stage of organization in the farmers' clubs and local agricultural societies, the National Farmers' Union was launched.

The ingrained reluctance of the majority of farmers to throw off their leading-strings was a crucial factor in the long continuance of tenant-deference, or what an outside critic like the *Economist* called 'modern feudalism'.[2] There had been many times before the 1880s when tenants had held the whip-hand and owners had had the utmost difficulty in letting all their farms. In the crises of 1834–5 or 1850–1, for example, tenants had it in their power to drive hard bargains, for it was only the few affluent owners who could afford to take a farm in hand, stock it, and risk running it at a loss for a few years, sooner than yield to extortionate demands. The Earl of Pembroke could afford to do this for a couple of years after 1834, and the loss of one-tenth of the capital of £5,400 which he had to lay out to stock a farm taken into hand was considered well worth while. 'It has been good policy to hold out and not yield to the offers of £700, 750 and 800 which were made [for a farm previously let at £950] which would have meant all the other tenants asking for reductions. It has shown that his lordship will not hesitate to keep a farm in hand rather than underlet it.' Lord Monson was differently and perhaps more typically situated when he wrote in 1850 that his steward, Brown, had 'been in a dreadful taking about this farm on our hands and it has worried me much. He had promised to look out for someone to manage it, but he owned it would be a dreadful pull to take it in hand and stock it – however at the eleventh hour he got a Mr Coupland to make a proposition to take it but at a great diminution of rent, he only offers £550 per an. and he requires a certain quantity of land drained for which he offers to pay £4 per cent. The old rent was £760 . . . however rather than have the farm on my

[1] A. H. H. Matthews, *Fifty Years of Agricultural Politics, 1865–1915* (1915), pp. 379–82.

[2] Many references in the 1850s and 1860s; for example *Economist*, 1 Feb. 1851, p. 116, 20 Feb. 1864, p. 230.

hands I have agreed . . . Brown thinks anything better than taking it in hand.'[1]

It is significant that on these occasions it seems to have been purely a rent question which was at stake. It did not appear to occur to either party that tenants might choose to exploit their strong position by defying landlords over, for example, game preservation, let alone on political matters. On the plain financial side of their relationship Lord Monson for one thought that his 'atrocious tenants' were a poor lot, 'leeches' lacking in energy or intellect, but still able to bully the agent mercilessly and force their landlord into granting abatements, because 'I must keep my tenants in some sort of good humour, I never could compass more farms being thrown up at once'. At the same time he never doubted that his tenants would continue to observe his wishes politically in supporting the Whig cause, and in the 1852 election received proof that they remained dutiful, since one of the candidates reported to Lord Monson that his tenants when canvassed 'say that they have received no directions how to act and therefore cannot promise'.[2] One reason for this state of affairs was that the periods when the advantage lay with tenants were relatively brief and infrequent, and the more normal situation was one in which there was keen competition for farms, particularly on good estates under generous landlords, and sitting tenants were not willing to run any risks of losing them. Scarth in the later 1850s and 1860s kept long waiting lists of applicants for farms on the Cleveland estates, both in Durham and Shropshire, and by the 1860s even Lord Monson was able to be selective in the choice of new tenants.

The more potent reason, however, was that even the fiercest financial bargaining between landlord and tenant took place within the framework of a traditional and accepted social order. It was not that landlord and tenant relations were kept in separate compartments, economic affairs not being permitted to impinge on social and political matters, nor was it a case of landowners continually and forcefully reminding tenants of their

---

[1] Wilton MSS, Memo. Book 1834–40, Dec. 1834 and Dec. 1837. Monson MSS, 25/10/2/4 no. 98, 27 March 1850.

[2] Monson MSS, 25/10/2/3 no. 5, 7 Dec. 1849; 25/10/2/4 no. 78, 13 June 1850; 25/10/3/1 no. 20, 17 Nov. 1851, no. 19, 22 Nov. 1851; 25/10/3/2 no. 77b, 2 March 1852.

inferiority and dependence. Rather was it a matter of the loyalties of a large family, the very paternalism to which the organs of the middle class so much objected. Struggles over rents, or game, or leases were domestic to an estate; to the outside world it presented a united front, and it was more natural and even rational for an unsophisticated tenantry to trust the political wisdom and wishes of worldly-wise landowners than it is for modern mass electorates to trust a television image. Acts of defiance or rebellion by tenants came, not when they felt they could afford to flout landlord power because its economic basis had weakened, but on the rare occasions when some issue close to their lives caused them to doubt whether their landlord's views could be trusted.

In 1832 Earl Fitzwilliam faced just this situation when seventy-six of his Irish tenants asked to be excused from voting again for the return of James Grattan for County Wicklow, on the grounds that he was turning out to be a pro-Catholic M.P. Though he ordered his Irish agent not to take any pains to see that these recalcitrants were entered on the new voting register, he made it clear to them that 'it is not for me to dictate to any man the mode in which he will exercise his franchise . . . or to injure any man in consequence of a vote conscientiously given, though that vote may not have been given in conformity with my wishes.' Fitzwilliam's to letter Grattan showed that this freedom of choice did genuinely exist. 'I foresee great difficulties in making what is called our interest effective in your favor. . . . In old times an Irish landlord would have merely consulted the registry, counted up the freeholders upon his own estate, compared them with those on others, and if there was a preponderance on his own and on those of his friends, the matter would have been settled, and the candidate who had such and such interests was sure of being elected. This will not do now, and in order to carry the freeholders with us, we must ask them to vote for somebody that they like to vote for . . . [hence] 'you should endeavour to ascertain as well as you can what are the inclinations both of tenants and of landlords generally through the county, not setting down such a landlord as worth so many votes and such another as worth so many, but rather considering what are the inclinations of the people. This will enable you to form a more accurate judgement of your prospects of success than you can derive from any declarations which I and a few others of the same class may make in your favour, for as I have suggested before I think it by no means certain that we can carry our people with us. The Catholics and the Anti-Tithe people we could carry for you, but I should be extremely sorry to see the great bulk of our Protestant tenantry voting against you, and your election carried by Priests and Tithe Robbers, or vice versa to see you defeated by the votes of our own tenants throwing themselves into the hands of Lord Wicklow and the Conservatives.'[1]

In Ireland religious issues were very deeply felt, but if eviction could not be contemplated as a political weapon in Ireland of all places, it is most unlikely that landowners of Fitzwilliam's stamp would be less squeamish towards their English tenantry. Differently-minded landlords, however, certainly continued to exercise pressure on their tenants, though in truth no landowner could ever afford to contemplate a mass eviction of his substantial tenants, so that in any pronounced difference of views the tenants, if united, were in the last resort bound to be irresistible. These political facts of life were well understood, particularly perhaps by the gentry, who whatever their private views on an issue like the Corn Laws tended to bend before the strong feelings of their tenants. Only a minority of the country gentry were Whigs in any case, and of them not a few were reluctant to tamper with protection. But even an aristocrat like Lord Monson, traditional Whig and sound on free trade, suspected that many of his tenants had been infected by talk 'about the loss of protection to native industry and such stuff' which has been put into their heads by interested politicians, and has done more harm to real industry than can well be conceived', yet felt unable to counteract the mischief.[2]

In normal times it was universally accepted that tenants voted with their landlords, and it was a binding convention of electioneering to write to the principal landowners soliciting the support of their interest, just as it was considered only prudent and polite to ask the permission of a landlord before canvassing his tenants. In the County Durham contest of 1820 it was noted on the Powlett side that 'owing to almost all engaged in this

---

[1] Fitzwilliam MSS, Letter book, 732, 23 Aug., 10 Sept., and 17 Sept. 1832.
[2] Monson MSS, 25/10/2/4 no. 39, 23 Sept. 1850.

contest being novices' certain cardinal points of electioneering had been 'grossly neglected'. High among the steps to be taken in any future election was the resolve to 'solicit either personally or by letter all the country gentlemen to embark in your cause and canvass for you', and a working list was drawn up of all the gentlemen with considerable property who 'ought always to be addressed by letter on the eve of a contest'.[1] When Earl Fitz-william went through this drill in the 1848 West Riding election, sending out 110 letters to the principal landowners requesting their support for his younger son Charles, the only surprise was that among all the usual replies promising to exert all influence and interest on his behalf there were quite a number offering a personal vote only, and stating that tenants were left free to choose. Sir W. Pilkington, for example, said that he never interfered with his tenants' votes, Sir J. Copley wrote similarly 'as far as my own vote is concerned I will support your son against any Radical or person of the Cobden school. With regard to my tenants I always leave them to vote as they like.' Even the Duke of Leeds answered that 'I have particularly assured my tenants that I will not in any way interfere with their opinions in the choice of their representatives.'[2]

The decline of voting by landlord's instructions, which Fitz-william had noted in 1832, can here be seen at work. The decline was doubtless slow, and was not felt to have gone very far by 1869, at the time of the inquiry which preceded the Ballot Act, when the Cheshire witness knew of only two landowners who had publicly stated that their tenants could vote as they pleased. The Select Committee on this occasion reported that it was certain 'that an influence, exceeding in a greater or less degree the legitimate influence which a popular and respected landlord must always exercise in his neighbourhood, is often brought to bear on tenant farmers, and other voters in agricultural districts. . . . The inducement to vote with the landlord', they concluded, 'may frequently proceed rather from the hope of future advantages to be conferred than from the fear of injury

---

[1] Raby MSS, Memoranda made during the Canvass of Co. Durham with Mr Powlett in 1820.
[2] Wentworth Woodhouse MSS, G.7, letter book of 1848 West Riding election, G.7.d, letters from prospective supporters of Hon Charles Fitzwilliam's candidature, nos. 93, 119, 121.

to be inflicted'. As late as 1904 it was supposed that when the Guest family reverted to Liberalism from Conservatism, over the free trade issue, their tenantry would change sides with them. Until 1904, the election trial judge remarked in 1910, 'whatever proper influence might be brought to bear, and it would be a poor thing for this country if those possessing wealth, position, and so forth, should not exercise some influence upon those who are, I was going to say under them, but in these days one ought not even to say that, but subject to their influence, in those days, up to 1904, I suppose whatever influence could be exercised properly and fairly with regard to the neighbours and tenants of the Wimborne estate, would be exercised in favour of the Conservative cause; but after 1904 the same influence would be exercised with regard to the opposite party.'[1]

Tenants were certainly anxious not to displease their landlords, and if left without guidance at an approaching contest might ask that their landlord's wishes should be made known. Their dutiful voting was partly a matter of prudence and partly a matter of accepted custom based on loyalty rather than fear. Contemporaries were much excited by the issue of landlord influence, but we need accept neither the view that it worked only through the threat of coercion nor that it never caused a tenant to vote against his convictions. The unanimity of voting on any one estate was astonishing, and the human race was not divided at birth into Whigs and Tories, so that Tory landowners could be certain of choosing only Tory tenants. Hereditary tenancies, however, did have something of that effect, and where they existed the chances of an individual violating his political convictions were perhaps least. The prevalence of this feature should not be overestimated. On the Fitzwilliam estates it might well be in the 1820s that 'the known and established rules of succession' were 'the boast and pride of the tenantry'. But on the Wilton estate, for example, only a quarter of the tenants in 1875 had been on their farms for twenty years or longer, while on the Northumberland estate in 1880 some 6 per cent of the 673 farms had been in the same family for three generations,

---

[1] *Parliamentary Papers*, 1868–9, VIII, S.C. on Parliamentary and Municipal Elections, Minutes of Evidence, Q. 6424, 6432, 6451–2. 1870, VI, Report, p. 5. *Parliamentary Papers*, 1910, LXXIII, Judgment on Trial of Election Petition for Dorset, E. Div., pp. 2–3.

and one-half of the sitting tenants had succeeded to their fathers' farms.[1] In such cases it was a fair assumption that the son also inherited his father's politics.

In the rare instances when a landlord changed his politics, as on the Wimborne estate in 1904, the chances of coercion were greatest, but even then the pressure was no more direct than the agent's presence at the polling booth to see that the tenants did vote. English landlords, indeed, seldom evicted tenants for political reasons, although a suitable instrument for the purpose lay ready to hand in the prevalent annual tenancies. Radicals and advocates of agricultural leases argued that the simple existence of tenancies-at-will was sufficient sanction for dutiful voting, so that actual eviction was unnecessary, and that the prevalence of these tenancies was chiefly due to political motives. The force of this argument cannot be ignored, but it requires qualification in several directions. There were powerful economic reasons for the spread of annual tenancies, and they were con-solidated as the normal form of tenure before the enfranchise-ment of the £50 tenants-at-will in 1832. No evidence was ever produced to show that the leasehold farmers of Norfolk, for example, were more independent politically than annual tenants, or that annual tenants felt that their practical security of tenure was peculiarly dependent on satisfactory political behaviour. In any case leasehold farmers were not immune from virtual eviction, and the most famous political eviction of the century, the Timpendean case, concerned a Scottish tenant holding under a long lease which was not renewed, because of political defiance of his landlord, the Marquess of Lothian.[2]

In the 'Celtic fringe', indeed, political evictions were not uncommon, but clearly the difference in this respect between Welsh and Irish farmers, and English farmers, was not due to tenurial differences, for all were likely to be annual tenants. The reason w. ; that there were social and religious barriers between landlord and tenant in Wales and Ireland which had no parallel in England. Although the Welsh may perhaps be more fiery

[1] Wentworth Woodhouse MSS, F.107k, W. Allen to Lord Fitzwilliam, April 1823. *V.C.H. Wiltshire*, IV. 107. Alnwick MSS, Business Minutes LXXIV, 11 Sept. 1880.

[2] S.C. on Parliamentary and Municipal Elections, 1868–9, Q. 7283–8054. See below, pp. 230–1. On landlord influence generally, see H. J. Hanham, *Elections and Party Management*, pp. 6–14, 32.

and unruly than the English, there seems no good reason to suppose that the English annual tenant was so supine that he would not have been ready to court eviction as readily as his Welsh counterpart if he had faced equally burning issues. In normal times, however, there were no burning issues dividing English tenants from their landlords. Where there were differences – over game, leases, or land laws – it was a perpetual source of disappointment and mystery to Radicals that farmers generally declined to treat them as critical issues.

Most English tenants did not have strong political views, or as a witness put it in 1869, 'do not care the least about politics'. This was inevitable when county politics were left to the domination of landlords, and were not a matter of choice between policies but of choice between persons, both of whom were likely to be members of the same landed class. This choice excited the liveliest interest of the landlords but was more or less a matter of indifference to the tenants. In this atmosphere it was unlikely to trouble a tenant's conscience when he voted in accordance with his landlord's wishes. Politics were left to the landowners not simply because tenant farmers had no other choice, but also because they usually trusted the political opinions of their landlords. The tenant farmers were certainly aware that they depended on the goodwill of their landlords, just as they were aware of loyalty to an estate as a social community. When the means of enforcing this dependence were weakened by the ballot, however, it made little difference to the nature of county politics. When the dependence itself was lessened by the Depression, when the idea of resort to pressure became less respectable, and when national politics became concerned with great issues, it remained likely that tenants and landlords would vote the same way. This likelihood was increased after the secession of the Liberal Unionists, for henceforth most landowners supported the same party, which had always managed to present itself as the true friend of the farming interest. By the end of the century tenants were less subservient than they had been, but support for their landlord's views which was now more freely given meant that the decline in the coercive element produced only a limited practical effect.

Political interest also played a very large part in the contributions of the great landlords to the poor of those places where they had both property and a political stake. In a proprietary borough like Malton, with a scot-and-lot franchise, many of the poorer tenements occupied by labourers avowedly existed only because votes were attached to them, and their votes were cast not out of tenurial attachment to Earl Fitzwilliam, but because he footed the bill for bribing them. After 1832 the scot-and-lot voters were a dying breed, but as long as any lived it was necessary to continue the treating in order to carry Malton. As the agent reported in 1847, 'it has hitherto been customary here on a General Election to entertain the Principal Electors at the Talbot Inn and one of the other inns (not limiting the expence), and the majority of the Electors with dinners at other inns at a cost of about 20s. each, but, since [the Act of 1842 against bribery and treating] a different course was taken, and at Lord Milton's election a friendly committee undertook the entire management of the treating, without my intervention, and without the presumed knowledge of the candidate – and I do not think it will be prudent or advisable on the present occasion to omit the like kind of treat . . . the scot and lot, and innkeepers (the only parties that care much about the treating) being almost enabled to turn the scale at an election. Every year their influence is decreased.'[1] Such expenses, reduced by this time to £370 from a pre-Reform £520 on the election of a single member, were naturally recorded as election expenses in the Fitzwilliam accounts.

The gift of £200 to Malton at every election, however, 'a customary payment for public improvements in the town', might easily slip into the category of a benefaction, in spite of its electoral purpose. While the 'annual payments to the charities etc. in the town, which amount to £100 or £120 a year', were accounted for as charitable payments even though they were acknowledged to be part of the cost of keeping up the Fitzwilliam interest. On the same pattern the Malton agent suggested in 1837 that Earl Fitzwilliam should make 'an unsolicited contribution' of £100 to the Methodists who were trying to liquidate the debt on their chapel, and thus 'rivet this large body to your interest'. Even rent reductions for the humblest cottagers, in pre-Reform times, were undertaken with political

---

[1] Wentworth Woodhouse MSS, G. 33, W. Allen to Lord Fitzwilliam, 24 June 1847, and Fitzwilliam MSS, do. to do., 24 June 1847.

interests in mind. Thus it was argued of this class of tenantry in 1818 that 'one consequence of the want of employment is, that they are driven to ask for relief of the Parish officer and thereby disqualify themselves for voting at an election. Every person paying scot and lot during half a year previous to an election and not receiving relief from the parish is entitled to vote. All the tenants down as low as 40s. and £3 are rated to the relief of the poor in order to qualify them to vote, and it is a material object that they should not lose their qualification. . . . An abatement of the rents of tenantry whose tenements are under £15 would be the means of enabling them to pay their parochial rates and would also secure their votes and interest in case of necessity. It would be the surest means of keeping out any opponents in the borough, for with the support of this class of tenantry I do not conceive it would be in the power of any other person to come into the borough with any chance of success.' Similar arguments for rent reductions, in order to calm 'a spirit of hostility to your lordship's interest which strongly pervades the minds' of the small tenants, were applied to 'the small farmers who principally occupy the land upon Old Malton Moor . . . who in addition to their small farms work for hire. The land is of a very inferior description and unproductive. They have likewise been deprived of the means of earning much by working for hire as those articles they have been in the habit of carrying now find their way up the country by means of the New Navigation from this place to Yeddington Bridge'.[1]

Other Fitzwilliam boroughs, Peterborough and Higham Ferrers, could also only be managed by extensive treating at elections, of voters and 'the populace' alike on different scales of liberality. Strong-arm methods too might be necessary, and as late as 1853 the accounts record 'paid Robert Richardson, solicitor of Oundle, for services performed by him when G. C. Lewis was a candidate for Peterborough, upon the retainer of J. D. Simpson, when amongst other things it was deemed advisable to get rid of Peter Vanderan (a voter) on the day of the election, and he was sent to London, this charge includes the expenses attendant thereon: £6 15s.' But maintenance of the patron's interest between elections called for proper attention to

[1] Wentworth Woodhouse MSS, G 33, W. Allen to Lord Fitzwilliam, 6 Feb. 1837; F.107k, W. Allen to Lord Fitzwilliam, Feb. 1818.

local charities, gifts to the poor, and pensions, and the level of these annual benefactions turned down sharply at Higham after its disfranchisement in 1832. At Peterborough, apart from the usual annual subscriptions, it was customary to make annual payments of 5s. each to the voters who paid scot and lot, and 1s. 6d. each to the 'poor housekeepers' who did not pay scot and lot. The tariff remained unchanged throughout the period from the 1790s until the accounts cease to record the payments in 1855. The number of 5s. people declined steadily after the loss of their special privileges in 1832, from 1,242 in 1831 to 140 in 1852; but the 1s. 6d. people, who had never had votes, grew equally steadily from 375 in 1831 to 583 in 1853, it being always important to propitiate the non-voters in order to prevent ugly scenes. At Grantham likewise the Duke of Rutland gave the 600-odd freemen 5s. each every year. These payments, as well as the refreshments which were provided on the pay-days, were accounted for as 'donations', though no doubt the recipients took them as a right and not as voluntary alms.[1]

Contributions to local causes have of course remained part of the price which politicians expect to pay in the cultivation of constituencies. Subscriptions from patrons, however, as distinct from subscriptions by sitting members or candidates, tended to fall by the wayside in the course of the century under the influence of the changing structure of politics. The actual cost to a wealthy landowner might not be much affected, for by the later nineteenth century he might in effect have commuted multifarious local payments into a single annual subscription to party funds. But his generosity as a local benefactor, and therefore part of the ties of local deference to him, had nonetheless diminished. A half-way stage in this decline may be observed in the case of a needy peer like Lord Monson, who felt that the family interest in Reigate did not need to be refreshed in this way until there was an imminent prospect of returning his eldest son as member. Thus when he was approached for a subscription to the National Schools in Reigate in 1852 Lord Monson wrote to his son 'while you are not member I think one need give but little', though he felt that the 100 guineas which others were giving was 'a fair sample of what would be required of a member.' By 1858, with

[1] Fitzwilliam MSS, Higham Ferrers Accounts 1789–1857, Milton accounts 1792–1886. Belvoir MSS, estate accounts 1788–1810.

his son just defeated at his first contest for Reigate and another election looming, Lord Monson was ready to think favourably of a request for the permanent endowment of a recently built church, for although 'it will be a fearful weight upon the owners of Gatton,[it] requires care at the present moment to manage all this Church interest for I consider the Keble [vicar] party as perhaps the least staunch of your supporters.' A year later, with his son now the sitting member, Lord Monson felt that to put up £100 towards the new Market House at Redhill was the least he could do: 'after all anything of this kind, or the improving the road, is decidedly the best mode of keeping up a legitimate interest in the place.'[1]

Politics did not provide the only ulterior motive for church building. There might, for example, be the frankly commercial reason of attracting a superior class of development to a building estate: 'a church may induce the letting of land for building leases', and 'church building is often an advantageous speculation', Lord Monson noted in respect of the new church at Gatton and the growth of villa residences on his land there.[2] More nearly religious motives naturally existed as well for the support of new churches, and concern for the spiritual welfare and the morals of local people no doubt merged with a feeling that Anglicanism provided a necessary bulwark of the social order, to inspire the church building activities of mid-Victorian landowners, of which the efforts of the Dukes of Northumberland in their home county were but one conspicuous example.

In much the same way philanthropy and religious feeling coincided with a desire to protect the establishment in landowners' support of the Anglican National Schools in villages on their estates. This educational effort, mirrored in annual subscriptions and gifts of sites, proceeded a little sporadically and lazily until galvanized into a sudden fury of action by the 1870 Education Act. Then, as on the Wilton estate, there was a flurry of activity to ward off the dread intrusion of a School Board, with its democratic control and its non-sectarian Cowper-Temple schools, by pushing up the number of places in church schools to the necessary minimum. Out of thirty Wiltshire

[1] Monson MSS, 25/10/3/2 no. 32, 14 Sept. 1852; 25/10/4/4 no. 61, 6 Aug. 1858; 25/10/5/1 no. 92, 1 March 1859.
[2] Monson MSS, 25/10/3/1 no. 132, 8 Jan. 1851, no. 130. 12 Jan. 1851.

parishes in which Lord Pembroke owned property, the existing schools in nine in 1870 were considered to be sufficient, in four it was proposed that Lord Pembroke should give a site and money for the erection of a school, in one he was to give £400 for a new school since the existing one was in the rector's stable, in nine he was to give varying sums for necessary enlargements, and in the rest it seemed that no separate school was needed. Not surprisingly this saving operation stepped up the annual contributions to schools from about £600 a year to £1,100 a year in the early 1870s. But it was a last-ditch operation, for the superiority of Board schools increased over the years and the standards which voluntary schools had to meet in order to qualify for government assistance were continually raised, so that the struggle was slowly conceded and landowners' contributions fell away. On the Wilton estate the annual contribution to schools had settled back to between £600 and £700 by the 1880s, had fallen below £400 by the early 1900s, and shrunk to £2 in 1909, £15 in 1912 and 3s. in 1915.[1]

It was only natural that philanthropic motives should be mixed up with utilitarian ones in a skein which it would be difficult to unravel. But it is plain that as other motives lost their power, whether it was through changes in the political structure, the development of public education or simply through the migration of the poor away from the villages, so the direct contributions of the great landowners diminished and their role as visible protectors and benefactors of their communities declined. There remained the more usual incidents of benevolence in discharge of the social responsibilities of landowners towards their parishes: the contributions towards church repairs or the augmentation of poor livings, the subscriptions to fuel charities, clothing charities and friendly societies, the provision of free bread for the needy and allotment gardens for the labourers, the support of hospitals and dispensaries, and on the more joyful side the subscriptions to village cricket clubs. To those who had been in their own service landowners might grant pensions, estate cottages for retirement, or simply employment on nominal duties about the park prolonged far beyond their able-bodied days. These, along with the local employment and trade pro-

---

[1] Wilton MSS, Memoranda for the attention of the guardians, 17 June 1870; estate accounts 1840–1915.

vided by the running of a great estate and a great house, were the sinews of the attachment of a community to its lord.

Many continued to set store by the employment of local labour, particularly when building was involved, as did the Duke of Northumberland on a great scale when the Alnwick alterations were made and Lord Sidmouth on a small scale when his country house was building. In some cases the amount of labour directly employed increased in the middle years of the century with drainage operations and programmes of modernizing farm buildings, but in general this factor must have been of declining importance with the growth of alternative employment and the means of reaching it by railway. Similarly, although tradesmen no doubt continued to value the prestige of supplying the great house, the growth of middle-class households must have lessened their dependence on the custom of the great. The charities themselves, however, seem to have been well maintained, at least until the end of the 1880s. Probably no individual landowner subscribed to them all, and individuals certainly varied in their generosity, but it would have been surprising to find a landowner who did not discharge some of these responsibilities. It is possible, indeed, that as at Longleat there was a general tendency for the level of charitable payments to rise in the half-century after Waterloo; the peak at Wilton was in 1876. By the middle of the century it seems to have been fairly normal on the great estates for something between 4 and 7 per cent of the gross income to be paid out in charities. Judging by the examples of the Blundells, Brooks, Orlebars and Senhouses, the gentry at this time might contribute only 1 or 2 per cent of their incomes, and this may understate the contrast since for the gentry genuine totals are known while for the great estates only payments which passed through the estate accounts are recorded.

From the 1880s the proportion of income devoted to charities probably began to decline. The £206 given to fuel and £207 to clothing charities at Wilton in 1882 had become £93 and £104 by 1902. Over rural England as a whole village paternalism had always been a patchy affair, those who lived in 'open' parishes without squires had never known much benevolence, and those who looked up to a country gentleman had probably always received less succour and protection than those living within the orbit of a magnate. One age is ever fond of regretting the faded glories of the past and bemoaning the niggardliness of the present: already in the 1790s some saw a decline in landowners' generosity and a consequent decline in the happiness of cottagers.[1] Within its limits, however, it would seem that in fact the central core of benevolence, shorn of some of its extraneous extremities, was well maintained until the late nineteenth century. Indeed, nowhere before 1914 did local communities altogether repudiate their traditional leadership or throw off their traditional respect, but the means by which deference was secured had everywhere been weakened by the passage of a century and the final onslaught of falling landed incomes.

[1] *Torrington Diaries*, p. 336.

VIII

Landed Estates in War and Peace,
1790–1835

'A large clear landed property is the foundation of dignity and respect in the county', Lord Sefton's advisers told him in 1791, 'for the populace now look to the person that has got the money and is accounted rich, they look more to a rich esquire with a large clear estate than a person with a title with a small one.' They were advising him on the means of clearing off his debts, and above all counselled him to avoid selling land because of 'the degrading and indignity that selling townships and lordships, etc. (and such number) brings to a noble family in the eyes and mind of the public.'[1] There must have been many families, with a century and more of debts behind them, who were reprieved from the sad fate of selling lands by the rise in rents after 1790. For others the same factor, with a rise in the selling price of land, presented a favourable opportunity for effecting sales which had been put off during the slump in the land market. A period of uncertainty which had lasted more or less from the outbreak of the American War of Independence, with fairly high agricultural prices and steady rents, but a pause in enclosures and farm building, as well as in those transport improvements which stimulated agricultural development, was

[1] Lancs. C.R.O., Sefton MSS, DDM 11/63, arrangements for paying Lord Sefton's debts 1791.

212

coming to an end. There followed twenty-five years during which, despite inflation and war taxes, landowners on the whole enjoyed great prosperity and great opportunities either for liquidating old debts or making new savings.

The great changes in eighteenth-century agriculture, the introduction of new farming techniques, the consolidation and rearrangement of farms, enclosures, and the movement towards greater regional specialization, which are often known as the agrarian revolution, proceeded somewhat jerkily in surges of activity separated by periods of pause. About 1790 such a surge was gathering momentum and, carried through the war period with some ups and downs, it ushered in the last age of enclosure. It was once the fashion when discussing agricultural progress to stress the importance of the efforts of a handful of great improving landlords and the interest in agricultural pursuits which their own enthusiasm engendered. It is now more usual to lay emphasis on the general economic and demographic causes of agrarian change: the rise in population which increased the market; the changes in consumer habits and in standards of living which, for example, increased the demand for wheaten bread, meat and livestock products; the transport improvements which made possible a move away from regional self-sufficiency towards regional specialization; and the shifts in prices and in the availability of capital which presented both the opportunities for making changes in farming methods and costs, and the means of implementing them. A run of bad harvests and high prices, holding out tempting visions of the profits to be made by bringing more land into more productive use, or a fall in the rate of interest paid by the government, meaning that funds were more plentiful or that lending to the state had become less attractive than other employments for savings, were more effective in producing a spate of enclosure acts than the efforts of progressive individuals preaching or practising the virtues of an enlightened system of agriculture.

Harvests and prices were highly important in the timing of the great bursts in agricultural investment, and explain why the number of enclosure acts rose from an annual average of twenty-five in the 1780s to fifty-eight in the 1790s and climbed to an all-time peak of 133 in 1811. In a more general way the rise and fall of prospects for landed property were mirrored in the number of private estate acts passed, for these were sought by limited owners desirous of being freed from some of their legal disabilities, sometimes in order to improve their estates, by granting leases or raising loans, more often in order to clear existing debts by sales of land. In the timing of these acts there was sometimes a crisis influence, when credit stringency forced embarrassed owners to resort to sales. But this was generally overlaid by the fact that fresh borrowing, or sales which were not the product of utter desperation, could be more profitably carried out when the outlook was bright and the market for land good. One year with another the number of private estate acts was fairly steady at around 20 a year from 1731 to 1761; it moved sharply up in 1762, and reached an average of 29 a year in 1766–70 and of over 37 a year in 1771–75. A break came in 1777, and the number fell towards a trough of 15 a year throughout the 1780s; another sharp upward turn in 1792 doubled it to about 30 a year, with a few leaner years like 1798, 1804 and 1806, until the average once again climbed to 37 in 1811–15. The crop of 47 estate acts in 1772 was not surpassed until 1813, when 52 were passed.

There were 1,672 private estate acts during the reign of George III, against 3,554 enclosure acts, and they fluctuated from year to year and period to period a good deal less markedly. Nevertheless, inasmuch as most of the estate acts were concerned with sales of land or timber and the discharge of incumbrances, their evidence indicates that disinvestment in land responded to the same influences, and in the same way, as new investment. When agricultural improvements were active, land prices were relatively high and sellers were encouraged to act. The sales perhaps added momentum to the improvements, by bringing in new landowners and by putting some spare resources into the hands of the sellers for investment in the residue of their estates; the repayment of mortgagees certainly placed new credit in their hands for use elsewhere.[1]

---

[1] T. S. Ashton, *An Economic History of England, The 18th Century* (1955), pp. 40–1. Annual numbers of enclosure acts in *Parliamentary Papers*, 1836, VIII, pt. ii, S.C. on State of Agriculture, p. 501; from 1788 in A. D. Gayer, W. W. Rostow and A. J. Schwartz, *The Growth and Fluctuation of the British Economy, 1790–1850* (1953). Private estate acts in G. Bramwell, *Analytical Table of the Private Statutes, 1727–1812* (1813), and H.M.S.O. *Index to Local Acts, Classified Lists, 1801–99*, Class XIII Personal and Private.

While some of the agricultural prosperity and the growing rents of the period after 1790 was the reward of change and improvement, this was not by any means always the case. In 1790 Great Britain was on the point of becoming a regular importer of wheat, with the likelihood that continued growth of population would make her increasingly reliant on imported supplies. In the short run at least this development by itself was favourable for domestic farmers, since prices had first to rise to the level at which it was profitable to import foreign corn and cover its transport costs. In the event the great French Wars complicated the situation, and presented English farmers with large extra profits. War did not interfere with supplies from Ireland, an important source of wheat and flour and the major source of imported oats. In all the course of the wars imports from foreign countries were never altogether cut off, and in fact reached considerable quantities in the years of grave domestic shortage, 1800–1, and again in 1810, when direct importation from France and Holland was encouraged by the government. Nevertheless there can be no doubt that the wars interfered seriously with the normal development of the grain trade, through the imposition of high freight and insurance charges to meet war-time risks no less than through the attempt to close Continental ports to British shipping. Such restrictions on the growth of imports helped to push up grain prices, quite apart from the effects of bad harvests. For some farmers and landowners this situation provided a great stimulus to expand output, to others it formed an opportunity for easily earned profits.[1]

One very general effect of the war period was to engineer a considerable transfer of income from the labouring and consuming sections to the agricultural community, at least to the landowners and farmers, who were thus presented with a sizeable unearned increment. Farmers' profits, particularly from cereals, went up and rents with them, by amounts in no way commensurate with any additional efforts, new practices or fresh outlays which were put into farming, while the real wages of farm workers and industrial workers probably went down. The unearned increment was no new phenomenon, being due to the general growth of the economy outside the agricultural sector,

[1] On this subject generally see W. F. Galpin, *The Grain Supply of England during the Napoleonic Period* (New York, 1925).

manifesting itself in greater demand and higher prices which made it possible to reap larger profits with unchanged techniques. But its force was much strengthened in the war years.[1]

In any case the easy profits and high prices of the war years granted a respite to the heavy land arable farmers from the pressure of competition from the technically more up to date light soil areas of the east where costs of production were being lowered by the spread of the four-course husbandry. The heavy clays, found typically in the Midland counties but also elsewhere in parts of Durham, Yorkshire, Essex, Sussex or Somerset for example, were cold and wet, stiff and therefore expensive to work, requiring three or four horses to the plough against one or two in Norfolk or on the wolds. They needed many cultivations to produce a seed-bed and then were usually behindhand for the sowing season because of their dampness, and at the end of it all generally produced low yields per acre. Their only redeeming feature was their ability to go on cropping almost indefinitely under the old three-course of two crops and a fallow, only one-third of the land furnishing a real cash crop each year. Comparatively unaffected by the eighteenth-century technical innovations, costs of production on such lands remained high and difficult to reduce. Rents could only be maintained with the aid of a favourable course of wheat prices, and could be improved only by conversion to pasture and stock-farming, where the nature of the land permitted. Yet on these lands in the war years were to be found prosperous farmers and doubled rents, alongside the unreformed fallowing ways, owing nothing to new skills or landlords' improvements and everything to 'a bad harvest and a bloody war'.

At the same time, however, that the heavy claylands formed one facet of the margin of cultivation, held there by the fortune of war, the lightest downlands formed another facet, where all was bustle and change. 'In the age when the swift growth of population was driving Ricardo's margin of cultivation visibly across the heaths and up the hills' war-time scarcities and war-time prices pushed forward the taking in of commons and wastes and the breaking in of thin downland soils for arable. Such extensions of the margin needed effort and outlay by landowners

---

[1] A. H. John, 'The Course of Agricultural Change 1660–1760', *Studies in the Industrial Revolution* (ed. L. S. Pressnell, 1960), pp. 152–4.

and farmers, in such things as enclosure, new access roads, new steadings or complete new sets of farm buildings, or new herds of livestock to impart the vital fertility to such marginal land. Provided that the advance of the plough was in general rationally ordered, the land most lately enclosed or most lately put under corn being the least profitable, then we would expect that the rewards in the shape of rents and profits were no more than barely adequate to call forth the necessary investment. Perfect rationality it would be unreasonable to expect, and indeed when the margin of cultivation retreated again a little in the 1820s while some of these newly tilled lands duly reverted to rough grazing, others stood up well and demonstrated a superiority, given the techniques of convertible husbandry, to lands anciently in tillage, a superiority which presumably had been there waiting to be discovered for a good many years before Napoleonic prices stirred someone to discover it.[1]

Economically speaking it is plain that the war-time rent increases ranged all the way from increases in 'pure' rent, as the difference between the best and the poorest land in use widened with the introduction of more and poorer land into cultivation, to reasonable interest on the fresh capital invested in bringing the new land into more productive use. In practice, of course, the picture was greatly complicated. There was, after 1797, currency inflation as well as an altered supply and demand situation operating on food prices.[2] Virtually every estate and not infrequently a single farm, contained different qualities of land. Rents on the whole moved stickily and jerkily, with very many landlords reluctant to put up rents on sitting tenants unless there was a glaring alteration in prices and farm profits, while others were prevented from altering rents by the existence of leases, and some preferred to take out part of the increase by shifting burdens onto their tenants. Nevertheless behind blanket statements of the rise in rents there can be distinguished wide variations in the conditions on which they were obtained, and it can be established that some landowners had an altogether easier financial passage than others.

[1] J. H. Clapham, *An Economic History of Modern Britain* (1950 ed.), I. 16, 19.
[2] Arthur Young, *An Enquiry into the Progressive Value of Money in England* (1812), p. 116, argued that increased demand for food since 1790, and interference with sources of imports, in fact accounted for all the increase in prices.

About the generality of rent increases there can be no doubt. Between 1776 and 1815 the rental of the Holkham estate in Norfolk rose from £12,332 to £25,789 on a constant acreage, and we may conjecture that the greater part of this increase came after 1790. On Lord Darnley's estate in Kent the rents in 1820 brought in £4,404, from the farms which in 1788 had brought in £2,229, the rise being over by 1812 and largely concentrated in the years 1805–11. In Cheshire rents per acre on the larger farms seem to have doubled or more than doubled between 1790 and 1820.[1] On the Alnwick estate in Northumberland the total rents, taking a constant area of 134,462 acres, seem to have risen by rather less than this, from £48,776 in 1790 to £79,790 in 1820, but this overall rise covers variations from a 50 to 60 per cent rise on clay farms in Alnham or Warkworth, to a rise of 150 per cent on the vast hill sheep farms of Redesdale. Also in Northumberland the rental of the Belsay estate, similarly adjusted to allow for intervening acquisitions, moved from £3,200 in 1774 to £4,015 in 1800, £7,600 in 1810 and back to about £6,800 in 1820. On the Milton estate in Northampton and Huntingdon rents moved from £7,639 in 1792 to about £21,000 in 1815 on the same acreage, while on Earl Fitzwilliam's other estate of Higham Ferrers and Harrowden further south in Northamptonshire the rents moved from £3,589 in 1790 to £6,160 in 1815. On Fitzwilliam's Yorkshire properties the rental of the Malton estate in the East Riding was £8,745 in 1800 and £15,610 in 1820, and of the Wentworth estate in the West Riding £10,849 and £22,827 respectively, but in both cases it has not been possible to make full adjustments for intervening purchases. On the Earl of Darlington's Durham estate the rents moved from £9,092 in 1790 to £14,766 in 1815 on a constant area, while as far as this can be accurately assessed on the Savernake estate in Wiltshire the rents there rose from £9,287 to £22,285 in the same period. In Hertfordshire the Gorhambury estate which brought in £4,295 in 1790 had advanced to £7,487 in 1816. In Essex the rental of the Mildmay estate in 1803 was £5,146, plainly a

[1] R. A. C. Parker, 'Coke of Norfolk and the Agrarian Revolution', *Econ. Hist. Rev.*, 2nd ser. VIII (1955), p. 157. H. G. Hunt, 'Agricultural Rent in South East England, 1788–1825', *Agric. Hist. Rev.*, VII (1959). C. S. Davies, *The Agricultural History of Cheshire, 1750–1850* (1960), pp. 45–46 and Appendices XVI and XVII.

long untouched figure since a valuer in that year put the actual value at £10,245, and the farms were in fact re-let on long leases between 1806 and 1810 at rents generally 10 per cent above this valuation; the Somerset estate was also raised, though less drastically, from £2,784 to £4,487.[1]

Similar illustrations of rent movements can be drawn from some of the gentry estates where the records are sufficiently detailed to make a comparison of like areas possible. On the Lancashire estate of the Blundells of Little Crosby the rents grew from £1,650 in 1795 to about £4,000 in 1815, though by this date purchases, some of them from Lord Sefton despite the 1791 advice, had swollen the total rental to £4,891. The great mass of rent increases were made between 1806 and 1815, and this was only partly because most of the Blundell tenants had held on seven- or eleven-year leases, since nearly all the leases in force in 1795 had come up for renewal by 1804. After 1806 some sitting tenants had their rents raised by 100 or 200 per cent, others by as little as 20 per cent. The rents of the Senhouses' small Baldersdale property of 431½ acres in the East Riding were £236 in 1808. The four farms were valued at £630 a year in 1809, and in order to test the market fully the farms were advertised for tenders. The highest offers were not in fact accepted, but were used to encourage the sitting tenants to renew their agreements in 1810 at rents slightly below them. The new rents totalled £685 10s. Here the landlord had obviously delayed long in taking any share of increased farm profits, and the delay was not due to the impediment of leases but to the inertia of management of a detached estate.

In 1790 the Orlebar estate in Bedfordshire was held on six-, nine-, and twelve-year leases, with a farm rental of £1,151 10s. Here the rents were edged up every time a lease fell to be renewed, and the length of leases was gradually reduced until by 1815 most of the farms were either held on yearly tenancies or for three-year terms. This policy produced a fairly even rate

[1] Alnwick MSS, Audit Accounts 1788–1820. Belsay MSS, Rentals 1774, 1800, 1810, 1820. Fitzwilliam MSS, Milton accounts 1792–1815, Higham Ferrers accounts 1789–1815. Wentworth Woodhouse MSS, Malton accounts and Wentworth accounts 1800 and 1820. Raby MSS, estate accounts 1789–1815. Savernake MSS, estate accounts, 1790–1815. Verulam MSS, XI. 64, XI. 86, Rent books 1774–96, 1816–28. Essex C.R.O., Mildmay MSS, D/DM.E4, Survey and Valuation 1803–4; T.94/6, Abstract of Title 27 June 1837, schedule of farms.

of growth in the rents, to £1,307 in 1800, £1,402 in 1805, and £1,679 in 1815, showing in fact no acceleration until six out of the nine farms chanced to be re-let together in 1814 and 1815. In a more southerly part of Bedfordshire the farms rents of the Brooks' estate at Flitwick rose from £321 in 1790 to £843 in 1815; but on their detached farms the increases were much less, an 88-acre grass farm at Irchester moving from £75 to £110, a 53-acre dairy farm at Cranfield from £40 to £52 10s., and a 45-acre grazing farm at Higham Gobion from £46 to £75. In Kent the rents of Pincke's four farms on the Sharsted estate moved from £200 in 1791 to £482 in 1815, the lowest increase being 100 per cent, and on the nearby Calehill estate belonging to the Darells, on the southern edge of the Downs, the rents seem to have moved from £1,318 in 1790 to £2,674 in 1815. Finally in Devon the rents of part of the Sidmouth estate which were £876 in 1818 appear to have been £414 in 1785.[1]

The fact that the overall increase exhibited by this collection of rents was about 90 per cent is of less significance than the wide variations between different estates, where the increases ranged from about 50 to 175 per cent, and the even wider variations between individual farms whose rents rose by amounts ranging from 20–30 to 300 per cent. Differences in situation, in the degree of competence of pre-1790 management in achieving an economic level of rent, and in the suitability of land for corn production obviously played a very great part in determining these discrepancies. In the 1800s in particular corn was king, and although the prices of livestock products also rose in this period they probably did not, except for butter and cheese, quite keep pace with the rise in the price of wheat. Indeed if there was a fairly general fall in living standards during the wars, as most contemporaries and historians believe, this would be the expected effect on food prices: a switch of consumption to

[1] Blundell MSS, BL.54/39, Guardians' accounts 1795–1806, BL.54/36, Rent ledger 1815. Senhouse MSS, 19/16, papers and correspondence concerning the Yorkshire estate 1803–20. Orlebar MSS, OR.1368–9, Rentals 1782–1815. Lyall (Brooks) MSS, LL. 17/276, Account Book 1784–1813, LL. 3/5, Rental 1791/2, BC. 487–98, Estate accounts 1813–31. Faunce MSS, U.145/A.11, Rentals and Accounts 1791–1828. Darell MSS, U.386/E. 10, Account book and notes 1772–85, C.4, Memo of rents 1815. Sidmouth MSS, Rentals 1777–85 and 1818, 1821–3. Subsequent references to rents and estate expenses are drawn from estate accounts except where otherwise mentioned.

the more basic foodstuffs, a relatively smaller demand for meat and a relatively smaller increase in its price. It was wheat above all which pushed at the margin of cultivation and pushed rents up. We can find dairy farmers as far apart as Devon and Bedfordshire, or sheep farmers in Cumberland, who eagerly switched into wheat and ploughed up old grass in most unpromising situations. Landlords might try to prevent this, normally the gravest crime in the farming calendar, or connive at it in return for increased rents. Brooks's great worry when a dairy farmer surreptitiously ploughed up a third of his farm was that the tenant, having entered at Lady Day, would brazenly claim on his quitting that he was entitled to take the final crop on this new arable without paying any rent for it. Other landlords might be more concerned by the probable long-term damage to the fertility of old grass land which would be caused by creaming off a few corn crops, and may perhaps have made more stir to enforce husbandry covenants forbidding the practice.[1]

If the corn left an indelible mark on many hillsides which have never been touched by the plough since, it also produced a more permanent change in cultivation in areas such as the Wolds of the East Riding which had been sheep walks but which were intrinsically suited to arable farming, given a high level of manuring. In 1776 Sir Christopher Sykes made a calculation of the probable effects of enclosing some of his property round Sledmere. He had many large tracts of low-rented rough grazing, at 1s. 3d., 1s. 9d. and 2s. an acre, and he supposed that these rents would be immediately doubled by enclosure. When he put their 'supposed value in 15 years' at 3s. 6d., 5s. 6d. and 6s. 6d. an acre, however, it is by no means apparent that he expected a wholesale conversion to arable to take place, and his other great project of large-scale planting points perhaps to an intended improvement in the quality of stock keeping as much as to an intended introduction of corn growing. The doldrums of the 1780s, as it turned out, postponed some of the projected enclosure until after 1790, and then its conjuncture with high prices produced a dramatic ploughing up of the Wolds. Earl Fitzwilliam's Malton agent, with no reason to like the Sykes for their Tory staunchness, reviewed the process perhaps with a

---

[1] References as above to Lyall (Brooks) MSS and Sidmouth MSS. For Cumberland, Dickinson MSS, farm journals 1807–22.

certain gloomy satisfaction from the vantage point of 1822. 'If the present low prices of corn continue', he reported, 'we may expect to see a great part of the Wolds laid down for sheep pastures. Many thousands of acres of the Wolds were purchased by the late Sir Christopher Sykes and Lord Middleton at not more than from £3 to £5 an acre expressly for sheep walks. The high prices of grain however tempted the tenants to plow them out, which the landlords consented to, on receiving 10s. and 15s. an acre instead of only 3s. The Wolds must now revert back to their original and natural state, and unless a reduction of almost one half of the present rental takes place, and soon, Sir Mark Sykes and some other great Wold proprietors must become the occupiers thereof themselves.' The gloom was in fact overdone, for much of the Wolds had been permanently won for sheep and corn husbandry.[1]

If corn raised rents, so did enclosures. The extent to which they did so permanently, by making possible changes in land use or economies resulting from a rearrangement of fields and holdings, might seem to be called in question by this letter, which implies that a good part at least of the increase was precariously based. In fact, however, the account evidence which has been consulted seems to show that the rents of lately enclosed farms proved no more vulnerable than the rents of old enclosed farms in the post-1815 period. The amount by which rents were increased after an enclosure may therefore be regarded as a fair measure of the return which a landowner received on his investment. The fact that rents were generally doubled, or more than doubled, by enclosure has perhaps created an impression that the yield obtained on this form of investment was exceptionally high. Such an impression could only be heightened by the conclusions of modern research that Arthur Young's idea that the average cost of an enclosure might go as high as £10 an acre was very wide of the mark, and that the normal cost was in the region of £1 to £2 an acre.[2] The lower figures, however, refer only to those costs which were covered by the

---

[1] Sledmere MSS, Letters and Papers 1770–82, A valuation of Sledmere by C. Sykes, 21 May 1776. Wentworth Woodhouse MSS, F.107 k, W. Allen to Lord Fitzwilliam, May 1822.

[2] Arthur Young, *An Enquiry.* . . . . (1812), p. vii. W. E. Tate, 'The Cost of Parliamentary Enclosure in England', *Econ. Hist. Rev.*, 2nd ser. V (1952), pp. 258–65.

rate levied on all the participating landowners by the enclosure commissioners, and information from private accounts shows that a landowner might easily have spent as much again by the time he had done all his fencing and made his new internal farm roads.

An enclosure of commons or waste, involving the breaking in of land which had hitherto been lightly used, might be expected to show a much greater profit than an enclosure of open fields, where a rearrangement of strips rather than a revolution in farming practices might be the only immediate consequence. In the former case, however, in order to produce effective results enclosure might well need to be accompanied by the creation of wholly new farms, involving the extra costs of building farmhouses and farm buildings, while in the latter case the buildings were already in existence. In practice of course any single enclosure was likely to include both the open fields and the commons attached to a village in the one operation, and it is difficult to distinguish the financial results. Some such factor, however, may go some way towards explaining some of the wide differences in yield which were experienced on the Fitzwilliam estates. The total costs of the enclosure of the Earl's 451 acres in Alwalton after 1806, for example, amounted to £16 per acre when the £1,971 spent on building a new farm is included, and the rate levied by the enclosure commissioners formed little more than one-third of this total. The Earl received a return of 3·4 per cent on this outlay in the form of increased rents. At the other extreme the Earl received a return of 33 per cent on his outlay on the enclosure of his 516 acres in Irthlingborough after 1808, where no new buildings were required and the cost per acre was only £4. The factor must not be overstressed, however, since on the enclosure after 1809 of Maxey and Helpstone on the edge of the fen country a return of 30 per cent was obtained on the outlay of £10,364, although this included £2,407 for erecting a new farm on Helpstone Heath.[1]

[1] The discussion of enclosure costs and returns is drawn from Fitzwilliam MSS, Milton and Higham Ferrers accounts 1789–1820, in conjunction with enclosure maps and awards Northants C.R.O., Maps 1051, 1107, 1948, Boxes 1140, 1219, 1224, 1227, and Fitzwilliam Misc. vols. 584, 663. Lyall (Brooks) MSS, LL. 17/249, Flitwick enclosure accounts 1806–11, LL. 17/222, extent and survey, in conjunction with award and map, Beds. C.R.O., M.A.68, 1808. Belvoir MSS, estate and guardians' accounts 1787–99.

Between 1790 and 1815 a dozen enclosures were undertaken on the Fitzwilliam estates in Northamptonshire and Huntingdonshire, ten of them after 1801. The costs were spread over a minimum of four years and a maximum of nine years after the act had been obtained in each case. The total cost amounted to £37,658, of which one-third went on the rates levied by the commissioners to cover their own and surveyor's fees, legal and parliamentary charges, the costs of new public roads and of attending to the rights of the church and tithe owners; one-sixth went on new farm buildings; and one-half was swallowed up by the costs of fencing and hedging and providing gates, in miles of mortised posts and rails and hundreds of thousands of quicksets. In the seven cases where the Fitzwilliam acreages can be accurately calculated, 3,208 acres were dealt with at an average cost of £8 an acre. The overall return to the landowner averaged 16 per cent on the outlay. This investment was financed out of income, an income which was increasing in this period quite apart from enclosure. Rents in fact rose by £10,000 a year, a rough doubling, on Fitzwilliam lands which were not affected by enclosure at this time, so that the owner was in effect using part of the unearned increment from his better lands to modernize most of the more backward parts of his property. A few places remained on the estate where enclosure had not been started by 1815. At Higham Ferrers itself enclosure was probably politically inexpedient on account of the disturbance and irritation which it might cause to voters, just as on the Belvoir estate Gonerby remained the only open field property in 1804, the Duke of Rutland's guardians having noted in 1797 that an enclosure would improve the rents but injure the Duke's interest in Grantham borough. At any rate the enclosure of Higham was not started until 1838, after its disfranchisement. But the postponement of enclosure at Old Weston until 1841, at Great Gidding until 1859 and 1865, and at Lutton until 1866 owed nothing to political complications, and probably stemmed from some tangle of proprietary rights rather than any lack of economic potential.

On other great estates also, such as the Duke of Rutland's, enclosure was financed out of income. Here in the 1790s the enclosure of the Vale of Belvoir and the conversion of the heavy valley lands to pasture was in full swing, turning everything upside down as the agricultural reporter said in 1809, the poorer soils on the hillsides which had been sheep walks becoming arable, while the rich wheat and bean lands became meadows.[1] It was also the time of the Duke's minority, and between 1787 and 1799 the guardians not only laid out £25,973 on enclosures and £6,240 on new plantations, but also discharged £87,195 of debts and made purchases of land totalling £62,391. All these operations on capital account helped to raise the income net of interest charges from £22,729 to £38,751 in a dozen years, one-quarter of the increase being attributable to the enclosures. The enclosures themselves, which seem to have averaged just under £4 an acre in total cost, yielded returns ranging from 10 per cent at Bisbrooke to 33 per cent at Bagworth, the overall return on the seventeen enclosures concerned being 19 per cent on the outlay, and the most frequently experienced return being 17 per cent, figures which correspond closely with the Fitzwilliam results of a decade later. In the same dozen years the rents of the Duke's lands which had been previously enclosed were raised by 30 per cent, thus furnishing resources which were used to make the new enclosures on which the growth in rentals was 60 per cent.

On smaller estates it was not so easy to meet out of income such a large and concentrated expenditure. In the Flitwick enclosure of 1808, for instance, part of common and part of open fields, Brooks had 327 acres affected. The entire process cost him £3,731, of which the commissioners' rate took half, and the return on this outlay in increased rents was about 7 per cent. Such a sum obviously could not be found out of a current income of about a thousand, and probably came from George Brooks's savings as a banker. On other smaller estates where the cost of an enclosure might be several times a year's gross income from rents the money would clearly have to be borrowed, and it was perhaps on this class of estate that variations in the rate of interest on loans produced their main effect in stimulating or retarding enclosures. The greater landowners, in so far as they were savers, were also affected by the ruling rate of interest on government securities, for if this was high they might be tempted to divert savings into the funds, or they might be

[1] W. Pitt, *General View of the Agriculture of Leicestershire* (1809), p. 14, quoted by W. Hasbach, *A History of the English Agricultural Labourer* (1920), p. 370.

discouraged by low prices from selling out their stocks. A landowner like Sir Christopher Sykes was well attuned to the vibrations of the stock market, and could instruct his broker in September 1788: 'In these wars and rumours of wars I think stocks will fall, and I will thank you if there should be any lowering or prospect of it to sell out my 5000 Reduced and 6000 of the 4 p. cts. for the opening in October.'[1] But when the prospective yield on an enclosure might be of the order of 15 to 20 per cent it seems unlikely that a difference of a few points in the yield on government stocks would deter a great landowner from making the investment. The primary consideration which weighed with the great landowners was the availability of tenants who were willing to pay the new level of rents which justified enclosing, and tenants naturally hung back unless farming prospects looked bright. It was, in other words, the demand of tenant farmers, based on their feelings about the market for farm produce, which broadly determined the pace of enclosure, rather than the conditions on which finance could be supplied to the landowners.

If farmers might be said to have exerted their underlying power in this fashion, in other directions landlords undoubtedly used the growing strength of their position in the war years. Enclosure was by no means the only improvement of which land was capable, although it was the most spectacular and most expensive. Other lasting improvements, such as those to buildings, might be regarded in normal times as falling within the landlord's province, while others again, of varying but limited duration such as marling, liming, or the primitive forms of field draining then known in some districts, were regarded as the tenant's business. Sometimes a landlord might assist in the financing of such tenants' improvements, either by making a specific allowance for them or by fixing a lower rent for the first couple of years of a lease, during which the tenant was supposed to be carrying them out. During the war period there is very little evidence in the accounts of estates, great or small, that the landowners were financing any permanent improvements apart from enclosures; there were for example only three or four years between 1792 and 1815 in which anything at all was spent on new buildings on the Milton estate, except for those

[1] Sledmere MSS, Letter book 1775–90, C. Sykes to J. Denison, 18 Sept. 1788.

directly occasioned by an enclosure, and on the Raby estate nothing was spent between 1794 and 1805. There is also some suggestion, on the Savernake and Longleat estates for instance, that landowners tended to become less generous in their financial encouragement to tenants' improvements.

It was also in normal times the landlord's responsibility to help keep the farm buildings in repair, though the arrangements varied from estate to estate, sometimes the owner bearing the whole cost of repairs, sometimes sharing half and half with the tenant, and sometimes providing the materials while the tenant had to find the labour. There was a tendency, particularly after 1810, for landlords to shift part of their accustomed burden of repairs on to their tenants' shoulders. This was neither very easy nor of very great moment on the Earl of Darlington's Durham estate, where the normal repairs outlay of the 1780s had been less than 1 per cent of the rental, but it was nevertheless accomplished when the average repair bill of £150 a year in the early 1790s dwindled to £1 in 1803. When the Earl inherited the Shropshire and Northamptonshire estates the total repair bill for all his estates again declined steadily from 10 per cent of the rental in 1808 to 4 per cent in 1815. On the Milton estate the repairs kept pace with increasing income from 1792 to 1810, at between 8 and 12 per cent of the rental, but then declined sharply to a level of 4 per cent in 1816. Similarly on the Alnwick estate repairs were kept up to nearly 10 per cent of the rental until 1810, after which they declined to 2 per cent or less from 1815 to 1817. There was a similar decline at Savernake and Longleat, but perhaps not at Belvoir. On the gentry estates the absence of adequate accounts makes it impossible to say what happened.

All these developments served to blur the distinction between landlord's capital and tenant's capital, and gave landowners a share of growing farm profits in addition to the share they took by openly raising rents. To nineteenth-century eyes the distinction had in any case not always been honoured in pre-1790 practice, for the long farm lease had been used partly as a device for transferring to the tenant responsibility for outlays which properly belonged to the landlord. Agricultural writers advocated leases principally on the grounds that the security of tenure enabled tenants to embark on long-term improvements to the quality of their land through intensive cultivation and manuring; not infrequently owners granted leases for the secondary reason that under them tenants could be induced to undertake alterations and extensions to their farm buildings. The conditions on which a twenty-one-year lease was granted on the Holkham estate in the 1770s illustrate this confusion of the landlord's and tenant's functions in the provision of capital. At the expiration of the lease of Castleacre Farm, Wicken, in 1771 it appeared that 'all improvements of marling, claying, new ditching and fencing were done at the sole expences of the occupier, and the additional building to Wicken barn, a stable, outhouse, garden wall etc. also at the expence of the tenant', for which the present tenant Boutoll 'at his entrance paid £1,100 to the creditors of the former tenant'. This Boutoll now agreed 'to pay all the labour and carriage for building within three years on the distant lands a new barn and cartlodge with granary over, the landlord allowing rough timber, bricks, lime and other materials.' He also agreed 'to build a cottage near the new barn at his sole expence.' This new building would enable a division into two nearly equal farms, both to be leased to Boutoll, 'and all necessary improvements of claying, marling, new ditches and fences (except gate stuff and layers only) shall be at the tenant's sole charge.' Here was a tenant bearing a considerable part of the cost of a permanent improvement in the creation of a new farm.[1]

Similar reasoning to justify long leases can be seen in operation on the Wentworth estate in 1810, when the steward reported: 'The claims of the tenants for money expended by them in substantial repairs and new buildings exceed my expectations, but as the rental is considerably increased by the value put upon such improvements, I found it, in most cases, more beneficial to make allowances in money, than abatements in rents, but there are some cases where people have made erections more calculated for their own occupation than general conveniences, in which instances, I have promised leases for 21 years.' Here was a landlord who normally gave his tenants cash on the nail for improvements made by them, but sometimes gave them leases instead.[2]

[1] P.R.O. Chancery Proceedings, C.12.572/13, Coke v. Cauldwell, f.4.
[2] Wentworth Woodhouse MSS, F.106a, C. Bowns to Lord Fitzwilliam, Dec. 1810.

On the whole, however, there was probably a move during the eighteenth century towards a clearer differentiation between landlords' and tenants' functions. Nowhere was this more apparent than in the changing attitude towards leases for lives of farm holdings. At one time these leases for three named lives had been regarded as an ideal method of ensuring that tenants undertook and financed all buildings and improvements, under the incentive of a long and perpetually renewable occupation, and ensuring that landlords creamed off part of the value added by their tenants' efforts, by stepping up the renewal fines whenever a life dropped. By the end of the century they were generally regarded as a perfect method for ensuring that land and buildings were allowed to decay and rot by tenants who could meet the nominal annual rents by slovenly farming, and whose capital was periodically raided by landlords taking fines. The great obstacle to their eradication was the reluctance of an owner to sacrifice present income, in the shape of renewal fines, in order to benefit a successor in some fairly remote future who would be able to charge rack rents when the leases ultimately ran out. It was an obstacle which on some west country estates was still being overcome in the 1870s and 1880s. Nevertheless opinion by the 1790s was decidedly of the view that the best farming was furnished by rack renting farms on which the owner provided the fixed capital and the tenant the working capital. Leases for lives were disappearing in Lancashire and Northumberland, for example, where they had formerly been as prevalent as in the south-west.[1]

It was a general movement towards clearer demarcation of the economic frontier between owner and tenant, of which this was the extreme instance, which was halted and partially reversed in the war years. At the same time as burdens were being shifted on to tenants their safeguard against frequent rent increases was being eroded by the decline of long leases. 'Long leases are now disliked by owners', Marshall noted in 1806, and tenancies from year to year were 'becoming more and more prevalent even

---

[1] Sefton MSS, DDM 11/63, arrangements for paying Lord Sefton's debts 1791. Blundell MSS, BL 54/42, Tenants' books 1728–1806. Alnwick MSS, Rental of Northumberland Estates as the same were let in 1748 and 1770. Longleat MSS, Report by J. Clutton 28 Dec. 1867. W. Marshall, *On the Management of Landed Estates* (1806), p. 378; cf. N. Kent, *Hints to Gentlemen of Landed Property* (1793), pp. 202–6 for old-fashioned praise of leases for lives.

where leases for terms of years were formerly granted.'[1] This is certainly borne out by developments on estates as far apart as Lord Darnley's in Kent, the Orlebars' in Bedfordshire, and Sir Charles Monck's in Northumberland, where yearly tenancies were fairly frequently substituted for leases because an owner was loath to tie himself to a fixed rent in a time of rapidly rising prices. At the same time it ought not to be assumed that this factor produced a wholesale collapse of long leases. At any given moment there were presumably some owners who thought that the price rise had reached its peak, and counted themselves fortunate to be able to secure a rent for the next twenty-one years which reflected a rise already achieved.

A much more serious decline in the popularity of leases seems to have occurred in the post-war period, especially in the troubled times of the early 1820s. It was then that owners discovered that they were obliged to make rent remissions even to tenants who held under leases, and that tenants became reluctant to commit themselves to the uncertainties of the future while prices tumbled round their ears and the air was filled with inspired talk of gloom, depression and disaster for farming interests. It is true that by 1824, when the immediate price upheavals were over, many of Lord Darnley's tenancies-at-will were converted into leaseholds once more, but this seems to have been against the main current of the times. At Alnwick, Wentworth, Raby and Gorhambury it was at this time that leases were largely discontinued, and yearly tenancies became the normal practice. Witnesses from Norfolk, the North Riding, Shropshire and Wiltshire all agreed in 1833 that it was scarcely possible to find a tenant willing to take a farm on lease, while ten to twenty years before they had been pressing to do so.[2]

Leases were by no means swept off the board. They remained usual for the light land farms of Norfolk and Suffolk, though it is notable that in the rather similar farming conditions of the Lincolnshire Wolds Lord Yarborough's tenants held under a form of the local tenant-right custom with a specified tariff of compensation for unexhausted improvements, and not under leases. They continued to be the practice on some Cumberland

[1] W. Marshall, *op. cit.*, pp. 378-9.
[2] Hunt, 'Agricultural Rent in South-East England 1788-1825'. *Parliamentary Papers*, 1833, V, S.C. on State of Agriculture, pp. 24, 54, 101, 111.

estates but not on others; they were still granted for some of Lord Sidmouth's Devon farms, though not for all; and a progressive landlord like the Duke of Bedford did not cease to offer leases. Nevertheless leases definitely gave ground after the war, and on the whole it was ground which was never again recovered. The yearly tenancy, more than ever before, became and remained the typical tenancy. For those who later in the century argued that this was a badge of farmers' subservience and landlords' political power it was paradoxical that the final spread of annual tenancies was a fruit of landlord weakness and not a demonstration of landlord strength.

The decline of leases was but one facet of the altered agricultural situation after 1815 and the changes which this produced in the landowners' position. It is now generally recognized that 'the agricultural depression' did not exist as a period of general and persistent gloom, loss and stagnation for all farmers stretching unbroken from the end of the Napoleonic wars to a recovery miraculously timed to start with the accession of the young queen in 1837. There was a series of short crises affecting cereal farmers, associated with abundant harvests and low prices, more severe but not essentially different from the crises which had punctuated the wars. The first brief break in war-time prosperity came when prices fell in 1814–15; the greatest crisis was in 1821–3 when the resumption of gold payments produced deflation; and 1833–6 were years of low prices and general complaint from arable farmers. Stock and dairy farmers were affected by the crisis of the early 1820s, but otherwise had little cause for complaint, apart from the attacks of sheep-rot at the end of the 1820s which in any case damaged sheep and corn farmers more than hill farmers. 'Very little evidence of agrarian distress has been found in Cheshire for the years after the French wars and no evidence at all of any reduction in rent', is the conclusion of Cheshire's agrarian historian. Rents in Lancashire on the Blundell estate, and in Cumberland on the Senhouse estate, were not reduced, though the Dickinson rents were brought down in the 1820s, as their farms grew oats and barley. On Lord Sidmouth's dairy farms in Devon there is evidence of rather more severe distress it is true. The farmers were given allowances from 1818 which averaged 15 per cent of their rents, and in 1823 these were increased to an average of 22 per cent.

But by 1827 the allowances had been withdrawn and rents at their full pre-1818 level were paid from then until the late 1840s.[1]

There remained the long-term fall in corn prices from their war-time level, wheat settling down in the 1820s and 1830s to a normal price which was about two-thirds or rather less of the average price of 1800–15. This fall hit particularly the clayland corn farmers, who in spite of rent and wage reductions had very great difficulty in reducing their costs of production sufficiently within the narrow limits set by their two crops and a fallow system, which Caird found still persisting in 1850. They were in fact exposed once more to the full force of competition from the farmers on lighter soils, where the altered price situation could be generally more easily withstood since barley, which concerned light soils but not heavy clays, fell rather less in price than wheat. On many light soils too the new situation could be met, once the first shock was over, by increasing production and reducing costs through higher feeding of stock and more manuring of the corn lands. It was in fact the greater output from such lands which generally succeeded, in spite of the growth in population, in keeping prices below the Corn Law import limits. The claylands were worst hit by the crises, they were most continuously depressed in the intervals, furnishing stories of farms thrown up and untenanted and farmers bankrupted, and it was from them that most of the evidence for agricultural distress was marshalled before the parliamentary committees of enquiry.

It is one of the ironies of agricultural history that an expansion in grain output, elicited by high prices and a measure of effective protection afforded by war conditions, was projected into the peace and contributed to an era of low prices in which the legislative protection from foreign competition was largely unnecessary and ineffective. In years of poor harvests there were large grain imports, in 1817–18 and again in 1828–31, and the Corn Laws served to make these imports more expensive than they need have been. But in half the years between 1815 and 1837 wheat imports were of trifling amounts, and it was precisely in the years of minimal imports and low prices, 1820–4

---

[1] Davies, *Agricultural History of Cheshire*, p. 47. Sidmouth MSS, Statement on allowances and valuation Nov. 1822, and estate accounts.

and 1833–6, that the loudest complaints of agricultural distress were heard. It was not foreign competition, but the internal competition of more efficient corn growers, from which the complainants were suffering. As a great Liverpool corn merchant put it in 1836, the distress of the clay lands was due to lands of superior quality having been brought into cultivation, and 'there is a fierce but silent contest carrying on between the productive lands of England and the unproductive.'[1] From 1838 onwards the supply situation altered, the rate of population growth at length out-stripped the rate of growth in grain output, and the country became an increasingly heavy and regular importer of corn in good as well as bad years.[2]

Nevertheless although depression for farmers may have been a selective process, landowners were more generally affected, and a basic alteration in their position was set in train. The times were difficult for the smaller landowners, particularly those who had been tempted to borrow heavily during the war years. Their debts, incurred at a time of high prices, left a burden of fixed interest payments which many were unable to meet from the lower money incomes of the post-war years, and considerable sales followed. By 1833 it was a matter of general comment that the body of yeomen occupying their own farms had undergone great changes since 1815, and had shrunk in size. When a yeoman was forced to sell, his land was sometimes bought by a local tradesman, who probably put in a tenant to farm the holding. More often in this period the small holding was bought by a neighbouring large landowner, or one of the rising new gentry, and concentration of ownership made a marked advance.[3]

The greater landowners were not seriously affected by this sort of pressure, because of their greater resources, but the post-war situation weakened their position in different ways. It was not merely a matter of rents, though this was important; it was above all a matter of the landowners' economic functions in relation to agriculture. Rent reductions varied very much from

[1] *Parliamentary Papers*, 1836, VIII pt. i, S.C. on State of Agriculture, Q. 6041.

[2] Import figures in G. R. Porter, *Progress of the Nation* (1847 ed.), pp. 137–8, and G. C. Brodrick, *English Land and English Landlords* (1881), pp. 477–90.

[3] S.C. State of Agriculture 1833, Report x, evidence pp. 65, 85, 109. E. Davies 'The Small Landowner, 1780–1832, in the Light of the Land Tax Assessments', *Econ. Hist. Rev.*, I (1927). See above pp. 116–27 on small landowners after the 1830s.

estate to estate though temporary remissions at least, of the order of 10 to 20 per cent, were very general in 1821–3. Estates with a high proportion of good turnip land and efficient sheep-and-corn farmers might well suffer in rents no less than estates dominated by strong land. Such a contrast can be drawn between the Duke of Cleveland's Durham estate, where in spite of the prevalence of strong land, rents remained completely stable between 1815 and 1855, and the Earl of Pembroke's Wilton estate, where in spite of the presence of good sheep-and-corn farmers, a depression allowance of about 15 per cent was started in 1821, increased by a further 10 per cent for the three years 1834–6, and not withdrawn completely until June 1839. On the nearby Savernake estate, with conditions broadly similar to those at Wilton, rents were permanently reduced by 5 per cent in 1815 and by a further 10 per cent in 1821. In the Midlands the farm rents on the Milton estate were reduced by 10 per cent in 1815, and by a further 10 per cent in 1821, at which level stability was achieved and arrears of rent declined, until they again rose slightly from 1833 to 1836; but on the Duke of Cleveland's Northamptonshire estate of Brigstock and Sudborough the rents remained unaffected throughout this period.[1]

In Hertfordshire Lord Verulam, in between attending meetings to protest at the agricultural distress, was surprised to find that his tenants paid up very well, until he was obliged to make a reduction of 10 per cent in most of his rents in 1822. 'We shall be ruined if we go on long thus', he then thought, and took some glee singers along to the audit dinner of 1824 to lighten the gloom, but in fact virtually all his farms had been restored to their 1821 rentals by 1825, while on his Essex estate at Messing, although the tenants grumbled badly in 1822, the rents were always met in full. Other Essex estates were not so fortunate, Lord Arran's rents being reduced by 15 per cent in 1822 and showing no recovery until 1835, while an Essex land agent in 1833 spoke of reductions of 20 to 30 per cent since 1820. On heavy lands in the North Riding rent reductions of 40 and 50 per cent were spoken of in 1833, while in 1836 a land agent from the East Riding who also spoke of reductions of 40 and 50 per cent since 1816, admitted that these applied mainly to the poor strong soils of Howdenshire and Holderness that had always

[1] Wilton MSS, estate accounts and Memo. Book 1834–40.

been wheat and bean lands, and that the farmers of the Wolds were generally prosperous.[1] On good corn land the Duke of Bedford reduced the rents of his Thorney estate on the Cambridgeshire-Lincolnshire border by about 17 per cent in 1821, and raised them again by about 20 per cent in 1828, while on his Bedfordshire estate rents were apparently reduced by about 10 per cent in 1822, and were certainly reduced by another 10 per cent in 1836. On the other side of the country the good mixed farms of the Duke of Cleveland's estate in Shropshire had their rents reduced by amounts varying between 10 and 15 per cent in 1817, and again by a further 5 to 7 per cent in 1837.[2]

It appears, therefore, that even where farmers rode out 'the alteration in the times' without grave discomfort they generally did so only with the assistance of varying amounts of rent reductions or remissions. In themselves, however, most of the reductions detailed were adjustments to altered prices rather than real sacrifices on the part of the owners, since the purchasing power of rents was kept up by the fall in the general price level. It was of much greater importance that generally speaking the level of estate expenditure was growing after the war, so that the proportion of gross rent which an owner received before tax was a declining one, perhaps falling on average from over 80 per cent at the end of the war to about 70 per cent in the 1820s. It was a long-established custom for landowners to meet times of agricultural distress by increasing their outlay on repairs and perhaps on improvements, hoping in this way either to maintain the existing level of their rents or at least to prevent a drastic reduction, for by such actions more of their tenants' capital was released for farming operations and farms were perhaps rendered capable of an increased output to compensate for lower prices. A move in this direction after 1815 not only reversed war-time trends, but also established on a firm footing in working practice the theoretically clear distinction between landlord's and tenant's capital.

[1] Gorhambury MSS, 1st Earl of Verulam's Diary, 28 Feb. 1821, 1 Feb. 1822, 27 March 1822, 1 April 1822, 27 June 1822, 4 July 1823, 2 Aug. 1824. Essex C.R.O., Oxley-Parker MSS, DD.Op. Box 2 bdle 12, particulars of late Lord Arran's estate 1837. S.C. State of Agriculture 1833, pp. 77–78, 110. *Parliamentary Papers*, 1836, VIII pt. i, S.C. on State of Agriculture, Q.5332–9, 5370–1, 5422–3.
[2] Duke of Bedford, *A Great Agricultural Estate* (1897), pp. 218–20, 230. S.C. State of Agriculture 1836, Q. 8211–8.

In the course of the 1820s the Duke of Bedford's outlay on repairs grew to 25 or even 30 per cent of the gross rental and on permanent improvements to nearly 10 per cent on the Bedfordshire estate, and of both together to one-third of the rental of the Thorney estate. On less munificently run estates the outlay on buildings and repairs moved up to 14 per cent of the rental at Alnwick, to 12 per cent at Milton, Savernake and Wilton, and to 9 per cent on the Duke of Cleveland's estates. The gentry perhaps were little affected by this movement, for as late as 1847 Senhouse spent less than 4 per cent of his income on repairs and Brooks about 5 per cent, while in the 1820s and 1830s the Blundells appear to have had no estate expenses whatever apart from taxes and the steward's salary, but the imperfections of other accounts make it impossible to frame any generalization.[1] To a great extent, indeed, these greater outlays were matched by a fall in the burden of taxation on landowners following the abolition of the war-time income tax. Thus by way of illustration the burden of taxation on the Raby estates fell from 11 per cent of the gross rental in 1815 to 2 per cent in 1830, and at Milton it fell from 12 per cent in 1816 to 4 per cent in 1830, the main fall of course being experienced in the one year 1817. To put it in another way, repairs and taxes combined took 15 per cent of the Raby rents in 1815 and 11 per cent in 1830, and at Milton they took 16·3 per cent and 16·5 per cent respectively. A transfer of resources from the central government to tenant farmers by way of landowners had never been intended, though it clearly helped to ease the owners' situation. But as the years slipped by and it became clear that the larger outlays were permanent, and not merely temporary expedients for tiding over a few years of low prices, nothing could obscure the fact that a definite modification of the agricultural structure was in progress.

In general tenant farmers, even those who remained fairly flourishing, could no longer afford to tie up their resources in the fixed assets of their farms or in semi-permanent improvements. They needed all their available capital and credit for farming operations, and for progressive farmers this was perhaps most

---

[1] Lyall (Brooks) MSS, LL. 17/200–204, Estate accounts 1833–49. Senhouse MSS, 19/165, Income and outgoings of the estate 1842–8. Blundell MSS, BL. 54/14, 54/15, 54/18, Steward's accounts 1820–31, 1835–6.

necessary of all, as they began to expand their outlays on purchased feeding stuffs and manures. Some land agents in 1833 still looked back to a time when tenants financed improvements. 'On the Duke of Bedford's estates there has of late years been a great deal of draining done', said one agent, 'he gives his tenants tiles and wood to do the drainage; but where the landlord will not be at the expense it remains as it was. . . . The tenant cannot lay out money on improving the land, he has not the means.' 'Draining was going on very rapidly', reported another of Wiltshire, 'and it is now much stopped unless the landlords do it. . . . I find the tenants will not do it, unless they are allowed a part of the expense, or the whole of it.'[1]

In fact the time was past when such things could be expected of tenants, and within a decade very many landlords were to fulfil their function of providing the permanent equipment of farming through financing improvements on a greatly expanded scale. In the meantime landowners had engaged in the defence of their rents not only with the political weapon of the Corn Laws, but also with the economic device of absorbing a greater share of farming costs. The shift was made under the pressure generated by the weakened resources of tenants, and if it did not register an outright weakness in the landowners' position it certainly did mark a decline in their strength. The shift also demonstrated in a practical way that farming was served by financial co-operation between landlords and tenants, and inasmuch as it impressed on landlords that they were obliged to co-operate it may be ranked among the ingredients which contributed to the background to Reform. In 1830–2 landlords listened to farmers asking for Reform just as politicians listened to the Birmingham Political Union.

[1] S.C. State of Agriculture 1833, pp. 16, 54.

IX

Estates in the Railway Age,
1835-79

'In these comparatively prosperous times for farmers', the Marquess of Ailesbury was assured in December 1838, it would be possible to withdraw four months of the period of grace hitherto allowed to his tenants for the payment of their rents, without causing them much embarrassment. It was done accordingly, and in 1839 his tenants in Wiltshire and Yorkshire were deprived of some £17,000 which in effect they had been accustomed to enjoy as interest-free loan from their landlord.[1] The times, indeed, had been better for arable farmers since 1836, as the run of abundant harvests in the mid 1830s came to an end. Paradoxically, in view of the farmers' attachment to protection and fear of foreign competition, prosperity and grain imports revived together from 1837. At the Wilton audit in November 1835 'depression still prevails' it was noted, with wheat at Salisbury down to 36s. a quarter and sheep fetching 18s. apiece; in the following May 'an improved aspect' was noted, with wheat up to 52s., and in November 1836 with wheat up to 60s., the special depression allowance was taken off and rents restored to their 1833 level. A year later, with wheat at 58s., sheep at 23s. and wool at 15d. a pound, 5 per cent was taken off the

---

[1] Hoare's Bank, Fleet Street, Ailesbury Trust MSS, Marquess of Ailesbury to R. W. Lumley, 10 Dec. 1838, Lumley to Marquess, 11 Dec. 1838.

allowance which had been made since 1821 without occasioning any of the murmurings that had been feared. Markets went on rising, in May 1838 Salisbury wheat was 70s. and wool 17d., in November 72s. and 18d., and in June 1839 the old depression allowances ceased altogether, wheat was 71s., sheep 21s. and wool 18d. and the audit passed off very quietly with no discontent.[1]

This was one of the more favourable periods for corn growers, and one of the most wretched for the rest of the community. In the years 1837–42, almost for the last time, farmers profited from bad harvests while the manufacturing districts were plunged into deep depression. There were exceptions, for some, like the Cheshire dairy farmers, realized for the first time their reliance on local industrial markets which could only take their farm produce in quantity when trade was brisk and wages and employment were high. They became corn-law repealers, acknowledging that 'their prosperity was thus identified with that of the manufacturers'.[2] Most farmers, however, remained protectionists with their eyes fixed on corn prices, which did not remain high for long. They dipped once more in 1843–5, and after a brief interval of scarcity conditions farmers were plunged into the post-Repeal distress of 1850–2; wool prices, sensitive to industrial demand, had already sagged to 13d. a pound at Salisbury in the course of 1840.

The effects on the finance of tenant farmers were perhaps very similar whether a landowner chose to exploit such a favourable short-term swing in market conditions by taking an increase in rents like the Earl of Pembroke, or by taking a single levy like the Marquess of Ailesbury. The psychological difference, however, was important. The first was felt to be a legitimate addition to the farmer's annual outgoings, the second an inroad into his working capital, depriving him perhaps of that tenth or fifteenth of his assets which he had been in the habit of expecting his landlord to provide. It was perhaps only an owner who was driven on by his own financial embarrassments that would dare run the risk of taking such action, for immediate gain might be outbalanced by long run loss if rents were placed in jeopardy

---

[1] Wilton MSS, Memo. Book 1834–40.
[2] W. Cooke Taylor, *Notes of a Tour in the Manufacturing Districts of Lancashire* (1842), p. 83.

through curtailing farmers' resources and encouraging niggardly farming. The whole tendency of the times was to hold that in general farmers did not have sufficient capital. It is true that there was no question of landowners supplying any of the tenant's working capital in any direct fashion, but until the 1880s the current flowed strongly in favour of large additions to landlord's capital with the express purpose of attracting and encouraging substantial farmers and liberal-handed farming. Particularly in bad years, but also in good times, landlords' outlays were increased, and the rewards they received were generally diminished. In this way the landowners bore a good part of the cost of the ascendancy of commerce and industry and the secondary position to which agriculture was being relegated. Behind the façade of the 'Golden Age of English Agriculture' which is said to have lasted for the twenty years after the outbreak of the Crimean War, a distinct weakening in the economic position of agricultural landowners can be detected.

The underlying developments were often obscured by the year-to-year movements which put fresh heart or fresh despondency into farmers, and brought well-paid rents or mounting arrears and renewed abatements. The crisis of 1850–2 was perhaps the sharpest for thirty years, but its effects on landowners varied very much from estate to estate and between different parts of the country. Abatements of 10 per cent were fairly common, and as one great landowner set the pace his neighbours generally felt obliged to follow suit in order to avoid the impression of being unfair to their own farmers. In this way Lord Monson with reluctance gave back 10 per cent to his Lincolnshire tenants in 1851, and Lord Verulam returned the same amount to his Hertfordshire tenants between 1850 and 1852, having observed that the example of richer neighbours was irresistible. Savernake, Wilton and Longleat all bowed to the 10 per cent, although the owners showed discrimination in respect of their estates in other parts of the country. On his North Riding estate of Jervaulx the Marquess of Ailesbury kept the remissions to a maximum of 5 per cent, and on his Shropshire and Herefordshire properties the Marquess of Bath apparently gave no remissions. Similarly on the Duke of Cleveland's Durham estate the rents remained unaffected and entirely clear of any arrears, while on his Shropshire estate an allowance was made in 1850 and the rents were permanently reduced by 10 per cent in 1851. The Duke of Bedford also seems to have treated his Bedfordshire and his Thorney estates differently. In Devonshire Lord Sidmouth gave most of his tenants an allowance of 10 per cent from 1849, and a new valuation in 1850 lowered most of the rents by 5 per cent or more. In Lancashire, however, rents seem to have been well maintained: the Earl of Derby made no general reduction or abatement, and at Little Crosby there is no trace of this depression. Likewise in Cumberland on the Netherhall and Lamplugh estates there are no evidences of strain.[1]

A general revaluation of all Earl Fitzwilliam's estates had been made in 1842, and this had produced an increase of rather more than 10 per cent in the rents of the Milton estate, which remained well paid throughout the early 1850s with no abatements and only a slight rise in arrears. On the West Riding estate also the agent was hopeful in 1850 that there would be no call for any abatement. The valuer had fixed the rents in 1842 'as if a lease of 21 years were about to be granted', even though the farmers were in fact annual tenants, and had fixed them on the assumption that the average price of wheat for the ensuing twenty-one years would be 53s. 4d. a quarter against an average of 58s. 5½d. for the twenty-one years which ended in 1842. The tenants were therefore expected to take in their stride individual years of below average prices, and in May 1850 the agent held strongly to the view that low prices were a passing phase, that free trade would bring advantages as well as disadvantages, and that the average price over the full twenty-one years would still work out as expected. The prescience of the valuer was indeed vindicated, for the average turned out to be 53s. 7d. a quarter. This, however, lay concealed in the future, and the pressure of another year of low prices did compel Fitzwilliam to return 10 per cent of the half-year's rents to his West Riding tenants in May 1851, though this was apparently the only concession from the twenty-one-year arrangement which he was obliged to make.[2]

[1] In addition to the estate account evidence already cited, see Monson MSS, 25/10/3/1 no. 99, 23 April 1851, no. 19, 22 Nov. 1851. Gorhambury MSS, 2nd Earl of Verulam's Diary, 11 Jan. 1850, 15 Jan. 1851, 12 Jan. 1853. Jervaulx MSS, estate accounts 1812–88. J. Caird, *English Agriculture in 1850–51* (1852), p. 266.

[2] Wentworth Woodhouse MSS, G. 49, W. Newman to Lord Fitzwilliam, 3 May and 7 May 1850, 17 May 1851.

Optimists had promised that free trade would bring advantages to farmers, in the shape of steadier prices, lower costs for some purchased farm inputs, and growing demand for farm produce from prosperous commercial and manufacturing centres. In the early 1850s such benefits appeared remote, and the worst fears about the consequences of repealing the Corn Laws seemed to be realized. For a few years, it could be held, the impact of free trade had been delayed, first by the poor harvests of 1846 and 1847, and then by the European revolutions which disrupted normal trade in 1848 and 1849. But in 1850 continental grain exporters could take full advantage of the fact that the British ports were open, and in conjunction with a good harvest at home this drove wheat prices down to 40s. a quarter, which might be about the normal level in future.

Prices stayed at, or slightly below, this level for the next two years, but then rose sharply, and in the following thirty years only once, in 1864, sank as low as 40s. again. Wheat imports rose, and in 1850-2 furnished perhaps a quarter of Britain's bread. With vicissitudes the volume of wheat imports continued to grow, and by the late 1870s had nearly trebled in quantity, accounting for half the country's wheat consumption. But in the quarter-century after 1850 import competition did not have a great effect on wheat prices, and the main effect of free trade was to bring world prices up to British levels rather than to depress British prices. In 1850-2 good harvests and low food prices were in fact helping to hasten economic recovery from the crisis of 1847, a recovery which ushered in the great mid-Victorian boom. The three years of agricultural distress turned out to be the prelude to the massive expansion of trade and industry which carried consumption upwards and for twenty-five years confirmed the League's claim that farmers had nothing to fear and much to gain from free trade.

While this lay in the future, the unsettled situation of the early 1850s induced many landowners to prepare for a new situation with a possible permanently lower level of agricultural prices. Many embarked on programmes of large investment in their estates, and many also made systematic revaluations of their farms, linking rents to prices. Typical of the more refined schemes was that elaborated at Wilton. A first step here had been to make the 10 per cent abatement conditional on the tenant actually expending that amount on artificial manures, in an attempt to foster higher output as an answer to depressed prices. The next step was to fashion a scheme for produce rents based on an index of the price of meat – an amalgam of London prices for beef, mutton, lamb, veal, hogs and porkers; wheat; and barley, in the proportions of two: two: one. The rent of a farm might be entered in the roll, for example, as 9,080 lbs of meat, 700 bushels of wheat and 645 bushels of barley. The maximum cash rent payable was pegged at the pre-Repeal level; 'the landlord does not go beyond the fair rent, it being considered that all profit above that should belong to the tenant.'[1]

About two-thirds of the Wilton tenants agreed to have their rents regulated on this basis. The result was that in most years down to 1867 the Earl of Pembroke received between 1 and 5 per cent less than the pre-Repeal rents. From 1868 to 1874 the average prices produced an excess of from 7 to 11 per cent over the standard, which was enjoyed by the tenants as extra profit. In 1874 all rents were converted into fixed money rents at the level of the standard rents, and the scheme came to an end. Its operation had been decidedly to the advantage of the tenants, for the landlord had accepted a self-imposed ceiling on rents at the pre-Repeal level less the manure allowance, over a period when other landlords had found it possible to raise rents.

Produce rents were commended by informed opinion as an equitable mode of dividing the fortunes of high and low prices between landlords and tenants, but if they were not very widely adopted the fault was not always on the side of the landlords. The Duke of Bedford offered his tenants the option of a corn rent, which apparently was not always taken up. Lord Monson wished to introduce a corn rent, but was frustrated by his tenants: 'I wish the tenantry would consent to a corn rent', he wrote in 1854, 'it is far more equitable, but as Brown said they would not hear of it even in low prices, of course at the present rates there is no hope. A corn rent would be easily done by me for I have Bartholomew's valuation of rent at corn at 56s., that would be the standard and as it rose or fell so would the rents. They could not then grumble in bad times, and in good times landlords would have a fund for improvements'. At Savernake the

[1] Wilton MSS, Memoranda to the Guardians 1862–71, esp. 17 Dec. 1862; Rent Rolls 1862–80.

tenants were given the choice in 1850 of having their rents determined by an index of wheat, barley and meat prices, rather as at Wilton, but less than a tenth of the tenants accepted the offer. In this case, however, no ceiling was fixed, and by 1856 the rents paid had risen well above the pre-1850 levels. At Alnwick any tenant was given the option, in 1848, 'to apply to have his farm valued . . . with a view to a lease not over 20 years; or he can go on from year to year, but without the benefit of the scale of corn rents'. In fact only two or three asked for leases, though they could not otherwise have the advantage of corn rents: 'they seemed apprehensive of the ultimate effect of the abolition of the Corn Laws, and have confidence from experience that no advantage would be taken of them under a simple contract'.[1]

The confidence was not misplaced, for the Duke of Northumberland not only allowed his tenants to apply for a revaluation at any time, but also ordered a thorough enquiry into the relationship between rents, prices and costs on the different classes of farm on his estate. The result was a long report in 1850 on the effect of free trade on tillage and pasture farms, setting out the output, costs and profits of six different types of farm, ranging from arable farms with two-thirds of their fallow quarter in naked fallow, the most common type on the estate, through the best turnip farms of Tillside in North Northumberland, to pasture farms almost wholly under grass, ending with small tillage farms in the colliery districts which kept small dairy herds. Not surprisingly this showed wide variation in the costs of production per acre, excluding rent, from £3 a year on the best turnip farms to 30s. on the pasture farms, the gross output being valued at £5 an acre and £3 respectively, and tenant's capital was found to vary from £4 12s. an acre on the dairy farms to £9 an acre on the turnip farms. Differential rents, however, had gone a long way towards ironing out differences in the rate of profit which tenants earned on their capitals, though with prices at pre-Repeal levels it was calculated that the pasture farmer had received 8·3 per cent and all the others 10 per

[1] *Parliamentary Papers*, 1846, VI pt. i, S.C. of H. of L. on Burdens on Real Property, Q. 687. Caird, *English Agriculture in 1850-1*, p. 441. Monson MSS, 25/10/3/4 no. 17, 30 Oct. 1854. Savernake MSS, estate accounts 1850-67. Alnwick MSS, Business Minutes, I (1848), p. 133, II, p. 9.

cent on their capitals, after allowing in each case a depreciation rate of 4 per cent. It was then assumed that all agricultural prices would fall in sympathy with wheat prices, though not in exact proportion: a fall of 12 per cent in the price of wheat was, for example, supposed to be accompanied by a fall of 4 per cent in the price of mutton. Labour costs were also assumed to fall in sympathy with the price of provisions for horses and men, though again not in exact proportion.

The result of applying these assumptions was to show up the superiority of the good turnip land farms over the most probable range of price falls, and to indicate that the pasture farms would have the advantage only in the case of absolute disaster. With the produce prices appropriate to wheat at 50s. a quarter it was considered that all farmers would still be able to earn more than 5 per cent on their capitals, which was felt to be the minimum rate of profit that would place a farmer 'in the lowest position he can occupy without encroaching upon his capital, which he can only improve . . . by still further reducing the cost of production'. But at this price level the turnip farmer would get a profit of 8 per cent, the bare fallow farmer one of 6·9 per cent, and the pasture farmer one of 6·7 per cent. If prices sank to the 44s. a quarter level, then in order to preserve the bare profit margin rents would need to be reduced by 6·4 per cent on the fallow farms, 5 per cent on the pasture farms, and nothing on the turnip farms. At 40s. a quarter these necessary rent reductions would become 17 per cent, 7·9 per cent, and 5·6 per cent, and at 36s. a quarter 26·5 per cent, 15 per cent, and 14 per cent respectively.[1]

Nothing as low as 36s. a quarter for wheat was in fact reached until 1884, but the experience of the period down to 1880 showed the error of one of the cardinal assumptions in these calculations, for while wheat prices after their recovery in 1853–5 settled down to a slowly declining trend, the prices of animal products continued to rise steadily. This divergent movement favoured pasture farmers, and created a situation to which some mixed farmers tried to adapt themselves. But the landowners' attitude, long conditioned to associate agriculture primarily with arable and corn, had been confirmed by the feeling that, in 1850, the advantages lay with the sheep and corn farmers

[1] Alnwick MSS, Business Minutes, VI (1850), pp. 1–51.

who had abundant green crops and large capitals, practised high feeding and high manuring, obtained high yields of grain and kept large flocks of beasts and sheep. Probably few landowners buttressed this opinion with the array of statistical support marshalled by the Duke of Northumberland, but it was nevertheless one which was widely held, and one which was broadly appropriate to the situation of the 1840s and early 1850s. Even Caird, although he stressed the favourable position of dairying and pasture farming, appeared to place his main emphasis in this direction since his main concern was to suggest positive action which could be taken to raise the condition of cold clay farms. It was in this environment that great schemes of agricultural investment were launched by many landowners, whose principal purpose was to render the clay farms as like the turnip farms as possible, rather than to assimilate them to the pasture farms. This effort was a last, expensive, homage to king corn, and largely because subsequent developments showed that it was misdirected the returns to landowners were on the whole disappointingly small. In these low returns, and in the higher levels of estate expenditure in general, we can see a weakening in the position of many landowners springing from the context of agriculture itself. It was not accidental that this was happening at the same time as a decline in the wealth and status of the landowners relative to the middle classes, and the conjunction of the two developments must be accounted an important factor in the weakening of the landed interest which had already proceeded far before the onset of the great depression.

Somewhat illogically the Duke of Northumberland used the information which had been collected to give differential abatements from February 1850 of 12 per cent on the tillage farms which had less than half their fallow quarter in turnips, 8 per cent on those which exceeded that ratio, and nothing on the stock farms. This was a short-term expedient, and was in addition both to the new valuations which he had offered to his tillage farmers as soon as he had succeeded to the title in 1847, and to the great improvement programme he had started in order to raise the productive and rent-paying capacity of his farms. Within five years over 77,000 acres had been revalued under this offer, covering virtually all the tillage farms, and the new rents represented a permanent reduction that averaged

11 per cent. This was effected in the main by the Duke taking over the payment of tithe rent charge, and by a reduction in rents equal to the amount of interest charged on drainage outlays, though in order not to give the tenants too much of a feeling that they were receiving something for nothing they were still formally charged with 5 per cent interest on these outlays. In any case from 1848 to 1854 over half the agricultural rental of the estate was spent on buildings, drainage and improvements, and a percentage was charged to the tenants on the drainage only. While the short-term returns on this investment were entirely negative, the longer-term returns, largely for this reason, were not encouraging.[1]

For very many landowners a great new age of agricultural improvement was launched in the half-dozen years after Repeal. Typically the landowners' outlays were expanded at times of depression in an effort to ward off or mitigate rent reductions. Unless improvements 'be heartily taken up and resolutely and intelligently followed out, loss of rent, and neglect of land' will follow, Lord Sidmouth was told in 1850. In 1849 Lord Monson's agent thought 'a general system for the whole estate of drainage is wanted and not to let the tenants do it, he thinks by that the present rental may in time be preserved'. Caird himself noted, of Lancashire's wet clays, that 'low prices bring demands for reduced rents, or such outlays in permanent improvements as will enable the farmer to meet the change of times'. In his general conclusions he stressed the advantages which lay, and would continue to lie, with rents and farmers which depended more on livestock products than on corn: 'as the country becomes more prosperous, the difference in the relative value of corn and stock will gradually be increased'. But he also insisted that the wet lands must be thoroughly improved, and as to the probable returns on such investment had only cold comfort to offer: 'the funds necessary must also be forthcoming, or the rent will fall to a far greater extent than the annual amount of a sinking fund to repay this outlay'.[2]

The technical foundations of the great surge of improvements

---

[1] Alnwick MSS, Business Minutes, V (1850), pp. 300–5, XI (1852) p. 60.

[2] Sidmouth MSS, Report on the Up Ottery Estate, 20 July 1850. Monson MSS, 25/10/2/3 no. 4, 14 Dec. 1849. Caird, *English Agriculture in 1850–1*, pp. 266, 483, 491.

had been perfected in the 1830s and early 1840s with developments in the practice of field drainage and the successful application of mass production methods to the manufacture of clay drainpipes. Soggy fields could now be laid dry at a cost of about £5 an acre, and the long stranglehold of naked fallows on the claylands was broken. On drained lands the essential green crops could be introduced into the rotation, particularly mangolds and swedes which suited heavy lands better than turnips. With the green crops came increased stocking of cattle or sheep, so that some form of the stock and corn farming which had been so successfully developed on the light soils could now be applied to the old wheat and bean lands. The livestock, however, had to be housed, for even on drained heavy land it was impossible to feed the roots in the field, since the beasts damaged the soil. Drainage without new buildings might be largely a waste of money, as the Earl of Ducie said of his estate in the Vale of Gloucester in 1845.[1] In any case on this sort of farm the existing buildings were often sadly dilapidated and required most expensive modernization to put them in keeping with the improvement in cultivation conditions which draining brought. Most landlords charged their tenants a percentage on draining outlays but very few on the great estates did so in respect of building outlays, the general practice being to fix rents on the assumption that adequate farm buildings would be provided by the landlord. On gentry estates it was perhaps more frequent to make a specific charge for new buildings, but it was rare indeed to find any landowner making an express charge for any of the associated landlord's improvements which might be provided, chiefly in farm roads and farm cottages.

Essentially landowners thought of this whole complex of improvements as a rescue operation, and for them its results were in sharp contrast to those of the age of enclosure. Here and there a few enlightened landowners, like Sir James Graham, might have embarked on such a course of systematic improvements in the 1820s. His rewards were not encouraging, for on a total outlay of £93,000 between 1819 and 1845 he received a return of barely 4 per cent. He had borrowed money at 3½ per cent as part of the scheme, and had had to wait many years for

---

[1] *Parliamentary Papers*, 1845, XII, S.C. of House of Lords on the Draining of Entailed Estates, Q. 1401, 1411.

his return, when the re-lettings of 1841–2 raised his rents.[1] Most owners, however, did not set about the energetic defence of their incomes until Repeal forced a careful appraisal of their position. Then the increased outlays in the poor years down to 1853, not unnaturally, did not produce any measurable returns at all; the most that can be said is that without them rents might have fallen rather further than they did. From the middle of the 1850s rents began to rise once more, and there was a chance that some positive reward might be shown for earlier investments, as well as for those which were still being made. In 1854, for example, the year's relettings on the Northumberland estate showed a small increase over the former rents for the first time, and it was not until the abatements were withdrawn in that year that the gross rental rose above that of 1847. This increase of £3,400 represented in fact a return of 1·4 per cent on the £225,900 which the Duke had laid out in buildings and improvements since the start of 1848, and on part of this investment he had waited six years before receiving even this return.

After 1856 rents began to move upwards more strongly, and furnished an increasing fund that might be looked upon as the reward for investment. Sometimes this increase was long postponed, as on the Duke of Cleveland's estate. The rents of his Durham estate remained unaltered, save by new purchases, from 1812 until a fresh valuation was at last ordered in 1864; this produced an immediate increase of 20 per cent and thereafter the rents continued to rise slightly until 1881. On his Shropshire estate, on the other hand, the rents did not even regain their 1850 level until a similar revaluation in 1865, and at their peak in 1879 were scarcely 7 per cent above 1850 and still 10 per cent below 1815. In this case the landowner had to wait at least eighteen years before he began to receive any return at all on the outlays he had been making since 1846, and then the rewards grew until by 1879 he was receiving 2½ per cent on the £450,000 which he had laid out, a reward which was maintained for only three years before rents began to decline.

In rent policy the Northumberland estate was more typical, with a steady annual stream of revaluations, almost entirely after 1854 occasioned by re-lettings when tenants died. These

---

[1] D. Spring, 'A Great Agricultural Estate: Netherby under Sir James Graham 1820–45', *Agric. Hist.* XXIX (1955), pp. 73–81.

showed substantial advances in 1856–7, a decrease in 1860 which was a cold wet year, and again in 1863 which was a bad year for wheat, and then a sustained run of advances from 1867 to 1875, when the rents flattened out at about 25 per cent above their level in 1847. The Duke of Northumberland, therefore, after the hiatus until 1854, was receiving a continuous return on his outlays, in fact a slightly increasing one. On the £653,000 expended down to 1868 the return reached the 2 per cent level in 1869, while on the £992,000 which was laid out in the entire period 1847–78 the return reached 2½ per cent for the four years ending in 1879. Much lower rates of return would be shown if we followed the estate practice of charging 5 per cent interest on the drainage outlays, and regarded any remaining rent increase as the sum available to recoup all the other building and improvement expenditure. On such a basis the non-drainage outlay yielded a maximum of 0·6 per cent down to 1868, and of 1·5 per cent over the whole period 1847–78.

Not every landowner was as wealthy and as generous as the Duke of Northumberland. His total outlay worked out at about £10 an acre, excluding his rough moors, and while this scale was matched by the Earl of Pembroke and exceeded by the Duke of Bedford, great landowners who were in straitened circumstances like the Marquess of Ailesbury achieved about £7 an acre, and those whose estates were in less need of drainage, as was Earl Fitzwilliam's Milton estate, could be content with £5 10s. an acre. On these estates and those of the Duke of Cleveland, the Marquess of Bath, and Lord Sidmouth altogether £3,450,000 was laid out in the period 1847–78, an average of just over £7 10s. per acre on the 450,000 acres involved, and at its highest point in 1878–9 the overall return on this outlay just reached 2·36 per cent in the shape of increased rents. The sample represents about 5 per cent of all the land in England held in great estates, and is undoubtedly overweighted by estates in the eastern half of the country. Nevertheless about a quarter of the sample lay to the west of Caird's line of division between the corn and the grazing counties, and the rate of return in this western quarter was only about a half per cent higher than the rate in the eastern three-quarters.[1]

[1] Following D. Spring, *op. cit.* and R. J. Thompson, 'An Inquiry into the Rent of Agricultural Land in England and Wales in the 19th Century', *Journal Royal*

It was not surprising that a committee of the House of Lords concluded in 1873 'that the improvement of land . . . as an investment is not sufficiently lucrative to offer much attraction to capital'. It was of the opinion that those who borrowed in order to finance draining might easily be out of pocket on that alone, without taking any account of outlays on farm buildings and cottages. Those who did not borrow, either from the government through its drainage loans of 1846 and 1849 or from the special agricultural credit institutions like the Lands Improvement Company, but instead financed their outlays out of current income as did the Duke of Northumberland, were equally making investments which did not pay. It might have been said of the whole complex of agricultural investments, as well as of drainage, 'that it is exposed to the risks of ordinary industrial undertakings, it must take its rank, not with the investments that are absolutely secure, but with the investments that depend for their yield upon the attention, the skill, and the good fortune of the investor.'[1]

In 1860 the *Bankers' Magazine* pointed out that in England interest generally varied between $3\frac{1}{2}$ and $4\frac{1}{2}$ per cent, that is 'the interest a man can get for the mere use of his capital upon good securities, without adding a fraction of labour'.[2] In business accounts it was the general practice to deduct 4 or 5 per cent as interest on the capital employed before declaring any profit. In 1846 Henry Ashworth, the great Bolton millowner, reckoned that the return on capital 'in the commercial world' was 8 or 9 per cent. In the same year Robert Hyde Greg, a large cotton manufacturer of Wilmslow as well as a considerable landowner in Hertfordshire and Norfolk, stated that the return on his firm's capital in the previous twenty years had averaged $7\frac{1}{2}$ per cent, 5 per cent of which he called interest and $2\frac{1}{2}$ per cent profit. It was a twenty-year period especially notable for pressure on

---

Statistical Society, LXX (1907), pp. 600–2, no distinction has been made between 'repairs' and 'improvements' in computing the total outlays given in the text, just as none was made in most estate accounts. If a distinction could be drawn between 'repairs' and 'new buildings', the maximum return on 'new investment' outlay might be raised to 3·6 per cent.

[1] *Parliamentary Papers*, 1873, IX, S.C. on Improvement of Land, Report, pp. iii–iv.

[2] *Bankers' Magazine*, XX (1860), pp. 409–10, quoted by D. Landes, *Bankers and Pashas* (1958), p. 57.

the profit margins of cotton manufacturers. The experience of many railway shareholders, it is true, was not much more favourable than that of the great landowners.[1] But it might have been expected that the normal returns on agricultural investment, if economically sound, would have compared with those in private commercial and manufacturing enterprises, rather than with those obtained from public utilities. An industrial capitalist who survived for many years with no return on his fixed capital, and eventually began to receive under $2\frac{1}{2}$ per cent would have been a great curiosity in mid-Victorian England.

It is impossible to be certain whether the gentry shared the fortunes of the great landowners in this matter, for virtually none of them kept accounts in sufficient detail or for sufficiently long periods to make comparable calculations feasible. The likelihood is that the gentry either allowed their land to remain in worse condition or succeeded in thrusting a higher burden on to their tenants, so that on smaller outlays per acre they would probably receive a higher rate of return. In 1907 an expert was of the opinion that on smaller estates of about 2,000 acres the depression had meant increased outgoings, because in the prosperous times farmers had not insisted on the landlord fulfilling his duty to repair buildings, while they went to the landlord for every little repair when they were depressed. On the other hand the only witness who was asked, in 1873, whether the large estates were in better order than the small, defined as those below £10,000 a year, had not 'observed much or any difference between them'.[2] Brooks, who was spending nearly 20 per cent of the rental of the Flitwick estate on repairs in the 1860s, was certainly not far behind the great landowners, and very many of the gentry undertook some draining. For example, out of the forty-eight loans raised by English landowners under the 1864 Improvement of Land Act in its first ten years, twenty-five were raised by members of the gentry, chiefly for drainage; these gentry loans, however, amounted to only one-third of the

---

[1] *Parliamentary Papers*, 1846, VI, pt. i, S.C. of H. of L. on Burdens on Real Property, Q. 3930, 4383–93. W. Farr, 'On the Valuation of Railways, Telegraphs, Water Companies, Canals, etc.', *Journal Statistical Society*, XXIX (1878), pp. 518–25.

[2] A. H. H. Matthews in discussion on R. J. Thompson's paper, *Journal Royal Statistical Society*, LXX (1907), p. 619. S.C. on Improvement of Land 1873, Evidence, Q. 2814–6.

sum borrowed under the Act.[1] Superior results for a more selective improvement policy on the part of the gentry might be indicated by the experience of the Orlebars, whose accounts for the twenty years ending in 1866 appear to show a return of 5 per cent on the estate expenditure of that period. In Essex, on the other hand, a land agent strongly advised a small squire against laying out money in improvements in 1861, on the grounds that there was no chance of an increase of rent which would pay for the outlay.[2]

Whatever the experience of the gentry, with the great land-owners the mid-century age of improvement was a matter of pouring money into their estates for very meagre rewards, a far cry indeed from the age of enclosure. Ironically enough, where enclosure remained to be done it could still show the old high profits for the landowner. The enclosures of Great Gidding in 1865 and Lutton in 1866 yielded Earl Fitzwilliam returns of 12 and 11 per cent on his outlays. Money was lavished on the other improvements partly because it was there to be lavished out of non-agricultural incomes, but it was spent by an impoverished owner like the Marquess of Ailesbury because a supreme effort to remedy years of neglect seemed to be the only way to conserve his rental. In his case the effort may not have been particularly successful, but it can be argued that in any event the whole direction of efforts like this was unfortunate for both landowners and farmers. For even when successful in establishing good farming the improvements all too often were directed towards encouraging good corn farming, when the trend of the times favoured animal husbandry.[3]

In this way when Thynne reported on the Up Ottery estate in Devon in 1850, although he acknowledged that 'the general system of agriculture is that comprised under the term of Dairy farming', he at once went on to observe that it was 'a system which seldom produces good corn farming. . . . Thatch and timber predominate [in the homesteads] so that much of the manure which should have been laid on the arable has been laid

---

[1] Ministry of Agriculture MSS, Register of Loans under the Improvement of Land Act, 1864, 1864–74. Scottish landowners borrowed nearly half the U.K. total, and the great landowners two-thirds of the English total.

[2] Oxley Parker MSS, DD. Op. Box 2, bdle 1, nos. 1–5.

[3] F. M. L. Thompson, 'English Landownership: The Ailesbury Trust 1832–56', *Econ. Hist. Rev.*, 2nd ser. XI (1958), pp. 130–2.

on the roofs'. His primary concern was to improve the corn farming, by draining, marling and better balanced rotations. When looking at the state of the buildings it was again admitted that 'depending so greatly on butter as this estate does, the dairies should be the first consideration', but it is apparent that the programme of improvements which Lord Sidmouth accordingly executed after 1850 was concerned much more with the interests of arable than with those of the butter or apples for which his property was so well suited. As to the returns to be expected, Thynne was not sanguine. 'Where the rents are low, any improvement done to the farm must be done with the agreement that an interest is to be paid on the outlay. Where they are above this, let the improvements be done without any interest being charged, and where they are unfairly high this course with an allowance in money for manure, or manure itself may be purchased and given. . . . Without such is done, I fear that the evils of heavy arrears, reduced rents, and neglected and perhaps unoccupied farms will be the result.' His rents continued to be regulated by wheat prices, and not surprisingly even by 1879 had not increased sufficiently to prevent Lord Sidmouth losing £300 a year on the £16,000 he borrowed between 1852 and 1866 in order to carry out drainage.[1]

Many landowners and agents may have had this bias towards arable farming, and thus helped to condemn themselves to uneconomic rates of return on their outlays. They were in any case used to regarding the ownership of land as a luxury, not a remunerative investment, providing social benefits which compensated for the low financial returns of 'at best only 2½ or possibly indeed only 2 per cent' that might be yielded by a purchase. A wealthy millowner would be well content with such a bargain, giving him the status of a country gentleman, a seat on the bench, sport for his sons when home from Eton and Cambridge, 'the sherrifalty, a squeeze of the hand from the Lord Lieutenant, the county balls for his wife and daughters, and perhaps an opening to the House of Commons'.[2] Equally low returns on improvements might not be regarded with any dismay.

[1] Sidmouth MSS, Report on the Up Ottery Estate, 20 July 1850, and estate accounts.
[2] *Economist*, 5 Jan. 1867.

But the orientation of improvements was at least connived at also by many farmers who were more traditional than commercial in their outlook. When Caird said that 'the Scotch tenants are practically the applicants for improvement loans' he might well have extended the observation to the generality of improvements in England as well. It was very usual, as on the Northumberland estate, for the owner to fix the total annual appropriation for expenditure on his estate, but for its detailed farm by farm application to be determined by the requests made by individual farmers for the draining of a field, the erection of a barn or the removal of a hedge. In this way, generally speaking, the type of improvements which an estate received was regulated by what the tenants asked for. Similarly anything which they failed to request was probably not carried out. Thus when the Duke of Northumberland, from 1863 onwards, tried to encourage his tenants on heavy clay farms to curtail their corn and lay down a good part of their arable to permanent grass, by offering to bear the cost of the conversion, the offer was virtually ignored. Such tenants were following their own preferences in remaining unduly vulnerable corn farmers, waiting to be swept away after 1878.[1]

The whole cycle of improvements therefore demonstrates the weakened position of agricultural landowners, particularly those who were held in thrall by corn. They were accepting financial sacrifices, in the sense that much greater returns could have been secured by putting their money elsewhere, and were therefore in effect 'paying ransom' long before Chamberlain suggested that they must do so. Moreover they accepted these sacrifices very largely at the behest of their tenants. The social and political consequences are perhaps visible in some degree in 1867 and 1884. The economic consequences, it can be argued, were to prolong the notion that corn farming was synonymous with agriculture, and to impede the proper adjustment of farming to the marketing possibilities of 'the Golden Age'. Farmers who had always grown corn no doubt liked to continue to do so, and their wishes were met by landlords, through this form of subsidy, because in the last resort landlords could not afford to antagonize their tenants. A more economic form of behaviour by land-

[1] J. Caird, *The Landed Interest and the Supply of Food* (1878), p. 101. Alnwick MSS, Business Minutes, XXXV (1866), pp. 36–40.

owners, however, would have mitigated the scale of the agricultural disaster after 1878, by ensuring an earlier and more gradual contraction of corn acreages.

When it did come many landowners were shielded from the full effects of the agricultural disaster because they had profited directly from the great industrial expansion of the times, and were by no means wholly dependent on their farm rents. For some, though not for all, mines, railways, docks or urban ground rents helped to provide the money which was poured into their farms. Of the landowners whose agricultural investments have been discussed, all owned some non-agricultural assets, of varying importance, save for the Marquess of Ailesbury: he only possessed some unrewarding house property in Marlborough, which had been acquired for its political importance. For practically all landowners railways, the great symbol of the age, had been more efficacious in increasing farm rents than had improvement outlays themselves. It was a factor noted by Caird in 1878 when discussing the increase in rents since 1857, and stressed by Thompson in 1907 when analysing rent movements over the 1845–72 period. It had been the subject of fairly extensive inquiry by Bailey Denton in 1868 when preparing a paper 'On the future extension of the railway system'. The consensus of opinion among the land agents he consulted was that the coming of a railway increased the letting value of farm land by 5 to 20 per cent according to the proximity of a station. Bailey Denton, however, was an undiscriminating enthusiast for all manner of improvements: he even expected that 'railways, by bringing in equipment for steam cultivation, will make the lands which have hitherto taken the lowest place, into the best wheat growing lands in the country – the heavy clay lands'. A more sober body of the Lords had concluded, in 1863, 'that the letting and selling value of land is in general greatly increased by its having the advantage of easy access to a railway'. They had heard evidence that 'about seven per cent. [on the rental] would be a moderate estimate of the benefit that all the land within five miles of a railway station . . . would receive'.[1]

[1] Caird, *The Landed Interest*, p. 94. R. J. Thompson, *Journal Royal Statistical Society*, LXX (1907), p. 594. J. Bailey Denton, 'On the future extension of the railway system', *Trans. Institution of Surveyors*, I (1868–9), pp. 128–31, 138. *Parliamentary Papers*, 1863, VII, S.C. of H. of L. on Charging Entailed Estates for Railways, Report, iii, Evidence, Q. 33.

The Lords' Committee was investigating ways of enabling landowners to raise money for investment in railways that were intended to benefit agricultural districts, for without the support of local landowners it was almost impossible to construct such branch lines. Their recommendation, that life-tenants should be empowered to borrow money on their settled estates in order to take up railway shares, the amount of interest being limited to 'the amount of increased annual value which the Enclosure Commissioners may be satisfied will accrue', was incorporated in the Improvement of Land Act of the following session. Even before this landowners had often subscribed largely to branch lines which intersected their estates. In the case of the Wansbeck Valley Railway in Northumberland, which was investigated by this committee, completion was ultimately financed by two neighbouring lines, the North British and the Blyth and Tyne, as it gave them a connecting link that avoided use of the rival North Eastern's rails. But of the £44,260 which had been raised from the public for this line, £30,000 was provided by Sir Walter Trevelyan in the interests of his Wallington estate, and £9,500 by the Earl of Carlisle because of his Morpeth land, while Sir Matthew White Ridley had found £500 since his interests in the port of Blyth stood to benefit.[1] This sort of thing was a long step from the early days when railways had often seemed to be built in the teeth of opposition from landowners.

Landowners who had been well schooled in the benefits which canals brought to their estates, through their effects in extending markets and lowering costs for the farm and the household, did not in fact take long to appreciate the greater benefits which railways might bring. Active encouragement of lines seeking to cross an estate may not have been forthcoming until the 1840s, when the railway had conclusively established its efficiency and superiority. Then we hear of Sir James Graham and the Duke of Buccleuch active in Cumberland, Sir James considering himself 'on velvet' when he was sure of three lines crossing his estate; or of Earl Fitzwilliam who was an active partisan in 1844 of the abortive scheme for a trunk line from London to Gainsborough, via Cambridge, Peterborough, and Lincoln, as the main route

---

[1] S.C. on Charging Entailed Estates for Railways, 1863, Report, iii. British Transport Commission, Edinburgh Archives, Minute Book of Wansbeck Valley Railway, II, 1 July 1864.

to York and the North. The Duke of Grafton may have been even earlier in the field, for he told Fitzwilliam in 1845 that for three acres of his land at Blisworth the London and Birmingham had paid him £600 for removing the top soil to make an embankment, leaving merely a bed of blue clay. This was given' to the company as an inducement to erect on it a first-class station and thus increase the value of the Duke's property in the district.[1] By 1845 it was a matter of notice that in fixing the price to be paid for land taken by a railway the surveyor did not 'take into consideration that the property of the individual is most likely benefited by the railway'. By 1852 it was a matter of routine for an Essex land agent to advise the trustees of the Hall Dare estate to make any farm leases granted terminable on twelve months' notice 'in order that they may take benefit of the value raised by the railway to Tilbury when that is finished'.[2]

Earlier than this it is perhaps too much to expect that land-owners should have been active partners in the first decade of railway promotions, although the contrary idea that as a body they were opposed to all railway ventures is certainly wide of the mark. The latter impression has arisen from several notorious instances in which peers used their obstructive parliamentary power either to steer lines away from close proximity to country seats, or to obtain enormously high compensation as a bribe for withdrawing opposition. Thus Lord Essex steered the London and Birmingham away from Cassiobury Park; a certain Lord A. was paid £11,025 for 27 acres of farmland on the Dover line, four or five times its agricultural value, because the line passed close to his mansion and he threatened opposition; and the Lancaster and Carlisle company silenced the opposition of a landowner who chanced to be an M.P. by agreeing to pay him 3,000 guineas for a quarter of an acre beside the Ribble. Resentment at the invasion of the privacy of parks and mansions, not unnaturally, continued to be expressed even by those who were friendly towards railways in general. Lord Fitzwilliam in 1845

---

[1] D. Spring, 'A Great Agricultural Estate: Netherby under Sir James Graham 1820–45', p. 77. Fitzwilliam MSS, Letter Book 733, 23 Jan., 23 Feb., 25 April, 8 May, 8 Oct. 1844; correspondence, Duke of Grafton to Lord Fitzwilliam, 29 May 1845.

[2] *Parliamentary Papers*, 1845, X, S.C. of H. of L. on Compensation for lands taken by Railways, Evidence, Q. 276. Oxley Parker MSS, DD. Op. Box 2 bdle 7, correspondence with trustees of Hall Dare estate, 1852.

wrote to Hudson about the Peterborough and Syston Railway Bill: 'I hope you will take the chance to make an arrangement entirely satisfactory to Lord Harborough. The intrusion upon his park is such as has never yet been sanctioned by Parliament, and such as I trust never will. My wish to see the measure pass makes me exceedingly anxious that it should be freed from this blot.' For himself, Fitzwilliam disliked the Great Northern route from King's Cross to York on public grounds, for it was 'ill judged and mischievous' neither to take the shortest and quickest line, since it went through Hitchin, Welwyn and Hatfield, nor to connect all the intervening places of importance, since it missed Lincoln, Newark (as projected in 1844), Stamford and Bedford. But in his private capacity, he also gave the first project his 'inveterate hostility as a landowner' and set his surveyor to work to map out a quarter-mile detour near Peterborough to protect his interests as a foxhunter: 'my object is merely to prevent the separation of some woods which in a hunting point of view are inseparable'.[1]

It was generally thought that the Great Northern missed Stamford because of the opposition of Lord Exeter, who desired to protect Burghley House against railway intrusion. A letter from Sir John Trollope of Casewick Hall near Stamford, of August 1844, seems to imply, however, that Lord Exeter only objected to the original route through Stamford and hoped to obtain a relatively minor deviation. There was terrible commotion in his district, Sir John wrote, because Stamford considered itself ruined by the line being taken to Peterborough, and the people blamed Lord Exeter 'as he opposed its coming into Stamford as originally intended'. Lord Fitzwilliam, he continued, had healed the angry feeling in Peterborough caused by his earlier opposition to the Peterborough–Blisworth project, by persuading the London and York promoters to go through Peterborough. Now Lord Exeter would have the same sort of feeling towards himself in Stamford 'as I really believe that if he had cordially supported the scheme in the first instance, you would have been unsuccessful in getting it to Peterborough, which is decidedly out of the straight line to York'. As it was,

---

[1] S.C. on Compensation for lands taken by Railways, 1845, Evidence, Q. 124–52. Fitzwilliam MSS, Letter Book 733, 24 Sept., 22 Nov., 25 Nov. 1844, 28 May 1845; correspondence, T. Dunn to Lord Fitzwilliam, 26 May 1845.

the line had been re-routed to pass within 400 yards of Casewick Hall, 'so close as to be an intolerable nuisance', and Sir John asked Lord Fitzwilliam to use his influence to get the line modified again. Within a year Lord Exeter had made some amends by arranging with Hudson a route for the Peterborugh–Syston line passing through Stamford.[1]

It has similarly been held that no main line ever passed through Marlborough because of the intransigence of the Marquess of Ailesbury in preserving the amenities of Savernake Forest and his mansion of Tottenham Park. In point of fact two schemes were put forward in 1846 for bringing main lines to the West through the district, and the Marquess made private, and lucrative, agreements with both sets of promoters before their bills were presented. He gave his assent to the proposals of the London, Bristol and South Wales Direct Railway, (which was never built) for a main line through Marlborough, including a principal station to be built on his land there, in return for a promise of £30,000. He also gave his assent to the proposed Great Western main route to the West from Hungerford to Westbury (which was built) on condition that they never applied for powers to make a branch line to Marlborough without the prior consent of the Marquess or his heirs. In return the Great Western agreed to pay at least £14,000 for his lands, up to a maximum of 70 acres, and a further £5,000 for residential damages to Tottenham Park, which lay a mile from the line.[2]

Even ten years before this the Earl of Pembroke had been in favour of the first proposals for the South Western Railway, when their route passed two miles away from Wilton House, and only changed his attitude when a revised scheme brought the line within three-quarters of a mile.[3] It is apparent that anxiety to protect residential pleasures had to be balanced against the desire not to inflame local feelings, and the notion of the landowners' complete opposition to the early railways must be qualified accordingly. A later generation might think them over-

[1] Wentworth Woodhouse MSS, G. 54, Sir John Trollope to Lord Fitzwilliam, 31 Aug. 1844. Fitzwilliam MSS, correspondence, G. Loch to Fitzwilliam, 18 March 1845.

[2] Savernake MSS, Deeds, Marquess of Ailesbury and the London, Bristol and S. Wales Direct Railway, 14 Feb. 1846; Marquess of Ailesbury and G.W.R., 15 April 1846 and 10 March 1847.

[3] Wilton MSS, Memo. Book 1834–40, May 1836, Sept. 1836.

sensitive, but it was very natural to be apprehensive of the 'snorting steed', or to pray like the Duke of Northumberland that 'arragements will be made for the steam engines to consume their own smoke'. Many landowners also certainly took their pound of flesh from the early trunk lines, and as late as 1845 Lord Fitzwilliam felt that they were fully justified in doing so, at least to the extent of receiving about double agricultural value for land compulsorily purchased. 'Railways', he observed, 'are speculations embarked on with a view to profit, without even any collateral view to the interest of the districts in which they are made. This is clearly demonstrated by the circumstance that a very small proportion indeed of the shareholders are locally connected with the districts which the railways traverse: and here is to be observed a marked distinction between them and the canals and roads, which have almost always been made with local funds subscribed by persons who have looked more to the benefit of the neighbourhood than to their own, except inasmuch as they might be incidentally benefited. With railways it has been directly the reverse. The profit of the speculator is the motive; the advantage of the public is the incident.'[1]

It was a view which Lord Fitzwilliam had formed as early as 1825, an antipathy towards the type of men and the speculative motives which were behind railroad schemes, not hostility towards the contrivance itself. When he was approached about a projected Leeds and Hull railway in 1825 he was favourable to the scheme, because the committee had endeavoured to exclude speculators and distribute shares among those who were locally interested in its success, and intended to consult the landowners whose estates were to be crossed. 'But by supporting what is reasonable we sometimes give an unintentional countenance to what is not so, and here lies the difficulty. It will not be easy to consider any railroad except as a part of a system, and to that system I feel no friendly disposition, as it is put forth by its authors.' Of another scheme in the same year, for a Grand Junction Railway through Sheffield, he wrote, 'I must see the measure in different hands before it can expect anything but opposition from me'. By 1836 he was fighting hard for the

[1] Alnwick MSS, 3rd Duke of Northumberland's Letter Book, Nov. 1836, Aug. 1844. Fitzwilliam MSS, Draft Report by Lord Fitzwilliam as chairman of S C. on Railway Land Compensation Bill, June 1845.

Rotherham and Sheffield Railroad Bill, a measure in respectable hands and calculated to benefit his coalfields in Greasborough and Rawmarsh, in a second attempt to overcome the Duke of Norfolk's opposition in the Lords' committee, an opposition based on that Duke's desire to protect his own collieries from competition.[1]

Many landowners made substantial capital gains from the railways from land purchase and compensation money, and until the days of the lesser branch lines in 1850s and 1860s few put anything into them. A case like that of the Furness Railway in the 1840s, largely financed by the Duke of Buccleuch and Lord Burlington, is not really exceptional, since it was designed purely as a mineral line, of the type which landowners were accustomed to construct for the transport of coal or ores from their royalties.[2] Similarly Earl Fitzwilliam became a shareholder in the South Yorkshire Railway and one of its directors from 1846, as it was of great importance to his collieries. His stake in the South Yorkshire, however, had only reached £16,000 by 1857, and this was his only railway holding; it was somewhat overshadowed by the £40,000 which he received for selling the River Derwent Navigation to the Malton Railway in 1854.[3]

In contrast the Duke of Northumberland, who also had great coal interests, received £23,000 in compensation from railways in Northumberland between 1847 and 1851, but held to a policy of declining to become an adventurer in such undertakings. This did not prevent him from taking credit, in 1855, for having 'suggested, facilitated or promoted the following new and improved communications' since 1829: in 1829 (by the third Duke) the Newcastle and Carlisle Railway and the Newcastle and North Shields; 1846, the Newcastle and Berwick, and the Tynemouth and Alnwick extensions; 1852, the Blyth and Tyne; 1853, the Tynemouth and Morpeth branches; 1854, the Border Counties. In the case of the Blyth and Tyne, in order to secure

[1] Fitzwilliam MSS, Lord Milton's Letter Book 731, 26 Jan., 7 Feb. 1825; correspondence, W. Newman to Lord Fitzwilliam, 8 March, 8 April 1836.

[2] S. Pollard, 'Barrow-in-Furness and the Seventh Duke of Devonshire', *Econ. Hist. Rev.*, 2nd ser. VIII (1955), p. 214.

[3] Wentworth Woodhouse MSS, G. 40, R. Baxter to Lord Fitzwilliam, 29 April 1846; G. 33, W. C. Copperthwaite to Lord Fitzwilliam, 1 Nov. 1853, 10 Oct. 1854, 18 March 1856; the Executors of Earl Fitzwilliam, Family and Impersonal Ledger, 1857, Share Account.

the rarity of a public railway run on the wayleave principle, the Duke had contributed £4,471, more than half the costs of the parliamentary contest. But it was not until the Border Counties line was started, with the object of opening up the North Tyne and especially the Duke's iron at Bellingham and coal at Plashetts, that the Duke reluctantly became a railway shareholder because without his financial support the line could not go forward. In the end the Duke supplied well over half the realized capital of this line, £15,500 in shares and £40,000 in an interest-free loan, and in order to obtain amalgamation with the North British in 1860, bringing financial salvation to a shaky concern, he was obliged to relinquish £15,000 of his shares.[1]

Landowners did not invest in the main line railways, but did move in to the support of secondary lines, easily and naturally where these were connected with mineral interests, later and less fortunately perhaps where these were primarily agricultural lines. Similar considerations determined the general pattern of other types of industrial investment. Landowners might engage in projects for the development of the resources of their estates, but very rarely provided any finance for concerns unconnected with their own landed property, or adjoining lands which they might acquire with a view to exploiting the mineral wealth. In several cases landowners built harbours for the development of the coal trade from their estates. In Cumberland Whitehaven had been virtually created by the Earl of Lonsdale, Workington by the Curwens, and Maryport by the Senhouses, while in South Wales the Marquess of Bute began to build his dock at Cardiff in 1839. In the creation of Seaham Harbour the Marquess of Londonderry expended about £162,000 between 1828 and 1831, and further extensions were said to have increased this sum greatly by 1850.[2] Sometimes, however, a preference for getting others to take the risks could be seen asserting itself. In the Northumberland Dock, the first coal-shipping dock on the north bank of the Tyne, the Duke expressly declined to become 'the proprietor and adventurer' although it was a project to improve his property and protect his wayleave revenues from

---

[1] Alnwick MSS, Business Minutes, XII (1853), pp. 120-5, 182-90; XIII (1855), pp. 344-8; XVII (1855), pp. 61-2; XXVI (1860), pp. 83-90.
[2] Marchioness of Londonderry, *Frances Anne*, p. 158; J. Caird, *English Agriculture in 1850-1*, p. 331.

marauders. The Tyne Commissioners were persuaded to take the risk, and the Duke's contribution was limited to £10,000 debenture capital out of a total cost for the dock of £133,789.[1]

This tendency for landowners not to run the risks of industrial undertakings was perhaps more evident in the case of the coal industry itself. Landowners certainly drew large and increasing incomes from coal, but these were predominantly and increasingly in the shape of royalty and wayleave rents. There was a persistent tendency for mineral landowners to withdraw from their enterprises into the more secure position of rentiers, and this should not be obscured by the fact that some of the great aristocratic undertakings still survived into the 1870s, like those of the Duke of Devonshire, the Bridgewater Trustees, the Marquess of Londonderry, or the Earls of Dudley, Durham and Lonsdale, and had indeed received large refreshments of new capital in the previous thirty years. By 1869 it appears that not many more than 5 per cent of the collieries in England were owned and managed by landowners, and a high proportion of those were owned by the half dozen coal empires which have been mentioned.[2] This figure undoubtedly registered a late stage in a long decline which ended in such events as the leasing of the Whitehaven collieries by the Earl of Lonsdale in 1888.

The decline can be illustrated in many districts: Earl Fitzwilliam, who had run four collieries in the late eighteenth century and five or six in the 1840s, apparently had only two left in his hands in 1869; and what remained of the ironworks which the Earl of Crawford had started in 1788 was leased out from 1835.[3] But it is perhaps plainest of all in the oldest established coalfield, the North East. The Duke of Northumberland had sunk some of his own pits in the later eighteenth century and worked some himself, as at Walbottle, and some through sub-contractors, as at Flatworth; by 1799 all his collieries were out to lessees and the Dukes never entered the colliery business again. The Delaval predecessors of Lord Hastings ran their own collieries

---

[1] Alnwick MSS, Business Minutes, IX (1851), pp. 64–8; XII (1853), p. 198; XVII (1855), pp. 57–60; XXXIV (1864), p. 6.

[2] *Parliamentary Papers*, 1871, XVIII, R.C. on Coal Supply, Appendix 27 to Report of Committee E, Collieries at work in 1869.

[3] *Ibid.* and Fitzwilliam MSS, Household General Accounts and Colliery Accounts 1780–1870. A. Birch, 'The Haigh Ironworks 1789–1856', *Bulletin John Rylands Library*, XXXV (1952–3), p. 332.

at Seaton Delaval through sub-contractors after 1756, but they were leased out after the death of Lord Delaval in 1808. The Ridleys had worked many collieries from the early eighteenth century, but the Sir Matthew White Ridley who succeeded in 1836 leased out the remaining Cowpen colliery in 1838 sooner than put up fresh capital which was needed for continued working. At the same time he withdrew from the Newcastle Old Bank, and within a decade the glass works in which the family had long been concerned was wound up, so that Sir Matthew White's withdrawal from business was complete. The Marquess of Bute won the Tanfield colliery in 1829, but sold it to the Joiceys in 1847. The aristocratic Grand Allies, Lords Ravensworth, Strathmore and Wharncliffe, had still been active colliery proprietors in the 1840s, but had sold out by 1860. North of the Tyne there was scarcely a landowner left operating his own colliery, and this was largely true south of the Tyne also except for the Lambtons and Vanes. The trend had been apparent by 1830 at the latest. 'Are the collieries usually won by the proprietors of the coal, or by adventurers?' John Buddle was asked, and he replied, 'They are usually won by adventurers. On the River Tyne there are only five proprietors out of the forty-one collieries who work their own mines, and on the River Wear there are only three; all the rest are in the hands of lessees or adventurers.'[1]

Landowners were ceasing to be an important source of mining capital basically because outside capital and managerial skill were becoming more plentiful, and the majority of landowners were thankful to be relieved of the great hazards and uncertain income of colliery ventures. By the 1860s the Lambs, Taylors, Joiceys, Strakers, Cooksons, Carrs and their kind were running the collieries of the North East, rich capitalists many of whom put some of their profits into landed estate. The landowners meanwhile, whether gentry like the Claytons, Crofts, Bates, Edens, Riddells or Wrightsons, or great landowners like the

[1] F. M. L. Thompson, 'The Economic and Social Background of the English Landed Interest, 1840–70' (unpublished D.Phil. thesis, Oxford University, 1956), pp. 336–42. A. J. Taylor, 'The Sub-contract system in the British Coal Industry', *Studies in the Industrial Revolution* (1960), pp. 222–3. Blagdon MSS, Report on Cowpen Colliery by J. Buddle, 31 Oct. 1837; Diary, 16 Aug. 1836, 16 June 1838, Aug. 1848. *Parliamentary Papers*, 1830, VIII, S.C. of H. of L. on State Coal Trade, p. 31.

Dukes of Northumberland and Portland, the Earl of Carlisle, Lords Hastings and Rokeby, or Sir Matthew White Ridley, drew their incomes in royalty and wayleave rents. These were not so spectacular as the profits of a capitalist like the Earl of Durham, but neither were they subject to the mercurial fluctuations which he experienced, a profit of £380,000 in 1873 and a dead loss of £65,000 in 1876.[1] The Duke of Northumberland's mineral income in fact grew from about £3,000 in 1800 to over £20,000 in the 1820s, suffered a setback after 1833 from which it did not properly recover until the end of the 1850s, and then settled down at about £25,000, not to expand again markedly until the middle of the 1880s. At this level it was not quite a quarter the size of the farm rents.

There were obviously wide differences between individuals in the size and importance of such incomes. The Duke of Cleveland, with rich lead mines in Teesdale, a little coal in Durham and a little more near Wolverhampton, had a mineral income which grew from about £6,000 in the 1840s to a steady £14,000 from the middle 1850s which continued until lead began to drop towards the end of the 1870s; it was about a fifth of the size of his income from land. Lord Sidmouth, with coal in Staffordshire, and ground rents in London, at the end of the 1870s had a landed income of £7,200 and other income of £3,900. Earl Fitzwilliam, before the estates were divided after his death in 1857, had an income from English lands of about £86,000 and a mineral income which had recently grown to about £23,000. At the other end of the scale the Marquess of Bath, in the 1870s, had a landed income of about £46,000 and a royalty income of a somewhat uncertain £3,000 from lead in Shropshire. The gentry, unless actually seated on the coal measures, were much less likely to enjoy any mineral income, since very few of their estates were scattered over several counties. Thus the Senhouses, who gave up working their own colliery at Maryport in 1844, had an income in the 1840s from royalties, ground rents, and all the miscellaneous rents from the quays, yards, rope walks and market place which went with the port, which was about equal to the £2,000 they derived from farms, and by the 1860s it provided well over half their total

---

[1] D. Spring, 'The Earls of Durham and the Great Northern Coalfield, 1830-80', *Canadian Hist. Rev.*, XXXIII (1952), p. 253.

income. At Lamplugh for a brief five years in the 1870s the Dickinsons had a mineral income of £600 against their land income of about £1,000, but Lamplugh was such a marginal colliery that in the 1880s the mineral income sank to £100 and soon disappeared altogether. But the Blundells, Darells, Harveys, Orlebars, and score upon score of others were passed by in the distribution of mineral riches; the Brooks were fortunate in being able to muster £20 a year from a sandpit.

Urban growth was another fertile source of wealth for landowners, either through the ground rents which many preferred in the south, or through the capital gains from outright sale of building land which was more characteristic of the north. Thus after some hesitation the Duke of Cleveland decided in 1867 to sell his building land on the fringe of Darlington rather than grant leases. He was at some expense, as were many developers, in laying out new roads and drains, but the return was generally very ample. In 1886 the Earl of Pembroke was reckoned to have spent £119,000 since 1853 on laying out roads on his 226 acres in Dublin, for which he was receiving ground rents of £11,719 a year and the prospect of eventual capital gains when the building leases should fall in.[1] The income of London's great landlords is difficult to assess, but was certainly vast and increasing. Already by the 1790s the Duke of Portland was receiving £4,000 a year from his Soho property, and he owned a large slice of Marylebone besides; by 1844 he estimated his London rents at £50,000 a year, half his net income.[2] The Grosvenors and Russells certainly did not fall behind.

London furnished a great array of smaller fortunes, replicas of Lord Sidmouth's properties in the City and the Strand or Faunce's property in Newington which have been noted. Outside London also there were many towns which had brought fortunes to individual landowners, all the way from Eastbourne which largely belonged to the Duke of Devonshire and the Gilberts of Truro, to Stockport which was shared between Lord Egerton of Tatton and the Scarisbricks who resided in Frankfort. Even Lord Monson received about £1,000 a year from Reigate

[1] *Parliamentary Papers*, 1886, XII, S.C. on Town Holdings, Evidence, Q.4896–905, 4970–8.
[2] Nottingham University, Portland MSS, Boxes 50, 125, Soho accounts, 1786–96, 1805–9. A. S. Turberville, *Welbeck Abbey and its Owners* (1939), II. 347.

ground rents. But the succour of urban site values was, like mining, most unevenly distributed among the members of the landed interest, and the majority of landowners were probably agricultural landowners. For the inquiry into housing in 1886 a solicitor circularized 261 provincial towns in England and Wales asking whether any considerable part of them was owned by large landlords. Great landowners were mentioned sixty-nine times as being considerable ground landlords, many of the magnates more than once, while the gentry were so named only thirty-four times. Moreover, half the towns answered that they had no large ground landlords at all.[1]

For those whose estates were fortunately placed the benefits of minerals or houses were very considerable, but the inequalities in the distribution of such benefits among the landed classes require much further investigation. It seems possible that the great landowners were benefited much more than the gentry, and that a new line of division was being created by the progress of industrialization between the great body of the mere gentry, and the landed aristocracy plus a minority of the squirearchy. The economic distinction was certainly becoming more marked year by year between landowners who were purely agricultural, and landowners who were guaranteed a share in the wealth generated by industry and commerce. For the beneficiaries the growing non-agricultural incomes helped to make possible the expanding agricultural outlays of the period, and provided solace for the weakened agricultural position which these implied. It may also have been that the magnates failed to make a stand for the protection of agriculture after 1879 because they were conscious of their position as industrial and urban landowners, and could afford to be more indifferent to falling rents than many of the gentry. But it would be a mistake to conclude that the simple fact of a spread of economic interests necessarily made an aristocrat feel any identification with industrialists or sympathy with middle-class objectives. Lord Cranborne, who impartially denounced Gladstone in 1866 and Disraeli in 1867 for undermining the landed interest, was firmly in the ranks of ground landlords; he spoke from centuries of Cecil tradition which took longer than this to bend before the realities of nineteenth-century economics.

[1] S.C. on Town Holdings, 1886, pp. 677-812.

X

The Decline of the Landed Interest,
1830–80

In spite of many forebodings the landed interest survived the great trials of the first Reform Bill and the Corn Law controversy, if not unscathed, then unbowed, and in the calm waters of the age of Palmerston once more exercised an easy and comparatively untroubled political dominance. Much of this, admittedly, depended on Palmerston's personality and policies, bluff, easy-going and averse to any great changes. Lord Monson might be suspicious of Palmerston, a slippery politician who 'might one day throw over the Whigs if he could do without them'; and in 1860 he observed, without any apprehension, 'there is little doubt but what Gladstone is the future Prime Minister'. It was more usual for the landed aristocracy to regard Palmerston as the prime bulwark of the established order. The fear that when Palmerston was gone the Whigs would revert to Whiggery and pernicious meddling with existing institutions, which was regularly expressed by the Marquess of Bath's political informant from 1862 onwards, must have been widely held. This was merely to anticipate the general reaction to Palmerston's death in 1865, for which Disraeli spoke in saying 'The truce of parties is over. I foresee tempestuous times, and great vicissitudes in public life'. They came, and Disraeli's own 'leap in the dark' was not the smallest of contributions towards a new age of reform, which as early as 1859 Lord Monson had seen must lead to equal electoral districts and the end of those traditional ties on which landed influence rested.[1]

It was one of the fortunate paradoxes of English politics that as often as not an aristocratic individual presided over the demolition of aristocratic institutions, perhaps ensuring power for his own lifetime at the expense of the future of his order. Thus Lord Derby presided over the passage of the Second Reform Act, and in spite of Lord Cranborne reform was treated in these years as a question of relative party advantage, not as a question of the defence of the landed interest. Indeed the most searing opposition to reform in the years 1865–7 came not from aristocrats in defence of interests, but from an intellectual, Robert Lowe, arguing for rule by the intelligent against rule by the ignorant masses. Again it was the same Lord Cranborne, grown to be Marquess of Salisbury, who compelled Gladstone to introduce equal electoral districts, as his price for allowing the Third Reform Bill to pass the Lords. It seemed that in succeeding to the leadership of the Conservative party he had succeeded to the idea that opportunist pursuit of immediate party advantage was the essence of politics, and that steady defence of established interests was no longer possible or desirable.

The feeling that the landed interest had been betrayed by its leaders, and denied any opportunity for standing in defence of its ground, because of misguided tactical manoeuvring, was trenchantly put to the Marquess of Bath in 1886. 'The establishment of electoral districts (to which I told you I was opposed)', the Marquess was reminded, 'involved a breaking up of old associations which must be prejudicial to the political influence of the landlords – an influence the good part of which rests more on old associations than on anything else. The calculation that electoral districts would be advantageous to the Tory party overcame the objection to them from the point of view of conservative principle, but I think the party were ill-advised even as regards their immediate result. . . . What I object to is the Tory attempt to outbid the Liberals by going beyond their

---

[1] Monson MSS, 25/10/4/4 no. 159, 5 Jan. 1858; 25/10/5/1 no. 85, 14 March 1859; 25/10/5/2 no. 80, 11 March 1860. Longleat MSS, Correspondence of Revd. Whitwell Elwin with Marquess of Bath 1860–77, esp. 1862 letters. W. F. Monypenny and G. E. Buckle, *Life of Benjamin Disraeli* (1929 ed.), II. 158.

proposals. When the Tories do this, and to do so is the essence of the neo-Tory method, their ultra proposals become at once the new Radical starting point; and the result is that events are forced, and instead of an orderly development of affairs, we are driven onwards to isolated triumphs of unripe sectional ideas. It was thus that we were brought to household suffrage, with the necessary sequel of manhood (Heaven only knows whether not also womanhood) suffrage. It was thus that we were brought to electoral districts. It is thus that, if Gladstone's Bill is rejected, we are likely to be brought to the establishment of a co-ordinate parliament in Ireland. Of all the delusions that have infected English political life in my time, there is none which seems to me more wonderful than the belief that genuine conservatism has any proper home in the party which was formed by Disraeli and is now led by Salisbury.'[1]

In fact, of course, when they were in positions of responsibility the leaders of either party were sensible enough to realize that they could not risk a head-on collision with the new forces, whether of the middle class or of the democracy, if only because in the last resort the established order did not dispose of sufficient physical force to resist determined and united attacks. Those in the wings of politics might contemplate the possibility of violent resistance, as the Duke of Buckingham did with the cannon taken ashore from his yacht in 1830 to fight Reform, or as Lord Monson did in 1860 on a wider and more organized basis. 'Has it ever struck you', he wrote to his son, 'that this Rifle Union may become a very important safeguard not only against a foreign enemy, but also against a too destructive democratic feeling among ourselves. It combines or will combine more or less everybody in its ranks that has anything to lose, and though I have no fear from its liberal constitution of its becoming a Tory agent, yet if anything of levelling plundering red republicanism was attempted here, it would be met by the élite of the nation already armed and disciplined.'[2] But even such a typically Whiggish readiness to rely on a voluntary union of all men of property for the armed defence of society was never shared by governments, except in such emergencies as the 1848 Chartist meeting when special constables were recruited to face an

[1] Longleat MSS, T. F. Wetherell to Marquess of Bath, 6 April 1886
[2] Monson MSS, 25/10/5/2 no. 65, 14 April 1860.

immediate threat of rioting. Governments on the whole were careful not to take up extreme positions, and to retreat in fairly good order and good time before serious manifestations of discontent. For this, to put it at its lowest, England had to thank the fact that there was no centrally controlled police force, and that the standing army was very small, so that governments were not tempted to risk a fight in defence of privilege or vested interest. From this power situation derived the long tradition of sensible moderation in government which had given England the reputation of possessing an essentially liberal-minded aristocracy. It is another way of saying that the rule of the landed interest was based on deference, on the whole voluntarily accorded, and not on outright power and coercion.

The quality of political leadership was one reason for the peaceful decline of landed power, and a most important one. It meant that there was a gradual long-drawn-out revolution, with no single episode, save perhaps Corn Law Repeal, which could be seized on convincingly as marking the point of no return. On occasion also what appeared to some traditional supporters as the vagaries or unreliability of their party leaders could act to reduce the actual extent of effective landed influence. The upkeep of an interest in a constituency was expensive work, and a landowner might well feel disinclined to continue the exertion if he had reason to disapprove of the course of the party which his members normally supported. Thus in 1868 the Duke of Northumberland, who felt that Derby and Disraeli 'have let the mob in upon us', contracted out of helping the Conservatives in Northumberland, while on the Whig side the Duke of Sutherland allowed his interest in Shropshire to lapse, Lord Yarborough was inactive in North Lincolnshire, and Lord Fitzwilliam was indifferent to the elections. Sometimes an interest might be revived successfully when the patron rediscovered a party enthusiasm, sometimes it might be allowed to go by default.[1]

A similar retreat into inaction had been hinted at a few years earlier when the Conservative Marquess of Bath took grave exception to Lord Derby meeting Garibaldi at a dinner given by the Duchess of Sutherland in 1864. 'It will reflect on you as leader of the Conservative party . . .', he wrote to Derby, 'you

[1] H. J. Hanham, *Elections and Party Management* (1959), pp. 26–8.

will mortally affront the Catholics who both in England and Ireland have not only dropped their hostility to the Conservatives, but have in many instances been disposed to support you . . . and last and least you will deeply wound the feelings of one who through the whole of his parliamentary career has made personal attachment to yourself the leading principle of his politics. . . .' Some of his reasons for disapproving of Garibaldi might be prejudices, 'but it is to prejudices such as these the Conservative party owes its present strength, and future hopes of success. They are prejudices such as these that have given me energy to win since 1852 three seats from the enemy and willingly and ungrudgingly to find myself involved in a certain expenditure of £5,000 and a possible one of £3,000 more to save these three and two others that were apparently in danger at the next general election'. Since Derby went through with his dinner, Lord Bath resigned his party post as one of the whips in the Lords, which he had held for twelve years. He remained lukewarm towards Derby, and thoroughly suspicious of Disraeli: 'I do wish Dizzy had accepted the peerage instead of his wife', his aunt wrote to him in 1868, 'we can never have a united party as long as Dizzy is the head of it'.[1]

Such factors, however, were not in themselves decisive in bringing about that weakening in the position of the landed interest which had already gone far, often beneath the surface, before the Third Reform Act seemed to lay it bare. In the 1885 election, it was said, 'the agricultural labourers have by their votes shown a spirit of rebellion . . . [against] the landlords and the established Church', which had been quite expected since 'it has for many years been recognised . . . that the predominant feeling among the agricultural labourers was on the liberal side. The landlords and the clergy were mainly on the other side, and it was well understood that they had been generally hostile to the enfranchisement'.[2] But in this half-century the weakening was more a matter of the changing relationship of the landed interest with the rest of society, than of the erosion of landed power within its own rural setting. In this field, in the broadest terms, the landed interest could not hope to prevent the industry

[1] Longleat MSS, Lord Bath to Lord Derby, 12 and 16 April 1864, Lord Derby to Lord Bath, 13 April 1864; Duchess of Buccleuch to Lord Bath, 17 Dec. 1868.
[2] Longleat MSS, T. F. Wetherell to Marquess of Bath, 6 April 1886.

state from coming of age; the most that could be expected, as we have seen, was that some would profit from the process. If the levers of power were still very largely held by members of the landed interest, increasingly they were held not by right of property but on sufferance from the rest of the community, and this conditioned the ways in which they could be pulled.

Even in a nomination borough like Malton, a modest market town serving the East Riding, Earl Fitzwilliam had to do more than pay bribes to the lower orders and support the chapels of Dissenters in order to retain his control. He had to pay heed to the interests of traders, merchants and small manufacturers, make sure in alliance with the Earl of Carlisle that Malton got its railway or 'we shall bleed for it', and adjust navigation tolls so that coal merchants or bone-millers could remain in business. Political interest had sometimes led to minor distortions of economic development here. 'As a further protection', the Earl was reminded in 1832, 'when the Navigation above the town was extended to Yeddington, the locks were so constructed as to admit small vessels only and the large vessels unload their cargoes into them below the bridge – this was done to prevent the trade of Malton getting to Norton. . . . The protection below the bridge is secured by charging the full dues (8s. per ton) for goods, wares and merchandize landed on the Norton side . . . and the same dues as Malton pays (2s. 6d. a ton) are only charged to the townships lower down. Without this protection the trade of Malton would soon change sides, at least would be greatly injured by it, and coal yards and warehouses would rise up in opposition to Malton to the ruin of many, who confiding in the continuance of this protection have expended their money in buildings and conveniences'. Certainly Fitzwilliam always got his man in for Malton down to the redistribution of 1885, but behind successful patronage lay a story of some attention to local commercial interests.[1]

At the other extreme in a wide constituency like the West Riding, filled with growing industrial towns as well as broad acres, landed influence could only be retained by consulting the 'feelings and interests of the trading part of the county'. The

---

[1] Fitzwilliam MSS, Lord Carlisle to Lord Fitzwilliam, 27 Dec. 1848. Wentworth Woodhouse MSS, G. 33, correspondence of the Malton agents 1828–57, esp. 27 Oct. 1832.

Fitzwilliams had never been able to control Yorkshire, since there had always been the opposition of the Tory nobility and gentry to contend with. In the thirty years after 1830 it became apparent that they could not control the Whig-liberal interests in the Riding, but must allow the townsmen a share in party management. After a troubled patch at the end of the 1840s when the Fitzwilliam influence was nearly extinguished, it re-emerged by 1859. But by then it was clear that Earl Fitzwilliam was in reality a figurehead for a party organization in which the leading liberals of Leeds, Bradford and Sheffield had at least a half-share.[1] Similarly as early as 1820 the Raby Castle party had eagerly solicited the support and interest of coal-fitters and shipbuilders in Sunderland, colliery owners and shipowners in Newcastle and Gateshead, sensing that the result of the Durham election hinged as much on these urban, industrial and commercial interests as on the dispositions of agricultural landowners. By 1841 it was even more apparent that the weight of voting power in South Durham lay in the industrial centres of Stockton, Darlington and the Aucklands, and the Raby party arrangements duly registered this fact.[2] There were quite a few counties in the Midlands and the North where similar partnerships with urban middle-class interests were the condition for the survival of country-house influence. For quite apart from the prolonged existence of many unrepresented towns embedded in county constituencies, it was possible from 1832 until 1885 for the wealthier property owners in parliamentary boroughs to have one vote for the borough and another for the county. The substantial citizens of Manchester, Liverpool, Leeds, or Birmingham, and many another great town, could thus make their views felt in the traditional centres of county politics.[3]

The redistribution of seats in 1885 had one small consolation for the landed interest, because it dealt with these dual voters and generally speaking ejected the alien town elements from

[1] F. M. L. Thompson, 'Whigs and Liberals in the West Riding, 1830–60', *English Hist. Rev.*, LXXIV (1959), pp. 214–39.
[2] Raby MSS, Memo made during the Canvass of Durham with Mr Powlett, 1820; Canvass book of South Durham elections, 1841.
[3] There is a return of these voters: *Parliamentary Papers*, 1857–8, XLVI, Return of Registered Electors, etc. Some of the poorer inhabitants of parliamentary boroughs, with freeholds worth over 40s. but under £10 a year, also had county votes.

rural seats, making the task of the landowners much less complicated, provided they could manage the agricultural labourers. By then, however, this was a salve to wounded feelings rather than an invitation to a renewed and purified landed dominance. Meanwhile where after 1832 great country houses had continued to provide leadership in such mixed counties, and had continued to seat members of the great political families, it was not simply because the middle classes continued to look up to them but also because they had learnt to pay proper attention to the interests, prejudices and opinions of the middle classes. This two-way traffic could only mean that members of the landed interest continued to enjoy the appearance of power on condition that they did not use it exclusively in the interests of land.

What was true of a number of the great electoral interests was even more true of Parliament itself. Landowners had long been accustomed to fill the House of Commons with themselves, their sons or their near relatives, and in spite of the Duke of Wellington's celebrated remark that the Reform Bill would render the House unfit for a gentleman to sit in, the custom was not much affected by the passage of the first Reform Act. Indeed the genuine landed gentry may have found it easier to get into Parliament after 1832 than before, for one of the many purposes of Reform was to rid the electoral system of those corrupt close boroughs through which nabobs and other *nouveaux riches* had bought their way into the House. Landed families, in any case, continued to furnish a majority of the House of Commons, a substantial one until 1868, still a slight one in the parliament of 1880; in 1885 for the first time 'the number of commercial men and manufacturers in the House of Commons was greater than the number of landowners'.[1] This did not mean that landed supremacy was prolonged without qualification until 1885, for many of this landed majority were seated not by farmers' votes but by those of the middle classes, and sat not for counties or minute rural boroughs but for genuine towns. They sat there because they were members of the hereditary political class, men with the self-confidence to govern and legislate, men with the independent means and the leisure needed for membership of the House

[1] Hanham, *op. cit*, pp. xv–xvii. And see J. A. Thomas, *House of Commons, 1832–1901* (Cardiff, 1939).

Above all it cost money to get elected. 'It appears that however Reform may extend the franchise it is not likely to extend the choice of members to any class that is not able to bear the bleeding by their constituents', Lord Monson wrote in 1860 after his purse had been stretched by Reigate. After 1830 many individuals might retire from the race because of the expense. £14,000 for the South Durham contest in 1841 was 'scandalously preposterous' Lord Harry Vane felt, almost but not quite enough to justify retirement from active politics. Sir F. Bathurst might not be available as a candidate for Wiltshire in 1860 because 'it seems he is laying out a good deal of money in building a new house – and he has a large family (or rather two) to provide for'.[1] But generally some other member of the landed class would be found ready to step forward and foot the bill for his turn in Parliament. In such conditions, as long as they pursued sensible policies with reasonable regard for the interests and opinions of others, many practical business men, as well as the shopkeeper and tradesman class, were well content to leave their representation in the hands of the landed gentlemen.

It is possible that the interest of historians in the composition of the House of Commons, analyzing the economic interests or social backgrounds of Members, or in the often irrational and sometimes purely pecuniary operations of the electoral process, has somewhat obscured the obvious facts that sometimes constituents mattered and that public opinion was a great and growing force. In the midst of the struggle for Reform Lord Grey referred to 'the middle classes who form the real and efficient mass of public opinion, and without whom the power of the gentry is nothing'.[2] It was an observation which was no less true of the succeeding decades than it was of 1831 itself. Money swayed elections precisely because the choice before electors was so often one between personalities whose policies were largely indistinguishable. What mattered to the 'efficient mass of public opinion', however, was what these policies were, what the members did once they had been elected. Here the quality of parliaments was to be judged not by the ancestry of members

[1] Monson MSS, 25/10/5/2 no. 55, 6 May 1860. Raby MSS, Election accounts 1841; Lord Harry Vane to T. H. Scarth, 8 Jan. 1842. Longleat MSS, Lord Derby to Marquess of Bath, 25 Dec. 1860.
[2] Quoted by N. Gash, *Politics in the Age of Peel* (1953), p. 15.

so much as by the record of current administration and legislation.

By this standard the record of parliaments between 1832 and 1868 was not conspicuous for its neglect of middle-class interests or for any pronounced emphasis on those of land. The combined force of the landed M.P.s might be able to 'ride roughshod over Government and capitalists and economists and all thinking people on such a question as that of indemnity for cattle' in obtaining legislation and public money to deal with the cattle plague in 1866.[1] It was one thing to be able to promote a sectional interest, quite another to maintain that it was the paramount interest. In the period between the Reform Acts the great institutional changes may have been largely completed by the end of the 1840s, leaving little but the budget as an instrument of domestic change in the 1850s and 1860s. But it would be idle to deny that the main tenor of these changes was to embody in law and institutions the requirements of that industrial economy in which by far the major part was played by the middle classes. It may have been a parliament of landowners which passed the Corn Laws in 1815. It was also a parliament of landowners, of course under outside pressure, amid confusion, and with no unanimity, which repealed the Corn Laws in 1846 – just as it was a Palmerstonian House of Commons which passed Disraeli's Reform Act, and just as it had been an unreformed House which reformed itself in 1832.

In a sense therefore the landed interest continued to hold sway politically by grace of the middle classes, whose ultimate reserve of political power was enshrined in their enfranchisement in 1832, and was reflected not in the composition of the House but in the course of legislation. The landed M.P.s of the 1860s, and still more of the 1870s, formed a thin upper crust resting on a middle-class electorate, whose power to thrust them aside was already in existence even if it as yet lay dormant and unused. Even more important than the dormant electoral sanction, which could not easily have been made decisive as long as the 1832 distribution of seats held good, was the sanction of public opinion. As government policy became more responsive to responsible opinion, from the middle 1820s onwards, an increasing influence passed to the opinion-forming bodies. The landed interest was certainly not unrepresented in the powerful

[1] *Economist*, 17 March 1866.

field of the serious London and provincial press or the quarterly reviews, but it was a field in which the intellectuals and professional men were dominant.

In the spate of reforms which followed 1868 could be seen the delayed entrance of the middle classes into their inheritance, at first through increasingly effective pressure on a slowly changing body of M.P.s. Then, as the spread of company organization freed more business men for other activities, and as the 1883 Corrupt Practices Act successfully limited the cost of getting into parliament, the inheritance was fully claimed, and the House itself became dominated by commercial men and manufacturers. It was a pattern of development in English political life which was to be repeated in the twentieth century, when the professional and business contingent of Liberal M.P.s formed an upper crust resting on a working-class electorate, which would thrust them aside as soon as it was equipped to support men of its own kind as members.

Because different answers must be returned to the questions, who holds power, and in whose interests is power exercised, and because rule by the landed interest did not mean rule for the landed interest, it must be conceded that the worm had eaten a long way into the essence of landed domination, as that had been understood until 1830, during the half-century before the end of that domination was laid bare for all the world to see. It was partly because this decline at the political level was gradual and not cataclysmic, half-concealed and well compensated by prolonged retention of the panoply of power, that the landed interest as a body never found an occasion to stand in defence of its position. It was also because a section of the landed interest, mainly to be found among the Whig magnates but also elsewhere and particularly among the Peelites, was brilliantly capable in the politics of compromise and concession. Such men appreciated that security and a large measure of stability depended on the solution of immediate practical problems. They refused to be distracted by Tory prophets of woe who were ever eager to announce their refusal to cross bridges long before they came to them, and to use long-range forecasts of future disasters as excuses for present inaction.

Twenty or fifty years after the event men could reflect on the realization of the fears of Alexander Baring, the Tories' chief spokesman in 1831, that 'In a Reformed Parliament, when the day of battle came, the country Squires would not be able to stand against the active, pushing, intelligent people who would be sent from the manufacturing districts'. 'The field of coal', he had said, 'would beat the field of barley.'[1] But it was thanks to the Whigs that the day of reckoning did not come in 1831 itself, and there can be no justification for the argument behind the Tory position, that it was better to have an immediate and violent revolution in 1831 than to have a gradual and peaceful one spread out over the next half-century. As Lord Fitzwilliam said, he was amply justified in the final Reform crisis of May 1832 in joining with the most radical elements in refusing to pay his taxes until the Bill was passed, the country then being on the very 'brink of a precipice' and it being of supreme importance to prevent the Crown, Lyndhurst and Wellington forming an anti-Reform government.[2]

If the Reform Act contained a contingent undermining of the power of the landed interest, and embodied their marriage with the middle classes in the defence of the constitution, it was not an isolated event, nor by itself the great cause of the decline of the landed interest. Reform had many roots, not least among that section of the landed interest which wished to curtail the power of government patronage and sweep away rotten boroughs in order to prevent any repetition of what was felt as the outrage of Catholic Emancipation in 1829. But among its roots was certainly the great transformation of the economy that had been long in progress, and the long-growing recognition that the great weight of responsible middle-class opinion was inadequately represented.

The Fitzwilliams, who must be ranked as very moderate Whigs since their association with Pitt in 1794, changed their minds on Reform over this very issue of opinion. 'I have hitherto been an opponent of Parliamentary Reform', Lord Milton wrote to a more extreme Whig in 1821, 'because it seemed the House of Commons fairly represented public opinion, even when the House of Commons did that which seemed to me unwise the public seemed to agree with the majority.' 'I have

---

[1] Quoted by Gash, *op. cit.*, p. 6.
[2] Fitzwilliam MSS, Lord Milton's letter book 732, Lord Milton to O'Bryan, 29 Nov. 1832.

never been satisfied (as to the necessity for reform)', he wrote at the same time in a summary of his own political philosophy, 'until the conduct of the House of Commons relative to the Queen [Caroline]. On this question one half of the higher ranks were on one side, while on the other side were the other half of the higher ranks and the whole of the middle and lower classes of society, and yet notwithstanding this extraordinary preponderance of public opinion in one scale, the members of parliament threw themselves into the other scale at the request of Ministers with as little hesitation as if they were voting upon the most trivial and uninteresting question. These considerations have persuaded me that public opinion has not its due weight in the House of Commons, and that therefore some measures ought to be taken to give the people a more adequate representation.'[1]

A long history of readiness to adjust the claims of the landed interest, and the institutions of the country, to the real facts of economic and social life led up to Reform, just as a long history of adjustments accomplished followed it. In one of these major adjustments, the establishment of free trade, it was again not a simple question of giving way to the clamourings of an insistent middle class. Lord Fitzwilliam was again to the fore, a prominent and consistent advocate of free trade at least since 1821, because he believed that the Corn Laws did not in fact provide protection for farmers, and because he held that the great interests of the 'highly educated commercial and manufacturing classes' must be respected.[2] He and his associates certainly did not intend that free trade, any more than parliamentary reform, should mean the abdication of the old landed interest in favour of the new middle classes, but neither did their conduct suggest that they meant the same thing by the preservation of the paramountcy of the landed interest as did their Tory and gentry opponents. 'If landlords think to get the better of right reason by means of great power, they cannot expect to be shown consideration', he had written in 1832, and he devoted much of the remainder of his life to seeing that they should continue to

[1] Fitzwilliam MSS, Lord Milton's letter book 731, Lord Milton to Sir G. Cayley, 11 March 1821, and draft by Lord Milton incorporated in this letter.

[2] *Ibid.*, Lord Milton to E. Ombler, 26 Feb. 1821; Lord Milton's letter book 732, Lord Milton to Bark, n.d. but *circa* Dec. 1832. And see D. Spring, 'Earl Fitzwilliam and the Corn Laws', *American Hist. Rev.*, LIX (1954), pp. 287–304.

receive consideration by showing that they were open to the persuasion, if not of logic, then at least of hard political and economic facts.[1]

Lord Fitzwilliam and his friends hoped that the landed aristocracy would remain the 'Master Interest' in the land. They experienced some uneasy moments when they feared that in fact it was doomed. The possibility was considered that the railway match-makers with their amalgamations and their territorial empires might be raising up a formidable rival interest. 'May they not be raising up a power, greater than any Colonial or even landlord interest, that may hereafter puzzle both Government and Parliament to deal with it?' a correspondent asked in 1845.[2] But skill and experience showed that the railway interest could be accommodated and absorbed, one wing to each of the old-established parties.

For a while after 1846, in spite of his principles, Fitzwilliam shared the view of his friend Evelyn Denison that the means by which Repeal had been secured had 'put the trading interest in ascendancy over the landed'. Denison complained that Lord John Russell had 'thought it necessary to buy up the mouthpieces of the great towns in the House of Commons', and Fitzwilliam echoed the grievance to the Duke of Bedford and others that the landed interest had been left out of the cabinet. He was only slightly reassured when the Duke of Bedford pointed out that 'I believe the Cabinet and its outworks to be remarkable for talent and integrity – but if anyone were to complain that there is not in the former a single representative of the Merchants and Manufacturers of this great community I should think there was more truth and better reason in his complaint than in Denison's, seeing that there are not less than six or seven to represent the land. John wrote to Denison . . . that he "was not aware till he heard his speech that Woburn Abbey was considered as a Cotton Factory" '. The troubles and affronts of West Riding politics in 1847 and 1848 only served to increase Fitzwilliam's alarm for the survival of the landed interest. But calm and reason returned, the Whig in him reasserted its presence, and the landed interest was seen to have emerged into

---

[1] Fitzwilliam MSS, Lord Milton's letter book 732, Lord Milton to Bark, c. Dec. 1832.

[2] Fitzwilliam MSS, G. Loch to Lord Fitzwilliam, 21 Feb. 1845.

the 1850s, not indeed altogether intact, but not yet mortally wounded either.[1]

Frontal assault on the aristocratic position by the middle classes was, indeed, perhaps the least effective of all in bringing about the decline of the landed interest. This was largely because the active leaders were inhibited in their choice of weapons by their principles. The campaign against the Corn Laws had been carried on with much fierce rhetoric against the 'aristocratic monopoly', and the radicals of the Manchester School had made it clear that they would not rest content with the immediate objective of total repeal, but intended this as a stepping stone towards sweeping reforms of the institutions in church, state and colonies which were dominated by the landed class. After Repeal Cobden still intended to proceed with the work of 'beating down the power of the aristocracy', but he declined to take up the obvious implement for the task, a programme of radical parliamentary reform, because he was fearful of its democratic implications and its likely association with Chartism in the public mind. Instead, arguing that power rested on wealth, and the power which he was attacking rested on land, Cobden for a time tried to rally the radical forces round a campaign for free trade in land. This movement for the abolition of primogeniture, entails and settlements, and the simplification of land transfers, had great intellectual attractions. It offered a means of securing the break-up of estates, the diffusion of land ownership and the end of landlordism in all its aspects without requiring any alteration of the franchise, and at the same time appeared to be a logical extension of the principles of political economy whose validity had just been admitted in the sphere of commerce. It had the overwhelming practical disadvantage of proving to be a mare's nest, devoid of strong attraction to potential supporters and bringing uncovenanted comfort to the intended victims.[2]

There were three main periods of active agitation for the reform of the land laws: that running concurrently with the anti-Corn Law campaign and carrying on until the middle of the

[1] Wentworth Woodhouse MSS, G. 18, J. E. Denison to Lord Fitzwilliam, 29 July 1846; Duke of Bedford to Lord Fitzwilliam, 4 August 1846. And see F. M. L. Thompson, 'Whigs and Liberals in the West Riding, 1830–60'.

[2] For this and the two subsequent paragraphs, except where otherwise stated, see F. M. L. Thompson, 'The Economic and Social Background of the English Landed Interest', *passim*.

1850s; the revived agitation for free trade in land after 1870 which issued into the rather wider land programme of the Chamberlainite radicals in the 1880s and then subsided after 1886; and the early twentieth century, particularly from 1909 to 1914, when the Liberals took up some of the old cries but focused their sights more on the urban landlords. All three periods succeeded in frightening the landowners and persuading them to draw somewhat closer together. In none were the fundamental objectives achieved, though the second and third periods could show secondary results of some importance. In the first period the known and far-reaching aims of the radicals caused the postponement of useful reforms in the laws governing land transfers, which in themselves had no revolutionary content. 'Take care of your coronets', the nobility were advised in 1847, 'and set your houses in order – for if you . . . do not adopt a more prudent line of public policy, your coronets and your title deeds will, ere long, be in danger'.[1] In the second period there was not only the Irish land legislation, but also English land legislation of importance on settled land, ground game and tenant's rights. And in the third period taxation of land values was started, and tenants were given protection against unreasonable disturbance by landlords.

Even after 1909, however, the success of any radical reforms in themselves in bringing about the downfall of the territorial system was very questionable and in any case very limited. It was of far greater importance that the espousal of land reform policies by radicals helped to show up the divisions within the ranks of the middle classes. A conservative section of the middle classes had of course always existed, but the realization that attacks on the free disposal of landed property by its owners were extensible to other forms of property undoubtedly helped to add to its strength. It was obvious during the campaign against the Corn Laws that a wide range of divergent interests and opinions was held together only for this single purpose. Nevertheless the attempt to carry on the movement after 1846 as one for free trade in land cost the support of many a wealthy millowner who had been a keen free trader, though Bright's desire to turn the movement in the direction of household suffrage lost the support of even more. Similarly when it seemed

[1] E. B. Denison, quoted in *Leeds Mercury*, 14 August 1847.

possible from the later 1870s that the English land question might become one of the dominant issues of the time, its association with interference with the rights of private property made it a contributory factor in the tendency for landowners and wealthy business men to range themselves on one side, and intellectuals and professional men on the other. It was a tendency which had been under way for years before the Home Rule crisis made it explicit.

The main effect of the attempts to attack the landed system at its roots, therefore, was to damage middle-class unity rather than wound the landed interest. In so far as it helped to rally all men of property to the defence of society, which had been one of the themes of 1832 and of Peel's conservatism, it did help to fuse the old landed and the new industrialists into a new ruling class, and therefore helped to undermine the ascendancy of the landed interest as such. This fusion, however, was helped much more by the intercourse of society, where wealth and lineage met; by the pressure of economic interests, which made the greatest in the land eager for the favours of railway king Hudson; by the action of the new model public schools, expanding in numbers at this time and moulding to a common type boys of the most diverse origins. And by the steady transfusion of new wealth into landed position: 'it would "pay" a millionaire in England to sink half his fortune in buying 10,000 acres of land to return a shilling per cent, and live upon the remainder, rather than to live upon the whole without land', it was said in 1870, 'he would be a greater person in the eyes of more people'.[1]

As time went by it became hard to tell whether the old order was successfully absorbing the new men and moulding them to its ways or whether the new had overwhelmed the old and produced another form of society, aristocratic, conservative in the sense that both Whig and Tory had been, but based on wealth and education rather than on land and tradition. The answer perhaps was only made plain in the thirty years after 1880, and it would certainly be a mistake to suppose that before 1880 there had been any great modifications in the distinctive way of life of the landed aristocracy.

A contrast is sometimes drawn between the reckless abandon and extravagance of aristocratic living in the Regency and late

[1] *Economist*, 16 July 1870.

Georgian period, and the sobriety and prudence of the mid-Victorian aristocrats, and there are doubtless many examples of such a change. Nevertheless there were always exceptions to the prevailing mood. Lord Verulam was God-fearing, upright, averse to high stakes at cards, and disapproving of mistresses in the 1820s: Lord Bessborough conducted a scandalous affair from Phoenix Park in 1846 while in the midst of dealing with the grave Irish distress. Lord Fitzwilliam kept innumerable personal accounts in a great effort to live within his income throughout the height of Regency dissipation: the Duke of Buckingham went bankrupt in 1848, when the Duke of Beaufort and the Earl of Mornington were also tottering, and in 1870 the Duke of Newcastle, the Earl of Winchilsea and Lord De Mauley were all before the bankruptcy courts, and in every case personal extravagance was a factor in their embarrassments.[1]

It may perhaps be a little misleading to suppose that the characteristics of an age are determined by the behaviour and amusements of the immediate entourage of the sovereign, so that at one time all are gay Regency bucks, at another sober Victorian family men, only to emerge once more as gay Edwardians. Certainly if there was a change in the social climate in the mid-Victorian age, there was also the ceaseless change in the attitude of individuals which was related to their years and the date of their inheritance rather than to any general social pressure. It was a theme which Lord Monson was fond of stressing: the recklessness of heirs and their saving habits when once in possession. 'It would never surprise me if the present Lord Yarborough turned henceforth a very saving man', he wrote in 1862, 'erring perhaps in the other extreme – it would be no change of character – the man who spends with reckless extravagance as long as he fancies the cost must be defrayed from the paternal pocket, the moment that he knows that he must himself and no other bear the weight of his expenses, he will look sharp after every shilling.'[2] At the very least, if the

[1] Gorhambury MSS, 1st Earl of Verulam's Diary, *passim*. Wentworth Woodhouse MSS, G. 18, J. E. Denison to Lord Fitzwilliam, 27 October 1846. F. M. L. Thompson, 'The End of a Great Estate', *Econ. Hist. Rev.*, 2nd ser., VIII (1955), pp. 36–52. D. and E. Spring, 'The Fall of the Grenvilles, 1844–8', *Huntington Library Quarterly*, XIX (1956), pp. 165–90. C. B. Patterson, *Angela Burdett-Coutts and the Victorians* (1953), pp. 103–4. *The Times*, Bankruptcy Court reports, 1869–71.
[2] Monson MSS, 25/10/5/4, no. 132, 23 Jan. 1862.

aristocracy generally did come to practice more of the virtues of prudence and thrift, we may be certain that they did not adopt a middle-class way of living, and in respect of domestic establishments or sporting habits the merger with the new wealth was conducted on their terms.

This fusion was perhaps apparent in the sphere of administration at the same time as it was apparent in high society, and in both before it was fully revealed in House of Commons politics. Caird could still write in 1878 that the professions, church, army and civil service were largely recruited from the landed interest. But in fact the conditions which secured this monopoly had already been swept away in Gladstone's first Administration by such measures as universities' and civil service reform and the abolition of the purchase of army commissions. It had already been conceded that employment in the public service, once the preserve of patronage, should be the reward for individual merit as tested by examinations. After this it was purely a matter of time, multiplication of tasks for civil servants and expansion of territories for colonial administrators, before the élite of the public schools and universities took over the running of the state from the sons of the landed families. The concession had been made because it was recognized that the resources of patronage could not provide sufficient competence for frugal administration, and because patronage was a method of appointment which offended current ideas of efficiency and equity. Before the forces of population growth, industrialization and large towns, the amateur administrator had to make way for the professional. It was something which had been admitted at least from the days of the Poor Law Amendment Act of 1834, though some of the further changes were a long time in coming.

In their own special sphere, that of county government, the landowners fought long and hard to preserve their control through the institutions of lords lieutenant and quarter sessions. In a sense they were highly successful, for there were at least a dozen bills put forward from 1837 onwards, proposing to establish elected county authorities, devices which nevertheless remained unknown until the establishment of county councils in 1888. Moreover the character of the bench remained largely unchanged, composed of the landed gentry and clergy – though including growing numbers of substantial businessmen in industrial counties – for the several efforts made to revise the property qualification for J.P.s were all frustrated. Thus in 1875 the Earl of Albemarle moved to allow on to the bench men with personal property worth £300 a year, asserting that the existing law was 'one of the last remnants of class legislation, vicious in principle and obstructive in operation, by which the administration of justice was subservient to the social elevation of a class', and he was supported by Earl Cowper who argued that large numbers of farmers would make good magistrates. They were overruled by less liberal peers, who were satisfied with the existing practice and held that there was no shortage of landed gentry to fill the benches.[1] Where, indeed, we seem to see such a shortage, as in the Essex of 1863 when Lord Braybrooke recommended the appointment as magistrate of the 'head of the very large Drug factory at Stratford, and a keen fox hunter', the reason was the fairly recent antipathy of Lord Chancellors to clerical magistrates. Nevertheless well over a thousand clergy were county magistrates in the England of the 1860s, perhaps half the magistrates of the country, and they and the landed gentry between them still reigned supreme in quarter sessions in the 1880s.[2]

Behind this stability, however, the functions of quarter sessions had been changing since the 1830s. In part their effective authority had been curtailed, as new local authorities, coterminous neither with one another nor with the counties, had been created piecemeal to discharge some of the duties of local government. Some of these new authorities discharged more effectively duties which had previously been under the supervision of quarter sessions, such as the Poor Law Unions and the Highway Boards; others, such as the School Boards and the Sanitary Districts which were created in the 1870s, were new bodies with new functions stemming from the growing demands of society. It is true that what the landed gentry lost in their capacity as J.P.s they frequently regained in a new capacity as elected members of Boards of Guardians or School Boards. It was a development which was to be repeated on a larger scale

[1] *Hansard*, 3rd ser. CCXXIII (1875), 765–70.
[2] Essex C.R.O., Braybrooke MSS, D/DBY.0.34, 0.35, and 0.38, Lord Braybrooke's diary as Vice-Lieutenant of Essex 1861–5, and correspondence on magistracies. *Parliamentary Papers*, 1861, LI and 1863, XLVIII, Returns of clerical magistrates.

after 1888, when the nobility and gentry found that they were easy winners in many county council elections. In a sense, therefore, the long resistance of the landed interest to the establishment of ratepayer's control of county government, through elected county financial boards, was unnecessary, since experience showed that as the natural leaders of local society the J.P. class did win local elections when they chose to stand. This did not prevent lugubrious spirits anticipating the 'dethronement of the squirearchy' in 1888, just as they had done for a similar measure in 1837.[1] In the elective bodies which did exist, however, the gentry had to share place with farmers and tradesmen, and on this score there is no doubt of the erosion of their exclusive control of local affairs from 1834 onwards.

Possibly of even greater importance in local government was the steady replacement of amateur administrators by professionals. County police forces, for example, were generally established in the later 1840s and the 1850s, replacing the old village constables and the newer, gentry-supported, voluntary associations for the apprehension and prosecution of felons which had become fairly common aids to rural security from the 1790s onwards. The county forces might be under the financial control of quarter sessions, and the chief constables might very often come, by way of the army, from the same gentry class as the J.P.s. But they were a professional force, and had the same tendency to establish an autonomous code of conduct, and a degree of control over their nominal masters, that is exhibited by all bodies of permanent and professional public servants. Similarly in the Unions the medical officers and relieving officers established a record of continuous and expert service which gave them much of the real work of administration and limited the effective range of the guardians' power from below, while central control limited it from above. All in all the landed gentry, in their various capacities of local authority, were by 1880 far removed from their former position as amateur unpaid administrators. Quarter sessions had moved a long way towards becoming a nominated county parliament, supervizing the services of a number of permanent professional officials. Prestige and position remained to the gentry, power had been curtailed.

[1] *Hansard*, 3rd ser. XXXVI (1837), 418; XXXVII (1837), 1128; CCCXXIX (1888), 918–23, 928–33.

Behind all these changes in the balance of forces within the community lay the fact that in the 1880s the landed interest still possessed an influence altogether out of proportion to their numbers. This they owed to the great social consequence which continued to attach to the owners of landed estates, a feeling of respect which had not been greatly affected by half a century's experience of adjustments to the new forces and new necessities thrown up by the industrial revolution. Several landowners had appreciated, by the middle of the century, that land was a luxury which gave very poor financial returns to its owners, and had wondered whether the time had not arrived to put their wealth to more remunerative uses. Sir James Graham in 1845 contemplated retreat from the position of a great landowner. Evelyn Denison expatiated to Lord Fitzwilliam in 1847 'about that "expensive luxury" Land. It is about to become infinitely more expensive than ever', he wrote, 'so great a luxury that many now in possession of it will be obliged to resign it'. This was because, he felt, interest rates on mortgages were about to be pushed to unprecedentedly high levels by the competition of railway debentures, 'which will put a pressure on encumbered estates (that is, speaking generally, on half or two thirds of the land of England) to which they have never before been subjected'. He himself, however, was going to sell land 'not because I am of the class of encumbered landlords, for I have luckily extricated myself from that, but because I do not think it worth while to keep a security paying 2 per cent, when I can get an equally good one paying 5.' Lord Monson put the matter more succinctly when he burst out in 1851: 'What an infernal bore is landed property. No certain income can be reckoned upon. I hope your future wife will have Consols or some such ballast, I think it is worth half as much again as what land is reckoned at.'[1]

None of these landowners did in fact sell up their estates, and it was only a very few of the very heavily encumbered owners who did find the pressure too great. The decision to hold on to landed property, despite its lack of economic attractions, was no doubt made unthinkingly by the majority out of respect for

[1] D. Spring, 'A Great Agricultural Estate', p. 81. Wentworth Woodhouse MSS, G. 20, J. E. Denison to Lord Fitzwilliam, 18 Aug. 1847. Monson MSS, 25/10/3/1, no. 19, 22 Nov. 1851.

family tradition, and by only a few after deliberate consideration. It was nonetheless a decision which prolonged the social influence of the landed order, for they would have been wealthier but lesser men without their estates. At the same time agricultural landownership did become an increasingly expensive luxury, and many landowners found that they were committed to a costly defence of the economic basis of their social position without reaping any increase in wealth at all commensurate with the effort. In this way, therefore, agricultural landowners more or less marked time while the wealth of the rest of the community surged forward, so that the very effort which secured a temporary prolongation of their social dominance made their decline in relative importance more certain, and ensured that the final triumph must go to the plutocracy of wealth.

There was no escape from the dilemma of wealth and status. Without land, they would no longer be a landed aristocracy. With land, only those whose estates were fortunate enough to benefit from industrial values were wealthy enough to remain dominant. The landed interest entered the late nineteenth century with its social position largely intact. The Percy dependants, at an annual dinner, could still state their position with frankness and enthusiasm:

> '. . . Those relics of the feudal yoke
> Still in the north remain unbroke:
> That social yoke, with one accord,
> That binds the Peasant to his Lord . . .
> And Liberty, that idle vaunt,
> Is not the comfort that we want;
> It only serves to turn the head,
> But gives to none their daily bread.
> We want community of feeling,
> And landlords kindly in their dealing.'[1]

But in political, economic and administrative essentials the landed interest had surrendered the keys of power before 1880. It remained for agricultural depression to make plain the extent of the accomplished fact, and for the landed aristocracy to enjoy a long twilight of great honour, prestige, and personal wealth, although their ascendancy was over.

[1] Alnwick MSS, Business Minutes, XXV (1859), pp. 106–7.

XI

<hr/>

Indian Summer, 1880–1914

<hr/>

O N E of the last intellectual defenders of the old landed aristocracy was the economist M'Culloch, who sang the praises of primogeniture and entails in 1848. Twenty years later Bagehot's admiration of the civilizing effects of the social power of the old nobility did not go so far as this. And when Robert Lowe defended aristocracy in 1865–7 he was not defending an order based on an hereditary nobility and inherited landed estates, but an aristocracy of intelligence and merit, in which each individual established his membership of the élite afresh in each generation.[1] What emerged as the dominant group in late Victorian England was a curious blend of these two ideas, and something more, practically effective if not intellectually satisfying. As well as the old territorial nobility it contained the new men who made their way by their own ability, and as often as not behind the new men lay industrial wealth, itself also liable to be inherited. Tradition, personal merit, and Bagehot's plutocracy made terms with one another, and nowhere is this more visible than in the history of the peerage after 1885.

Until the fall of Gladstone's Ministry in 1885 the nobility had remained very largely the preserve of landed wealth and aristocratic connexions. Gladstone himself, although he had been offending Whig principles and shedding Whig allies for several

<hr/>

[1] J. R. M'Culloch, *Treatise on the Succession to Property Vacant by Death* (1848). W. Bagehot, *The English Constitution*, p. xxxiii. A. Briggs, *Victorian People* (1954), chap. ix.

years, had not yet abandoned Whig standards in the creation of peers. Disraeli had perhaps come nearer to innovation: his final creations in 1880 had included the Guest barony of Wimborne and the Guinness barony of Ardilaun, the first direct entry of beer into the Lords. Both these new peers, however, had inherited baronetcies, possessed considerable landed estate, and had made aristocratic marriages, so that their acceptability was already established. Nevertheless it can be seen that Lord Salisbury was building on a newly-founded Conservative tradition when in his short first Ministry he created Henry Allsopp, Lord Hindlip. Allsopp had a modest country seat at Hindlip Hall in Worcestershire, but he was notable as a large-scale Burton brewer, a self-made man, and an active Conservative. In retrospect it is clear that with this creation Lord Salisbury had opened a new road into the peerage for industrial and commercial wealth and started a development in which landed qualifications were before long lost to sight.

For Gladstone his first Home Rule Ministry was in this respect at least a liberating experience, and he at once countered in 1886 by creating the rival Burton brewer, Michael Bass, Lord Burton, and by advancing to the peerage Thomas Brassey, son of the famous railway contractor. The new trend was consolidated in Lord Salisbury's second Administration of 1886–92, when a third of the new peers were men whose fortunes rested on trade and industry. In this band there were some, like John Hubbard, Lord Addington, whose position as a Russia merchant and Governor of the Bank of England was similar to that of earlier banking peers; while the second Guinness peerage, that of Iveagh in 1891, was plainly a case of having the other half. Yet others showed the full variety of this new stream of recruits: H. F. Eaton, Lord Cheylesmore, was a silk broker; Samuel Cunliffe-Lister, Lord Masham, made his fortune in wool-combing; Lord Armstrong of Cragside was famous in engineering and armaments; and the leader of the House of Commons, W. H. Smith, is commemorated in his bookstalls rather than in the title of Hambleden which was granted to his widow.[1]

[1] On this whole section see R. E. Pumphrey, 'The Introduction of Industrialists into the British Peerage: A Study in Adaptation of a Social Institution', *American Hist. Rev.*, LXV (1959), pp. 1–16. The figures in the text differ from Pumphrey's, since royal dukes and promotions within the nobility are not counted among the new peers; the general conclusions are similar.

Two hundred and forty-six new titles were granted between 1886 and 1914; discounting those recipients who were members of the royal family or who were receiving promotion within the peerage, there were some two hundred individuals entering the nobility for the first time. More than a third of these new peers, some seventy, represented the new wealth of the industrial revolution; another third had risen in the professions, the law chiefly, and service to the state in diplomacy, colonies or the armed forces; and scarcely one-quarter were the heads of old-established landed families, the group which had formerly furnished the backbone of the peerage. From a different point of view the decline of the landed classes looks less precipitous. A number of the industrialist peers were, like Lord Joicey, the sons of men who had acquired landed status; if we eliminate those who had inherited a landed position, though nevertheless remaining active in business, not more than a quarter of these new peers were self-made men. Furthermore a goodly proportion of the second group, particularly the diplomats and colonial governors, were younger sons of the nobility and gentry, and thus belonged to the landed classes although not landowners themselves. Hence in terms of their family backgrounds slightly more than half the new peers still came from landed circles. This registered a steep decline from the years before 1885, when more than three-quarters of the new peers came from this kind of family background. It also meant that the landed classes continued to provide a share of the recruits to the peerage out of all proportion to their total numbers, and is some indication of the relative position which they still occupied within the influential classes as a whole.

The influential classes, as measured by the grant of titles, continued in the main to be politicians. Two-thirds of the new peers had rendered political services, either in the cabinet or in the Commons alone, only a slight decline from the proportion in earlier years. Within this group of politicians the changed emphasis is most marked: one-third came from the landed classes, one-fifth from the middle-class professions, and the remainder, the largest single section, from the world of industry and commerce, clear reflection of the transfer of power. Such a division, indeed, corresponds roughly with the altered social composition of the House of Commons, the landed element continuing to receive a share of new titles larger than was warranted by its share of the total membership of the Commons. The granting of political honours in effect necessarily mirrored the changing character of the Commons, the more rapid entry of Members with middle-class origins after 1868 and the dominance of the middle classes after 1885. From this point of view the diversification of the peerage is much less remarkable than the tenacity of the landed interest in maintaining its over-representation. This tenacity was most clearly exhibited in the highest reaches of political leadership, where members of the landed aristocracy and gentry continued to supply a majority in every cabinet until Campbell-Bannerman's in 1906. Campbell-Bannerman himself, although he has been described as a status-seeking Glasgow businessman, was also the younger son of a new and wealthy Scottish laird, James Campbell of Stracathro. Apart from Disraeli, Asquith was the first Prime Minister who did not come from a landed family.[1]

The admission of new blood to the peerage, therefore, saw the old order accepting members of the newly important classes while itself only gradually giving ground. It was appropriate that Lord Salisbury, the traditionalist defender of the landed interest in 1866–7, should have been the first instrument of this change, showing the recognition of political necessity and disregard of tradition which has been the hallmark of successful modern conservatism. It would be tempting to regard his peerage policy as consolidating the party alliance of landowners with big business, were it not for the fact that the Liberals ennobled at least an equal number of businessmen. Both parties acknowledged their growing reliance on the world of business, and indeed in the nine years of Liberal rule after 1905 more peers were recruited from that world than in the seventeen years of government by Salisbury and Balfour. Nevertheless, since the old landed interest became overwhelmingly Conservative or Unionist in this period, it was the Conservative creations which were the most telling indication of the willingness of the

[1] H. R. G. Greaves, 'Personal Origins and Interrelations of the Houses of Parliament', *Economica*, IX (1929), pp. 173–84. J. A. Thomas, *The House of Commons, 1832–1901* (1939), pp. 14–20. W. L. Guttsmann, 'The Changing Social Structure of the British Political Elite, 1886–1935', *British Journal of Sociology*, II (1951), pp. 122–34. W. L. Guttsmann, 'Aristocracy and the Middle Classes in the British Political Elite, 1886–1916', *ibid.*, V (1954), pp. 12–32.

old aristocracy to accept a large infusion of new wealth into the citadel of the upper class.

There was some distinction in the varieties of new men which the two parties drew into the peerage, reflecting the predominant political attitudes of different sections of the business world. The Conservatives ennobled eight or nine bankers and made three newspaper barons, while the Liberals contributed only three and one in these groups. The Liberals drew largely on manufacturing industry: linoleum (Ashton); chemicals (Overtoun and Glenconner); tobacco (Winterstoke); and cotton (Marchamley, Rotherham and Emmott), whose traditional political sympathies were thus at length rewarded. The Conservatives offered no parallels here. On the other hand there was also much overlapping. Both parties honoured merchants, shipping and shipbuilding interests, and building contractors, while the three Conservative brewers were matched by two Liberals. On the whole party polarization of economic interests did not extend very far at this level.

Most of the merchants, manufacturers and financiers who entered the peerage were, as we have seen, politicians. Hence the alteration in the social and economic character of the peerage appears as a reflection of previous political changes rather than as a separate phenomenon. Besides the politicians, however, there was a smaller but significant group of new men who received titles without having pursued active political careers. This group included such new peers as Masham and Armstrong of Cragside; Mount Stephen, Strathcona and Leith of Fyvie, all North American industrialists; Inverclyde of Cunard and Pirrie of Harland and Wolff; Merthyr of South Welsh collieries; and Northcliffe and Rothermere of the Harmsworth press. In all there were more of these industrialists among the new peers than there were law officers and judges, or servants of the state. Some of them had of course rendered valuable party services without becoming politicians; others had reached special eminence through imperial concerns, philanthropy, or promotion of education. Whatever their individual contributions, however, their presence in the nobility meant that the intake of new men went beyond the strict limits of political necessity, and indicated a general broadening of the social origins of the upper class.

By the time of the Parliament Act crisis the public was so

familiar with the social changes in the peerage that 'Beer Barons' and 'the beerage' were epithets commonly used by opponents of the Lords. The brewers had hardly earned such prominence, since there were only five in the House and only one very recent creation, Marchamley in 1908; but it was doubtless too great a temptation not to use beer to call attention to the arrival of a 'plebeian aristocracy'. The new elements had not, in fact, made a very profound impression on the character of the whole body of the nobility in 1911. There were then more than 570 hereditary members of the House of Lords, and not more than one-eleventh came from the business world, although perhaps as much as one-sixth were first generation peers from non-landed backgrounds. The great constitutional struggle was over the powers of a still predominantly territorial nobility, whose mass was only gradually being altered by new accretions.[1]

Some of the newcomers were themselves altered by the territorial habit, and acquired country seats as well as peerages, thus continuing at an accelerated pace the time-honoured practices of social elevation. W. H. Smith built up a sizeable country estate in East Anglia and the Home Counties. Sir W. G. Armstrong already owned Cragside and some 2,265 acres in Northumberland by 1873; he made further large purchases in the Rothbury district in the 1880s, including some from the Duke of Northumberland, and before his death in 1900 possessed an estate of about 16,000 acres and a second seat at Bamburgh Castle.[2] Samuel Cunliffe-Lister became a great Yorkshire land-owner, also purchasing extensively in the 1880s; his chief moves were to purchase the Swinton Park estate in 1882 for £457,000 and the Marquess of Ailesbury's Yorkshire estate in 1886 for £310,000, Jervaulx Abbey becoming his principal seat. In the end he owned about 34,000 acres.[3] These three excursions into landed estate were a natural and traditional preparation for the grants of peerages which followed a few years later in each case. Sir Edward Guinness also tried to acquire a suitable country

---

[1] Pumphrey, *op. cit.*, p. 2. George Whiteley (Lord Marchamley), Chief Liberal Whip 1905–8, was both a cotton spinner and a brewer.

[2] Alnwick MSS, Business Minutes, LXX (1882), pp. 27–28, 178–9; LXXI (1883), pp. 71–4.

[3] Jervaulx MSS, Estate accounts. *Estates Gazette*, 1 Jan. 1887, 7 Jan. 1888.

estate in anticipation of his peerage, and made an offer of three-quarters of a million pounds for the Ailesbury family heritage, the Savernake estate. The fourth Marquess, the spendthrift and bankrupt William, was most anxious to sell, but his uncle and eventual heir, Lord Henry Bruce, was even more determined that Savernake should remain in the family and out of the hands of the 'mere upstart merchant, a *nouveau-riche* Irishman' who had been so presumptuous as to suppose that an inheritance of centuries could be bought for cash. Lord Henry's resistance was so resourceful that Guinness became Lord Iveagh in 1891 when the legal fight to contest the Marquess's power to sell was only just beginning. By 1893, when the case had been up to the Lords and the law offered no further devices for preventing the sale, Iveagh not unnaturally lost his patience at the continued delay in making over Savernake, and called off his bargain.[1] Hence he had to look elsewhere, in Suffolk, for an estate in keeping with his new dignity.

Such men became in due course landed magnates, and others such as Inverclyde, Furness or Strathcona were not far behind them in their propensity to invest part of their fortunes in landed position. It was more usual, as in earlier times, for the industrialists to acquire status through more modest investment in an estate of one or two thousand acres, the course adopted for example by Lords Blyth, Burton, Cheylesmore, Mount Stephen, Nunburnholme, Overtoun, Swaythling and Winterstoke, to name but a few. Land, therefore, by no means lost its attractions as a means of advancement. Indeed in some respects the attractions increased, since as we shall see it could be acquired on much more favourable terms than before 1880. Many of the industrialist-peers entered society in the grand manner, brought a new vitality to old stately homes, and presently cited 'country pursuits', 'hunting, shooting and fishing', or 'cattle breeding' as their recreations.

On the other hand it seems that the acquisition of land was no longer the obligatory step towards a peerage which it had once been. The available works of reference are not a sure guide that the fact was always recorded when a new man purchased landed estate, and the following statement probably underestimates such

---

[1] Earl of Cardigan, *The Wardens of Savernake Forest*, pp. 318–28.

purchases without, however, being grossly inaccurate.[1] Taking those new peers who had not been born into landed families it appears that between 1886 and 1905 about one-third of them acquired landed estates, a proportion which fell to one-sixth under the Liberal government of 1906–14. It is perhaps not surprising that the proportion which remained unlanded was so high, since the total includes the lawyers and public servants who may not have amassed large fortunes. Even with those of great wealth, however, the ennobled bankers, brewers, merchants, manufacturers and newspaper proprietors, it appears that not much more than one-half acquired a landed position between 1886 and 1914. Many of the remainder, no doubt, contented themselves with a country house without surrounding it with property extensive enough to be called an estate.

A picture emerges of a partial but definite transformation of the titled upper class. The old nobility remained dominant, in numbers and in social standing if not always in wealth, but they were fused with a significant group thrown up by the new industrial England. Many of the new men, following a familiar path from fortune through land to title, rose in a single generation at a pace unprecedented since the sixteenth century. Many others disregarded the territorial foundations of the aristocratic way of life, and in their rise demonstrated in even more emphatic fashion the arrival of a monied nobility. In this way the peerage offered a reflection of the real distribution of power in society, and recorded the transition from an aristocracy of landowners not to democracy but to an aristocracy of business and professional talents.

This fusion was a good deal more than a mere formality, and extended beyond the ranks of the titled aristocracy into the ordinary life of society. By the end of the century it was much easier for newcomers to gain entry into London political society than it had been fifty years earlier, a necessary consequence of the changed face of politics. Men of old families, those of Cecil, Cavendish, Churchill or Balfour for example, mixed freely with the new men like Asquith, Chamberlain, Gorst or Haldane in

---

[1] *The Complete Peerage, Who's Who*, and editions of Burke's *Landed Gentry* immediately prior to dates of ennoblement have been searched for indications of the purchase of estates, as distinct from simple possession of an address in the country. Many landowners, but not all, entered their holdings in *Who's Who*.

society drawing rooms as well as in the House. Similarly in country house weekends the house parties were no longer closely confined to aristocratic circles: politicians of varied origin could be found at Hatfield for example, while the set of society intellectuals known as 'the Souls', and their friends, were being entertained at nearby Panshanger. Moreover London society was by the 1890s no longer so exclusively political as it had once been, but luxuriated in a more variegated life, in which the frivolity and extravagance heralded by the arrival in force of the millionaires was perhaps more prominent a feature than the appearance of a spearhead of upper-class socialist intellectuals led by the Webbs. An air of rich vulgarity and indecent opulence was beginning to permeate society. 'There might just as well have been a Goddess of Gold erected for overt worship – the impression of worship in thought, feeling and action could hardly have been stronger', wrote Beatrice Webb after dining at Bath House, Piccadilly, with Sir Julius Wernher and a company of financial magnates and their hangers-on.[1]

In the long run the old aristocratic influence could not resist the force of the intellectuals, for charm and cultivated manners were no match for reason, investigation and administrative vigour. The representatives of the old order were either too indolent to produce a coherent reasoned defence of their position or too well aware of the impossibility of justifying privilege. Instead they concentrated on the tactics of expediency and the preservation of as much as possible of the power of property for as long as possible, manipulating the machinery of political democracy through mass ignorance, prejudice and apathy to delay the spread of social equality. In the short run, however, the old aristocracy might have absorbed and dominated the new wealthy elements and imposed the pattern of their standards of behaviour on the plutocrats, had it not been for the fact that these standards themselves were shifting towards a greater pre-occupation with pleasure and money.

The means of exercising social influence still lay ready to hand. Some of the millionaires, like Sir Julius Wernher with his fortune from South African diamonds, were eager to adopt the outward conventions of the old aristocracy. He purchased Luton

---

[1] Barbara Drake and Margaret I. Cole, eds., *Our Partnership by Beatrice Webb* (1948), p. 347.

Hoo, Beatrice Webb recorded, because 'part of the minor convention of his life has been the acquisition of a great country mansion, with an historic name as counterpart of Bath House, Piccadilly. This was no doubt to please his "society"-loving wife – a hard, vainglorious woman, talkative and badly bred, but not otherwise objectionable.'[1] A set like the 'Souls', highminded as well as socially brilliant, might not in fact aspire to civilize the boors, but it was a decidedly aristocratic group – Balfour, Curzon, Lyttleton and Wyndham among the men, Lady Elcho, Lady Frances Horner, Lady Mary Jeune among the women – even if Margot Tennant, the leading spirit, and her sister Lady Ribblesdale were comparative newcomers.[2] Above all the great London society hostesses of the time, although they included such brilliant figures as Margot Asquith (née Tennant) and Mrs George Keppel, were still mainly drawn from the circle of great titled ladies. Such figures as Millicent, Duchess of Sutherland, daughter of the Earl of Rosslyn; Lady Wimborne, daughter of the Duke of Marlborough; Lady Dorothy Nevill, daughter of the Earl of Orford; and Lady Elizabeth Balfour, daughter of the Earl of Lytton, were the leaders of London life and had the power to set the tone.

A number of factors conspired to ensure that this tone became increasingly less exclusive and more tolerant towards the brash display of wealth. One should not discount a broadening of the mind of the old nobility, a greater readiness to accept the nonaristocratic as equals, a liberalization which proceeded quite independently of calculations of personal advantage. The seventh Duke of Northumberland did have the Webbs to lunch at Alnwick Castle, although 'struggling to keep us at a distance, scared by the assumed attempt of these notable Socialists to get access to the records of his manor courts.'[3] Personal advantage, though probably not financial benefit, was indeed mirrored in the veritable wave of marriages between the old nobility and actresses which was started by Earl Bruce (subsequently fourth Marquess of Ailesbury) when he married Dolly Tester in 1884. From then until 1914 there were nineteen such marriages, featuring a Duke of Newcastle, a Duke of Leinster, a Marquess

[1] *Ibid.*, pp. 412–13.
[2] Lord Haldane, *Autobiography* (1928), pp. 120–1.
[3] *Our Partnership* by Beatrice Webb, p. 355.

of Headfort, an Earl of Orkney, and the 25th Lord de Clifford among the highest and most ancient nobility. The charms of the Gibson girls clearly had something to do with this outbreak, especially pronounced in the years 1905–8, but they won husbands in an atmosphere of relaxed conventions: there had only been ten such marriages in the hundred years before 1884.[1]

The influence of Edward, as Prince of Wales and as Edward VII, was undoubtedly important. 'This utterly commonplace person' was social sovereign, and through his rule 'the new vulgarians, those loud, extremely rich men for whom the Prince had an abiding taste' made their way into the centre of courtly society. Men like Sir Ernest Cassel or Sir Thomas Lipton caught Edward's fancy, and in such an atmosphere the adulation of gold and diamond millionaires, financiers, and rough self-made men became fashionable and respectable.[2]

These movements, however, were largely on the surface. More deeply, aristocratic society changed its outlook because it had a new respect for money, especially money not furnished by agricultural estates, and growing affinities with those who made money in large-scale enterprises, particularly overseas. This was to be seen in the serious aristocratic marriages, where marriage with American heiresses was a widely noticed feature of the times, a movement in which the Churchill family were notable pioneers. The novelty and glamour of these moves to call in young and vigorous dollar stock to refresh the old, and sometimes decaying, English aristocracy naturally attracted attention, but they were in fact no more than a striking new version of the old established practice of marrying into new wealth. There had always been a trickle of marriages with bankers' daughters, kept up for example by the 13th Earl of Strathmore who married a niece of the 1st Lord Carrington, and the 5th Earl of Chichester who married Alice Carr Glyn, daughter of the 1st Lord Wolverton.[3] Inter-marriage with the newly ennobled families was kept up at the same time as the American matches. Sir Henry Stafford Northcote, himself created Lord Northcote in 1900, had married in 1873 Alice,

[1] J. M. Bulloch, 'Peers who have married Players', *Notes and Queries*, CLXIX (1935), pp. 92–94.

[2] *Our Partnership by Beatrice Webb*, p. 138. C. Sykes, *Four Studies in Loyalty*, p. 24. Sonia Keppel, *Edwardian Daughter* (1958), chap. ii.

[3] See above p. 100.

adopted daughter of the future Lord Mount Stephen, the Canadian railway and banking magnate; and the eldest son of Viscount Peel married Ella Williamson, daughter of Lord Ashton the linoleum manufacturer. We do not know whether the American marriages were more numerous than the marriages with wealthy English or Anglicized families, nor whether the American brides paid more handsomely for their aristocratic connexions, on account of the risks involved in their greater strangeness, or less handsomely on account of their superior beauty. The general impression is that down to 1914 it remained normal for the aristocracy to marry within their own circle, choosing daughters of landed families or joining with the allied groups of generals' and parsons' daughters, but that alliance with wealthy new families, English or foreign, was increasingly common. The need for injections of new wealth, after all, was clearly on the increase.

Many landowners found that their agricultural incomes fell steeply in the fifteen or twenty years after 1878, sometimes by as much as a half. Though the general price level also fell, the aristocratic cost of living, with its large elements for wage bills and luxury goods, certainly did not fall in proportion. For many the situation posed the alternatives of drastic retrenchment or efforts to find new sources of income by entry into the world of finance and commerce. Retrenchment might mean withdrawal from an active social life, leaving the field more open to the *nouveaux riches*. A story went round the London clubs in 1882 of a large landowner who had met falling rents by letting his London house: 'We have five farms on our hands', he said. 'We have hired for a trifling rent the Rectory in our parish, which chanced to be vacant. We have broken up our establishment, and shut up our house here [in the country], and we have a better balance at our bankers than we ever had in our lives before.'[1] A better balance achieved by looking for income outside the boundaries of an estate, on the other hand, might mean a growing identity of outlook and interest with the world of the stock exchange and company promoter. Either way, therefore, led to social abdication.

The changing fortunes of the Earls of Verulam provide a good

[1] W. Bence Jones, 'Landowning as a Business', *The Nineteenth Century*, XI (1882), pp. 346–68.

illustration of these developments. In the 1870s the second Earl's ordinary expenditure was running at over £19,000 a year, and the unexpected items which added a thousand or two to this almost every year were a constant source of worry. This was most understandable, since his regular income was not much over £17,000, made up of £13,500 from rents, about £1,000 from timber, and £2,500 in dividends on one King's share and one-sixth of an Adventurer's share in the New River Company which had been in the family since the eighteenth century. Beyond this he had a steadily dwindling holding of Consols, yielding in 1878 an income of some £700. Economy and retrenchment had been preached for many years without being practised, but were begun in earnest when rents started to fall after 1881. By 1889 the annual expenses were down to about £15,000 and any extras over this had been curbed. Income, meanwhile, had fallen to about £14,000: timber receipts remained much as before; rents now brought in about £9,000, the receipts from the Essex estate of Messing having utterly collapsed from £1,964 in 1878 to £547 in 1889; the New River dividends had risen to £3,000; and Consols brought in about £1,000. The Earl had in fact been enabled to survive thus far, without being forced to try to sell land, through the unexpected inheritance of £100,000 from one of his brothers in 1884. Much of this legacy had been used to pay off his brothers' and sisters' portions, and thus reduce the annual charges, but the Earl was also living on this capital and by 1889 the remnant was only £21,500. At his current rate of spending this would have lasted a further ten to fifteen years.[1]

The second Earl of Verulam died in 1895. It is difficult to tell just how far retrenchment in his lifetime had meant a real change in style of living. A large reduction in annual expenditure had been achieved by paying off the portions, reducing family charges from some £3,000 in 1876 to £2,000 in 1886. In addition the fall in the prices of provisions made some contribution to the reduction of tradesmen's bills: but the London tradesmen's bills fell from about £1,200 a year in the late

[1] This section is based on Gorhambury MSS, 2nd Earl of Verulam's Diary, 1846–90; 3rd Earl of Verulam's Diary, 1868–97; 3rd Earl of Verulam's Accounts, 1896–1914; 3rd Earl of Verulam's Pocket Diary, 1901–20; Gorhambury Cellar Book, 1858–82; Gorhambury Game Books, 1820–1923.

1870s to £800 in 1889, and the St Albans bills from £1,100 to £800, which the Earl certainly felt reflected some genuine economies in housekeeping. The staff had been reduced a little by dispensing with some of the helpers in the stables. The London season had been cut from four or five months to two which were spent in houses rented for the purpose at 30 guineas a week. Drinking habits had been tempered to the times: against the 590 bottles of sherry and 255 bottles of brandy drunk in 1870 the consumption in 1880 was down to 298 and 75 bottles; the consumpion of champagne, however, had only fallen from 161 to 126 bottles, and of port from 101 to 83 bottles, while in recompense the quantity of claret drunk had risen from 687 to 740 bottles. In 1887 the allowance given to his eldest son for running the shooting on the estate had been cut from £500 a year to £320, and the hand-rearing of pheasants was given up. There were thus some real economies, and this sort of pruning of expenses was perhaps as much as could be accomplished by an old man of settled habits. It was still not enough to enable him to live within his income.

His son, the third Earl, was altogether more business-like, as befitted one who became something of a businessman. He kept his total annual expenditure at around £15,000, which included a strict allowance for his own living expenses of £3,600 in 1896 growing to £4,000 by 1913, and he contrived to keep within his income. At first this needed great economy. In his father's lifetime he had been living at Sopwell, a house on the estate. After his father's death he continued to live there, and Gorhambury and the shooting were let, first to J. B. Taylor and then to Lord Bingham. The rent of £1,500 to £2,000 a year, and the small staff and reduced scale of entertaining at Sopwell, were vital to solvency in these early years. Then from 1901 the family were able to return to Gorhambury and resume some of the former way of life. But the shooting, for example, was never revived in its full glory: the pheasants remained entirely wild-bred, and the shooting parties were informal family affairs rather than revivals of the grand parades of dukes, marquesses and earls who had come down in the 1870s.

If the recuperation was based on temporary evacuation of the family seat, revival was firmly based on the City. Already in 1896 the Earl held shares in three other companies besides the

New River, including 605 in the South African Gold Trust which paid a dividend of 100 per cent in 1895/6. The portfolio was extended from the later 1890s onwards, and by 1913 included holdings in at least fifteen companies, with a distinct bias in favour of investments in colonial and overseas ventures – American Freehold Land Mortgage Company, Intercontinental Trust, British North Borneo Rubber, Tali Ayer Rubber, and Gold Coast Mines, to name a few. Such investments, however, gave only a passive contact with the world of finance and the stock exchange. It was Lord Verulam's development into a considerable company director which created his close links with the City. In 1896 he was on the board of four companies, all domestic concerns: a brewery (Colchester), an insurance office (Imperial Life), a housing company (Harrietsville), and Accles Limited. Two more directorships were added in 1897, showing the interest in gold: Palmarejo Mexican Mines and the South African Gold Trust. In 1898 came the Pacific N.W. Railroad, and in 1900 the Klondyke Consolidated. By 1913 he was a director of thirteen companies, with a heavy emphasis on mining – Abboutiakoon Mines, Effluenta, Fanti, Wassau (Gold Coast), and Nigeria Tin had been added to the list, as well as the quaintly named Cinnamon Bippo. The directors' fees varied considerably, from the £50 of the Colchester Brewery to the £500 of Accles or Borneo Rubber, and in aggregate provided a substantial income. The fees, moreover, were not paid merely for the advantage of being able to put Lord Verulam's name on the prospectuses: he attended board meetings regularly. Fees and dividends together supplied nearly one-third of his total income in 1897, and over one-third by 1913. It is no surprise to find that he installed a domestic hot-water system of his own devising, complete with calorifier, nor to find that one of his daughters married Felix Cassel, a successful barrister and nephew of Sir Ernest Cassel.

It had long been quite common for members of the peerage to appear on the boards of railway companies, though these had usually been lines of local importance to particular estates. The case of the third Duke of Buckingham, who was chairman of the L.N.W.R. in the 1850s, was unique for the times. Until the 1880s it was not at all usual for peers to become directors of any other sort of company. Then the rush started to get peers on the boards, and by 1896 there were 167 noblemen, over a quarter of the peerage, holding directorships, most of them in more than one company.[1] A very few of these, like Aldenham, Hillingdon or Rothschild, were recently created peers who were directors in their own businesses. Some of the older nobility, such as the Duke of Devonshire or the Earl of Durham, were directors of companies which operated on their estates. The vast majority, however, had taken directorships in companies with which they had no previous associations, and had lent their titles and talents to the business world in general. The late 1890s saw the season of Hooley, the great company promoter who made 'large gifts to obtain the names of titled and other persons as directors.'[2] The rewards may not always have been very magnificent, except for those like Lord Verulam who had half a dozen or more directorships: these included Lords Castletown, Colville, Donoughmore, Ebury, Gifford, Playfair, Rathmore, Ribblesdale, Stratheden and Tweeddale. But the directors' fees were pure income, and the presence of so many of the oldest and noblest families on the boards reveals both the financial exigencies and the changing social outlook of the aristocratic order.

It is also highly likely that from the 1880s onwards there was a general movement by landowners to spread their assets through investment in stock exchange securities, though this is not yet adequately documented In the 1880s the Marquess of Salisbury's trustees were investing heavily in railway stock, debentures, and London ground rents, partly by switching from Consols, whose yields sank to under 3 per cent from 1882 to 1910, and partly by selling some land.[3] In the 1890s the Earl of Durham and Earl Fitzwilliam undertook large-scale conversions of their assets into stocks and bonds.[4] Also in the 1890s the Duke of Portland invested in a wide range of industrial debentures and ordinary shares, taking in home breweries, collieries and stores, South African gold mines, and Burmese, Indian and South American railways; by 1907 the nominal value

[1] G.E.C., *The Complete Peerage*, V, App. C.
[2] Quoted by J. H. Clapham, *An Economic History of Modern Britain*, III (Cambridge, 1938), p. 238.
[3] Gorhambury MSS, 2nd Earl of Verulam's Diary (Lord Verulam was one of the Salisbury Trustees).
[4] D. Spring, 'The English Landed Estate in the Age of Coal and Iron, 1830–80', *Journal Econ. Hist.*, XI (1951), p. 7.

of his personal holdings was over £75,000, and the trustees of his settlement may easily have held very much more.[1] The gentry also joined in the movement. Until the middle of the 1870s Major Best had been investing steadily in Consols; then he began to diversify his portfolio, choosing colonial and foreign government bonds, and Indian and South American railways: the Brooks in the 1880s and 1890s also invested in colonial government and railway stocks, getting about one-fifth of their income from such investments by 1899.[2] It would be of great interest to know how far the aristocracy and gentry participated in the export of capital in this period, and in particular how much they were involved in the financing of Empire, but sufficient information is not yet available. It is clear, however, that a considerable section of the landed interest was acquiring the habit of frequent dealings with stockbrokers, and was becoming increasingly familiar with the world in which the great financial magnates of the day, Beit, Cassel, Speyer and Wernher, had their being.

Behind all these changes lay the Great Depression in agriculture of 1873–96 and its profound effects on landownership. Most contemporaries saw this as an unparalleled disaster, caused by a run of atrocious weather in 1878–9 and again in 1893–4, and by a swiftly rising flood of imported foodstuffs, which left English agriculture prostrate. Most historians have agreed with them. The evidence is impressive and appears to admit of little doubt. First American prairie wheat in the 1870s, and subsequently Canadian, Indian, Australian and Argentine wheat, knocked the price of English wheat down from an average of 56s. a quarter in 1867–71 to 27s. 3d. in 1894–8, with a low point of 22s. 10d. in 1894. The price of other grains did not fall by so much as wheat's 50 per cent, but still fell substantially, as did the price of wool. With the perfection of refrigerating techniques the import of frozen and chilled meat grew apace from the middle of the 1880s, and meat prices also fell, while the traditional English breakfast of Danish bacon and eggs was being established at the same time. The effects were to be seen in mounting arrears of

---

[1] Nottingham University, Portland MSS, 125/3.
[2] Best MSS, U 480, C. 26, Notices from bankers 1870–87; C. 17, list of Major T. C. H. Best's investments, 1888. Brooks MSS, LL. 17/278, 17/279, account books 1888–1903.

rent, bankrupt and ruined tenants, and falling rent rolls: and they were to be seen written across the countryside in a dwindling arable acreage, in farms thrown up, and in land suffered to run to weed and waste.

Nevertheless the universality of the depression and its severity have been much exaggerated in the past, and the period in fact emerges as a continuation, in greatly intensified fashion, of the previously apparent diverging fortunes of corn and livestock farming.[1] It was above all a depression in wheat, and to a lesser extent in barley and wool. Sheep-and-corn farmers were badly hit, especially on the lightest of light lands like the tops of the Wiltshire Downs, and worst hit of all were farmers on the heaviest arable lands, perhaps recently drained at great expense, such as were to be found almost everywhere in Essex. The sufferings of the corn farmers were taken to indicate the sufferings of farmers generally, partly because landowners and farmers from the corn regions were greatly over-represented before the Royal Commission on Agricultural Depression of 1879–82, and partly because the general public continued to identify farming with corn growing. Falling grain prices in fact benefited stock and dairy farmers in two ways. Cheaper bread released purchasing power for the more expensive foods, and helped to stimulate the demand for meat and dairy produce, which in any case expanded with rising living standards. In the second place cheaper grains meant cheaper feeding stuffs for the livestock producers, and thus lower costs of production, for they were large consumers of grains. Imports of beef, mutton, bacon, eggs, cheese and butter certainly increased in this period, but so also did home production. Each article had its own price history, but in general the prices fell from the middle of the 1880s by about 10 per cent or slightly more; though milk scarcely altered in price at all. The home product, when of good quality, generally held its price better than the imported variety. The modest price fall was plainly more a product of lower costs

---

[1] T. W. Fletcher, 'The Great Depression of English Agriculture, 1873–1896', *Econ. Hist. Rev.*, 2nd ser., XIII (1961), pp. 417–32, to which this section is heavily indebted. F. M. L. Thompson, 'Agriculture since 1870', *V.C.H. Wiltshire*, IV (1959), pp. 92–114. The best general account of agriculture in this period remains that of J. H. Clapham, *An Economic History of Modern Britain*, II (Cambridge, 1932) pp. 279–84, and III (1938), chap. ii, though he is inclined to speak of all areas as suffering from depression, some much more so than others.

and increased productivity than of import competition. The livestock farmer who had increased his output may well have maintained or raised his money income, and since most of the non-food articles which he wished to buy had fallen in price he had almost certainly improved his real income considerably. Such farmers might experience a short crisis, as did the cheese producers when their market collapsed in 1879, but they experienced no depression.

The different fortunes of arable and livestock farmers were reflected in the experience of landowners. There can have been few great landowners who could show an actual increase in rents between 1870 and 1896, as did Lord Derby on his Fylde estate in Lancashire.[1] The general experience was that rents fell from a peak reached in 1874–8 until the middle of the 1890s, and that thereafter they were stabilized at a new level. But the amount of the fall varied markedly between different parts of the country. In a sample covering just short of half a million acres, drawn from the accounts of great and lesser estates, rents fell by an average of 26 per cent between 1874–8 and 1894–8, a somewhat smaller fall than that shown in other rent series.[2] The estates in the sample may be divided into two groups, a south-eastern and a north-western, unequal in acreage but roughly equal in value in 1874–8, each group then yielding about £225,000 in rents. In the south-eastern group, with estates in Bedford, Buckingham, Cambridge, Essex, Hertford, Huntingdon, Kent, Northampton and Wiltshire, rents had fallen by 41 per cent by 1894–8. In the north-western group, with estates in Cumberland, Devon, Durham, Northumberland, the North Riding, Shropshire, Stafford, Somerset and West Wiltshire, rents had fallen by 12 per cent by 1894–8.

The contrast between these two groups probably does less than justice to the reasonably good fortune of landowners in the grazing and dairying counties, since the geographical division was not identical with the agricultural division. The Shropshire

[1] T. W. Fletcher, 'Lancashire Livestock Farming during the Great Depression', *Agric. Hist. Rev.*, IX (1961), pp. 32–36.
[2] R. J. Thompson, 'An Inquiry into the Rent of Agricultural Land in England and Wales in the Nineteenth Century'. H. A. Rhee, *The Rent of Agricultural Land in England and Wales, 1870–1943* (1949), table II, pp. 44–46. The rents compared in the text are gross rents less abatements or remissions, and less tithe rent charges paid by the landlord.

estate in the north-western group included many arable farms where corn was important, and its rents in fact fell by nearly a quarter, while both the Duke of Northumberland's estate and the Duke of Cleveland's Durham estate included many arable farms of indifferent quality. On the other hand the south-eastern group was not all corn; for example, the Duke of Cleveland's Brigstock estate in Northamptonshire included a good deal of grass land, and during this period it was virtually re-equipped with new farmsteads suited to more intensive stock-keeping.[1] The geographical division cannot be pressed too closely; neither can the difference in average rent movements of the two groups, for on individual estates changes ranged from a fall of 66 per cent on Lord Verulam's Messing estate in Essex to a rise of 1 per cent on the Jervaulx estate (late Marquess of Ailesbury's) in the North Riding.

The Duke of Cleveland's agent was quite clear that the prosperity of Durham farmers depended on the prices of beef, mutton and dairy produce, and on the state of local industrial activity. 'There is a general depression in the surrounding coal district', he reported in 1884, 'they are working short time generally, and in some cases I hear pits are closed. This has a general effect upon all classes round here.' In 1886 mining was more active, and in 1890 he could report that 'the farmers round here are in good spirits at the improved state of things. The iron and coal industries are in a most flourishing condition, and cause a general prosperity in this neighbourhood'.[2] He held to the view that the grass land farmers ought to be able to continue without any permanent reduction in rents, and that their occasional difficulties from poor seasons or poor markets should be met by temporary remissions. In making these the distinction between farmers was always clear: in 1881, for example, 50 per cent of the half-year's rent was returned to tillage farmers and only 20 per cent to grassland farmers. Nevertheless these remissions were fairly frequent, in 1881–2, 1886–9, and 1893–4, and Scarth slipped into the habit of assuming that there was an agricultural depression in Durham, only not so bad as in Northamptonshire.[3]

[1] Raby MSS, Letter Book III, W. T. Scarth to Duke, 4 June 1889.
[2] *Ibid.*, W. T. Scarth to Duke, 15 April 1884, 5 April 1886, 15 Jan. 1890.
[3] *Ibid.*, W. T. Scarth to Duke, 26 May 1885, 2 Jan. 1893.

On the Duke of Northumberland's estate rents declined by a maximum of 19 per cent from 1878 to 1893, and were stabilized in the period 1894–8 at a level about 11 per cent below the average of 1874–8, after remissions had been discontinued and new permanent rents had been fixed. Here also the agent was keenly aware of the distinction between corn and grass farmers, and when framing a policy in 1879 to meet 'the great depression in the Farming Interest' he recommended a return of 20 per cent of rent to tillage farmers for all corn lands in the four-course rotation, 'leaving the grass land entirely out of consideration, inasmuch as so long as beef can be sold at from 8s. to 9s. per stone, and mutton from 8d. to 9d. per lb. (which are about the present prices) it may be assumed that grass land is producing profits equal to the existing rental paid for it'.[1] This remission showed that corn farmers contributed a little over one-third of the rental of the estate. In the following fifteen years livestock prices did fall, sometimes with such suddenness from one year to the next that, as in 1892, the hill farmers faced disaster. A remission of 10 per cent was given on grass land in 1885, which subsequently became a permanent reduction in rent, and again in 1893, which was withdrawn after 1895. This fall in the rents of all types of farm, and recurrent anxiety over falls in meat prices, had led the agent by the early 1890s to think in terms of a general depression affecting the livestock farmers only less severely than the corn farmers.[2]

Similarly on the Marquess of Bath's Longleat estate severe depression was felt only on the part – about one-third of the property – which lay in the Wiltshire chalk country and was characterized by sheep-and-corn farming. Here arrears mounted sharply after 1878, farms fell into hand, bankrupt and absconding tenants inflicted considerable losses on the landlord, and rents were ultimately reduced by about a quarter. The rest of the estate, however, lay in the dairying part of Wiltshire and in the Cheddar and Frome districts of Somerset, and here there were few signs of strain and rents were well maintained. As a result the total rents of the estate in 1894–5 were only 11 per cent

---

[1] Alnwick MSS, Business Minutes, LXIII (1879), pp. 97–99.

[2] *Ibid.*, LXXVII (1885, pp. 76–80; XCI (1892), pp. 48–50; XCIII (1894), pp. 109–16. Rents of dairy farms close to Tyneside, however, appear to have been raised.

below the level of 1874–8. Nevertheless in 1889, when the auditors prepared a statement showing a fall of 9½ per cent in the rents, they made no comment on the causes, but simply felt that the estate was weathering the depression very well.[1]

When remissions had to be granted and rents were permanently reduced, even though by a fairly slight amount, it was natural that landowners and their agents, dealing with stock farming estates, should feel that they were suffering from a depression. In fact where rents fell by little more than 10 per cent, while the general price level fell by nearly a quarter, it may be doubted whether landowners, any more than their tenants, experienced anything which deserves to be called a depression. Such a fall, at least, seemed to make little difference to a landowner's style of living. The Marquess of Bath's net money income from the Longleat estate, for example, was about the same in 1894–5 as it had been in the 1870s, for estate expenditure had been reduced all round, and the cost of repairs and improvements in particular had fallen from about 23 per cent of gross rents to 15 per cent. Expenditure on such items of aristocratic living as the park and gardens was as high as it had been in the early 1870s, and expenditure on the game department was considerably higher. Similarly the Duke of Northumberland's expenditures on the Alnwick household, gardens, park, and game were all higher in 1895 than they had been in 1870.

It was the landowners of arable estates who felt the effects of real depression, for where gross rents might be reduced by as much as a half it was inevitable that the whole mode of life should be altered. Where such a landowner was favourably placed, owning relatively unaffected estates in other parts of the country or enjoying substantial non-agricultural income, he could afford to treat his corn farmers generously and be comparatively indifferent to the financial results. In this way the Duke of Cleveland made a substantial investment in re-equipping his Northamptonshire farms for livestock farming, and the Duke of Northumberland paid £3 an acre for inferior arable land laid down to permanent grass, as well as providing suitable buildings for the new type of farming.[2] On the Wilton estate, where fixed

---

[1] Longleat MSS, Rawlence and Squarey's Reports on Accounts 1878–91, esp. 3 Sept. 1889.
[2] Alnwick MSS, Business Minutes, XCVII (1897), pp. 105–20.

interest charges on the improvement loans of the 1860s were a rising burden, Lord Pembroke allowed the level of estate maintenance to decline, but increased his outlay on game. He drew less and less from the estate for his personal use, until in 1896 the estate expenses exceeded the income, while he lived on the growing bounty of Dublin ground rents.

Less fortunate owners found, like the Earls of Verulam, that drastic economy was inescapable. At Savernake the fifth Marquess of Ailesbury succeeded in 1894 to a much neglected estate which was saddled with £5,000 of 'terrible jointures' payable to the dowagers, out of a gross rental which had shrunk from £38,000 in 1867 to £17,700 in 1896. Assisted by an agent who charged no salary, resolving that 'so far as my supervision goes [the estate] shall no longer be regarded as a milch cow', everything was subordinated to the rehabilitation of the property. The Marquess lived in a small house on the estate, leaving Tottenham Park empty; the game and the deer in the Forest were made self-supporting by greatly expanded sales of birds and venison and by widespread letting of shooting; and the estate kept going on a bank overdraft until 1911, yielding no personal income to the Marquess. In the early twentieth century he was able to move into the great house, but only opened up one wing of it. And he continued to lead the frugal life of a modest country gentleman, with no attempt to resume the grand manner of aristocratic living.[1]

It is difficult to tell what proportion of landowners were compelled to adopt a more modest manner of life and to renounce the great world. But it is quite likely that a good number of the 'backwoods' peers who came to town in 1910 to fight a last ditch battle against the Parliament Bill were returning with the frustrated bitterness of long exile imposed by agricultural depression. Their relative impoverishment lay behind the façade of the gay and lavish life of Edwardian society, last flowering of an aristocratic world now supported by a shrunken band of the more fortunate landowners and a constantly growing contingent of the *nouveaux riches*. The gentry in the arable districts were perhaps the hardest hit financially, since at their smaller

---

[1] Savernake MSS, Letter books, E. B. Merriman to Marquess, 18 March 1895, 22 March 1896; estate and household accounts. Earl of Cardigan, *Wardens of Savernake Forest*, pp. 331–9.

level of income it was exceedingly difficult to absorb a cut of one-half. One Kent landowner commiserating with another in the 1890s on the ruinous consequences of letting farms 'at half what rents used to be', wished that 'we and you had a little of the superfluous cash of some of our neighbours. Land is no longer an enviable possession unless it is coupled with a good income from other sources'.[1] One of these owners, Major Best, although he did have a fair income from other sources, spent a large part of his time abroad and in quiet English resorts in the 1890s, in order not to have to play the part of squire too constantly, 'becoming very economical to suit my reduced income'.[2] The reduced incomes of many of the gentry could no longer stretch to the old social and political activities, and they retired from the Commons at an accelerating pace before the new men who could better afford a parliamentary life. 'In the existing development [of the House of Commons],' a foreign observer commented in 1904, 'as in its social environment, the last of the long line of squires, with only a few thousands for revenue, knows there is no place for him.'[3] But it was probably the landed magnates in reduced circumstances who suffered the most severe social decline, even if their remaining income was adequate for a retired country life of ease and comfort.

The difference in the fortunes of arable and pasture estates tended to be self-perpetuating. After a few years of depression most arable landowners abandoned the traditional expedient of trying to stem pressure on rents by increasing their outlays on repairs and improvements. There are signs that this was tried in Bedford, Cambridge, Huntingdon, Northampton and Wiltshire, for instance, but from the middle of the 1880s the effort was given up as fruitless, and the amount of estate expenditure was allowed to drop. On most estates, indeed, it appears that the proportion of gross rents spent on repairs and improvements was only very slightly, if at all, lower in the twenty years before 1914 than it had been in the 1870s. But such a constant proportion meant, in view of the reduced rentals, that the actual money

---

[1] Best MSS, U. 480, C. 16, L. Whatman to M. Best, 21 May n.d. ?1895.

[2] *Ibid.*, C. 22, bdles. 1–3, correspondence with agent, 1886–98, esp. M. Best to C. Loth, 3 May 1896.

[3] A Foreign Resident, *Society in the New Reign* (1904), p. 123, quoted by O. R. McGregor, Introduction to Sixth Edition of Lord Ernle, *English Farming Past and Present* (1961), p. cxxxix.

spent on the estate fell by 40 or 50 per cent. Although some materials became cheaper, labour on the whole became more expensive, so that this decline in cash outlay involved a considerable decline in the amount of physical equipment and maintenance provided by the landlords. Such a slow deterioration in the fixed equipment of farming could only prevent any recovery in rent-producing capacity. It also meant that landowners were being forced to surrender some of those agricultural functions which were at the base of their influence in the countryside.

Even where the farming on an estate was radically altered to meet the times it was likely to halt the decline rather than lead to a recovery, at least from the landowner's point of view. Thus S. W. Farmer, who was introducing large-scale dairying and beef production into the Vale of Pewsey, held five farms on the Savernake estate from the 1890s, totalling 3,500 acres, at an average rent of 8s. 2d. an acre against the former rent of about 19s. an acre. These rents did improve slightly after 1905, and by 1914 had reached 9s. 2d. an acre, but even at their peak in 1925, after a spell of inflation, they barely topped 12s. an acre. In this instance grass land farming was the salvation of the tenant but provided only small cheer for the landlord.[1] In general the structure of agricultural society was severely shaken and the landowners' power much weakened. With many farmers ruined in the 1880s there was a great turnover of tenants, and very often the newcomers were strangers to the estate. Long-standing family associations with an estate were broken, and the new tenants – who came, it might be, from Scotland, the West Country, or only from a neighbouring parish, – had none of the traditional attachment to the landowner and his family. In any case in times when farms were hard to let and owners were afraid of being left with untenanted land, the bargaining power of all tenants was greatly strengthened. Enforcement of farming covenants was largely abandoned, and tenants farmed much as they pleased, receiving perhaps the agent's advice rather than being subject to his control.

Rents on the arable estates were stabilized by the middle of the 1890s, and after about 1900 the more cheerful prospects for corn farmers, with wheat prices above 30s. a quarter, were slowly reflected in rentals. On those estates where account

[1] Savernake MSS, estate accounts 1895–1930.

material is available rents rose by about 10 per cent at Savernake and Wilton between 1900 and 1914, as they did on Lord Sidmouth's Devon estate, where by 1914 the rents were back to their 1882 level though still 12 per cent below their peak of 1876; but on the Duke of Northumberland's estate they remained untouched. There was a very general reluctance to raise rents on sitting tenants, and the returning confidence in arable farming was not reflected in any return to the old structure of landlordism.

The difference between corn and grass landowners tended to reinforce the difference between purely agricultural and partially industrial landowners, since the corn counties of southern and eastern England lay far from coal measures and major industrial centres. Incomes from coal, though they suffered some setbacks after 1873 for a decade or so, generally continued to rise alongside output until 1914. The Duke of Northumberland's mineral income, for example, made great strides in 1883–4, 1889–92, 1899–1902, 1908–9, and 1914. In 1914 it amounted to £73,445, over 40 per cent of his gross income, against less than 20 per cent in 1870; when estate expenditure had been deducted the minerals furnished nearly 60 per cent of the net income in 1914. In the same way Lord Sidmouth's Staffordshire collieries flourished, yielding over £5,000 in rents in 1913–14, not a particularly good year, against £2,000 in the 1870s; in the same period his London ground rents grew from £2,700 to £4,250: in 1913–14 these two sources provided 59 per cent of his gross income and 70 per cent of his net income. Moreover it is plausible to suppose that it was chiefly this type of landowner who invested in stocks and shares, since they had the buoyant incomes which gave room for this sort of financial manoeuvre. If so the financial distance between them and the stricken landowners was further widened, to the benefit of individuals but to the detriment of the social cohesion of the landed interest, which was increasingly split into the wealthy and the poor relations.

In one respect, however, depression affected all landowners. Land prices fell steeply after 1878, with little regard to the amount by which rents had fallen, and the land market entered on thirty years of almost unbroken dullness and restricted activity.[1] By 1890 land was selling at 20 to 25 years' purchase

[1] See F. M. L. Thompson, 'The Land Market in the Nineteenth Century', for a fuller discussion of these points, and further references.

in place of the former 30 to 40 years', so that quite apart from any reductions in rent the capital value had fallen by something between one-sixth and a half. The Marquess of Ailesbury, for example, received about 23 years' purchase for his Jervaulx estate in 1886–7, even though the rents were the same as they had been ten years earlier.[1] In privately negotiated sales and purchases, where some special residential or sporting values were involved, it is true that the Duke of Northumberland's valuers continued to calculate prices on the basis of 30 to 37 years' purchase of current rents. But at public auction, for example, the Duke bought in 1893 a flourishing dairy and market garden farm, rented at more than £4 an acre, at 22 years' purchase.[2] As far as the *Estates Gazette* was concerned only Wales escaped the fall in capital values: in 1887 'a large number of Welsh estates were brought into the market, in almost every case successfully, the prices being extraordinary, 30 years' purchase being rather the rule than the exception. However bad may be the state of agriculture in England, farming appears to be still a very profitable pursuit in the Principality, for in the majority of cases the tenants were the purchasers of their holdings.'[3] In fact in Wales the market saw the persistent land-hunger of a peasant society, while in England it saw the persistent loss of confidence of capitalist investors. Though it is well to remember that in peasant Ireland as little as 15 years' purchase was the rule in 1885.[4]

In spite of the lower prices only a fraction of the land coming on to the market found purchasers. The demand for land collapsed, partly because of a decline in the political and social advantages attached to landownership, but mainly because of a general belief in the universality of depression in agriculture and despondency over its future. Until 'the future conditions of agriculture can be more clearly foreseen', said the President of the Surveyors in 1883, 'we shall probably look in vain for any great increase in the demand for land, and the market will be filled, as at present, with anxious owners, of whose offers to sell no heed is taken by capitalists'. 'The truth is, we suppose', said

[1] *Estates Gazette*, 1 Jan. 1887, 7 Jan. 1888.
[2] Alnwick MSS, Business Minutes, XCII (1893), pp. 102–14.
[3] *Estates Gazette*, 7 Jan. 1888.
[4] Longleat MSS, Bath Estate Purchase Act (1885), Ireland, Register of Sales.

The Times a few years later, 'that for purposes of sport capitalists prefer to hire rather than to buy, while for purposes of investment they mistrust the security which land offers in present circumstances in England.'[1]

Many old-established owners tried to sell at least portions of their estates in the 1880s and 1890s. Some were faced by an insupportable burden of debts, such as those presented to the third Marquess of Ailesbury by his son. Some were faced by acute pressure of falling rents on irreducible expenditure. And some felt that the time had come to spread their assets over a variety of securities; for the Settled Land Act of 1882 had given the power to sell to life-tenants, and under it, wrote the Duke of Marlborough in 1885, 'were there any effective demand for the purchase of land, half the land of England would be in the market tomorrow'.[2] Many of these estates were sold, occasionally to old families but most often to new men. The largest transaction of 1889 was stated to be the purchase from the Marquess of Ripon by a Bradford manufacturer of the 7,000-acre Lincolnshire estate of Norton Hall. Other new purchasers of this year included H. McCalmont, 'the thrice-millionaire' who 'bought out the Partridges of Bishops Wood on the Wye', James Joicey, M.P. who bought the Ulgham estate from the Earl of Carlisle, five other M.P.s, and four other businessmen.[3] Prominent purchasers in the following year included J. Colman, the mustard king, Cunliffe-Lister who secured the Ackton Hall estate in the Yorkshire coalfield, and J. Robinson, a Nottingham brewer, who bought Worksop Manor from the Duke of Newcastle; they also included one of Lord Fitzwilliam's sons, H. W. Fitzwilliam, who bought the 4,500-acre Wiganthorpe estate near Malton for £100,000. Successful sellers in these two years, besides those already mentioned, included the Earl of Carlisle, selling outlying portions of his Cumberland and Northumberland property, Lord Grantley, selling part of his Surrey estate, Lord Tollemache and Benyon of Culford Hall, both selling heavily in Suffolk.[4]

In spite of this appearance of activity, however, there were generally many more fruitless offers to sell than there were

---

[1] *Trans. Inst. of Surveyors*, XVI (1883-4), p. 8. *The Times*, 14 Oct. 1887.
[2] *Ibid.*, 3 Oct. 1885.
[3] *Estates Gazette*, 4 Jan. 1890.
[4] *Ibid.*, 17 Jan. 1891.

successful sales in the 1880s and 1890s, and the total amount of land changing hands declined steeply from the level of the prosperous years. Among the properties which were put on the market but remained unsold perhaps the most famous case was the 20,000-acre Hesleyside estate in Northumberland, since the fact that the Charltons were trying to sell after 600 years in possession, no less than the fact that they failed to find a purchaser, attracted the notice of a *Times'* leader.[1] After the best part of another century the Charltons are still happily in residence in the 1960s. Other notable estates which remained unsold in these years for want of purchasers included the Marquess of Cholmondeley's Houghton Hall estate in Norfolk, Lady Gage's Hengrave Hall in Suffolk (which was later sold to John Wood, cotton spinner of Glossop, who was created a baronet in 1918), Lord Westmorland's Apethorpe in Northampton (which was finally sold, in 1904, to Henry Brassey who was created Lord Brassey of Apethorpe in 1938), Lord Saye and Sele's Lincolnshire estate, Lord Rodney's Berrington estate in Hereford, Sir Robert Loder's Whittlebury estate in Northampton, Sir Geers Cotterell's Garnons near Hereford, and in Shropshire the Pemberton's Millichope estate and the Oakeley estate which had belonged to those families since the sixteenth century.[2] There were many more besides, and it is for this reason unlikely that there was any major transfer from land into stocks and shares before 1900, although many old-established landed families gave evidence of a desire to make the switch.

In the majority of cases the potential sellers were trying to sell a part only of their family estates, in order to clear off debts and increase income by making alternative investments, and it must not be assumed that there was as yet a general desire to abandon country life. The loans raised by owners of settled estates, under a special Act of 1870, for the alteration and improvement of their country houses, provide some indication of the continued attachment to the family seats.[3] Most of the loans were raised for such purposes as providing mansions with sewers, piped water, minor additions, and, from 1896, electric light. In the whole period

[1] *The Times*, 14 Oct. 1887.
[2] *Estates Gazette*, 1885–95.
[3] Ministry of Agriculture MSS, Register of Loans under the Limited Owners' Residences Act (1870), 1870–1930.

down to 1930 only one new mansion was financed under the Act, for Algernon Freeman-Mitford in 1888, though in 1884 Lord Strafford raised £22,147 for rebuilding Wrotham Park, Barnet. It may be assumed that the great majority of borrowers under the Act were not well off, since the affluent landowners would scarcely need to resort to a procedure which added 10 per cent to the cost of works. In the first decade of its operation £229,033 was borrowed under the Act; in the second decade, to 1890, £336,301, and in the third decade £241,936. Only after 1900 did this borrowing fall steeply, £56,566 being raised from 1901 to 1910, the last loan in the decade being approved in June 1908. The trend was continued, with one application in 1911 and three in 1919–20, yielding a total of £5,524 for the decade, and two final applications in 1922–3 amounted to £1,356, one of which was from Orlando Orlebar to put drains into Hinwick.

It would be unwise to read too much into these figures. Slightly dearer money after 1906 may have contributed to the decline in borrowing. Owners of settled estates may have found alternative methods of financing alterations to their mansions, especially under the judicial interpretation of the Settled Land Acts of 1882 and 1890. In 1905 the courts allowed the installation of heating and electric light as legitimate applications for the proceeds of sales of settled land, when such improvements formed part of a general rebuilding project, although earlier decisions had disallowed heating or lighting schemes in isolation.[1] But the sudden cessation of applications, when there had been six in 1901, does suggest that declining confidence in the future of country house life was one of the factors present.

This decline coincided with the return of an overwhelmingly strong Liberal Government and revived fears of discrimination against landowners and an attack on the 'land monopoly'. After the legislation of 1908 had further strengthened the tenant's claims to compensation from his landlord for any disturbance 'inconsistent with good estate management', and had given County Councils compulsory powers to purchase land for use as small holdings, the frontal attack seemed to have arrived in the 1909 Budget with its Increment Value Duty and Undeveloped Land Duty and its provision for a valuation of all the land in the

---

[1] *Wolstenholme's Conveyancing and Settled Land Acts* (10th ed. 1913), pp. 420–1, 498.

kingdom. In 1910 a flood of land sales started, continuing through to the outbreak of war in 1914, and it was easy to argue that these were politically induced sales. For the first time there was talk of the break-up of estates, and its likely effects on agriculture. 'Not for many generations has there been so enormous a dispersal piecemeal of landed estate as in 1911 and 1912', it was reported, 'and the supply of ancestral acres in the provinces is apparently unlimited'. It was calculated that at least 104,000 acres changed hands in 1910 and 174,000 in 1911, with 1912 and 1913 showing even higher figures; one firm of estate agents had so many estates for sale in 1911 that it took the unprecedented step of publishing a special illustrated catalogue. The Duke of Bedford, who was not under any personal financial pressure, was credited with starting the process by disposing of nearly half his estates which had become financially unattractive.[1] In 1912 nineteen noblemen were listed as selling large estates, ranging from Lords Londesborough and Winchilsea who were probably substantially indebted, to the Dukes of Sutherland and Westminster who clearly were not. In 1913 the nobility in the land market were said to be more numerous than ever, and the half-season of 1914, interrupted by the war, brought 'the enormous dispersal during the last five years' to a total of about £20 millions, or perhaps 800,000 acres.[2]

Walter Long, announcing in 1910 the forthcoming sale of a great part of his Wiltshire estate, good dairy farms let at £2 an acre, stated that he reached his decision because the policy of the Government towards large landowners 'compels all of us who are interested in land to most carefully consider our position. We who are owners have done our best to act as if in partnership with our tenants and have not been governed by purely mercenary considerations. A change, however, is coming over the scene, and those of us who do not possess other sources of income must regulate our affairs accordingly'.[3] He added, in his public letter to his tenants, 'I hope you may decide to become

---

[1] *Parliamentary Papers*, 1912/13, XLVII, Rep. and Evidence, Departmental Committee of Board of Agriculture on Tenant Farmers, Q. 1723–4; the Duke of Bedford sold his Thorney estate in 1909 to the tenants, after the breakdown of a negotiation to sell to the Crown in one lot.

[2] *Estates Gazette*, 16 Dec. 1911, 4 Jan. 1913, 3 Jan. 1914, 2 Jan. 1915. *The Times*, 30 Dec. 1911.

[3] *Ibid.*, 24 Sept. 1910.

the owner of your own holding', thus setting the Conservative seal on the old radical programme of peasant proprietorship. As it turned out, most of the Long estate was bought by the sitting tenants, but it emerged that there had first been a negotiation for a sale to Lord Carrington in a single lot.[1] Walter Long, as a front-bench Conservative, had an interest in making political capital out of his move. But his most important motive in selling may have been to make financial capital, rather than to escape the effects of recent government policy. For no new taxation had been imposed on agricultural land, and even the $\frac{1}{2}$d. in the pound undeveloped land duty, as the *Estates Gazette* pointed out, 'really sounds worse than it is', and applied only to land ripe for building.[2] Long countered that it was not present impositions, but what governments might do in the future, that made it prudent to sell portions of family estates. This may well have been true, but it was a more demonstrable truth that it had for many years past been prudent for landowners to possess other sources of income, for reasons unconnected with the Liberal Government or radical land policy.

The inducements to sell were increased by 'a feeling of apprehension among owners as to the probable tendency of legislation and taxation in regard to land'. But the older desire persisted, to pay off mortgages and increase net incomes by re-investing the balance of capital. And a new motive appeared when owners found that their farms were under-rented and preferred to sell rather than to raise rents.[3] The outstanding feature of the situation, however, was that the sellers found someone to sell to, and that the great unloading of landed estates did not glut the market as had happened twenty or thirty years earlier. Demand was firm in these pre-war years, and prices ruled comparatively high. Some purchasers bought entire estates as of old: Lords Brackley and Egmont were noticed among the nobility, and Sir Ernest Cassel among the new men.[4] In very many cases, however, tenant farmers bought their holdings, and the disintegration of estates on a national scale had thus begun. The farmers bought, with some reluctance,

---

[1] *Ibid.*, 22 Nov. 1910.
[2] *Estates Gazette*, 17 Dec. 1910.
[3] Report of Departmental Committee of Board of Agriculture, 1912, p. 5.
[4] *Estates Gazette*, 4 Jan. 1913.

because confidence in agriculture had revived and with it competition for farms, empty farms were hard to come by, and they feared eviction by new owners. Many, from the side of the farming interest no less than from Conservative ranks, urged that the State should make loans to enable tenants to purchase.[1] This was not in fact done, but the support for the proposal indicated the extent to which the estate system was regarded as moribund.

When an owner was selling only a part of his estate and retained his country seat, which was the most frequent case at this time, it made sound economic sense for the land to be sold farm by farm to the tenants. The farmers gave good prices, and an investor who would take a non-residential property as a single lot was hard to find, so that the break-up of estates in these circumstances imposed no financial sacrifice on the seller. It was another matter that it might well bring hardship to the new owner-occupiers in the future, when they no longer had a land-lord to reduce rents or provide extra capital in times of distress. When an entire estate was sold, however, as happened in many cases, the break-up meant that the seller lost the value which had once attached to the estate as an entity, the embodiment of the country gentleman's position. Potential purchasers were as much scared of the possible future taxation of large landowners as were the existing owners. There was also the slow decline in the social prestige attached to land, and a change in social habits: 'many who used to shoot in England now take a shoot in Scotland, and go abroad much earlier than they used to, often in October and November . . . and many now prefer golf'. As a result, although 'farms and small holdings sell well, residential and sporting estates as a whole are difficult to realize. This causes certain owners to break up their estates in order to sell at all. Consequently many large country houses are empty.'[2]

In these cases, therefore, fears for the future engendered by the trend of policy produced their effect, though it must be set alongside the more deeply rooted decline in the social and economic attractiveness of landed estates. Landowners, after all, had survived previous political alarms. Some, like Lord

[1] A. H. H. Matthews, *Fifty Years of Agricultural Politics*, pp. 204–7; cf. pp. 210–11 for earlier hostility to such proposals in the 1880s.
[2] *Estates Gazette*, 17 Dec. 1910, 16 Dec. 1911.

Carnarvon and Lord Rosebery, had felt that the establishment of County Councils in 1888 was a revolutionary measure which meant 'the dethronement of the squirearchy', but in practice the nobility and gentry provided most of the chairmen of the new councils[1].

A Government supporter, George Russell, had expected that the establishment of parish councils in 1893 would end the age-old alliance of the clergy 'with the squire and the privileged classes in the attempt to rule full-grown men against their will, to order them about like children, and to check the least symptom of independence', and that 'the hereditary right to dominate in social and civil matters would be . . . rudely shaken'. Knatchbull-Hugessen felt himself to be 'the only Tory left in the House' to protest against this revolutionary legislation: but again in practice it produced no startling changes.[2] Harcourt's death duties of 1894 had been hailed as harbingers of ruin for agricultural landowners, but in fact their burden was comparatively easily borne out of income or special insurance policies, reaching the maximum rate of 8 per cent only on the very large estates worth a million pounds, with rentals of well over £40,000.[3] The alarms of 1909, though somewhat more serious especially with the increased rates of death duty, did not on the surface justify fears of real catastrophe any more than these earlier scares.

It was therefore in part a coincidence that many owners chose to act upon the scares of 1909. These provided self-justification for a course which had long seemed wise, the realization of some of their landed assets so soon as a favourable market should appear. To blame the radicals provided some salve for the wrench of parting with the family inheritance. Paradoxically the estates system was already beginning to crumble just as Lloyd George was getting ready to launch a great new radical campaign in 1914 against the 'land monopoly'. The beginning of the break-up, however, may more profitably be seen as the natural culmination of the whole trend of the preceding generation. The landed interest had lost its pre-eminence, and now land was losing many of its attractions. On the surface much

---

[1] *Hansard*, 3rd ser., CCCXXIX (1888), 918–33.
[2] *Ibid.*, 4th ser., XVIII (1893), 128, 387–9.
[3] Matthews, *Fifty Years of Agricultural Politics*, pp. 113–6.

remained unaltered in 1914, with the younger sons of the landed classes entrenched in the diplomatic service and the army and the old aristocracy flourishing in London society. Beneath the surface it could be seen that many of the old landowners had made terms with the capitalists and become involved in the business world themselves. Now a further section of the landed interest began to regard their estates in the cold light of investments, and decided that they would be better off if they sold land, deciding in so doing that the social advantages of landownership had so diminished as to be no longer worth paying for. The apparently stable Edwardian society had in fact resolved upon a social revolution, the liquidation of the landed interest, whose full accomplishment was but deferred by the First World War.

XII

◇◇◇

Eclipse, 1914-39

◇◇◇

THE First World War brought grievous sacrifices to the whole nation, and it perhaps brought greater losses to the landed families, with their long military traditions, than to any other class. It would be impossible to measure how much the quality and vitality of landed society in the post-war years suffered from the absence of the sons killed in France, or from the natural hedonism of the survivors of the holocaust. It would be unfair to suggest that in the higher reaches of military leadership the hereditary principle vindicated itself with such *éclat* in modern warfare as it had done in the campaigns against Napoleon. But at the regimental level the service was as valuable as it was unstinted. The war also brought great changes at home. Higher taxation, especially of large incomes, and greatly increased death duties; greater equality between classes, as government tardily enforced an equal sharing of physical shortages, and as rising wages overtook inflated prices from 1917; a growing scarcity of domestic servants, as female as well as male labour was drawn into the war effort; and, when the government at length took the food situation seriously after the end of 1916, a vigorous effort to expand food production, especially of wheat, under state control.

Death duties compelled sales, especially when an owner's death was quickly followed by that of his heir, killed in action, or when such double deaths in the reverse order left an estate to pass to a distant relative with no strong ties to the family estate. Thus when Sir Edmund Antrobus's death closely followed that of his only son, in action, the whole of his Amesbury Abbey estate was put on the market in 1915. The Abbey and park remained unsold, but the farms were bought by the tenants, and Stonehenge was bought by a Salisbury man, C. H. E. Chubb, for £6,600. It had been fenced, and a charge made for admission, only since 1901; it was reckoned an excellent bargain, as the receipts averaged £360 a year, though Chubb did not buy it as a speculation, having decided on the spur of the moment during the auction that a local man ought to own it.[1] Taxation made inroads into aristocratic living standards which had not been apparent before the war. Income tax, which took barely 4 per cent of gross rents at Wilton and Savernake before 1914, was taking over a quarter by 1919, and the burden of all direct taxes taken together (land tax, rates, and income tax) had risen from 9 to 30 per cent of the rental. Moreover landowners generally did not appropriate any of the great increase in agricultural prices by raising rents, at least in war-time. Between 1914 and 1920 the prices of barley, wool, meat and dairy produce trebled, and the price of wheat doubled; at Savernake, for example, rents were not touched until 1920, when they were raised by 16 per cent.

War-time restrictions and hardships, however, were not all-pervasive. Foxhunting was generally given up by 1917, but shooting continued, on a somewhat reduced scale. At Gorhambury, for instance, there was little gamekeeping staff left by 1918, so that practically no rabbits were shot in that season. But the bag of partridges and pheasants was kept up at little less than half its pre-war figure, and fairly frequent shooting parties were held throughout the war, with many officers among the guests. Farm building and repair was generally restricted by shortage of labour and materials, but it was still possible in the middle of the war to have the magnificent ceiling of the Sledmere library replaced, from the original mouldings still preserved by the London plasterers. The life of the great town houses became much curtailed, but Sonia Keppel still came out in the New Year of 1918 in full debutante's style, in the midst

[1] *The Times*, 27 and 28 May, 15 and 16 June, 12 Aug., 21, 22 and 23 Sept. 1915.

of her war-work at a Forces' canteen.[1] Nor was it simply the pressure of war-time taxation, the difficulty of running large houses without large establishments, or the need to meet death duties, which released the great flood of land sales immediately on the return of peace.

The land market had not been entirely inactive, but on the whole transactions had fallen to a trickle until the last year of the war, as both buyers and sellers waited to see how high agricultural prices would go, and as surplus money was diverted into lending to the state. In the sales that did take place the break-up of large estates continued. In 1917, for example, Lord Pembroke sold off his detached estate in North Wiltshire, and Sir Francis Astley-Corbett, whose seat and main estate was in Lincolnshire, sold his entire Wiltshire estate of Everleigh Manor. This estate of 4,500 acres was bought in a single lot, the purchaser at once ordering the resale of all the outlying farms totalling 3,000 acres. In 1918 Lord Alington sold off 2,630 acres of his outlying property in Dorset, Ernle-Ernle-Erle-Drax, primarily a Dorset landowner, sold off his Wiltshire estate, and Lord Pembroke sold a further 8,400 acres, this time the outlying portions of the Wilton estate itself. Such sales were generally described as 'forced', induced by taxation and death duties, but in none of these cases was there a death immediately preceding the sale and it is more plausible to regard them as a continuation of the pre-war trend towards the contraction of family estates by sale of outlying parts, liberating capital for more profitable uses.[2]

The season of 1918 saw a big revival in land transfers: one firm alone, Knight, Frank and Rutley, sold 454,972 acres in the year, which however included nearly a quarter of a million acres in Scotland belonging to the Duke of Sutherland.[3] The avalanche came with the spring of 1919. The Duke of Sutherland offered a further 144 square miles of the Highlands, with Dornoch Castle, and in England his Shropshire seat of Lilleshall House, and he was joined by the Duke of Westminster, Lords Aberdeen, Aylesford, Beauchamp, Cathcart, Middleton, Northampton,

---

[1] Sonia Keppel, *Edwardian Daughter*, chap. xiii.
[2] *Estates Gazette*, 6 Jan, 14 April, 16 June, 30 June, 18 Aug., 1917; 5 Jan., 23 Sept., 23 Nov., 1918; 4 Jan. 1919.
[3] *The Times*, 31 Dec. 1918.

Petre, Tollemache and Yarborough, Sir Hamilton Hulse, Sir Thomas Neave, Sir H. J. Vansittart-Neale and Sir Hereward Wake, to name but a few, until by the end of March about 1,000 square miles or well over half a million acres was on the market.[1] All this land had been offered for sale before the 1919 budget, although Lord Hugh Cecil, the Duke of Marlborough and others suggested that it was the 'confiscatory' taxation of this budget in raising death duties to 40 per cent on estates of £2 million and over which obliged large landowners to sell. 'The old order is doomed', wrote Marlborough, the great part which the landed aristocracy had played in the social and political life of the nation would survive no longer in the face of a fiscal policy which deliberately aimed at preventing the inheritance of great houses and great estates: 'These fortresses of territorial influence it is proposed to raze in the name of social equality'.[2] The old order was indeed doomed, had in fact already passed away in many respects, but it was from causes of much longer standing than the 1919 budget, though the desertion of the cause of the landed aristocracy by the Conservative Ministers in the Coalition Government no doubt was painful. The Duke's predecessor had said in 1885 that 'half the land in England would be in the market tomorrow' were there any effective demand for its purchase: now, in 1919, 'tomorrow' had at last arrived.

By March 1919 a 'revolution in landowning' was proclaimed by the *Estates Gazette*. Then more and more estates were put on the market, and by May an advertisement announced 'England changing hands'. By the end of the year the market reports were full of the phrase 'England is changing hands'; it was the 'annus mirabilis' of the property market, one firm had announced three-quarters of a million acres for sale in the course of the year, within a few weeks in the summer over two million acres had been advertised for sale in *The Times*, and probably well over a million acres had actually been sold during the year.[3] In 1920 the records were broken again, with the Duke of Beaufort and the Marquess of Bath in the ranks of the sellers: the biggest sale of the year was by the Duke of Rutland, who

[1] *The Times*, 22 March 1919.
[2] *Ibid.*, 19 May 1919.
[3] *Estates Gazette*, 29 March 1919, 3 Jan. 1920. *The Times*, 15 May, 30 and 31 Dec. 1919.

sold 28,000 acres or about half his Belvoir estate, for £1½ million, closely followed by the sale of the 12,500-acre Scarisbrick estate in Lancashire for £1 million. By May 1920 'we all know it now', *The Times* was saying, 'England is changing hands. . . . Will a profiteer buy it? Will it be turned into a school or an institution? Has the mansion house electric light and modern drainage? . . . For the most part the sacrifices are made in silence. . . . The sons are perhaps lying in far away graves; the daughters secretly mourning some one dearer than a brother, have taken up some definite work away from home, seeking thus to still their aching hearts, and the old people, knowing there is no son or near relative left to keep up the old traditions, or so crippled by necessary taxation that they know the boy will never be able to carry on when they are gone, take the irrevocable step'.[1]

During 1921 the boom collapsed, alongside the general recession in business, and in particular because in June came the thunderbolt of the repeal of the Corn Production Act and hence the removal of guaranteed prices for grains. The turnover of land in 1921 was less than half that of 1920, though it was still very large by pre-war standards; the Duke of Northumberland, for instance, successfully sold his Yorkshire estate of Stanwick in this year. Nevertheless land prices fell and sales became uncertain. Farmers were frightened by the signs of coming depression, and far less eager to purchase than before, and many owners unsuccessfully stood out for the high prices they could have realized in 1919–20.[2] Some selling continued: for example the Duke of Northumberland sold the bulk of his Albury estate in Surrey, except the mansion, in 1922; and there was some revival of sales in 1924 and 1925. After 1925, however, selling largely ceased, and the Marquess of Ailesbury had plainly missed his market in disposing of the bulk of the Savernake estate in 1929. He sold 25,000 acres, retaining the mansion, the Forest, and 16,000 acres in all. It was bought by a middleman who at once broke it up into lots and resold the sixty farms and ten complete villages. The middleman received barely £11 an acre for the 22,000 acres which he succeeded in reselling, which

---

[1] *Estates Gazette*, 1 Jan. 1921. *The Times*, 19 May 1920.
[2] *Ibid.*, 15 Oct., 31 Dec. 1921. *Estates Gazette*, 31 Dec. 1921.

was perhaps fourteen years' purchase on their existing rents; the middleman may have made a loss on the transaction, but the Marquess can scarcely have got a very good price. The average selling price of agricultural land in the good years was about £35 an acre.[1]

Looking back from the end of 1921 over the four hectic years of land sales the *Estates Gazette* concluded that one-quarter of England must have changed hands.[2] The sales reported in the journals would hardly admit of so high a figure, but undoubtedly many sales were never reported there at all. For example, the Marquess of Bath's sale in 1920 of his outlying estates of Minsterley in Shropshire and Weobley in Hereford was reported. But his more extensive sales, between 1919 and 1921, of at least 8,600 acres of his Longleat estate in Wiltshire and Somerset, which brought him £350,000, were not reported in the national papers.[3] An independent check also suggests that the figure of one-quarter of England changing hands was a plausible estimate. In 1914 some 11 per cent of the agricultural land in England and Wales was occupied by its owners, a figure which included the home farms which were occupied by the larger landowners. By 1927 the owner-farmers occupied 36 per cent of the total acreage.[4] Precisely one-quarter of England and Wales had therefore passed from being tenanted land into the possession of its farmers in the thirteen years after 1914. Insofar as a proportion of the estates which were sold continued to pass into the hands of large landowners, established or new, and did not swell the ranks of the owner-farmers, it is possible that in the four years of intense activity between 1918 and 1921 something between six and eight million acres changed hands in England. Such an enormous and rapid transfer of land had not been seen since the confiscations and sequestrations of the Civil War, such a permanent transfer not since the dissolution of the monasteries in the sixteenth century. Indeed a transfer on this

[1] *The Times*, 29 July 1922, 25 July, 3 and 26 Sept. 1929, 21 June 1930. *Estates Gazette*, 27 Dec. 1924, 9 May 1925. Savernake MSS, Estate accounts 1929–30.

[2] *Estates Gazette*, 31 Dec. 1921.

[3] *Ibid.*, 1 Jan. 1921. *The Times*, 14 Jan. 1920. Longleat MSS, Sale particulars, Cheddar, Frome and Warminster, 1919–21.

[4] Figures of owner-occupation are summarized and discussed by S. G. Sturmey, 'Owner-Farming in England and Wales, 1900–50', *Manchester School of Economic and Social Studies*, XXIII (1955), pp. 246–68.

scale and in such a short space of time had probably not been equalled since the Norman Conquest.

The transfers also marked a startling social revolution in the countryside, nothing less than the dissolution of a large part of the great estate system and the formation of a new race of yeomen. Within the lifetime of the generation of social historians who in the 1900s had examined the historical problems of the disappearance of the small landowner this character made a dramatic reappearance.[1] Some purchasers of the old type still came forward. A classic instance was the sale in September 1921 of Compton Verney, the family seat of Lord Willoughby de Broke, the famous Diehard leader of 1911. It was bought by Joseph Watson, soap-boiler and racehorse owner, who was created Lord Manton of Compton Verney just three months later. It is typical of the common over-emphasis on taxation as the cause of sales that the *Complete Peerage* comments that Willoughby de Broke was compelled to sell 'doubtless by death duties', when he had succeeded to the estate in 1902 and did not die until 1923.[2] In 1923 the *Estates Gazette* commented on the reappearance of one or two of the 'older' nobility as extensive purchasers, instancing Lord Wimborne.[3]

In these years, however, the sitting tenants formed the overwhelming mass of purchasers. Sometimes they purchased direct from the old owner, who might consent to leave most of the purchase money on mortgage at 5 per cent, thus gaining for himself an increased gross income which was free from all the previous deductions for estate management and upkeep. Sometimes the owner helped his tenants to form a syndicate to purchase the entire property and then break it up amongst themselves. But very often, especially when an owner had mortgages pressing at his back, the estate was first sold entire to a syndicate of speculators and the tenants bought from them at second hand. There was a good deal of grumbling from farmers at the speculation in land, and resentment that they had to pay a middleman's profit, which was said to have amounted to £250,000 on the turnover of 50,000 acres in Lincolnshire.[4]

[1] For example A. H. Johnson, *The Disappearance of the Small Landowner* (1909); R. H. Tawney, *The Agrarian Problem in the Sixteenth Century* (1912).

[2] G.E.C., *The Complete Peerage*, XII, pt. ii, 701.

[3] *Estates Gazette*, 29 Dec. 1923.

[4] *The Times*, 17 and 19 May, 1919.

As had been predicted throughout the nineteenth century in comments on radical plans for greater diffusion of landed property, the new owner-farmers generally found that they were paying more in interest on mortgages than they had paid in rent. With the general price fall of 1921, moreover, they were at once plunged into an agricultural crisis without the landlord shield to protect them. In the ensuing years of adjustment to a lower price level and a higher labour cost, and of renewed conversion of a war-inflated corn acreage to grass, owner-farmers found that fixed interest charges aggravated their difficulties. In the 1930s it was said, for instance, that the banks virtually owned half Norfolk, and that the new owner-occupiers had fared the worst of any section of the agricultural community since 1920.[1]

In a primarily industrial and urban society, preoccupied with its own problems of finance, foreign trade, and unemployment, it is perhaps hardly surprising that no Radical appeared in 1920 to celebrate the triumph of the dissolution of estates, nor yet in the 1930s to comment on the effects this had produced in the farming world. Nevertheless the dissolution was certainly due in part to the climate of opinion about equality which Radicals had done so much to create. It was this which moulded ideas of taxation and accustomed governments to look to inherited wealth as a source of revenue. It was this which created the sense 'that landowning on a large scale is now generally felt to be a monopoly and is consequently unpopular', which Lord Northampton gave as one of his reasons for selling in 1919. But neither landlord unpopularity nor the burdens of existing taxation were the sole reasons for the great post-war sales.[2]

Apart from the effects of the actual level of taxation in forcing some landowners to live on capital there were special fiscal considerations which made it desirable to sell land. Farms were very generally under-rented by the end of the war, since landlords had not tapped the extra profits of war prices by raising rents. Farms could be sold at prices based on their current annual value, not on their existing rents, so that the seller capitalized this difference and took his share of increased land values as an untaxed profit. If rents had been raised the increment

[1] *Ibid.*, 3 May 1935.
[2] *Ibid.*, 19 March 1919.

would have been liable to income and super taxes. Moreover under the 1919 budget land was to be valued for death duties at its current selling price, in place of the former valuation on the basis of existing rents, and this gave a similar incentive to sell land rather than other assets in order to pay the duties, since the amount on which duty was levied was greater than the capitalized value of the existing income from land.

Such factors reinforced the more deep-seated inducements to sell. As in so many other fields, the effects of war emphasized trends which had already been apparent before 1914. The social and political influence of the landed interest had already declined, and it declined still further during the war, when power and influence belonged to the strident men of affairs and not to the old families. The costs of estate management and maintenance increased as a result of the war, and the smaller net incomes from land simply confirmed that the low return in relation to capital value imposed a price on landownership which was no longer balanced by social advantages. Alongside those who were literally forced to sell, therefore, came hosts of the nobility and gentry who realized the wisdom of adjusting the scale of their landed possessions to the altered social and economic conditions, while the going was good and the market land-hungry. The more detached views of the spate of selling acknowledged this interpretation. 'Landowners everywhere seem to have come to the conclusion that it is the best policy to divest themselves of any land that can at all be regarded as outlying,' it was said, 'and many are taking a very broad view of the term, and selling land quite near their own seats.' Another comment was that an owner could do very well for himself by selling an asset which perhaps yielded him 3 per cent, clearing off mortgages whose burden had risen during the war, and reinvesting the surplus in trustee securities yielding 7 or 8 per cent.[1]

The movement, moreover, was not confined to the sale of country estates. Early in 1919 the Marquess of Salisbury sold his town house in Arlington Street, which had been the Cecil house for generations, and this was hailed as doing for the great town houses what the Duke of Bedford's sales before the war had done in initiating a general movement for agricultural estates. The possibility of demolition for the erection of hotels was

Ibid., 29 March 1919. *Estates Gazette*, 7 Aug. 1920.

canvassed, which would have begun a general process of evacuation of town houses since 'the presence of an hotel does not contribute to the social amenities of a first class district.' Town houses, it was conceded, might be able to survive alongside blocks of flats, provided these were let in large suites at rents high enough 'to exclude tenants who do not keep up the character of the position.' Though one or two other town houses were sold, such as Lord Dartmouth's, the process was perhaps not quite the landslide which had been forecast, since Lord Salisbury having obtained £120,000 for his old house from Lady Michelham then moved into the next-door one for £60,000. Nevertheless the process had clearly started, which over the next generation saw the eclipse of the great town houses and the disappearance of their society life, and the abandonment of Mayfair to hotels, flats and offices.[1]

Urban estates were broken up in 1919 no less than agricultural ones, and here the drive to convert into cash and then into other investments was plainer for all to see. The Duke of Bedford sold £2 million worth of his Bloomsbury ground rents, Lord Portman 7 acres of Marylebone, Lord Camden part of Camden Town and Lord Southampton a part of Euston. When selling country estates, it was pointed out, 'it was customary for owners proposing to sell to express their regret at the severance of old associations and all that sort of thing, and to declare that the welfare of their tenants was their primary aim. But there are no sentimental attachments to town properties . . . with some conspicuous exceptions, the great ground landlords of London have not identified themselves at all with the social life of the boroughs in which their properties lie . . . and it is a matter of indifference to the tenants whether they pay the ground rents at one office or another.'[2] Since 'London lessees are not as a rule very eager to sink capital in acquiring the freehold of their premises' the partial break-up of the great London estates did not then result – and on the whole has not since resulted – in the creation of large numbers of home-owners. Instead it has substituted property companies, or a large number of small private ground landlords, for the few great landlords, a change of some economic but little social significance. In the 1950s

[1] *The Times*, 1 Feb. and 26 April 1919.
[2] *Ibid.*, 9, 15, 16 and 17 May 1919.

further and larger sales of this kind, of the Bedford, Portman or Westminster estates, were occasioned by the immediate need to pay death duties. In 1919 and 1920 the sales were a part of the landowners' new investment policy.

In many cases, no doubt, the proceeds of the great sales were at once swallowed up in payment of death duties or satisfaction of creditors, leaving the sellers in reduced circumstances. It is significant, however, that of forty noblemen who sold part of their estates in the first half of 1919 in only six cases had any death duties become payable since 1914. The great landed magnates, therefore, emerged into the inter-war period still in residence in their country seats, with their territorial empires considerably reduced, but with their incomes – once debts had been cleared and reinvestments made – probably much healthier than they had been for very many years. Several more estate sales followed in these years, such as the Savernake sale which has been noted, occasioned perhaps by death duties or by schemes to avoid the payment of death duties. A few new landed aristocrats continued to appear, still converting wealth into social position, more delighted with their new toys of landlord's rights than the old owners, mourning the passing of the great days, had come to be. Such, for example, was the brewer, Newall-Cain, who purchased Lord Melbourne's old home of Brocket Hall and its estate – somewhat curtailed by the sales of Lord Walter Kerr, an intervening owner – and was created Lord Brocket in 1933. But on the whole the social balance of the countryside was not greatly disturbed between 1921 and 1939. In 1941, when the next farm census was taken, the area occupied by owner-farmers was much the same as it had been in 1927, even slightly smaller: by 1950 the process of breaking up the great estates had been resumed, and 38 per cent of England's farmland was in the hands of owner-farmers. It has since continued, and in the 1960s England is about to become a predominantly peasant country: only the new twentieth-century 'peasants' bear little resemblance to those with the homespun smocks and small holdings which nineteenth-century reformers had in mind.[1]

The landed aristocracy in the inter-war years gradually settled down to a circumscribed style of living, which had

[1] Sturmey, *op. cit.*

previously been typical only of the impoverished arable land-owners. We know very little of the size of their non-agricultural incomes in this period, but their dividends presumably fell away after 1929, and were in any case subject to income tax and super tax. Mineral incomes also presumably suffered from the troubles of the coal industry, and their decline may have been one of the reasons why the nationalization of mineral rights in 1939 caused so little stir. Even at the height of these incomes, during the war, there had been much feeling at the large share taken by taxation. In 1918 the Duke of Northumberland's mineral income was £82,450: this was reduced to a net income of £23,890 after payment of the 5 per cent Mineral Rights Duty, the 80 per cent Excess Mineral Rights Duty on the amount by which tonnage rents exceeded the pre-war levels, income tax at the standard rate of 6s. in the pound, and super tax at the maximum rate of 4s. 6d. in the pound. Public opinion, in any case, was moving strongly against the royalty owners. In answer to the question: 'As a coal owner what service do you perform to the community?' the Duke could only say 'As the owner of the coal I do not think I perform any service to the community – not as the owner of the coal.'[1]

Their incomes as agricultural landowners definitely declined sharply. Rents which had very generally been raised soon after the end of the war almost at once began to fall away again with the break in prices in 1921. By 1933 they were back to their pre-1914 level, and by 1936 reached their lowest point in the period since 1870 and perhaps their lowest point since 1800; they had fallen by about a quarter since 1921.[2] Although the general price level had fallen considerably since 1921, it was still in the middle of the 1930s about 50 per cent above the pre-war level, and the cost of labour, which entered so largely into the aristocratic cost of living, was between 60 and 100 per cent more than before 1914. Landowners once more reacted to falling rents by cutting down their improvements and their standards of estate maintenance, in an effort to conserve as much net income as possible. This marked a further decline in their contribution to agriculture, but the restrictions in outlay were not sufficient to prevent their personal incomes from being a dwindling

[1] *Parliamentary Papers*, 1919, XII, R.C. on the Coal Industry, Q. 15,033,15,184. Rhee, *Rent of Agricultural Land in England and Wales, 1870–1943*, pp. 41–43.

proportion of gross rents. Before 1914 estate expenditure of all kinds, on maintenance, management and improvements, had generally taken about 35 per cent of gross rents. Rising costs and largely stationary rents had increased this proportion to 62 per cent by 1921; although a combination of rent increases, lower costs, and economy reduced outlays to 48 per cent of gross rents by 1923, the proportion absorbed by estate expenditure thereafter rose steadily, in spite of further economies, and by 1938 had again reached 62 per cent of gross rents. The implication of these figures, in conjunction with the movement in gross rents, is that estate expenditure in the 1930s was about 70 per cent higher than it had been before 1914, an increase somewhat less than the rise in the cost of materials and labour, and that the residual personal income of landowners was about half its pre-1914 amount.[1]

These reduced incomes were subject to permanently higher levels of income tax and super tax. Domestic staff, after the end of the war, was once more not too difficult to find, but wages remained so high that it was out of the question to re-create the vast establishments and the way of life that had depended on them. The sixth Duke of Portland, surveying the scene in the middle of the 1930s, pinpointed the changes which marked the passing of the aristocratic world. 'Fifty years ago', he wrote, 'there was little or nothing of vital consequence at issue between Liberals and Conservatives. . . . Now . . . there is no longer a powerful and moderate Liberal Party standing between the National Parties and those who support socialistic or communistic principles.' It is instructive to find the Liberals of the 'Unauthorized Programme' and Joseph Chamberlain's land reform movement dwindling into moderates in the perspective of a nobleman's world which had been turned upside down. In the old days, the Duke continued, the great London houses 'were thrown open every season for large social gatherings', and he listed Hertford, Grosvenor, Dorchester, Londonderry, Lansdowne, Devonshire, Spencer, Chesterfield, Stafford, Bridgewater, Apsley, Montagu and Holland Houses. 'At present only Londonderry, Apsley, Bridgewater and Holland Houses remain as private residences'. The rest had been closed, turned into

[1] *Ibid.*, p. 50. D. K. Britton, *An Enquiry into Agricultural Rents and the Expenses of Landowners in England and Wales, 1938 and 1946* (1949), pp. 7, 27.

museums, or pulled down, and 'from a social point of view restaurants, cabarets and night-clubs have risen in their place'. In the country 'large estates . . . have been and still are being broken up, and the houses attached to them sold to individuals most of whom have had little or no connexion with the land . . . farmers no longer have the old landlords to whom they were accustomed to turn for help when times were bad.' 'Many of the great country houses, when not in the occupation of strangers, or used for other purposes, quickly become derelict. . . . When I first lived at Welbeck the great neighbouring houses, such as Clumber, Thoresby and Rufford were all inhabited by their owners, who . . . employed large staffs. . . . Now not one . . . is so occupied, except for a few days in the year, and the shooting attached to them is either let or abandoned. . . . Whether this is for the general good I leave for others to judge. It is certainly the fact.'[1]

The Duke of Portland was chiefly interested in hunting and shooting, and what he mainly regretted was the passing of the days when his friend Lord Ripon, between 1867 and 1900, had been able to kill 142,343 pheasants, 97,759 partridges, 56,460 grouse, 29,858 rabbits, and 27,686 hares, not to mention 2 rhinos, 11 tiger, 12 buffalo, 19 sambur and 97 pig bagged in big game shooting. He recalled the 1909 season, though with some shame, when 2,500 pheasants had been shot daily for three successive days.[2] The reduction of such slaughter, or its transference to syndicates of businessmen, however, was not the most important aspect of the aristocratic eclipse. As the great town houses closed down, so the old families left the centre of the stage of London society. At the same time, amidst the scandals of the sale of honours under Lloyd George's Government, connected with the mobilization of a party campaign fund, the new peerage finally became a nobility of newly acquired fortunes.[3] There were 280 new peers created between 1916 and 1945, of whom just over half had been M.P.s. A tiny fraction of the politicians, thirteen, had been Labour members, and thus introduced a new element to the Lords. The great phalanx of ennobled Conservative politicians was, indeed, largely

---

[1] Duke of Portland, *Men, Women and Things* (1937), pp. 1–3.
[2] *Ibid.*, pp. 228–9, 237.
[3] See G. Macmillan, *Honours for Sale* (1954), on this episode.

composed of men with upper-class backgrounds who had been educated either at one of the 'aristocratic' public schools or at one of the socially favoured Oxford and Cambridge Colleges. But even the great old-Etonian element in the Conservative ranks in the House of Commons contained but a small section from the old landed families in the 1920s and 1930s. Apart from the politicians, there were sixty-six new peers who were prominent businessmen, beside whom the nine magnates, 'men of great eminence in local life and generally possessed of inherited wealth and land', only barely maintained the old traditions.[1] Moreover, within the Conservative party, the commanding influence of the inner ring of notabilities, in which members of the old families had continued to wield much power, was rudely challenged when the rank and file made a bid for self-government in forming the 1922 Committee. Thenceforward, though the party leaders reasserted their sovereign authority, the business interests were in charge.

The Duke of Portland acknowledged that some things were better in the 1930s than they had been a generation earlier: for his examples he chose dentists' equipment and motor transport.[2] The motor car, indeed, is the symbol of the new age, slowly dawning in the inter-war years, triumphant by the 1960s, the age of final mechanization, of mass consumption, of labour shortage, an age in which there is little place for a leisured aristocracy. Before 1914 the motor car had made its way into the aristocratic stables, accepted as a useful adjunct to the horses and carriages: in 1910 Lady Wimborne had a fleet of four Daimlers and Mercedes at Canford, and one of her sons had five Darracqs and Napiers of his own, all in charge of a 'chief of the engineering department'.[3] By the 1920s it was a normal part of life, and made possible some reduction of establishments as one or two chauffeurs replaced a dozen or more grooms and helpers. As car-ownership spread in other classes, moreover, and as charabanc trips became popular, the commercial possibilities of country-house visiting were opened up. This new source of income from

[1] Bromhead, *The House of Lords and Contemporary Politics,* pp. 20–30. J. F. S. Ross, *Parliamentary Representation* (1948), pp. 77–83.
[2] *Men, Women and Things,* p. 4.
[3] *Parliamentary Papers,* 1910, LXXIII, Trial of Election Petition for Dorset, East Division, Q. 1854–1904, 3343, 5144.

half-crown trippers, more widely and vigorously exploited since 1945, was beginning to make its appearance before 1939.

Apart from some commercialization of their country houses it does not seem that the nobility and gentry generally made any very energetic efforts to develop new sources of income in the inter-war period. Probably rather more had active business careers than formerly, and more joined in the search for company directorships. But the advice to run their own estates as businesses, farming for profit, which had been freely given in the 1880s, was not more generally followed then than it had been earlier.[1] And when, for example, fortunes were made out of gravel, they were made by contractors leasing the pits and not by the owners of the land. The traditions of gentility died hard, and only the scourge of the Second World War and yet higher taxation at length released a spirit of vigour and enterprise which may arrest the further decline of the old landed families.

This decline has been most marked in the landed gentry. Of the gentry families of Essex, Oxford and Shropshire, which were discussed in Chapter V, only one-third in each county still survived in 1952 in possession of their country seats. In addition a quarter of the gentry families of the 1870s were still listed in the 1952 edition of the *Landed Gentry* but had sold their family seats and moved, some to smaller houses in the country, some to London addresses, and some to Kenya or Rhodesia. The rest had disappeared, and for the most part their former homes had disappeared with them. Sometimes, of course these had been acquired by new gentry. But in Shropshire, for instance, of the ninety-odd country houses of the 1870s at least thirty-five seem to have left no trace in 1952. Out of the dozen gentry families whose records have been mentioned in this book, only the Middletons of Belsay, the Blundells of Little Crosby, the Orlebars of Hinwick, and the Dickinsons of Red How are still in residence. In the last case, characteristic of the times, the owner runs a tree nursery and garden contracting business.

The landed gentry, who stood firm during the greatest political and social changes of the nineteenth century, have suffered from economic adversity more severely than the landed aristocracy. Their decline in the twentieth century, given the

---

[1] W. Bence Jones, 'Landowning as a Business', *The Nineteenth Century*, XI (1882), pp. 346–68.

conditions of high taxation, rising costs and falling incomes, is no more surprising than their decline in the early eighteenth century. The novel feature of the present century has rather been the end of the rise of the new gentry. New men no longer come forward in sufficient numbers to replace the old, and in consequence estates are broken up and country houses lie forlorn and derelict, themselves broken up for their mantelpieces and door-frames. The reason is not that life in the country has lost its attractions, for if anything these have grown and become increasingly accessible to the motorized commuters. A place in the country is still an object of ambition and carries with it considerable social prestige, but with some exceptions the new men do not care to buy entire estates. This is because an estate is no longer generally regarded as a worthwhile investment in status. As an economic unit an estate is still viable, and the landlord-tenant arrangement may still be defended as the most efficient way of providing agricultural capital and management. An agricultural estate has powerful fiscal attractions, since it is liable to death duties on only half its capital value. The upkeep of a country house is indeed a formidable task, and houses designed to be run by large staffs of inexpensive servants are not easily adapted to modern ideas of comfort and convenience; but at a price it can be done. The life of a leisured country gentleman is no longer possible, and a landowner needs other occupations besides landowning and other sources of livelihood besides rents. But fundamentally estates have been suffered to disintegrate because they no longer embody great social power, for where power lies all obstacles are overcome in finding the means to acquire and exercise it.

In contrast, the landed aristocracy has survived with far fewer casualties, though everywhere with much reduced landed estates. Among the great ducal seats, for example, Stowe now houses a public school, Welbeck Abbey an Army College, and Eaton Hall is dilapidated and partly demolished. Clumber stands empty and the Duke of Newcastle lives in Rhodesia, while Kimbolton no longer seats a Duke of Manchester, who resides in Kenya. Forsaking Hornby Castle and the Gogmagog Hills the Duke of Leeds finds a home in the Channel Islands. But Badminton, Woburn, Chatsworth, Euston Hall, Blenheim Palace, Arundel Castle, Alnwick Castle, Albury and Syon House, Goodwood,

Belvoir Castle, Berry Pomeroy, and Strathfield Saye are all lived in by the descendants of their nineteenth-century owners. In some only a small part of the house is occupied, it is true, and most are open to the public. To take another example, we may look at the other great houses which have figured most prominently in this book. Burton Hall, the home of the Monsons, has been demolished and Gatton has passed away from the family; Jervaulx Abbey is the home of a new owner, and Tottenham Park houses a school, as does Canford, while Wentworth Woodhouse is tenanted by a physical training college. But a Lord Fitzwilliam still lives at Milton, and Gorhambury, after an abortive attempt to sell it in 1930, is the residence of a Lord Verulam: the late Earl, an energetic and noted industrialist, did much to restore the house and ensure its survival in the family. In the same way, Blagdon is still in the Ridley family, the present Lord being a skilled mechanical engineer and chairman of the Consett Iron Company. Raby Castle is the home of Lord Barnard, descendant of the last Duke of Cleveland, and Alresford Grange, Castle Hill, Longleat, Sledmere, Up Ottery, and Wilton are all residences of the present heads of the old families associated with them.

It would be misleading, therefore, to conclude on a note which emphasized the passing of the old order. It has certainly vanished, leaving a still highly class-conscious society in which, however, the landed classes are no longer accorded a separate existence. Its passing has left some curious results. At the centre the crown and the court have been left in splendid isolation, deprived of the society of equals which was furnished by the town palaces of the great magnates. In the countryside the farmers, largely deprived of landlord protection as well as landlord interference, have been left face to face with the state. Though their voting power is small, it is strategically spread over the constituencies and highly organized, and the farmers have obtained far more public assistance for agriculture than the great landowners, in the days of the Corn Laws, could ever procure. Even in family arrangements there has been a curious revolution. With death duties increasingly treated as a voluntary tax on inheritance it has become prudent to put an eldest son into possession during the father's lifetime, and the traditional provisions of family settlements have been cast to the winds.

Gone also is the life of excessive leisure and little purpose, in which the overmastering aim was to avoid boredom. 'Look here, young fellow,' the Duke of Portland was told by his senior officer on succeeding to the title in 1879, 'you'll be able to amuse yourself more or less as you like now. My advice to you is, be a bit of a jack-of-all-trades. Don't just stick to hunting and sport, but try and enjoy everything as it comes. Always intersperse your pleasure with business, and then things that might otherwise bore you will act as spice to your enjoyment.' 'I have tried to take his advice,' the Duke commented, 'and have always found it excellent; for it seems to me to be the best way of enjoying not only sport but life as a whole.'[1] Hunting and shooting still enjoy great popularity, but as recreations rather than as the chief activity of life.

There remain the representatives of a number of old landed families, which have shown remarkable powers of survival. Most are great men in their counties: they serve on local councils and as chairmen of county councils, they are appointed to the governing bodies of schools, hospitals and other institutions, and are widely sought after as presidents of charitable and voluntary societies. In the past the landed aristocracy has done great service as well as enjoyed great wealth, and the most important service has been the peaceful surrender of power. In the present, with the age of dominion long past, it continues to serve as the respected symbol of order and continuity in a changing world.

[1] *Men, Women and Things*, p. 29.

Bibliography

THIS bibliography is not intended to be comprehensive, but it includes all the MS collections and printed material found useful in the preparation of this book. The majority of the items are referred to in the text at some point, while those marked with an asterisk may be regarded as suggestions for further reading.

The material is arranged under the following heads:

1. Manuscript Collections
2. Parliamentary Papers
3. Newspapers and Periodicals
4. Works of Reference
5. Diaries, Memoirs and Biographies
6. Other Works

1. *Manuscript Collections*

For each collection of Papers a brief description is given of the main classes of records consulted. In the case of estate account material the following categories are noted in brackets: 'series', indicating a continuous run for a fifty-year period or longer; 'intermittent', indicating a number of short and discontinuous runs; and 'occasional', indicating that accounts for single isolated years only have survived.

(i) *In Libraries and Record Offices*

Ministry of Agriculture MSS, Loans under the Improvement of Land Act, 1864.
— Loans under the Limited Owners' Residence Act, 1870.
Ashburton MSS, Hampshire C.R.O. Deeds; Business and Estate Correspondence.
Best MSS, Kent C.R.O. Business, Estate and Family Correspondence; Estate Accounts (occasional).
Blundell MSS, Lancashire C.R.O. Business, Estate and Family Correspondence; Diaries; Estate Accounts (intermittent).
Braybrooke MSS, Essex C.R.O. Business Correspondence.
British Transport Commission, Edinburgh Archives. Records of the Border Counties and North British Railways.

Darell MSS, Kent C.R.O. Deeds; Estate Correspondence; Estate Accounts (intermittent).

Faunce Delaune MSS, Kent C.R.O. Deeds; Business and Estate Correspondence; Estate Accounts (intermittent).

Fitzwilliam MSS, Northamptonshire C.R.O. Business and Estate Correspondence; Personal and Household Accounts; Estate Accounts (series).

Harvey MSS, Bedfordshire C.R.O. Estate and Family Correspondence; Estate Accounts (occasional).

Lyall (Brooks) MSS, Bedfordshire C.R.O. Estate and Family Correspondence; Diaries; Estate Accounts (intermittent).

Mildmay MSS, Essex C.R.O. Deeds; Estate Correspondence.

Monson MSS, Lincolnshire C.R.O. Estate and Family Correspondence; Estate Accounts (intermittent).

Orlebar MSS, Bedfordshire C.R.O. Estate Correspondence; Household Accounts; Estate Accounts (series).

Overstone MSS, Northamptonshire C.R.O. Deeds; Business Correspondence.

Oxley-Parker MSS, Essex C.R.O. Estate Correspondence.

Portland MSS, Nottingham University Library. Business and Estate Correspondence; Estate Accounts (occasional).

Sefton MSS, Lancashire C.R.O. Business Correspondence.

Senhouse MSS, Cumberland C.R.O. Business, Estate and Family Correspondence; Estate Accounts (occasional).

Sidmouth MSS, Devonshire C.R.O. Deeds; Business, Estate and Family Correspondence; Estate Accounts (series).

Tithe Redemption Commission, Finsbury Square, London. Tithe Awards.

Verulam MSS, Hertfordshire C.R.O. Household Accounts; Estate Accounts (intermittent).

Wentworth Woodhouse MSS, Sheffield Central Library. Deeds; Business and Estate Correspondence; Estate Accounts (series).

(ii) *Private Collections*

Ailesbury Trust MSS, Hoare's Bank, Fleet Street, London. Business and Estate Correspondence; Trust Accounts.

Alnwick MSS, Alnwick Castle, Northumberland, by courtesy of the Duke of Northumberland. Business and Estate Correspondence; Estate Accounts (series).

Belsay MSS, Belsay Castle, Northumberland, by courtesy of Sir Stephen Hugh Middleton. Estate Accounts (intermittent).

Belvoir MSS, Belvoir Castle, Leicestershire, by courtesy of the Duke of Rutland. Household Accounts; Estate Accounts (series).

Blagdon MSS, Blagdon, Northumberland, by courtesy of Viscount Ridley. Deeds; Business and Estate Correspondence; Diaries; Estate Accounts (occasional).

Castle Hill MSS, Castle Hill, Devonshire, by courtesy of Earl Fortescue. Household Accounts.

Dickinson MSS, Red How, Lamplugh, Cumberland, by courtesy of R. F. Dickinson, Esq. Deeds; Business and Estate Correspondence; Estate Accounts (intermittent).

Gorhambury MSS, Gorhambury, Hertfordshire, by courtesy of the Earl of Verulam. Diaries; Household Accounts and Ledgers.

Hoare's Bank MSS, Hoare's Bank, Fleet Street, London. Ledgers.

Jervaulx MSS, Jervaulx Abbey, Yorkshire, by courtesy of H. Lorenzo Christie, Esq. Estate Accounts (series).

Longleat MSS, Longleat, Wiltshire, by courtesy of the Marquess of Bath. Business and Estate Correspondence; Estate Accounts (series).

Raby MSS, Raby Castle, Co. Durham, by courtesy of Lord Barnard. Deeds; Business and Estate Correspondence; Household Accounts; Estate Accounts (series).

Savernake MSS, Savernake, Wiltshire, by courtesy of the Marquess of Ailesbury. Deeds; Estate Correspondence; Household Accounts; Estate Accounts (series).

Sledmere MSS, Sledmere, Yorkshire, by courtesy of Sir Richard Sykes. Business and Estate Correspondence.

Wilton MSS, Wilton, Wiltshire, by courtesy of the Earl of Pembroke and Montgomery. Business and Estate Correspondence; Estate Accounts (series).

2. *Parliamentary Papers*

1810, IX, Report of Committee on Saleable Offices in Courts of Law.

1826/7, VI, S.C. on Criminal Commitments and Convictions.

1828, VI, S.C. on Criminal Commitments and Convictions.

1828, VIII, S.C. on Game Laws.

1830, VIII, S.C. of H. of L. on State of Coal Trade.

1833, V, S.C. on State of Agriculture.

1836, VIII, S.C. on State of Agriculture.

1845, X, S.C. of H. of L. on Compensation for Lands taken by Railways.

1845, XII, S.C. of H. of L. on Draining of Entailed Estates.

1846, VI, S.C. of H. of L. on Burdens on Real Property.

1846, IX, S.C. on Game Laws.

1847/8, VII, S.C. on Agricultural Customs.

1857/8, XLVI, Return of Registered Electors.

1861, LI, Return of Clerical Magistrates.

1863, VII, S.C. of H. of L. on Charging Entailed Estates for Railways.

1863, XLVIII, Return of Clerical Magistrates.

1868/9, VIII and 1870, VI, S.C. on Parliamentary and Municipal Elections.

1870, XX, Part II, Thirteenth Report of Commissioners of Inland Revenue.

1871, XVIII, R.C. on Coal Supply.

1873, IX, S.C. of H. of L. Improvement of Land.

1874, LXXII, Return of Owners of Land, 1872–3 (England and Wales).

1874, LXXII, Part III, Return of Owners of Land, 1872–3 (Scotland).

1876, LXXX, Return of Owners of Land (Ireland).

1881, XV, 1881, XVI, and 1882, XIV, R.C. on Agricultural Interests.

1886, XII, S.C. on Town Holdings.

1894, XVI, 1895, XVI, and 1896, XVI, R.C. on Agricultural Depression.

1910, LXXIII, Judgment on Trial of Election Petition for Dorset, East Division.

1912/13, XLVII, Report of Departmental Committee of Board of Agriculture on Tenant Farmers.

1919, XII, R.C. on the Coal Industry.

3. *Newspapers and Periodicals*

Blackwood's Magazine.
The Builder.
The Economist.
Estates Gazette..
Gentleman's Magazine.
Leeds Mercury.
Newcastle Courant.
Newcastle Journal.
The Times.
Transactions of the Institution of Surveyors.
Transactions of the National Association for the Promotion of Social Science.

4. *Works of Reference*

J. Bateman, *The Great Landowners of Great Britain and Ireland* (final ed. 1883).
The Black Book (1820).
The Extraordinary Black Book (1831).

G. Bramwell, *Analytical Table of the Private Statutes, 1727–1812* (1813).

Burke's Landed Gentry.

Burke's Peerage, Baronetage and Knightage.

Cobbett's *Parliamentary History.*

G. E. Cockayne, *The Complete Peerage.*

H. M. Colvin, *Biographical Dictionary of English Architects, 1666–1840* (1954).

C. R. Dod, *Electoral Facts, 1832–52* (1852).

Hansard, *Parliamentary Debates.*

G. R. Porter, *Progress of the Nation* (1847 ed.).

E. Walford, *The County Families of the U.K.: The Titled and Untitled Aristocracy, A Dictionary of the Upper Ten Thousand* (1860).

R. Welford, *Men of Mark 'Twixt Tyne and Tweed* (1895).

Whitaker's Almanack.

Who was Who (1920–   ).

Joshua Wilson, *A Biographical Index to the present House of Commons* (1808).

Wolstenholme's Conveyancing and Settled Land Acts (10th ed. 1913).

5. Diaries, Memoirs and Biographies

Boyd Alexander, ed., *Correspondence of William Beckford* (1957).

C. Bruyn Andrews and Fanny Andrews, eds., *The Torrington Diaries* (1954 ed.).

The Earl of Bessborough, ed., *Diaries of Lady Charlotte Guest, 1833–1852* (1950).

Life and Times of Henry Brougham by Himself (1871).

Barbara Drake and Margaret I. Cole, eds., *Our Partnership by Beatrice Webb* (1948).

J. K. Fowler, *Recollections of Old Country Life* (1894).

J. Greig, ed., *The Farington Diary* (1922–8).

J. Gore, ed., *Creevey* (1948).

The Greville Memoirs (1888).

A. L. Kennedy, ed., *My Dear Duchess: Social and Political Letters to the Duchess of Manchester, 1858–69* (1956).

Sonia Keppel, *Edwardian Daughter* (1958).

Edith, Marchioness of Londonderry, *Frances Anne* (1958).

J. Morley, *Life of Gladstone* (1903).

C. B. Patterson, *Angela Burdett-Coutts and the Victorians* (1953).

*Lord Eustace Percy, *Some Memories* (1958).

The Duke of Portland, *Men, Women and Things* (1937).

The Journal of Thomas Raikes (1856–7).

*The Duke of Sutherland, *Autobiography* (1958).

BIBLIOGRAPHY

G. Ticknor, *Life of William Hickling Prescott* (1863).

6. Others Works

*W. S. Adams, *Edwardian Portraits* (1957).
Mabell, Countess of Airlie, *In Whig Society* (1921).
Arthur Arnold, *Free Land* (1880).
W. Bagehot, *The English Constitution* (1929 ed.).
James Beal, *Free Trade in Land* (1855).
The Duke of Bedford, *A Great Agricultural Estate* (1897).
A. Birch, 'The Haigh Ironworks, 1789–1856,' *Bulletin John Rylands Library*, XXXV (1952–3).
Sheila Birkenhead, *Peace in Piccadilly* (1958).
H. R. Brand, 'Free Land,' *Fortnighlty Review*, n.s. XVI (1874).
Asa Briggs, *Victorian People* (1954).
*—, *The Age of Improvement* (1959).
D. K. Britton, *An Enquiry into Agricultural Rents and the Expenses of Landowners in England and Wales, 1938 and 1946* (1949).
G. C. Brodrick, *English Land and English Landlords* (1881).
P. A. Bromhead, *The House of Lords in Contemporary Politics, 1911–1957* (1958).
J. M. Bulloch, 'Peers who have married Players,' *Notes and Queries*, CLXIX (1935).
J. B. Burke, *The Vicissitudes of Families* (1st and 2nd ser. 1861, 3rd ser. 1883 ed.).
*W. L. Burn, 'The Age of Equipoise: England, 1848–1868,' *The Nineteenth Century*, (1949).
J. Caird, *English Agriculture in 1850–51* (1852).
—, *The Landed Interest and the Supply of Food* (1878).
The Earl of Cardigan, *The Wardens of Savernake Forest* (1949).
Sir A. M. Carr-Saunders and P. A. Wilson, *The Professions* (1933).
*O. F. Christie, *The Transition from Aristocracy, 1832–1867* (1927).
*—, *The Transition to Democracy, 1867–1914* (1934).
J. H. Clapham, *An Economic History of Modern Britain* (1926–38).
F. Cross, *Landed Property: its Sale, Purchase, Improvement and Management* (1857).
T. F. Dale, *The History of the Belvoir Hunt* (1899).
C. Stella Davies, *The Agricultural History of Cheshire, 1750–1850*, Chetham Society, 3rd ser. X (1960).
E. Davies, 'The Small Landowners, 1780–1832, in the Light of the Land Tax Assessments,' *Econ. Hist. Rev.*, 1st ser. I (1927).
Lord Ernle, *English Farming Past and Present* (6th ed. 1961, with an Introduction by G. E. Fussell and O. R. McGregor).
*T. H. S. Escott, *England: Her People, Polity and Pursuits* (1885).

W. Farr, 'On the Valuation of Railways, Telegraphs, Water Companies, Canals, etc.,' *Journal Statistical Soc.* XXIX (1878).

T. W. Fletcher, 'The Great Depression of English Agriculture, 1873–1896,' *Econ. Hist. Rev.*, 2nd ser. XIII (1961).

—, 'Lancashire Livestock Farming during the Great Depression', *Agricultural Hist. Rev.*, IX (1961).

W. F. Galpin, *The Grain Supply of England During the Napoleonic Period* (New York 1925).

*R. M. Garnier, *History of the English Landed Interest* (1893).

N. Gash, *Politics in the Age of Peel* (1953).

A. D. Gayer, W. W. Rostow and A. J. Schwartz, *The Growth and Fluctuation of The British Economy, 1790–1850* (1953).

H. R. G. Greaves, 'Personal Origins and Inter-relations of the Houses of Parliament,' *Economica*, IX (1929).

W. L. Guttsmann, 'The Changing Social Structure of the British Political Elite, 1886–1935,' *British Journal of Sociology*, II (1951).

—, 'Aristocracy and the Middle Classes in the British Political Elite, 1886–1916,' *British Journal of Sociology*, V (1954).

H. J. Habakkuk, 'English Landownership, 1680–1740,' *Econ. Hist. Rev.*, 1st ser. X (1940).

J. L. and Barbara Hammond, *The Village Labourer* (Guild Books ed. 1948).

H. J. Hanham, *Elections and Party Management* (1959).

*—, 'The Sale of Honours in late Victorian England,' *Victorian Studies*, III (1960).

W. Hasbach, *A History of the English Agricultural Labourer* (1920).

J. J. Hecht, *The Domestic Servant Class in Eighteenth-Century England* (1956).

James Humphreys, *Observations on the Actual State of the English Laws of Real Property, with the Outlines of a Code* (1826).

H. G. Hunt, 'Agricultural Rent in South-East England, 1788–1825,' *Agricultural Hist. Rev.*, VII (1959).

Llewellyn Jewitt, *The Stately Homes of England* (n.d.).

A. H. John, 'The Course of Agricultural Change, 1660–1760,' *Studies in the Industrial Revolution* (ed. L. S. Pressnell, 1960).

A. H. Johnson, *The Disappearance of the Small Landowner* (1909).

W. Bence Jones, 'Landowning as a Business,' *The Nineteenth Century*, XI, (1882).

L. Kennedy and T. B. Grainger, *Present State of the Tenancy of Land in Great Britain* (1828).

N. Kent, *Hints to Landed Gentlemen* (1793).

D. Low, *Landed Property and the Economy of Estates* (1844).

*H. M. Lynd, *England in the Eighteen-Eighties* (1945).

G. Macmillan, *Honours for Sale* (1954).

J. R. M'Culloch, *Treatise on the Succession to Property Vacant by Death* (1848).

W. Marshall, *On the Landed Property of England* (1804).

—, *On the Management of Landed Estates* (1806).

A. H. Matthews, *Fifty Years of Agricultural Politics, 1865–1915* (1915).

*D. C. Moore, 'The Other Face of Reform.' *Victorian Studies*, V (1961).

J. Mordant, *The Complete Steward* (1761).

J. L. Morton, *The Resources of Estates: being a Treatise on Agricultural Improvement and General Management of Landed Property* (1858).

Sir Lewis Namier, *The Structure of Politics at the Accession of George III* (1957 ed.).

Sir Nicholas Harris Nicolas, *A Letter to the Duke of Wellington on the Propriety and Legality of creating Peers for Life* (1830).

R. A. C. Parker, 'Coke of Norfolk and the Agrarian Revolution,' *Econ. Hist. Rev.*, 2nd ser. VIII (1955).

S. Pollard, 'Barrow-in-Furness and the Seventh Duke of Devonshire,' *Econ. Hist. Rev.*, 2nd ser. VIII (1955).

R. E. Pumphrey, 'The Introduction of Industrialists into the British Peerage: A Study in Adaptation of a Social Institution,' *American Hist. Rev.*, LXV (1959).

H. A. Rhee, *The Rent of Agricultural Land in England and Wales, 1870–1943* (1949).

J. C. Rogers, 'The Manor and Houses of Gorhambury,' *Transactions of the St. Albans and Herts. Architectural and Archaeological Soc.* (1933).

J. F. S. Ross, *Parliamentary Representation* (1948).

J. L. Sanford and M. Townsend, *The Great Governing Families of England* (1865).

D. and E. Spring, 'The Fall of the Grenvilles, 1844–8,' *Huntington Library Quarterly*, XIX (1956).

D. Spring, 'The English Landed Estate in the Age of Coal and Iron, 1830–80,' *Journal Econ. Hist.*, XI (1951).

—, 'The Earls of Durham and the Great Northern Coalfield, 1830–80,' *Canadian Hist. Rev.*, XXXIII (1952).

—, 'Earl Fitzwilliam and the Corn Laws,' *American Hist. Rev.*, LIX (1954).

—, 'A Great Agricultural Estate: Netherby under Sir James Graham, 1820–45,' *Agricultural Hist.*, XXIX (1955).

—, 'English Landownership in the Nineteenth Century: a critical note,' *Econ. Hist. Rev.*, 2nd ser. IX (1957).

*—, 'The Role of the Aristocracy in the late Nineteenth Century,' *Victorian Studies*, IV (1960).

S. G. Sturmey, 'Owner-Farming in England and Wales, 1900–50,' *Manchester School of Economic and Social Studies*, XXIII (1955).

E. B. Sugden, *Letter to James Humphreys* (1826).

Christopher Sykes, *Four Studies in Loyalty* (1946).

W. E. Tate, 'The Cost of Parliamentary Enclosure in England,' *Econ. Hist. Rev.*, 2nd ser. V (1952).

A. J. Taylor, 'The Sub-Contract System in the British Coal Industry,' *Studies in the Industrial Revolution* (ed. L. S. Pressnell, 1960).

W. Cooke Taylor, *Notes of a Tour in the Manufacturing Districts of Lancashire* (1842).

J. A. Thomas, *The House of Commons, 1832–1901* (Cardiff, 1939).

F. M. L. Thompson, 'The End of a Great Estate,' *Econ. Hist. Rev.*, 2nd ser. VIII (1955).

—, 'The Economic and Social Background of the English Landed Interest, 1840–70,' (unpublished D.Phil. thesis, Oxford University, 1956).

—, 'The Land Market in the Nineteenth Century,' *Oxford Economic Papers*, n.s. IX (1957).

—, 'English Landownership: the Ailesbury Trust, 1832–56,' *Econ. Hist. Rev.*, 2nd ser. XI (1958).

—, 'Whigs and Liberals in the West Riding, 1830–60,' *English Hist. Rev.*, LXXIV (1959).

R. J. Thompson, 'An Inquiry into the Rent of Agricultural Land in England and Wales in the 19th Century,' *Journal Royal Statistical Soc.*, LXX (1907).

A. S. Turberville, *Welbeck Abbey and its Owners* (1938–9).

—, *The House of Lords in the Age of Reform* (1958).

H. B. Wheatley and P. Cunningham, *London Past and Present* (1891).

R. J. White, ed., *The Conservative Tradition* (1950).

Victoria History of Leicestershire, III (1955).

Victoria History of Lincolnshire, I (1906).

Victoria History of Wiltshire, IV (1959).

Arthur Young, *An Enquiry into the Progressive Value of Money in England* (1912).

Index

In the case of peers the family name of the first holder of a title is given in brackets. In general members of the nobility are indexed under the title which they finally held. Irish titles (I), and Scottish titles (S), are so marked.

STUDIES IN SOCIAL HISTORY

Editor: *HAROLD PERKIN*

Professor of Social History, University of Lancaster

Assistant Editor: *ERIC J. EVANS*

Lecturer in History, University of Lancaster